TERRIBLE
SWIFT
SWORD

Major General Philip Sheridan. *National Archives*

TERRIBLE
SWIFT
SWORD

The Life of
GENERAL PHILIP H. SHERIDAN

Joseph Wheelan

DA CAPO PRESS
A member of the Perseus Books Group

Set in 10.5 point Garamond Pro by The Perseus Books Group

Library of Congress Cataloging-in-Publication Data
  Wheelan, Joseph.
  Terrible swift sword : the life of General Philip H. Sheridan / Joseph Wheelan.
    p. cm.
  Includes bibliographical references and index.
  ISBN 978-0-306-82027-4 (hardcover : alk. paper)—ISBN 978-0-306-82109-7 (e-
book) 1. Sheridan, Philip Henry, 1831–1888. 2. United States—History—Civil
War, 1861–1865—Campaigns. 3. Indians of North America—Wars—1866–1895.
4. United States. Army—Biography. 5. Generals—United States—Biography. I.
Title.
  E467.1.S54W54 2012
  355.0092—dc23
  [B]

                                                                    2012018587

First Da Capo Press edition 2012
Published by Da Capo Press
A Member of the Perseus Books Group
www.dacapopress.com

Da Capo Press books are available at special discounts for bulk purchases in the U.S.
by corporations, institutions, and other organizations. For more information, please
contact the Special Markets Department at the Perseus Books Group, 2300
Chestnut Street, Suite 200, Philadelphia, PA 19103, or call (800) 810–4145, ext.
5000, or e-mail special.markets@perseusbooks.com.
10 9 8 7 6 5 4 3 2 1

In memory of the late

EDWARD W. KNAPPMAN
(NOVEMBER 1943–MARCH 2011)

a first-rate literary agent, editor, and mentor

———————

CONTENTS

Illustrations following page 168

MAPS

ACKNOWLEDGMENTS

The genesis of this book was a two-volume set of Philip Sheridan's *Personal Memoirs* that came to me after my father's death. For years, it sat neglected on the shelf while I pursued a career and wrote books about the early nineteenth century.

When I finally got around to reading the *Personal Memoirs*, I realized that Sheridan would make a fine subject for a book.

As I delved more deeply into Sheridan's life and times, librarians and historians from Washington, D.C., to Tennessee, Virginia, and North Carolina aided me in tracking down the information that I needed to write this book.

The University of North Carolina's Davis Library and its Southern Historical and Rare Book collections offered a rich trove of Civil War–era diaries, journals, and papers.

During my visits to the Library of Congress in Washington, the staff, as always, was courteous and eager to assist.

Wake County Public Libraries—particularly the Interlibrary Loan staff and the West Regional Library—helped me to obtain microfilms of Philip Sheridan's papers lent by the Library of Congress.

The staff historians at the Civil War battlefields where Sheridan became a household name were generous in sharing their valuable knowledge with me.

Jimmy Blankenship, the historian at the City Point Unit of the Petersburg National Battlefield, guided me through General Ulysses S. Grant's City Point headquarters, and answered my questions about Sheridan's and President Abraham Lincoln's visits in 1864 and 1865.

James Ogden, historian for the Chickamauga and Chattanooga National Military Park, clarified Sheridan's movements during the Battle of Chickamauga.

Finally, my wife Pat's unflagging support and interest were as essential to this project as to every historical journey that I have undertaken.

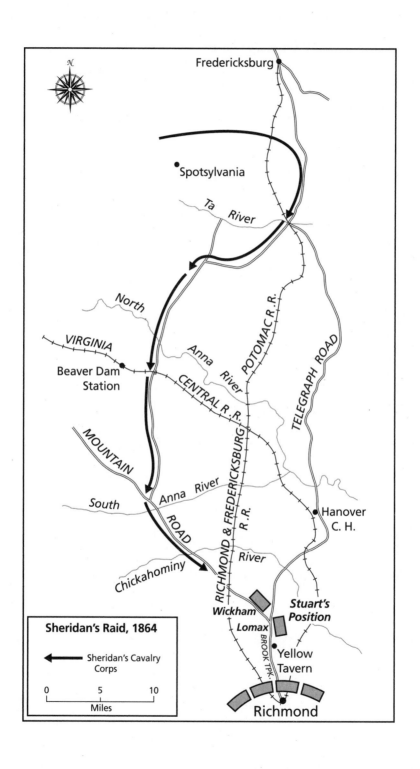

Fredericksburg

N

Spotsylvania

Ta River

North

VIRGINIA

POTOMAC R. R.

Anna River

TELEGRAPH ROAD

Beaver Dam
Station

CENTRAL R. R.

MOUNTAIN

South

Anna River

ROAD

RICHMOND & FREDERICKSBURG R. R.

Hanover
C. H.

Chickahominy

River

Wickham

Stuart's
Position

Lomax

BROOK TPK.

Yellow
Tavern

Richmond

Sheridan's Raid, 1864

⬅ Sheridan's Cavalry
Corps

0   5   10
Miles

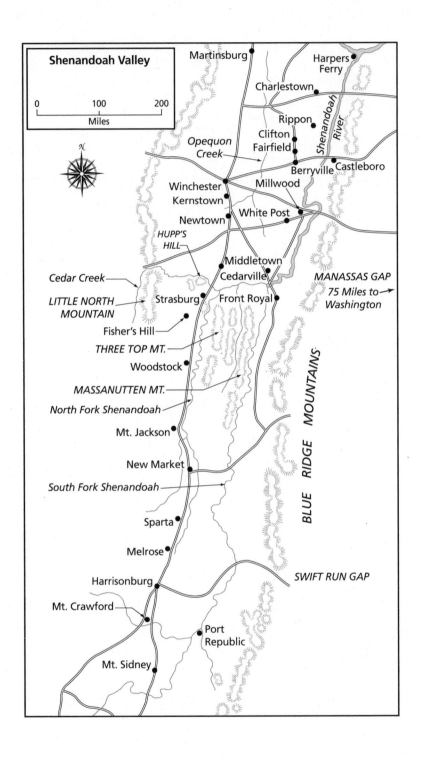

Shenandoah Valley

0   100   200
Miles

N

Martinsburg

Harpers
Ferry

Charlestown

Rippon

Clifton
Fairfield

*Opequon
Creek*

Berryville   Castleboro

*Shenandoah
River*

Winchester
Kernstown

Millwood

White Post

Newtown

*HUPP'S
HILL*

Middletown
Cedarville

MANASSAS GAP
75 Miles to
Washington

Cedar Creek

*LITTLE NORTH
MOUNTAIN*

Strasburg

Front Royal

Fisher's Hill

THREE TOP MT.

Woodstock

MASSANUTTEN MT.

North Fork Shenandoah

Mt. Jackson

New Market

South Fork Shenandoah

BLUE RIDGE MOUNTAINS

Sparta

Melrose

Harrisonburg

SWIFT RUN GAP

Mt. Crawford

Port
Republic

Mt. Sidney

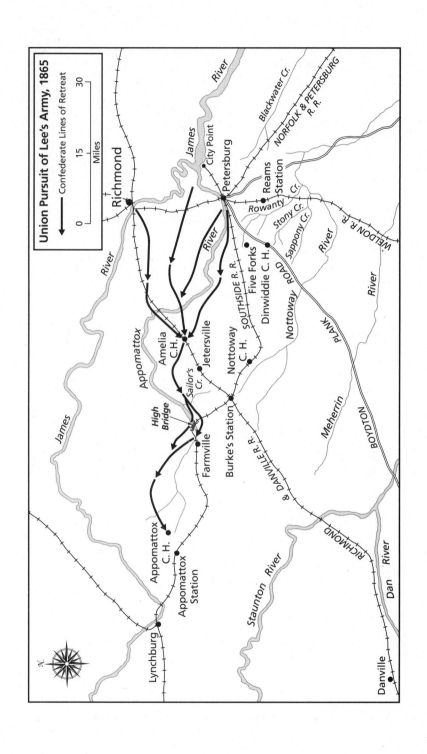

Union Pursuit of Lee's Army, 1865

→ Confederate Lines of Retreat

Miles
0   15   30

Richmond

James River

City Point

Petersburg

Blackwater Cr.

NORFOLK & PETERSBURG R. R.

Reams Station

Rowanty Cr.

Stony Cr.

Sappony Cr.

WELDON R. R.

Five Forks

Dinwiddie C. H.

SOUTHSIDE R. R.

Nottoway C. H.

Nottoway River

NOTTOWAY ROAD

Appomattox River

Amelia C. H.

Jetersville

Sailor's Cr.

High Bridge

Farmville

Burke's Station

Meherrin River

BOYDTON PLANK

RICHMOND & DANVILLE R. R.

James River

Lynchburg

Appomattox C. H.

Appomattox Station

Staunton River

Dan River

Danville

N

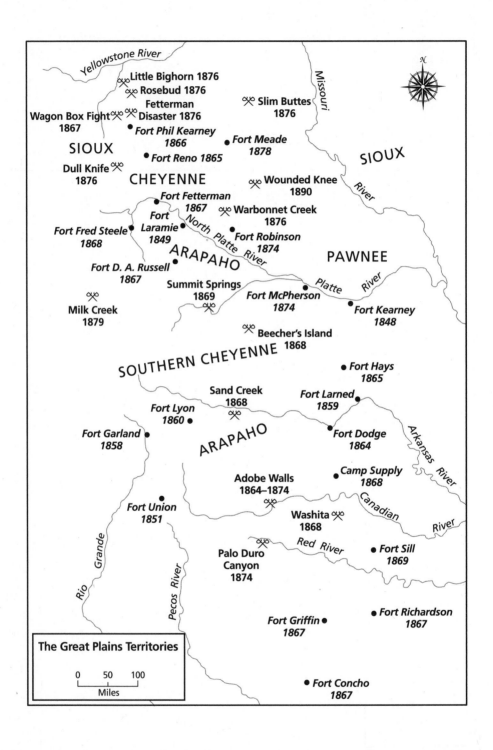

The Great Plains Territories

0   50   100
Miles

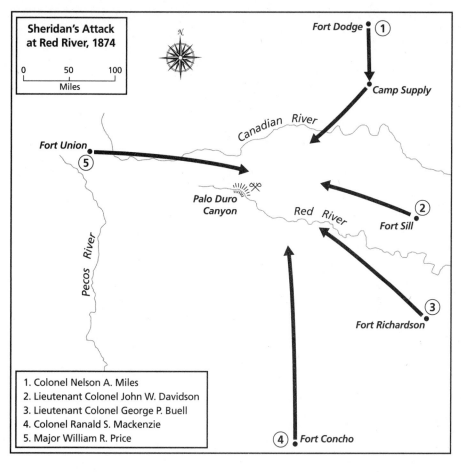

Sheridan's Attack at Red River, 1874

0   50   100
Miles

Fort Dodge (1)

Camp Supply

Canadian   River

Fort Union
(5)

Palo Duro
Canyon

Red   River

Fort Sill   (2)

Pecos   River

Fort Richardson
(3)

1. Colonel Nelson A. Miles
2. Lieutenant Colonel John W. Davidson
3. Lieutenant Colonel George P. Buell
4. Colonel Ranald S. Mackenzie
5. Major William R. Price

(4) Fort Concho

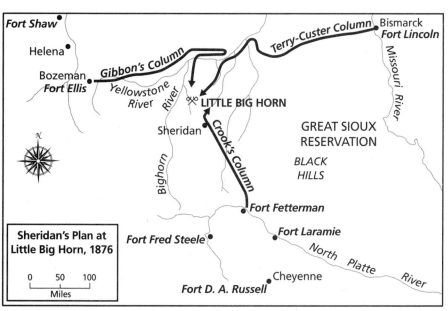

Fort Shaw

Helena

Bozeman
Fort Ellis

Gibbon's Column

Yellowstone
River

River

Terry-Custer Column

Bismarck
Fort Lincoln

Missouri River

LITTLE BIG HORN

Sheridan

Bighorn

Crook's Column

GREAT SIOUX
RESERVATION

BLACK
HILLS

Fort Fetterman

Fort Fred Steele

Fort Laramie

North   Platte   River

Sheridan's Plan at Little Big Horn, 1876

0   50   100
Miles

Cheyenne

Fort D. A. Russell

They want war too methodical, too measured; I would make it brisk, bold, impetuous, perhaps sometimes even audacious.

—ANTOINE HENRI JOMINI

PROLOGUE

OCTOBER 19, 1864–WINCHESTER, VIRGINIA—Major General Philip Sheridan and his three-hundred-man escort rumbled through the streets of the oft-captured strategic crossroads city in the early morning. All around them, the Shenandoah Valley was ablaze with vivid autumnal yellows and reds under a serene, blue sky. It might have been a glorious day for picnicking—except for the disturbing sound of distant cannon fire.[1]

After an absence of three days, Sheridan was returning to his Army of the Shenandoah. His 32,000 veterans were camped to the south among an accordion-like series of ridges along the north bank of Cedar Creek. On the creek's other bank, Massanutten Mountain—and, significantly, Three Top Mountain, with its Confederate signal station—loomed over the Union encampment.

Sheridan had been in Washington to confer with War Secretary Edwin Stanton and Army Chief of Staff Henry Halleck about his army's next move. They liked his plan to send most of his men to General Ulysses S. Grant at Petersburg, leaving just a small force at the Valley's north end to check any Rebel advances.

Major fighting in the Valley seemed at an end. In September, Sheridan's army had defeated Lieutenant General Jubal Early's Army of the Valley at the Third Battle of Winchester and then, three days later, had driven the Rebels from Fisher's Hill. The Confederates had withdrawn seventy miles to the south, to Waynesboro.

But then, on October 12, Early's army had suddenly reappeared at Strasburg, just a few miles south of the Yankee positions. Sheridan had already sent VI Corps marching east to join Grant. He ordered it to return.

On October 16, Union signalmen intercepted a Rebel communication indicating that Lieutenant General James Longstreet's I Corps was marching to Early's aid. A courier had overtaken Sheridan on his way to Washington. After reading the message and obtaining intelligence on recent enemy movements, Sheridan concluded that it was a red herring (it was). But he was unable to rid himself of nagging second thoughts, and he had returned as quickly as possible.

When Sheridan left his army, the Rebels occupied Fisher's Hill, about ten miles south of Cedar Creek.

But today the Rebels were no longer at Fisher's Hill.

LIKE MANY CIVIL WAR generals, Sheridan had risen fast, after being stuck in rank at lieutenant for eight years in the peacetime army. He was still just a captain in 1862 when he was given his first field command, the 2nd Michigan Cavalry in Mississippi. His career had taken off with a series of battlefield promotions. He was now responsible for parts of three infantry corps and the Cavalry Corps.

In December 1862 at Stones River, Sheridan's division had slowed the Confederate onslaught long enough to save Major General William Rosecrans's Army of the Cumberland from destruction. In 1863, his division had reached the crest of Missionary Ridge first and pursued Braxton Bragg's retreating army the longest. In May 1864, Sheridan's Cavalry Corps had defeated the Rebel cavalry at Yellow Tavern and mortally wounded the celebrated Jeb Stuart.

When Jubal Early threatened Washington in July 1864, President Abraham Lincoln, General Ulysses Grant, and War Secretary Edwin Stanton decided that the Shenandoah Valley had to be cleared of Rebel armies. They combined four military departments and made Sheridan commander of some of the best fighting men in the Union army.

Sheridan had impressed Grant at Missionary Ridge and later, too, when he transformed the Cavalry Corps into a mobile strike force. He was increasingly seen as a man who got things done fast, a man who could think on his feet.

He was small, five foot five at most, and thin but wiry and broad shouldered; his men called him "Little Phil." On horseback, Sheridan appeared larger because his torso and arms were disproportionately long, and his legs were short. He possessed incredible stamina that enabled him to function at a high level without sleep or food.

For a man of slight stature, Sheridan's appearance was striking. With his heavy, arched brows, piercing, Tartar-like hazel eyes, chin beard, and curling moustache, he bore a strong resemblance to a Mongolian horse soldier. He kept his hair cropped short because he hated his curls; someone once observed that his hair looked painted on. A Southern civilian declared Sheridan the most savage-looking man he had ever seen—but then related a kindness that Sheridan had shown him.

In the Shenandoah Valley, Sheridan became a favorite of Lincoln and Grant—not only because he struck hard and won battles but also because he believed, as they did, in ruthlessly waging a "total war" on all of the Confederacy's resources. They, along with Major General William Tecumseh Sherman, believed that destroying the enemy's army, burning his farms, killing his livestock, hanging his guerrillas, and freeing his slaves would win the war quicker and save lives.

AS HE RODE THROUGH Winchester's streets on Rienzi, his big warhorse—seventeen hands high, or nearly six feet at the withers—Sheridan noticed that townswomen were standing in their windows and doors, "shaking their skirts at us and . . . otherwise markedly insolent in their demeanor." Initially, he thought nothing of their behavior.

But when the sound of artillery fire grew louder at the edge of town, he began to wonder whether the women had been "in raptures over some good news, while I as yet was utterly ignorant of the actual situation." He knew that a XIX Corps detachment was conducting a reconnaissance that morning, but the gunfire seemed to suggest a large-scale engagement, not a skirmish.

Sheridan was correct in surmising that the Rebel women knew something that he did not. Mrs. Hugh H. Lee wrote in her diary that earlier that morning, the "glorious news" that Early had routed two-thirds of Sheridan's army had reached Winchester.

After riding a short distance farther, Sheridan "leaned forward and listened intently," wrote Major George A. "Sandy" Forsyth, an aide. He was trying to locate and interpret the gunfire. Then, he dismounted and placed his ear near the ground, "seeming somewhat disconcerted as he rose again and remounted."[2]

Alarming signs began to appear as they traveled south on the Valley Turnpike. A supply train bound for the front lines was stopped in the road, "seemingly in great confusion." Sheridan sent Forsyth ahead to find out what was wrong. The quartermaster told Forsyth that an officer from the front had warned him to turn back—the army had been attacked and was being driven down the Valley.

From the crest of the next ridge, everything became shockingly evident. Spread before them was "the appalling spectacle of a panic-stricken army."

Sheridan ordered most of his escort to remain on the ridge. He sent instructions to Colonel Oliver Edwards, who commanded a VI Corps brigade in Winchester, to deploy a "straggler line" across the Valley Turnpike to stop fleeing soldiers, yet to allow wagons to pass through so they could park north of town.[3]

Then, with Major Forsyth, Captain Joseph O'Keefe, and a dozen troopers, Sheridan rode on at a fast trot, gray dust rising in a plume in their wake.

They met a flood of men and wagons headed toward the rear and soldiers who had stopped beside the road to brew coffee. Sheridan shouted to them, "Turn back, men! Turn back! Face the other way!"

When the soldiers saw the towering charger bearing the familiar, fierce-featured man in the flat-brimmed hat, an "echoing cheer" arose.

"God *damn* you, don't cheer me!" Sheridan shouted at them. "If you love your country, come up to the front! God *damn* you, don't cheer me! There's lots of fight in you men yet! Come up, God damn you! Come up!"[4]

Wild enthusiasm traveled from regiment to regiment along the Valley Pike. "Flags were waving, men were throwing their hats high in the air, shouting for joy, for now we had a leader," wrote Frank Flinn of the 38th Massachusetts Infantry. "We . . . knew now that there was to be no more retreat."[5]

The men began chanting, "Sheridan! Sheridan!" They "swung their hats in glee," and by the hundreds and then the thousands, they began to follow him back to the front.

Forsyth was astonished by the effect that Sheridan had on the men. "It is no exaggeration to say that as he dashed on to the field of battle, for miles back the turnpike was lined with men pressing forward after him to the front."[6]

Sheridan was going to attempt what no commander had ever done during the war: to lead an army beaten in battle to victory on the same day.

IN SHERIDAN CIRCLE IN Washington, DC, stands the iconic equestrian statue of Phil Sheridan, green with age. Reaching backward with his hat in hand, Sheridan rallies his men at Cedar Creek. He and Rienzi are action incarnate, captured in medias res. The sculpture accurately depicts a man who led from the front and believed it was almost always best to take the offensive.

Phil Sheridan's legacy, of course, is richer and more complex than a statue representing him at a climactic moment can convey. Cedar Creek was only one point along an ascending line that ended with Sheridan becoming the Union commander most responsible for bringing Robert E. Lee to bay—as well as Grant's most trusted troubleshooter.

At the war's conclusion, Grant, Sherman, and Sheridan were recognized as the Union's victorious triumvirate, forever linked by their invaluable collaboration in defeating the Confederacy.

Supremely confident that Sheridan could rise to any challenge, Grant gave him a broad spectrum of postwar assignments that tested and stretched his abilities. They ranged from governing defiant Louisiana and Texas, to waging the nation's first "cold war," to subduing the Plains Indians. In suppressing the Indians, Sheridan conceived the idea of striking their winter camps—a ruthless strategy that succeeded brilliantly.

When Grant became president in 1869, he pulled Sherman and Sheridan up with him, with Sherman becoming general of the army and Sheridan taking Sherman's old position as commander of the Division of the Missouri. The three remained close friends and allies until the end of their days. Sheridan succeeded Sherman upon his retirement.

Scores of biographies have been written about Grant and dozens about Sherman. But Sheridan has remained somewhat of an enigma, the reason being that all of his diaries, journals, personal papers, and documents were destroyed in the Great Chicago Fire of 1871.

With his source material gone, Sheridan had difficulty writing his *Personal Memoirs*, and it is no wonder that biographers have struggled too. The inner man remains indistinct, although his letters and reports, as well as the accounts of contemporaries, provide glimpses of him.

One thread running through Sheridan's life was his readiness to defend what he believed needed protecting, utilizing every available resource. After fighting to save the Union, he defended black freedmen against ex-Rebels in Texas and Louisiana; settlers against pillaging Indians; reservation Indians against corrupt agents and contractors; and Yellowstone National Park against vandals, poachers, and corporate exploiters.

He believed ends justified practically any means, no matter how harsh. In Virginia's Shenandoah Valley, Sheridan's name will always be associated with "the Burning"—his systematic destruction of Virginia's breadbasket. In some parts of the West, his name evokes images of bloody daybreak attacks on Indian villages in wintertime.

However, his friends and comrades, Grant and Sherman, believed there was no better military leader than Sheridan. In 1876, then president Grant spoke to Representative George F. Hoar of Massachusetts with unusual feeling on the subject: "I believe General Sheridan has no superior as a general, either living or dead, and perhaps not an equal. People think he is only capable of leading an army in battle, or to do a particular thing when he is told to." According to the president, however, those people were wrong. Sheridan was capable of directing "as large a territory as any two nations can cover in a war."[7]

CHAPTER I

———

Rise from Obscurity

1831–1862

He is worth his weight in gold. He would not make a stampeding general.
—THREE GENERALS RECOMMENDING PHIL SHERIDAN'S PROMOTION TO BRIGADIER GENERAL IN JULY 1862[1]

PHILIP HENRY SHERIDAN's birthplace is a rare opacity in an otherwise transparent life spent largely in uniform. Four versions exist. In his *Personal Memoirs*, Sheridan states that he was born in Albany, New York, on March 6, 1831—fittingly, the month of Mars, the Roman god of war. Somerset, Ohio, the village where he grew up, claims Sheridan as a native son. Strangely, no written record of Sheridan's birth exists in either place.

Sheridan's mother once said that Philip was born at sea during the family's migration from Ireland to America, but in 1888 she insisted that his birthplace was Somerset and named the priest who had baptized him. Others have asserted that he was born in County Cavan, Ireland; a stone marker in front of a stone house in Killinkere reportedly commemorates the event.

Not in dispute is that Sheridan's father, John Sheridan, was a County Cavan tenant farmer who claimed lineage from Irish kings and married his second cousin,

I

Mary Meenagh. Together they worked John Sheridan's lease holding on the Cherrymount estate near Killinkere in north-central Ireland.

In 1831, the family immigrated to America at the urging of John Sheridan's uncle, Thomas Gainor, an émigré who lived in Albany. The Sheridans loaded a horse cart with their worldly possessions, and a neighbor drove them to Dublin. Historian Eric Wittenberg writes that the neighbor reported that Mary Sheridan held young Philip in her arms. In Dublin, the Sheridans booked passage on a ferry to Liverpool, where they boarded a packet ship to America with their two older children, Patrick and Rosa, and possibly Phil too. Rosa died during the ocean voyage and was buried at sea.[2]

Some historians have suggested that Sheridan pointedly claimed Albany as his birthplace because he entertained presidential ambitions, and being foreign-born would have made him ineligible. But this seems far-fetched, because Sheridan never evinced the slightest interest in seeking any elective office.

More plausibly, if Sheridan did lie about his origins, he probably was trying to distance himself from the Irish immigrants swamping Boston and New York in the wake of the potato famine just as Sheridan was matriculating at West Point in 1848. Between 1847 and 1854, the arrival of nearly 1.2 million Irish—at least one-sixth of Ireland's population—aroused widespread xenophobia and helped inspire the rise of the nativist Know-Nothing Party. Albany may have been Sheridan's self-inoculation against the intense hostility toward Irish immigrants.[3]

JOHN SHERIDAN DID NOT linger in Albany. Lured by the prospect of steady work, he moved on to Somerset, a village of 1,400, southeast of Columbus, Ohio. He got a job building the National Road, a federal project to link the Potomac and Mississippi Rivers. Later, he became an independent contractor for the National Road, the Hocking Valley Canal, and the Zanesville and Maysville Turnpike in Ohio.[4]

Because John Sheridan's work often kept him away from home, Mary Sheridan raised Phil, his three brothers, and his surviving sister. Mrs. Sheridan was a devout Catholic in a village that was overwhelmingly Catholic because of its large Irish immigrant population.[5]

A small boy with long arms and a bullet-shaped head, Sheridan belonged to the west-side Pig Foots, one of Somerset's two warring factions of boys (the other being the east-side Turkey Foots), and was a respected street fighter, although not a boy who started fights. He and his friend Henry Greiner liked to play hooky and go fishing and swimming.

In 1840, Colonel Richard M. Johnson of Kentucky campaigned in Somerset while challenging President Martin Van Buren for the Democratic nomination.

Most of Somerset's Democrats turned out to meet Johnson, the man reputed to have killed Shawnee Indian chief Tecumseh at the Battle of the Thames in 1813.

Sheridan and some other boys who claimed Whig affiliation hung back, but when Johnson approached to shake their hands, the boys shoved Sheridan to the front of the crowd. When Johnson offered his hand, Sheridan refused to shake it. Johnson asked him why. "Because I am a Whig!" Sheridan replied. Johnson said that it didn't matter, but Sheridan would not relent. Finally, Johnson, laughing along with the crowd, said, "Boys, give way and let the little Whig out. We can't force or coax him to shake hands with a Democrat."[6]

When he was fourteen, Sheridan left school and took a job at John Talbot's grocery and hardware store for $24 a year. After one year, Sheridan quit Talbot, known as a humorless skinflint, to work in David Whitehead's store for $60. A few months later, Sheridan again changed jobs—going to Finck & Dittoe dry goods for $124 a year. As head clerk and then bookkeeper, Sheridan displayed an aptitude for creating order and keeping track of things.[7]

Sheridan first considered a military career during the Mexican War, after reading newspaper reports about the exploits of a local volunteer company, the Keokuk Rifles. The boys who were too young to enlist formed their own unit, the Kosciuszko Braves; they wore green uniforms gaudily trimmed in plaid and turbans with black plumes.

The uniforms and the battle accounts ignited Sheridan's new ambition to attend the US Military Academy at West Point. A cadet was often seen in Somerset courting a girl attending St. Mary's Female Academy, and Sheridan and Greiner enjoyed spying on them. The cadet was William Tecumseh Sherman, and the girl was his future wife, Ellen Ewing.[8]

At Finck & Dittoe's, Sheridan became acquainted with Congressman Thomas Ritchey, who sometimes handed out apples from his orchard to the store employees. Sheridan asked Ritchey to secure an appointment for him at West Point. Ritchey had already selected another boy, but when that boy failed his entrance examination, Ritchey recommended Sheridan in his place.

After a few months of intensive studying and tutoring by the local schoolmaster, Sheridan boarded a train to West Point. He easily passed the entrance exam and was admitted to the Corps of Cadets on July 1, 1848.

West Point's influence was becoming strongly felt throughout the US Army. Established under a law signed by President Thomas Jefferson nearly fifty years earlier, it was modeled upon France's L'École Polytechnique. West Point was not only the army's institution of higher learning but also its proving ground for tactics and new weapons and war materials, such as cast-iron gun carriages, pontoon bridges, and breech-loading pistols. During the Civil War, nearly 450 West Point graduates served as Union or Confederate generals.

Sheridan found the course work challenging, but he was fortunate in his assigned roommate—Henry W. Slocum. A former schoolteacher, Slocum would later serve as a Union corps commander at Gettysburg and during Sherman's march through Georgia. After "Taps" at 10 p.m., Slocum draped a blanket over their window and, by candlelight or whale oil lamp, tutored Sheridan in algebra and other subjects with which he struggled.[9]

In an attempt to compensate for his uneven academic background, Sheridan read widely during the weekends, when cadets were permitted to use the academy library for recreational reading. The records show that among other items, he withdrew four books on Napoleon and his campaigns; biographies of Samuel Johnson, Lord Byron, and Mohammed; works on the geography of Ireland, Greenland, California, and Oregon; and Sir Walter Scott's Waverly novels.[10]

ANTEBELLUM WEST POINT HAD an unofficial caste system. At its pinnacle were the Southern Episcopalians, with Virginians occupying the very top echelon. Sheridan and the other Irish American Catholics from the North ranked far down in the pecking order, an arrangement that was amenable to those on top and resented by those who were not.[11]

On the West Point parade ground one day in September 1851, at the beginning of Sheridan's fourth year, a sergeant cadet from Virginia, William Terrill, peremptorily ordered him to "dress," or step closer to the man beside him. Sheridan, who believed that he was already properly closed up, snapped.

Crying, "God damn you, sir, I'll run you through!" he charged Terrill with his bayonet lowered. Before Sheridan could make good this threat, however, a dawning awareness of what he was about to do caused him to stop and return to the ranks, where he continued to berate and menace Terrill.

Terrill rightly put Sheridan on report, which only stoked Sheridan's anger further—precipitating an explosion the next day when Sheridan encountered Terrill on the barracks steps. With a curse, Sheridan clouted Terrill in the head. Terrill fought back. The larger Virginian had the upper hand over the former Pig Foot scrapper when an officer separated them.

After the cadets submitted their respective explanations for the altercation, Sheridan, who admitted to starting the fight, was suspended from West Point for one year. In choosing to suspend rather than expel Sheridan, which he would have been justified in doing, Superintendent Henry Brewerton taught Sheridan a lesson in self-control that he took to heart during the long months that he spent in Somerset, working at his old job of keeping the books at Finck & Dittoe's.[12]

SHERIDAN RETURNED TO WEST Point during the summer of 1852 to complete his senior year. His former classmates—who included Slocum; another ex-roommate, George Crook; and Alexander McCook, Sheridan's future corps commander—had graduated and left for their first postings as commissioned officers. Sheridan joined the 1853 class of James McPherson, John Bell Hood, John Schofield, and Terrill, his nemesis. His new roommate was Joshua Sill, and Robert E. Lee was the new superintendent.

Sheridan was not an exemplary cadet; he graduated in the bottom third of his class with plenty of demerits. But one important lesson stuck with him down the years—an abiding belief in offensive warfare. It was the central lesson of Dennis Hart Mahan's six-lesson "Science of War" seminar, a springtime pregraduation rite for West Point first classmen.

Mahan, toting the iconic umbrella that he carried in all weathers, spent his entire teaching career at West Point. The cadets nicknamed him "Old Cobbon Sense," because he emphasized common sense and suffered from a chronic nasal infection.

Mahan's senior-year class in civil engineering, draftsmanship, military engineering, and the building of permanent and field fortifications was the capstone of a cadet's academic career. West Point was essentially an engineering school whose top graduates went into the Corps of Engineers, while those in the bottom tier became infantry officers.

In his warfare seminar, Mahan, a devotee of Napoleon and French military theorist Antoine Jomini, literally shaped the antebellum graduates' tactical and strategic military philosophy. A leader, he said, should make it his object to destroy the enemy's army and not simply to capture territory. Furthermore, he wrote, war must be carried into the enemy's homeland to make the civilian population suffer—the very definition of "total war." Always concentrate one's forces and attack the enemy's flanks, Mahan counseled, and then relentlessly pursue him when he is beaten.

"Successful warfare is almost always offensive warfare," Mahan wrote in his slender booklet with a long title, "Elementary Treatise on Advanced-Guard, Out-Post, and Detachment Service of Troops, and the Manner of Posting and Handling Them in the Presence of the Enemy." During the coming conflagration, Mahan's six lessons would become integral to the battle plans of both sides, and his booklet would occupy a place in the saddlebags of both Union and Confederate officers.[13]

Having graduated in the bottom third of his class, Brevet Second Lieutenant Sheridan did not bother to apply for assignment to a particular branch of the army; he knew he was unlikely to get it. He was sent to the 1st US Infantry at Fort Duncan, Texas, on the Rio Grande. It was a relief to put West Point behind him and to be "looking forward with pleasant anticipation to the life before me."[14]

Sheridan reached western Texas in March 1854. On his two-hundred-mile overland journey from Corpus Christi to Fort Duncan, he marveled at the big, open country and its abundant wildlife. In Laredo, he rode out a "blue norther'"—heavy rains followed by three days of strong, northerly winds and piercing cold.

Because of recent Comanche and Lipan raids, Sheridan was sent to Camp La Pena sixty miles east of Fort Duncan for scouting duty with Company D of the 1st Infantry. Throughout the spring and summer, he was on the move almost continually, tracking and chasing small bands of Indians without ever engaging in direct combat.

He made maps, learned some Spanish from the Mexican guide, and trapped and studied the bright-colored birds whose migrations brought them through the Rio Grande Valley. He learned to stalk, kill, butcher, and dress game. He and his hunting companion kept Sheridan's company supplied with meat.

One of Sheridan's duties as company subaltern was to ensure that each morning the soldiers drank their ration of pulque. Pressed from the maguey plant and left to ferment in bottles, it was repulsive, vile tasting, and sulfurous smelling. But it inoculated the troops against scurvy in a place where fresh vegetables and fruit were rare. Sheridan learned to gulp it down as quickly as possible.

The soldiers went into winter quarters at Fort Duncan. Sheridan and the other young officers passed many pleasant evenings attending dances across the Rio Grande in Piedras Negras at the home of the Mexican commandant. The commandant's family invited the town's upper-class young women to dance with the American officers. Light refreshments were served, and the occasions, wrote Sheridan, were marked by "the greatest decorum."

In November 1854, Sheridan was promoted to second lieutenant, without the "brevet," or provisional, designation, and was transferred to the 4th US Infantry in California. The following spring, he left for Fort Reading.[15]

March 26, 1856–Washington Territory—At the bustling Fort Vancouver dock, Second Lieutenant Phil Sheridan and his forty dragoons, with a small iron naval cannon in tow, were poised to board the steamer *Belle* and sail up the Columbia River to rescue white settlers barricaded in the Middle Cascades blockhouse. Hundreds of US Army regulars were urgently collecting food, weapons, and clothing, as steamers stood ready to take them upriver. It was reminiscent of Fort Vancouver's heyday, back when it was an important Hudson's Bay Company trading center for the upper Oregon Territory.

Indians had massacred seventeen white settlers at the Cascades of the Columbia, midway between the fort and the Dalles's churning rapids. The survivors had taken refuge in the old military blockhouse at the Middle Cascades.

Nearly all of the Washington Indian tribes, angry over white encroachments on their lands, were on the warpath. Men, women, and children had been murdered in their cabins and settlements.

The previous fall, tribal leaders had ceded the lands and agreed to move to reservations. Under the agreement, whites could not move into the areas until Congress had ratified the treaty. However, the settlers and gold prospectors had not waited. Washington Territory's governor, Isaac Stevens, had encouraged the flouting of the treaty, declaring the lands open for immediate settlement. When gold was discovered in the Colville mines during the summer of 1855, the rush was on.

As so often happened in the collision of the white and Indian cultures, the tribal leaders had signed the 1855 treaty without their people's consent, during secret negotiations with Washington Territory leaders. When the tribal members learned about the treaty, they rejected it and warned that there would be a war if whites encroached on their lands.

The Indians killed six miners bound for the Colville goldfields and murdered the Indian agent sent to investigate the deaths. Under a flag of truce, militiamen seized Walla Walla chief Pio Pio Mox Mox, shot him when he tried to escape, scalped him, and cut off his ears. The Walla Wallas, Yakimas, Cayuses, and Umatillas—as well as members of other Washington tribes—donned blue paint and went on the warpath.[16]

The commander of the US Army's Northwest Department, Major General John Wool, whose service dated to the War of 1812 and who had led an expedition during the recent Mexican War, blamed the Washington and Oregon territorial governors for starting a war "to promote their own ambitious schemes." Now, he disgustedly observed, they wanted the army to win the war for them.[17]

THE WIRY, COMPACT SHERIDAN had been on duty in the Pacific Northwest for just seven months. Upon being reassigned to the 4th US Infantry in California,

Sheridan had traveled to New York, where he temporarily commanded a detachment of three hundred recruits at the army fort on Bedloe's Island before sailing to San Francisco, crossing the Isthmus of Panama in suffocating July heat.

At Fort Reading, California, he was ordered to catch up with an army expedition that had left four days earlier to survey a railroad route between the Sacramento Valley and the Columbia River in the Oregon Territory. He relieved Lieutenant John Bell Hood, a Class of 1853 classmate and future adversary, and assumed command of the expedition leader's mounted escort. The expedition's quartermaster was Lieutenant George Crook, a friend and former West Point roommate.[18]

When the expedition reached the Columbia River, Sheridan was assigned to Major Gabriel Rains's expedition against the Yakima Indians; they had killed their Indian agent and repulsed a punitive expedition under Major Granville Haller.

Rains's column, consisting of a small detachment of regulars and Oregon mounted volunteers, did no better. After trailing six hundred Yakima to a ridge, where the Indians taunted the soldiers and made lewd gestures, Sheridan proposed that he lead his dragoons into a canyon behind them while Rains charged the hill with his infantry, trapping the Indians between them—a strategy Sheridan would employ over the years with success.

But the hypercautious Rains rejected the plan, and the Indians continued to mock the soldiers before disappearing into the mountains. After the troopers foundered in the deep snow in futile pursuit, the expedition ended without achieving any of its objectives. Sheridan fumed over Rains's "incompetency."[19]

Sheridan was optimistic as 1856 began, although the Nez Perces, Spokanes, Cascades, Walla Wallas, and Umatillas had now joined the Yakimas on the warpath. Rains was gone, replaced by Colonel George Wright of the 9th Infantry, an able thirty-year veteran. Better still, the twenty-five-year-old Sheridan was leading his first independent command, small though it was, on a rescue mission.[20]

CLOAKED BY THE COLD, early-morning fog on March 27, the *Belle* deposited Sheridan and his damp dragoons on a narrow neck of land about five miles downriver from the Middle Cascades blockhouse. The runoff-swollen Columbia River had made a peninsula of the shelf of vegetation-clotted dry land, hemmed on one side by a flooded slough and on the other by the river.

Yakima and Cascade Indians were also on the neck of land, Sheridan and his men quickly discovered. The Indians commenced taunting and shooting at the soldiers. With six men, Sheridan advanced under cover of the thick underbrush to determine the Indians' position and strength.

There was another gust of gunfire, and a bullet nicked Sheridan's nose and struck a soldier crouched beside him in the neck, severing his carotid artery and spinal cord and spraying blood everywhere. It was Sheridan's first close brush with death under fire. Buoyed by the kill, the Indians rushed the scouting party, but other soldiers brought up the naval gun and opened fire with solid shot. The Indians withdrew.

All day long, the dragoons and Indians traded gunfire, with neither side able to advance. At nightfall, Sheridan sent the *Belle* back to Vancouver with his written report on the situation.

After a day's desultory combat—Sheridan's first—the blockhouse still lay five miles distant. But rather than wait for a relief force, Sheridan devised a new plan of attack.

Early the next morning, after firing the cannon into the solid wall of green in which the Indians lay hidden, Sheridan and half of his forty dragoons boarded a large Hudson's Bay bateau brought up on the *Belle* and crossed to the Columbia's south shore.

In the middle of the river, just below the blockhouse, lay Bradford's Island, two miles long and a mile wide. Sheridan planned to row the bateau upriver along the island's south side, concealed from the Indians on the north shore, and then to cross the river to the blockhouse.

But the south channel was choked with rapids, and Sheridan saw that the bateau would have to be dragged by rope through the rocks and rapids to the smooth water opposite the blockhouse. Sheridan and ten men landed on the island and began hauling the boat upriver by a rope attached to its bow.

It was slow, laborious work—until the soldiers happened upon a camp of Indian squaws. Commanding their silence, so as not to alert the warriors on the river's north shore, Sheridan and his men forced the squaws to help them pull the boat. "They worked well under compulsion, and manifested no disposition to strike for higher wages," Sheridan sardonically observed.[21]

Sheridan and his dragoons landed just below the blockhouse and, anticlimactically, rescued the settlers without further resistance from the Indians. A couple hours later, an army detachment under Lieutenant Colonel Edward Steptoe arrived from Vancouver.

The Cascades on the north shore had fled to the island, while the Yakimas had bolted for the mountains. Sheridan, Steptoe, and their men crossed to the island, formed a skirmish line, and rounded up the Cascades—men, women, and children.

The headmen denied playing any role in the settlers' massacre or in the battle on the north shore. But when Sheridan lined up all the Indians with their muskets in hand and checked them for powder residue, he found that all had been fired recently.

Sheridan arrested thirteen of the "principal miscreants." Colonel Wright convened a drumhead court, which convicted Chief Chimoneth and eight braves of participating in the massacre. They were hanged.[22]

WHILE SHERIDAN AND HIS dragoons were camped near the blockhouse, a frontier guide, Joseph Meek, asked Sheridan whether an Indian named Spencer or his family had passed through the area. They were traveling to Fort Vancouver, where Spencer, an influential, peaceable Chinook chief, was an interpreter and mediator for Colonel Wright.

Meek said that Spencer, believing it safe for his family to travel alone, had gone ahead, but the family had not yet reached Fort Vancouver. Meek glumly remarked that they were probably all dead.

Sheridan and his dragoons began a search and soon found the bodies of the mother and six children. All had been strangled. The bodies were arranged in a semicircle, with short lengths of rope knotted around their necks—except for the baby, around whose neck was looped a red silk handkerchief, probably taken from the mother.

The killers, Sheridan surmised, were probably whites avenging the deaths of their relatives during the recent settler massacres. He never forgot what he saw that day.[23]

IN HIS GENERAL ORDERS No. 14, General in Chief Winfield Scott recounted the successful Cascades campaign and "the gallant conduct of the troops, under, in most cases, circumstances of great hardship and privation." He added, "Second Lieutenant Philip H. Sheridan, Fourth Infantry, is specially mentioned for his gallantry." In his first combat, Sheridan had displayed initiative, bravery, and a knack for improvisation.[24]

In 1857, the army and the militia got the upper hand in the Yakima War, and the tribes were compelled to cede enormous tracts of land west of the Cascade Mountains. The massacres and revenge killings had blighted the countryside. A traveler to the Washington coast in 1857 observed deserted, ruined homes and desolate fields.[25]

GENERAL WOOL SENT SHERIDAN and his dragoons to Fort Yamhill to prod the 1,500 Indians on the Grande Ronde reservation in Oregon's Coastal Range to adopt an agrarian life. For the next four years, the reservation was Sheridan's home base.

The Oregon Indian tribes had submitted tamely to the whites, except for the Rogue River bands, which refused to abandon their hunting-and-gathering ways. Sheridan and his men tried to persuade them at least to give up their self-destructive traditions, such as honoring the dead by destroying the deceased's possessions and killing their horses on their graves. Another tradition permitted a family to kill a medicine doctor if a relative died under his care.

One day, a band of Rogue River Indians murdered a medicine woman on Fort Yamhill's parade ground after her patient died. Sheridan met with the Indians—by now, he was fluent in Chinook, the coastal tribes' lingua franca—and demanded that they give up the sixteen men who had each fired a bullet into the woman's body. The tribe refused. During the unsuccessful parley, someone stole Sheridan's pistol.

That night, Sheridan and fifty troopers raided the Indians' camp and captured the chief. Sheridan threatened to kill him unless his tribesmen handed over the sixteen men. They surrendered the killers, and Sheridan placed all of them in chains. There were no further clashes between the Rogue River Indians and Sheridan's men.[26]

Sheridan now had time to enjoy coastal Oregon's beauty. He described watching squaws and their children gathering crabs at night on the beach at Yaquina Bay. With a torch in one hand and a sharp stick in the other, they impaled the crabs and deposited them in baskets that they carried on their backs. "The reflection by the water of the light from the many torches," wrote Sheridan, "with the movement of the Indians while at work, formed a weird and diverting picture of which we were never tired."[27]

And then there was Sidnayoh—her white friends called her Frances—the daughter of a Willamette Valley Indian chief and Sheridan's lover in Oregon. Sidnayoh never forgot Sheridan and even traveled to Washington, DC, after the Civil War to see him. However, Sheridan evidently made it clear that their romance was over; when she returned to Oregon, Sidnayoh married a Canadian trapper. In early 1869, Sheridan declined President-elect Ulysses Grant's appointment to the army's Pacific Northwest District command, citing "many reasons, some of which are personal."[28]

WHEN THE CIVIL WAR began in April 1861, Sheridan and his fellow officers watched the developments 3,000 miles away with sharp interest. Several Southern officers left the 4th Infantry to join the Confederate army, part of an exodus of Southerners throughout the US Army.

A wave of promotions swept the ranks, much to the relief of the remaining Union officers. Sheridan, who had spent eight years as a second lieutenant, became a first lieutenant and then, three months later, a captain. While his regiment was ordered east, Sheridan remained at Fort Yamhill, awaiting the arrival of his replacement, Captain James Archer of the 9th US Infantry.

But when Archer arrived, Sheridan refused to relinquish command to him, believing that his sympathies lay with the Confederacy and that he might commit "some rebellious act." Indeed, Archer resigned his commission and left Fort Yamhill in July to join the Rebels. Sheridan remained in charge until September, when another captain—who convinced Sheridan of his fealty to the Union—relieved him.

Eager to get in on the fighting, Sheridan headed east.[29]

HIS PATRIOTISM, SHERIDAN WROTE, "was untainted by politics, nor had it been disturbed by any discussion of the questions out of which the war grew." To friends and neighbors whom he visited in Somerset on the way to his new duty station in St. Louis, he said, "This country is too great and good to be destroyed."[30]

In November 1861, he reported to the 13th US Infantry, commanded by Brigadier General William Tecumseh Sherman, whose courtship more than a decade earlier Sheridan had covertly watched.

But no sooner had Sheridan reached Jefferson Barracks, Missouri, than the Department of the Missouri's new commanding general, Major General Henry Halleck, assigned him to audit the department's disordered ledgers. Millions of dollars were unaccounted for at the end of the chaotic hundred-day command of Halleck's predecessor, Major General John C. Fremont.

Fremont had built up his command and raised an ironclad fleet on the Mississippi River, but he had also run up shocking costs and quarreled with—and even jailed—his patron, Frank Blair, the brother of Postmaster General Montgomery Blair. Fremont's "emancipation proclamation" for the states that he administered—Missouri, Iowa, Minnesota, Illinois, Arkansas, and western Kentucky—was too much for President Abraham Lincoln, who demanded that Fremont withdraw it. When Fremont refused and the Blairs then leveled serious charges against him, Lincoln fired Fremont on October 7, 1861.[31]

Fremont's chief quartermaster, Brigadier General Justus McKinstry, was in jail when Sheridan reached Jefferson Barracks. McKinstry and his agents had overcharged the government for building materials, horses, clothing, and other goods, pocketing huge sums of money without Fremont's knowledge.

Sheridan joined an army committee trying to find out where the money had gone. It was just one of three committees sifting through the Fremont department books, the others being a congressional subcommittee and President Lincoln's three-man Commission on the Debts of the Western Division.

"The duty was not distasteful," Sheridan wrote, "and I felt that I was qualified to undertake it." Indeed, Sheridan's familiarity with quartermaster and commissary paperwork, together with his Finck & Dittoe's bookkeeping experience, undoubtedly had recommended him to Halleck for the job.

When Sheridan and the other investigators finished their work, McKinstry was court-martialed, convicted of fraud, and dismissed from the army.[32]

HALLECK GAVE SHERIDAN A new assignment: chief commissary and chief quartermaster of the Army of the Southwest. Its commander, Brigadier General Samuel Curtis, was assembling troops and supplies for a campaign to drive Confederate major general Earl Van Dorn's army from southwestern Missouri.

Sheridan was an extremely efficient, if ruthless, commissary quartermaster. A staff officer described him as "a modest quiet little man" with a forceful personality and "vitalizing energy." As the army marched toward a major clash with Van Dorn's Rebels at Pea Ridge, along the way Sheridan built mills where his men threshed corn and wheat. And all over southern Missouri, Sheridan's commissary agents purchased grain, produce, and livestock from the region's often hostile, pro-Confederate farmers.

Sheridan paid fair prices, but he also dealt harshly with uncooperative growers who claimed they had nothing to give the Yankees—by coercing them to reveal hiding places. Decades later, Colonel Grenville Dodge of the 4th Iowa Infantry would write that the brutal methods employed to obtain this information from these holdouts "would astonish those of our people who have been so horrified at the mild persuasions used for similar purposes in the Philippines."[33]

When Sheridan discovered that some troopers were stealing horses from civilians and selling them to the commissary department, he seized the horses as captured property, branded them with "US" markings, and refused to pay for them. An assistant quartermaster in on the scam circulated a false report that Sheridan was withholding money that the foragers had earned honestly. Without first looking into the matter, Curtis, preoccupied with the Battle of Pea Ridge—an important victory that gave the Union control of Missouri—ordered Sheridan to pay the men.

Sheridan refused. "No authority can compel me to jayhawk or steal. If those under my supervision are allowed to do so, I respectfully ask the general to relieve me from duty in this District." Curtis's staff drew up charges against Sheridan, alleging disobedience of orders and neglect of duty. Sheridan promptly turned to Halleck, and the general sent orders for Sheridan to report to St. Louis. The charges were never preferred—they were pronounced "nil-void" in August 1862.[34]

"Forlorn and disheartened at the turn affairs had been taken," Sheridan wrote, he returned to St. Louis. Halleck gave him no time to brood, sending him north to buy horses for the army. In Wisconsin and Illinois, he bought four hundred mounts and shipped them downriver.

SHERIDAN WAS IN CHICAGO when he learned that a bloody battle had been fought at Shiloh (Hebrew for "place of peace") in southwestern Tennessee on April 6 and 7. He left immediately for St. Louis, hoping to get into the fighting that was continuing in Mississippi.[35]

Caught by surprise and apparently beaten on the battle's first day, Major General Ulysses Grant's Army of the Tennessee, reinforced during the night by 30,000 troops from Major General Don Carlos Buell's Army of the Ohio, had won a narrow victory on the second day. Calls for Grant's removal were met by President Lincoln's declaration, "I can't spare this man; he fights."[36]

When Sheridan reached St. Louis, Halleck was not there. He was on his way to Shiloh to take personal command of the Armies of the Mississippi, Tennessee, and Ohio that were massing for an offensive in Mississippi.

Sheridan persuaded the commander's assistant adjutant general, Colonel John Kelton, to give him an assignment in Mississippi. Kelton drafted orders for Sheridan to report to Halleck, and Sheridan hitched a ride down the Mississippi on a hospital boat bound for Pittsburg Landing.

"This I consider the turning-point in my military career, and shall always feel grateful to Colonel Kelton for his kindly act which so greatly influenced my future," Sheridan later wrote in his *Personal Memoirs*.[37]

A YEAR AFTER GENERAL P. T. G. Beauregard's batteries fired on Fort Sumter, Captain Phil Sheridan at last reached the war zone. But he was again disappointed in his hope of joining a combat unit. Halleck sent him to Colonel George Thom, his chief topographical engineer, who gave Sheridan the unglamorous job of building corduroy roads across the swampy bottomlands between the supply depot at Pittsburg Landing and the front near Corinth, Mississippi. By Sheridan's own admission, "it was rough, hard work, without much chance of reward, but it was near the field of active operations, and I determined to do the best I could at it till opportunity for something better might arise."

Such an opportunity soon presented itself. While Halleck labored mightily to supply his army of 100,000, his headquarters camp was in bad straits—poorly sited and provisioned. At the suggestion of one of Halleck's staff officers, Sheridan was assigned to fix the camp's problems. Conditions rapidly improved, thanks to Sheridan's knack for creating order. Everyone, including Sheridan, was happy with the changes. "My stay at General Halleck's headquarters was exceedingly agreeable," he wrote.

The great benefit of Sheridan's assignment to the army's headquarters was the regular access he now had to all of the Mississippi army's important figures. It moved

Sheridan out of the army's shadows, where he had toiled for eight long years, into the bright light where decisions and careers were made.[38]

In his unoccupied hours, Sheridan went to the front to watch Brigadier General Sherman's men skirmish with the Rebels. Sheridan and Sherman discovered that, besides their common Ohio backgrounds and Sheridan's acquaintance with Sherman's in-laws, the Ewings, they had other qualities in common: their eloquent profanity, their loquaciousness when among friends, and their passion for order.

Sherman understood what Sheridan had been through in Missouri. In Kentucky, Sherman was relieved of command by Buell due to newspaper reports alleging that he was unstable and possibly deranged. Sent to Halleck, Sherman was given a division—one of those driven back during Shiloh's first day. Nonetheless, Halleck retained confidence in Sherman.[39]

Sherman was eleven years older than Sheridan, and he took a big-brotherly liking to the younger man. Would Sheridan be interested in a field command with an Ohio regiment if Sherman could arrange it? Of course, this was the very thing that Sheridan wanted. But Ohio governor David Tod appointed someone else.

Sheridan's name remained in circulation, however. Brigadier General Gordon Granger, the Army of the Mississippi's cavalry corps commander, recommended Sheridan to Michigan governor Austin Blair while visiting his state's volunteer regiments. Blair was seeking a regular army officer to lead the 2nd Michigan Cavalry.

On May 27, 1862, Captain Russell Alger, a former Michigan governor, delivered a telegram to Sheridan informing him that he had been appointed commander of the 2nd Michigan Cavalry. Thrilled with his first field command, Sheridan persuaded Halleck to waive the usual War Department clearance so that he could join his new regiment immediately.

Sheridan set out with Alger and the regiment's quartermaster for the 2nd Michigan, which was poised to mount a raid near Rebel-held Corinth. As he rode away from Halleck's headquarters camp, Sheridan wore the coat and trousers of an infantry captain, but on his shoulders rested a pair of well-used colonel's epaulets given to him by General Granger.

That very night, Sheridan embarked on his first raid of the war with his new command.[40]

CORINTH WAS HALLECK'S OBJECTIVE as he inched his massive army southward for seven weeks—digging, digging at every stopping point. "Old Brains," as Halleck's men nicknamed him because he was a lawyer, author, and military theorist and had helped write California's constitution, was a brilliant administrator but an obsessively cautious field commander. At last, his grumbling, sweating men scooped out trenches on the northern edge of the railroad hub in anticipation of a siege—and a climactic, possibly war-ending battle.

But when the Union army finally entered Corinth on May 30, the Yankees found only deserted works, dummy guns, and even wooden cannoneers with mocking grins painted on their faces; the Rebels had slipped away to Tupelo, fifty miles to the south. Halleck pronounced it a great victory and sent Major General John Pope and his Army of the Mississippi after the Rebels.[41]

SHERIDAN'S 2ND MICHIGAN RODE east, almost into Alabama. With the 2nd Iowa Cavalry, the other regiment in Colonel Washington Elliott's cavalry brigade, it captured Iuka. The brigade then seized Booneville, twenty-two miles south of Corinth, and destroyed the tracks of the Mobile and Ohio Railroad, preventing the retreating Confederates from using it.

As the Rebels approached Booneville on their way to Tupelo, the Union cavalrymen repelled an attack by enemy mounted troops, capturing five hundred prisoners. They burned twenty-six railroad cars and their contents, about 10,000 small arms, and three cannons. Sheridan's regiment and the Iowans then joined in Pope's pursuit, clashing often with the withdrawing Confederates.[42]

On June 11, when Colonel Elliott was promoted to brigadier general and became Pope's chief of staff, Sheridan became the brigade's commander—just two weeks after joining the 2nd Michigan. "Whenever my authority would permit I saved my command from needless sacrifices and unnecessary toil," he wrote. "Therefore, when hard or daring work was to be done, I expected the heartiest response, and always got it."[43]

ON JULY 1, COLONEL Phil Sheridan and his cavalry brigade awaited the Confederates in the wilting heat outside Booneville. Scouts had reported that 5,000 Rebel cavalrymen led by Brigadier General James Chalmers were swarming up two roads that converged southwest of Booneville.

Just north of the junction, Sheridan and his 820 men guarded the southern approaches to Corinth. He recognized that his men, outnumbered five to one, must make a supreme effort if they hoped to withstand the Rebel attacks, much less prevail.

In a matter of minutes, his pickets were falling back and firing at two Rebel regiments advancing on either side of the road. After dismounting, the Confederates occupied strong positions north of the junction. Sheridan sent Captain Archibald Campbell and the rest of the 2nd Michigan to reinforce his pickets and positioned the 2nd Iowa behind Campbell.

He informed the cavalry reserve commander, Brigadier General Alexander Asboth, who was in Rienzi, ten miles from Sheridan, that Chalmers had eight regiments, and Sheridan's two regiments needed support, particularly artillery. "Let me have them at once, if it is possible," he wrote.[44]

The Rebels attacked Campbell across an open field, their eerie, keening cry sending shivers down the spines of the Union cavalrymen. The Yankees waited until the attackers were thirty yards away before driving them off with heavy fire from their Colt revolving rifles, which could fire six shots without reloading but were prone to powder fires.

Chalmers's cavalrymen attacked Campbell's flanks, forcing him to withdraw to a stronger position. Then, they mounted another frontal assault. There were too many of them, and this time the Rebels overran Campbell's position. During the brutish hand-to-hand combat, the Yankees fended off the Rebels with rifle butts. The 2nd Iowa rushed to the 2nd Michigan's assistance, and together they repelled the attack.

The roar of small arms fire subsided, and there was a lull in the fighting as Chalmers prepared to launch a strong attack on the brigade's left flank. Sheridan knew that he must act quickly; his brigade faced annihilation. He asked the cavalry division headquarters for two battalions, along with artillery and infantry. "I have been holding a large force of the enemy—prisoners say ten regiments—all day, and am considerably cut up."

At the same time, Sheridan was also making an offensive plan to defeat the Rebels with just his small force. In his *Personal Memoirs*, Sheridan wrote, "My standing in drawing at the Military Academy had never been so high as to warrant the belief that I could ever prove myself an expert." But at West Point he had learned how to make rough maps; he had notebooks full of them.

He had in fact drawn a map of Booneville and the surrounding countryside. It was about to come in handy as he prepared to put into practice the overriding principle taught in Dennis Mahan's "Science of War" class: "Successful warfare is almost always offensive warfare." Attack the flanks, Mahan had said, and pursue the enemy until he was beaten.[45]

On his map, Sheridan noted that a meandering woodmen's road looped around the Rebels' left flank. A small mounted force might slip down that road, get around Chalmers, and strike his rear—while Sheridan simultaneously launched a frontal attack. Only by making such "a bold and radical change in our tactics," thought Sheridan, could his brigade beat the heavy odds against it.

He selected four saber companies—cavalrymen who fought principally on horseback. Two were from the 2nd Michigan, and two were from the 2nd Iowa, for a total of ninety-two men. Captain Russell Alger, the former Michigan governor, was ill and resting in his tent when Sheridan asked him to lead the flank attack. Alger eagerly consented. Sheridan directed him to follow the woodmen's road until it joined a road about three miles from Booneville, turn up it immediately, and charge in column formation, employing it as a battering ram to pierce the Rebels' rear.

It would take about an hour for Alger's men to get into position. They should cheer loudly when they attacked, said Sheridan, so that the rest of the brigade could launch its assault on the enemy's main force. The element of surprise, he believed, would swing the prospects for victory in his favor.

He assigned to Alger a "thin, sallow, tawny-haired Mississippian" named Breene, whom Sheridan had used as a guide and who knew all of the backcountry roads. Sheridan did not attempt to downplay the great risk involved. It would be the sort of "quick and desperate work that is usually imposed on a forlorn hope," he told Alger.[46]

Sheridan moved all 730 of his remaining men into his front line, where the fighting was steady and sharp as the Confederates pressed his brigade's left flank. An hour passed, and no cheering from Alger's men reached Sheridan's ears.

Unwilling to wait any longer, he ordered his men to attack.[47]

At nearly that very instant, as the 6,000 men in the opposing armies braced for a bloody collision, they heard a whistle announcing the arrival of a train in Booneville. It was a locomotive and two railcars filled with grain for the Yankees' horses. But Sheridan's men, knowing that he had earlier sent a courier requesting reinforcements, believed that reinforcements had arrived from Rienzi. They let loose a wild cheer and charged the Rebel line with abandon.

Seeing that the misperception might indeed also serve the purpose of demoralizing the Rebels, the quick-thinking Sheridan sped instructions to the train engineer to blow the whistle loudly and repeatedly. "This stratagem," Sheridan wrote afterward, worked beautifully; the Confederate line began to disintegrate in confusion before Sheridan's small force.

This was not the doing of the train whistle alone, though. Alger's men had struck the rear of the Confederate lines just as the brigade launched its frontal attack. Either because of distance or the train whistle's shrieks, their cheering had not carried to the brigade's lines. Yet the two attacks occurred almost simultaneously, just as Sheridan had planned, and the Rebels stampeded. The Yankees pursued them for four miles.

Sheridan finally got a reply to the stream of dispatches he had been sending to headquarters without receiving any acknowledgment. The reply was an order for him to fall back.

Sheridan quickly wrote out an answer: "I have driven the enemy back and hurt them badly. I do not see any necessity of falling back." He sent another dispatch a short time later: "I will not want any infantry supports; I have whipped the enemy to-day."

With just one man lost, Sheridan had defeated a much larger enemy force and killed sixty-five Rebel cavalrymen in his first battle leading an independent command.[48]

MAJOR GENERAL WILLIAM ROSECRANS, who had succeeded Pope as Army of the Mississippi commander, issued an order complimenting Sheridan. In a telegram to Halleck, now in Washington, DC, where he was the army's commanding general, Rosecrans wrote, "More cavalry massed under such an officer would be of great use to us. Sheridan ought to be made a brigadier."[49]

On July 3, Generals Gordon Granger, Horatio Wright, and Alexander Asboth added their endorsements in another dispatch to Halleck: "Brigadiers scarce; good ones scarcer. The undersigned urge the promotion of Sheridan. He is worth his weight in gold. He would not make a stampeding general."[50]

Sheridan was busy patrolling the scorching-hot Mississippi woods in order to divine the intentions of Major General Braxton Bragg, the new Rebel commander in Tupelo. On July 28, a detachment from Sheridan's brigade raided Ripley and seized a cache of Confederate letters left behind by the fleeing 26th Alabama.

As he sifted through the letters, Sheridan spotted a piece of valuable intelligence: the Rebels were planning to send a large army to discourage Buell from marching on Chattanooga. He forwarded the information up the command chain. It was intelligence of "immense value," wrote Rosecrans, who added his name to those lobbying for Sheridan's promotion.[51]

ON SEPTEMBER 13, HALLECK confirmed Sheridan's promotion to brigadier, effective July 1, the day of his Booneville victory. Sheridan had risen to the rank of general just weeks after being promoted from captain to colonel.

Orders arrived for Sheridan, his brigade, and the rest of Granger's division to join Buell's Army of the Ohio in Louisville. Bragg had successfully diverted Buell from his supposed designs on Chattanooga and marched into Kentucky, where his army threatened to shatter the state's shaky allegiance to the Union and lay open the entire Ohio River valley.

Before leaving Mississippi, Sheridan was presented with a new horse by Captain Campbell of the 2nd Michigan. The jet-black, three-year-old gelding stood seventeen hands high and was said to possess extraordinary stamina.

Sheridan named the horse Rienzi, for the Mississippi town near Booneville where he had recently skirmished with the Rebels. For the rest of the war, Sheridan would ride Rienzi in every campaign and battle. Henry Greiner, Sheridan's lifelong friend, wrote that its "favorite gait was a swinging pace from which she [sic] would go if urged by word, or the bridge rein into a rack, or canter, always with the ease of a cradle and the grace of an antelope."[52]

SHERIDAN WAS IN CORINTH to entrain with his brigade for Kentucky when he encountered Major General Ulysses Grant, who was disconsolately watching some of his best troops ship out. Grant was unhappy to see Sheridan's brigade leaving too. "He was much hurt at the inconsiderate way in which his command was being depleted," Sheridan wrote.

Sheridan was eager to go to Kentucky, because he knew he would see action there. He made it clear to Grant—"somewhat emphatically, I fear"—that he did not want him to attempt to keep Sheridan's unit in Mississippi.

Grant later wrote that while he was sorry to see Sheridan leave, "his departure was probably fortunate, for he rendered distinguished service in his new field."[53]

———

CHAPTER 2

Stones River

SEPTEMBER 1862–SEPTEMBER 1863

My division, alone and unbroken, made a gallant stand to protect the right flank of our army. . . . My troops gave time for a re-arrangement of our lines.

—SHERIDAN, IN HIS BATTLE REPORT[1]

DECEMBER 31, 1862, 2 A.M.–STONES RIVER, TENNESSEE—Cold rain had soaked the central Tennessee woods all day long, but it had finally stopped when Phil Sheridan was awakened from a brief slumber in his tent. Sheridan sat on the edge of his cot, fully awake, studying the worried face of his 1st Brigade commander, Brigadier General Joshua Sill, his former West Point roommate and friend.

Hours earlier, just after nightfall, the regimental bands had serenaded the 43,000 men of the Army of the Cumberland with "Yankee Doodle" and "Hail Columbia." The Southern bands in the 37,000-man Army of the Tennessee barely a quarter mile away, in a cedar grove on the other side of an open cotton field, had riposted with "Dixie" and "Bonnie Blue Flag."

Then a band had struck up "Home Sweet Home." All the musicians, Yankee and Rebel alike, had joined in, with soldiers on both sides singing along, many of them choking up over the words "There's no place like home."[2]

Methodical and precise as always, Sheridan had met with his three brigade commanders to review the offensive planned for just after dawn on the far left of the Union line. Sheridan's 3rd Division and the two other divisions of Major General Alexander McCook's right wing were to play only a peripheral role, while the left wing, led by Major General Thomas L. Crittenden, folded back Braxton Bragg's right and got behind the Rebel center. At the same time, Major General George Thomas, commanding the Union center, would attack the Confederate center, sandwiching the Rebels between him and Crittenden.[3]

It had all sounded reasonable enough in the orders issued by Major General William Rosecrans, the Army of the Cumberland's commander. Sheridan planned to have his men up and ready for action by daybreak.

What no one in Rosecrans's army knew was that Bragg had made an identical battle plan—to strike the Union right with his left wing. Bragg's assault was planned for about the same time as Rosecrans's attack. If Bragg and Rosecrans attacked simultaneously, in theory they might twirl around like two dancers. In practice, something entirely different would occur.[4]

In Sheridan's tent, Sill told Sheridan that Confederate infantry and artillery had been moving along his front all night long. He believed that Bragg was massing troops for an attack on the Union right—the sector where no offensive action was planned that morning. Sheridan rode with Sill to the lines and listened. After a few minutes, he told Sill that General McCook needed to be informed.[5]

At McCook's headquarters, Sheridan and Sill awakened their commander and described the incessant rumble of artillery and the tramp of infantry that they had heard along their front. Clearly, they expected to receive orders to ready their men for a possible Rebel assault.

But McCook was unconcerned. In just five hours, he told them, the Rebels would be too busy trying to fend off Crittenden's attack on their own right to attempt an attack on the Union right. McCook was confident that Sheridan's division and his corps's two other divisions, commanded by Brigadier Generals R. W. Johnson and Jefferson C. Davis, could handle anything the Confederates threw at him. There was no need for further measures, said McCook. He sent Sheridan and Sill away.[6]

McCook HAD NOT ALLAYED their concerns. Sheridan decided to ready his 5,000-man division, at least, in case the Confederates confounded McCook's expectations by attacking the Union right.

Sheridan awakened his regimental commanders and gave each the same message: feed your men and have them in battle formation before daylight. He sent two reserve regiments to reinforce Sill's brigade.[7]

The 3rd Division was under arms and standing in ranks when the camps of Generals Davis and Johnson were just stirring to life. Across the valley, in the enemy camp in the black cedar grove opposite Sheridan's division, where there had been cheerful fires and band music hours before, followed by the sound of marching men, an unnatural hush reigned.

IN THE CREPUSCULAR PREDAWN light, a fog arose from the soaked ground that lay between the armies. It thickened with dawn's approach.

And then, at 7:15, before the Union left wing's scheduled attack on Bragg's right flank, there emerged from the fog two long, dense battle lines of butternut troops, incongruously heralded by a wave of flushed jackrabbits that scampered over the cotton fields. Eerily silent, the Rebels advanced steadily, with a firm tread, colors flying, the dark host conducting itself "as if on the parade ground."

Advancing upon Sheridan's men was Major General J. M. Withers's division of Lieutenant General Leonidas Polk's corps; to Sheridan's right, Lieutenant General William Hardee's 10,000-man corps was tidally surging toward Davis's and Johnson's camps, where the troops were unconcernedly making coffee and breakfast. The Rebels had risen early and gotten ready for action without any sustenance except whiskey, to fortify them for the daredevil feat of charging an armed enemy across open ground.[8]

As Sheridan's men watched from good defensive positions amid jumbled rock slabs and thick-growing cedars riddled with holes and fissures, the Rebels lowered their bayonets. When they were about one hundred yards away, they began jogging toward the Union lines with their keening cry.

Three of Sheridan's batteries shredded the Confederate column, but it did not stop. Fifty yards from Sheridan's lines, Colonel Francis Sherman, who commanded the 88th Illinois in Sill's brigade, ordered his infantrymen to fire, aiming low. They rose to one knee and loosed a volley from their charged muskets. The Rebels wavered, as though they had met a strong wind, and then resumed their double-quick-time approach.

Reloading, Sherman's men riddled the Rebel column with a second volley. Some of the Confederates flung themselves to the ground and tried to fire back. Sherman ordered a counterattack, and the bluecoats repulsed the Rebels—but not for long, and not without heavy loss. Among those killed was General Sill, shot in the head while leading his men.

Withers attacked twice more, failing to break Sheridan's lines both times. Sheridan "was everywhere present in the thickest of the battle," wrote Sherman. His men recognized him at a glance, with his uniform coat buttoned to his throat and his trademark flat-brimmed hat clamped on his distinctive bullet-shaped head.

As nearly 20,000 Rebel troops crashed into the right wing's three divisions, Sheridan prowled his lines, shouting encouragement. On this day, as would always be the case during combat, Sheridan was energy incarnate; a newspaper correspondent wrote that he was "more than magnetic, he was electric."[9]

WHILE SHERIDAN'S DIVISION WAS repelling the first Confederate attacks by Withers's troops, Hardee's onslaught caught Johnson's division of McCook's right wing completely unprepared. When the Rebels struck, the Yankees were shaving, boiling coffee, and cooking bacon. Their arms were stacked and unloaded.

Hardee's corps slammed into them before they could react; a Rebel private compared the Confederates' swooping attack to "a whirl-a-gust of woodpeckers in a hail storm." For some of McCook's veterans, the overwhelming assault bore a nightmarish resemblance to Hardee's triumphant attack at Shiloh nine months earlier—as on this day, it had come in the early morning and from the south. Some of them even shouted, "Shiloh!"[10]

Johnson's division crumbled, abandoning its frontline batteries because there was no time to bring them into action. Hardee's tough veterans wheeled to their right and plowed into Davis's division, driving it, too, back in wild disarray. In the now chaotic camps of McCook's men, the storming Rebels snatched up food cooking in frying pans and killed Yankees still in their nightclothes inside their tents. One Union soldier was shot dead while clutching his coffeepot.[11]

Sheridan's division had stood its ground during the attack, but the rout of Johnson's and Davis's divisions exposed its right flank and rear. Sheridan hastily swung his division to the right, like a door on a hinge, placing it on a new line perpendicular to his initial position.

Hardee's corps surged toward the Nashville Pike, hoping to cut off Nashville, the Union operations base, from Rosecrans's army. It would be an enormous strategic accomplishment, for if Nashville then fell into Confederate hands, the way into Kentucky might be reopened for Bragg's Army of the Tennessee, possibly all the way to the Ohio River. It would expiate Bragg's indecently swift withdrawal from Kentucky after the confused Battle of Perryville three months earlier.[12]

McCook's two shattered divisions retreated pell-mell for three miles. The panicked troops poured through the Union regiments in the center. It was "a yelling mob, officers weeping or swearing, soldiers demoralized and shivering," wrote Captain Henry Castle. Another observer, Henry Freeman, saw "men retiring with guns, and men without their guns; men limping, others holding up their blood-stained arms and hands. . . . Riderless horses dashed out of the woods . . . ran for a distance, and stopped and stared back at the tumult."[13]

Two fresh divisions from Polk's corps now attacked Sheridan—Irish-born Major General Patrick Cleburne's division targeting his flank and Major General Benjamin Cheatham's division attacking frontally—to make a clean sweep of Mc-Cook's right wing. Low on ammunition, Sheridan's division slowly fell back. During a two-hour fighting retreat, Sheridan's men joined Brigadier General James Negley's division from George Thomas's center corps in new positions.

Sheridan placed Colonel George Roberts's brigade at right angles to Negley's men. The brigades of Colonel Nicholas Greusel—Sill's replacement—and Colonel Frederick Schaefer were then put at right angles to Roberts's brigade, forming an inverted "U," with Sheridan's artillery in the center. Along the Wilkinson Pike, on a limestone ridge, amid sinkholes and rock outcrops, screened by a dense cedar brake, Sheridan faced Hardee's and Polk's advancing corps, determined to prevent them from reaching the Nashville Pike.[14]

When Rosecrans learned that his right wing had been crushed by Bragg's surprise attack, he suspended the offensive against the Rebel right wing and sent two divisions from his left running to try to staunch the breakthrough. But he knew they wouldn't reach the front in time to stop the Rebels.

Informed that Sheridan's bloodied division had survived the attack and in fact occupied a strong position between the Confederates and the chaotic Union lines, Rosecrans told Sheridan that he must, at all costs, hold his position to give the rest of the Army of the Cumberland time to establish new defensive positions. Sheridan understood the import of Rosecrans's words: "It would probably require a sacrifice of my command."[15]

Outnumbered two to one, Sheridan and his men hunkered down among rocks and cedar logs and made one of the great stands of the war. Hardee's corps assaulted Sheridan's right, and the Rebels "seemed . . . present on every side."

But Sheridan occupied a strong position, although his and Hardee's batteries lay just two hundred yards apart. The Rebels attacked, yelling, across an open field, and the Yankee gunners cut them to pieces. "Men fell around on every side like autumn leaves," wrote Lieutenant Colonel J. J. Scales of the 30th Mississippi, "and every foot of soil over which we passed seemed [dyed] with the life blood" of his men.[16]

"For the first time since daylight, General Hardee was seriously checked in the turning movement he had begun," wrote Sheridan.

The Rebels attacked a second and third time—also without success. Sheridan's division was hemorrhaging; about one-third of his men were wounded or dead, among them another brigade commander, Colonel Roberts, followed by Roberts's replacement, Colonel Fazilo Harrington.

During ninety minutes of intensive combat, in which Rebel troops with glittering bayonets battled to within a few feet of Sheridan's lines, his 3rd Division stood off three Confederate divisions.[17]

There was a lull, as the two sides assessed the shocking bloodletting. Sheridan discovered that two of his three brigades had no ammunition and that the Confederates had captured the right wing's ammunition train. He would have to withdraw.

Sheridan ordered his men to fix bayonets and to counterattack if the Rebels launched an assault during the division's withdrawal. Roberts's brigade fired the last of its ammunition as Sheridan's troops slowly retreated toward the Nashville Pike, where Rosecrans's divisions from the center and left had dug in.

Under heavy fire, Sheridan's depleted division, blackened by powder, blood streaked, and bandaged, withdrew through the cedar brake. Eight guns had to be abandoned because no horses were alive to pull them—eighty lay sprawled dead on the ridge—and the gunners were unable to manhandle the guns over the rocky ground.[18]

At the pike, Rosecrans encountered Sheridan, his face flushed and powder smudged, swearing wonderfully as he directed the orderly withdrawal. A devout Catholic, the commanding general admonished Sheridan to watch his language. "Remember," warned Rosecrans, "the first bullet may send you to eternity," where Sheridan would have to answer for his profanity.

Sheridan protested that he couldn't help it. Pointing to the bloodied, powder-smudged men filing past them, he said they were all that remained of his division. Sheridan had lost 1,600 of his 4,100 men.[19]

THE EPIC STAND BY Sheridan's 3rd Division saved Rosecrans's army from destruction. Sheridan's and Sill's alertness and preparations during the predawn hours enabled them to repel the initial Rebel onslaught and retain unit cohesion. The sole intact division in McCook's right wing, the 3rd Division had then delayed the Rebels two hours so that the Army of the Cumberland could establish a strong defensive line along the Nashville Pike. "My division, alone and unbroken, made a gallant stand to protect the right flank of our army. . . . My troops gave time for a rearrangement of our lines," Sheridan proudly wrote in his battle report.

Given no time to rest, the 3rd Division obtained fresh ammunition just as four Confederate formations marched toward the pike. Rosecrans sent Sheridan's men to support General Thomas Wood's division—one of the two that Rosecrans had moved from his left wing to stop the Confederate juggernaut. It was now under attack. "Shot and shell that came in torrents" met Sheridan's division as it took its place in the line and then helped drive off the Rebel attack. Here, Sheridan lost the last of his original brigade commanders, Colonel Schaefer.

Expecting yet another attack, Sheridan massed his troops in close formation and ordered them to hug the ground. The assault never came, but his division was heavily shelled. "The torments of this trying situation were almost unbearable," Sheridan wrote. Twenty more men died during the bombardment.[20]

Sheridan joined Rosecrans as he supervised the reorganization of his line. The Rebel gunners took aim on the mounted group of officers. A round of solid shot suddenly took off the head of one of Rosecrans's staff officers, Colonel Julius Garesché, spattering blood on Rosecrans, Sheridan, and some other officers. The headless body rode on twenty paces, until the horse pulled up and the corpse slid to the ground. Even after witnessing carnage all day long, Sheridan and the other officers were horrified by the death of the dedicated twenty-one-year army veteran, described as "half mystic, half saint."

There was no time to mourn though. "We cannot help it," Rosecrans told his officers. "Let us push on; the battle must be won." Rosecrans later clipped the buttons from his bloody coat and put them in an envelope labeled "Buttons I wore the day Garesché was killed."[21]

The Confederate divisions now attacked the Union left, in the hope that it might be turned and the Yankees yet driven from the Nashville Pike. Bragg concentrated on a salient where a four-acre patch of dense woods rested on a slight elevation in front of cotton fields. Locals called it the Round Forest; it became known that day to Union soldiers as "Hell's Half-Acre" and to the Confederates as "The Slaughter Pen."

All afternoon, Bragg sent waves of Rebels against the Union brigades packed shoulder to shoulder under cover in the cedars, from which they raked the attackers with sheeting musket fire. Fifty Yankee guns, arrayed hub to hub, stood on higher ground near the forest and poured down shot, shell, and canister at nearly point-blank range. The din was so terrific—"equal to the falls of Niagara," wrote John Magee, a Mississippi artillery captain—that the charging Rebels stopped to pick cotton and stuff it into their ears. The concentrated Yankee firepower broke every attack. "Men were swept down by hundreds—trees, shrubs, and everything was torn up, cut off, or shivered," said Magee. J. Morgan Smith's 32nd Alabama went into action with 280 men and left the field with 58.

One massive attack might have swept aside the Union defenders, but the Rebel brigades were sent in piecemeal—just as Bragg and Polk had ruinously done at Shiloh. At 4:30 p.m., after ten hours of carnage, the Rebels could attack no more; lack of rest and food had caught up with them.

But Bragg's army had driven back the Yankees along a two-mile arc and could rightfully claim a hard-won victory for the day. Sheridan, while justifiably pleased with his division, was "sorely disappointed at the general result."[22]

THAT NIGHT, NEW YEAR'S Eve, in a cabin where rain drummed on the roof, Rosecrans polled his three corps commanders and some other generals about whether to stay or to withdraw to Nashville and leave the field to Bragg. There was no consensus; while the corps commanders appeared to favor remaining on the field, they pledged to support Rosecrans's decision. With some staff officers, the commanding general left the meeting to inspect the lines and ponder the options. He returned to the cabin with his decision: the Army of the Cumberland would not retreat. "Prepare to fight or die," he told his generals.

That night, the two armies camped a half mile apart. No fires were permitted. "As I walked along . . . watching the men sitting on the rocks and cold ground shivering from frost, I could not help but think how little the people at home know of the suffering of the soldier," observed Colonel Hans Heg.

About 14,000 dead and wounded men from both armies were scattered over a six-square-mile area on this bitterly cold New Year's Eve; many died, frozen to the ground in their own blood, as the year 1863 was born.

Under an unofficial armistice, Union and Confederate squads ventured out to bury the dead and bring in the wounded, who were laid in rows, irrespective of their allegiance, between warming fires. At the field hospitals of both armies and in makeshift hospitals in churches in nearby Murfreesboro, the overworked surgeons amputated limbs, tossing "the quivering flesh into a pile."

At daybreak on New Year's Day 1863, Sheridan's division was busy building breastworks of stone and logs. Within the hour, the Rebels attacked, but the Union troops easily repulsed them, and did so again several hours later. The skirmishing ebbed. Neither army left the field.[23]

BRAGG CLAIMED VICTORY, BUT when Rosecrans did not withdraw as expected, the Confederate general grew uneasy. On January 2, he ordered an attack across Stones River against a hill on the Union left flank, which had not been tested on December 31. Major General John Breckenridge, whose division would lead the attack, objected. Union troops dug in on a hill behind his objective would cut the Confederates to pieces, the former US vice president predicted. Bragg instructed Breckenridge to attack anyway. The assault was scheduled for 4 p.m., late enough in the day, Bragg calculated, to forestall the possibility of a Union counterattack.

It went just as Breckenridge had feared. Rosecrans's troops closely watched the Rebel preparations, and they were ready when Breckenridge attacked. His five brigades stormed the hill in rain and sleet and easily—too easily, it turned out—

drove away Brigadier General Horatio Van Cleve's division. Then, fifty-eight Union guns on the crest and at the base of the second hill opened fire, decimating the Rebel troops. Yankee infantrymen counterattacked and reclaimed the hill. Just 2,800 of Breckenridge's 4,500 troops recrossed the river alive and unwounded.

When the shooting stopped, hungry Union soldiers cut steaks from horses that Confederate cannonballs had mowed down like ten pins on the Murfreesboro Pike and cooked them over fires.

During the night of January 3, Bragg's Army of the Tennessee withdrew from its position straddling the river and marched south through Murfreesboro. By ceding the battlefield, Bragg had conceded victory to Rosecrans, such as it was. Union losses at Stones River totaled nearly 13,000 of the 44,000 troops in the field; about 12,000 of Bragg's 37,000 effectives were killed, wounded, or captured.[24]

For his conduct at Stones River, Sheridan was promoted to major general of volunteers. General Ulysses Grant later told newspaperman and author John Russell Young that Sheridan's fighting withdrawal and gallant stand in the cedar brakes on Wilkinson Pike was "a wonderful bit of fighting. It showed what a great general can do even in a subordinate command; for I believe Sheridan in that battle saved Rosecrans's army."[25]

THREE MONTHS EARLIER, SHERIDAN had fought in his first major battle as a division commander at Perryville, Kentucky. His frustrating experience reflected the leadership problems that pervaded the then named Army of the Ohio.

Upon reaching Louisville from Mississippi on September 14, 1862, Sheridan reported to Major General William "Bull" Nelson. Nelson gave him command of 1,500 infantrymen—the Pea Ridge Brigade, veterans of their namesake Union victory in southwestern Missouri, where Sheridan had played a supporting role. It was composed of the 2nd and 15th Missouri, and the 36th and 44th Illinois. Nelson told Sheridan that Major General Don Carlos Buell, who was shadowing Braxton Bragg's army through Kentucky, might assign more regiments to Sheridan's brigade.

But the command structure changed when Brigadier General Jefferson C. Davis shot Nelson dead in a hallway of the Galt House. The shooting climaxed a dispute that had swiftly metamorphosed from hot words to action, with Davis flinging a balled-up calling card in Nelson's face and Nelson backhanding Davis. Davis had then borrowed a pistol from a bystander and shot Davis in the chest, killing him. Placed under house arrest, Davis was never prosecuted. He commanded the right wing division beside Sheridan's at Stones River.[26]

Buell was appointed the Army of the Ohio's commander and overhauled the command structure. One change rankled with Sheridan—Buell's promotion of

Captain Charles Gilbert to major general with command of III Corps. Sheridan argued that he deserved at least a division if an officer whom he ranked in tenure got a corps. Buell agreed and assigned Sheridan the 6,500-man 11th Division.[27]

Officers and enlisted men were united in their dislike of Gilbert and Buell. War correspondent William F. G. Shanks of the *New York Herald* described Gilbert as a "martinet of the worst sort." Gilbert rummaged through his men's baggage for contraband, and he had arrested a colonel for allowing his men to climb some persimmon trees. At one point, Gilbert ordered everyone in III Corps to stand at attention every morning from 3 a.m. until daylight.

Buell, openly contemptuous of the volunteer units, tried to impose army regulations on the independent-minded Westerners. Consequently, he made powerful enemies, including Andrew Johnson and Oliver Morton, the war governors, respectively, of Tennessee and Indiana. One night, two dozen officers met secretly to sign a petition to President Abraham Lincoln seeking Buell's removal for incompetence and disloyalty.[28]

BUELL AND BRAGG REACHED the battleground north of Perryville on October 7, both operating under huge misconceptions. Bragg believed he faced only a fragment of Buell's army, when in fact he faced Buell's entire 58,000-man force, while Buell was under the impression that he faced Bragg's 45,000-man Army of the Mississippi, when Bragg had only 20,000 men with him. Bragg confidently planned to attack; Buell cautiously resolved to stay on the defensive until his entire army had assembled and then to attack on October 9.

October 8 began with one of Sheridan's brigades, commanded by Colonel Daniel McCook—one of Ohio's "Fighting McCooks"—seizing Peters Hill in front of Doctor's Creek, thereby providing fresh water for the thirsty army. The Rebels counterattacked two hours later but were flung back. Sheridan's men drove them south across Chaplin Creek and captured the next hill.

But Gilbert feared that Sheridan's aggressiveness might bring on a general engagement before Buell was ready for one. He ordered Sheridan to pull back to Peters Hill. Sheridan's men dug rifle pits there. Throughout the late morning and into the afternoon, Gilbert sent Sheridan a stream of nagging signals from the rear reminding him not to advance.[29]

While Gilbert handcuffed Sheridan's division and the rest of III Corps, I Corps, commanded by another "fighting McCook," Major General Alexander McCook, was in Bragg's bull's-eye on III Corps's left flank.

Bragg attacked I Corps as it was forming a battle line and getting drinking water, driving it back a mile. There, a desperate battle raged all afternoon. III Corps and II Corps, positioned to III Corps's right, did not assist McCook, except for Sheridan's artillery batteries, which raked the Rebel columns.[30]

THE EXTRAORDINARY SITUATION ON the Union side was due to the fact that Gilbert and Buell were absent and uninformed of developments. Buell had fallen from his horse the previous day and could not ride. He and Gilbert were at the army headquarters camp three miles in the rear. Because of an acoustical anomaly due to the wind and the rolling Chapin Hills, they were unaware that the army was fighting a major battle.

Both were in their tents—Buell on his cot, reading—when the sound of heavy cannonading brought them outside at 2 p.m. Buell told Gilbert to put a stop to "that useless waste of powder." He then invited Gilbert to stay for dinner. It was leisurely. The two men discussed the next day's battle, unaware that it was being fought there and then.

At about 4 p.m., they heard more loud gunfire, and Gilbert finally rode off to find out what was happening. Along the way, he met couriers who told him that McCook's corps faced annihilation. Gilbert promptly ordered one of his idle III Corps divisions—not Sheridan's—to reinforce McCook. Then, a message from Sheridan arrived: Rebel infantry was poised to attack Peters Hill.[31]

AFTER BEING REPEATEDLY THROWN back by I Corps, the Confederates had finally broken McCook's lines and forced I Corps's withdrawal to secondary positions, where the Yankees were now under severe attack.

Among the I Corps dead was Brigadier General William Terrill, the West Point cadet whom Sheridan had memorably fought—and with whom, a few days earlier, he had reconciled. The night before the battle, Terrill, Brigadier General James Jackson, and a Colonel Webster had been overheard speculating about their chances of being killed or wounded. None survived the battle.[32]

At about 4 p.m., as Sheridan watched from atop Rienzi, Confederate infantry charged up Peters Hill, the Rebel commander unaware that he faced not only Sheridan's division but also two others behind it. Unsurprisingly, the assault and two subsequent attempts to take the hill failed. "We found ourselves confronted with more than ten times over our numbers," wrote Colonel William Dowd of the 24th Mississippi, one of the four regiments that stormed the hill.

The unsuccessful late-afternoon Rebel attacks marked the end of the day's fighting, and the Confederates withdrew toward Perryville. To Sheridan's disappointment, no orders came for a general counterattack.

GILBERT INVITED SHERIDAN TO Buell's headquarters, and he stayed for supper. Listening to Buell and his staff officers discuss the day's events, it dawned on the amazed Sheridan that they "were unconscious of the magnitude of the battle that had just been fought." Indeed, Buell's army had lost 4,200 men, and Bragg's, 3,400.[33]

Later that night, Buell issued orders to II and III Corps to attack Perryville at first light. I Corps, severely depleted by losses, was excused. In the meadows where I Corps had stood off the Rebel attacks all afternoon, so many dead men lay on the ground "that one could walk on them for rods and not touch the ground," wrote Emerson Calkins of the 8th Wisconsin Battery. Under a full moon, the living slept among the dead, amid the piercing cries of the wounded.[34]

By daybreak, the Rebels were gone. They had left during the night and were marching south, back to Tennessee. Buell did not pursue them.

The Union army at Perryville turned back the Confederate invasion of Kentucky, but if an energetic leader had been in command, the Army of the Ohio might have destroyed Bragg's army. In his *Personal Memoirs*, Sheridan wrote, "The battle of Perryville remains in history an example of lost opportunities."[35]

In the first report of the battle sent to Northern newspapers, Sheridan was listed among the dead. Concerned that his family in Ohio might see the false report, he eagerly read the newspapers that reached the army a few days later—and was relieved to find "that the error had been corrected before my obituary could be written."[36]

In the battle's aftermath, Buell and Gilbert were sacked. Neither held field command again during the war.

Buell's successor, General William Rosecrans of the Army of the Mississippi, pursued Bragg into Tennessee. He rechristened his force the Army of the Cumberland, reflecting its new theater of operations.[37]

After Stones River, during the 169 days between January 9 and June 23, 1863, the Army of the Cumberland did little active campaigning. It remained in its camps near Murfreesboro. Bragg's army occupied positions thirty miles to the south along the Duck River, straddling the roads and railroads connecting Nashville and Chattanooga. Bragg's chief operating base was Tullahoma, fifty-five miles northwest of Chattanooga and a primary Rebel supply depot.

Confederate officers clamored for Bragg's removal. At Perryville, he had attacked when he should not have, and at Stones River, he had retreated when he should have stood fast. Despite the dissident officers' best efforts to get Bragg fired, he remained in command.[38]

Because Stones River was heralded as a great Union victory, Rosecrans and his command escaped criticism for having allowed Bragg to catch the army napping—Sheridan's 3rd Division excepted—and narrowly avoiding a crushing defeat.

After fighting two major battles in three months, the Army of the Cumberland had time to recuperate. During the long hiatus, Rosecrans made some organizational changes; for one thing, he renamed the center and the right and left wings. Alexander McCook's right wing became XX Corps; George Thomas's center was now XIV Corps; and Thomas Crittenden's left wing was renamed XXI Corps.[39]

The divisions also underwent changes, some superficial, some substantial. Sheridan's 3rd Division remained under McCook's XX Corps, but with new brigade commanders to replace the men killed at Stones River: Brigadier General William Lytle and Colonels Bernard Laiboldt and Luther P. Bradley.

WHEN HE BECAME A division commander weeks before Perryville, Sheridan had to learn quickly how to manage his 6,500 men. After Stones River, Sheridan was able to school himself properly in divisional command, and he applied himself with his habitual intensity. "I had to study hard to be able to master all the needs of such a force, to feed and clothe it and guard all its interests," Sheridan wrote. "When undertaking these responsibilities I felt that if I met them faithfully, recompense would surely come through the hearty response that soldiers always make to conscientious exertion on the part of their superiors."

Toward that end, Sheridan dedicated himself to their comfort, inasmuch as it was possible for an army in the field to be comfortable. He selected good campsites and made sure that his men had enough food, forage for the livestock, good clothing, and proper equipment to do their jobs. His background as a quartermaster and commissary general—and even his Texas experiences as a hunter—proved valuable. His men approved of his efforts.[40]

In return, Sheridan expected obedience and discipline. Mistakes he might tolerate but never cowardice—especially in his officers. In such cases, he did not hesitate to make a "mortifying spectacle" of their disgrace.

After Stones River, four 3rd Division officers who had abandoned their colors and regiments were marched to the center of a hollow square formed by the division. Sheridan ordered them to surrender their swords—to his black servant, for Sheridan said he would not "humiliate" any soldier by requiring him to touch the sullied weapons. The servant then cut all rank insignia from the men's coats, and an order was read announcing their dismissal from the service. They were drummed out of the camp. No division officer abandoned his colors after this ritual humiliation, Sheridan wrote.[41]

DURING THE LONG ENCAMPMENT at Murfreesboro, Sheridan's command style came into sharper focus. He was like many successful Union generals in his high levels of energy and stamina, and he was able to think clearly even when he had

not slept for days. Leading from the front and exhorting his men from his big gelding, Rienzi, Sheridan was an inspiring figure.

He was also surprisingly modest. Henry Castle, acting quartermaster sergeant
for the 73rd Illinois, one day went to division headquarters seeking information.
He nearly rode over a young man in shirtsleeves sitting on a stump, smoking a cigar.
The startled man asked, "Who the—are you, anyhow?" Castle replied that he was
seeking the division quartermaster's advice on obtaining cattle.

The man proceeded to advise Castle on selecting and butchering cattle and distributing the meat. As the man was concluding his soliloquy on these subjects, a
staff officer rode up, saluted, and addressed him as General Sheridan. Horrified by
his mistake, Castle stammered out an apology for his "unceremonious approach."
It was entirely understandable, replied Sheridan, because he was not wearing rank
insignia. He added that Castle should not hesitate to consult him if he had further
questions about his military duties.[42]

During the interregnum Sheridan improved his intelligence operations, convinced by the Rebel surprise attack at Stones River of the great importance of gathering accurate information about the enemy. One day, a stranger appeared at his
headquarters, offering to supply him with information about the Army of the Tennessee. An intelligent, bustling little man, James Card was from eastern Tennessee,
a region of hills and hollows where subsistence farmers eked out a marginal living.
Most of them also supported the Union. From selling religious tracts throughout
Middle and East Tennessee and Georgia, Card had gained a thorough knowledge
of the roads and people. Sheridan hired him to serve as a scout, guide, and intelligence agent.[43]

THERE WAS A STRATEGIC reason for keeping the Army of the Cumberland idle at
Murfreesboro until summertime. With General Ulysses Grant marching on Vicks-
burg, Bragg's army must be kept pinned down in Middle Tennessee so that it would
not reinforce the Mississippi Rebels. And so, Rosecrans's army scarcely stirred until
June 23, when James Card and his brothers reported that Bragg was on the move.
The Union army broke camp and headed south.[44]

The Army of the Cumberland's march through Middle Tennessee and Bragg's
deft withdrawal were at once a master's seminar in maneuver and a maddening
game of cat and mouse. Every Rosecrans movement designed to place Bragg's army
in jeopardy was foiled by Bragg slipping away. By marching on Liberty Gap, Rosecrans hoped to turn Bragg's army at Shelbyville. But when the Yankees reached
Shelbyville, Bragg was gone. Sheridan approached Tullahoma, halting six miles
away so that the army could mass for an all-out attack on the Rebel storage depot.
When the Yankees finally pounced, the Confederates were not there.[45]

Sheridan learned that a Rebel cavalry brigade and some infantry had stopped on Monteagle Mountain, where the University of the South had been founded three years earlier by several Episcopal bishops—one of them Confederate general Leonidas Polk. But when Sheridan reached the mountaintop on July 5 with 1,200 cavalrymen and an infantry brigade, the Rebels were gone. Sheridan sent the units back to his division.

Weary after ten days of campaigning, Sheridan requested that a handcar be sent to the mountaintop to carry him and Colonel Frank Sherman to the bottom. He and Sherman began walking down the track to meet the handcar. But no handcar came, and it grew dark.

The anticipated easy trip down the mountain became a dangerous adventure: in the nearby cabins lived hostile Southerners; the tracks on which they walked tie to tie dropped off into black chasms. Falling often on the uneven roadbed in the dark, they slogged eleven miles without meeting the handcar. They reached their camp around midnight. Sheridan later learned that the handcar crew was captured after taking a wrong turn. Sore and bruised for months, Sheridan had many occasions to repent his lark.[46]

BRAGG'S LONG WITHDRAWAL ENDED at Chattanooga, a ragged town of wooden sidewalks and rutted dirt roads ringed by picturesque mountains and ridges. Located on the banks of the foaming Tennessee River, it was the crossroads of the Confederacy's two most important railroads: the East Tennessee & Virginia, which ran north and south, and the Memphis & Charleston, running east and west. It was the perfect springboard for any new Rebel offensive.[47]

To prepare the ground for operations against Chattanooga, Sheridan's division was sent to Bridgeport, Alabama, southwest of Chattanooga. There, he established a supply depot and chose a place to build a bridge over the Tennessee River to provide Rosecrans's army a pathway into Chattanooga.

On August 29, Sheridan began building the bridge. In one day, 1,500 men felled trees to make 1,500 logs while foragers stripped planking from nearby barns and homes. On September 1, the bridge was completed—an astounding feat to accomplish in so short a time. Sheridan's division and other units crossed the bridge the next day.[48]

Newspaper correspondent William F. G. Shanks happened to witness a vivid display of Sheridan's temper when he was accompanying Major General George Thomas by train to show off the new bridge and the repaired railroad line. When the train inexplicably stopped and the delay dragged on, Sheridan asked the conductor, a burly six-footer, to get the train moving again. The conductor boorishly replied that he only obeyed orders from his military railroad superintendent.

At that, Sheridan sprang to his feet, slugged the conductor two or three times, and kicked him off the train, Shanks wrote. Sheridan ordered the train forward, and he and Thomas resumed their conversation as though nothing had happened. When informed of the incident, Rosecrans admonished Sheridan not to interfere with railroad employees. Sheridan replied that the man was "saucy and impertinent."[49]

The Army of the Cumberland finally marched on Chattanooga, only to discover that Bragg's army had withdrawn from the city on September 8.

Rosecrans sent two of his three army corps through the mountain gaps southeast of Chattanooga in the hope of locating Bragg's army, presumed to have withdrawn deep into Georgia. The third he kept in Chattanooga. The two corps probing southeastward—one of them Alexander McCook's XX Corps, to which Sheridan's division belonged—lost contact with one another.

SHERIDAN, TOGETHER WITH MOST of the division and brigade commanders, began to suspect that Bragg was not marching to Atlanta. This was a disturbing thought because if Bragg's army was nearby, it might attack Rosecrans's now dispersed army corps and cut them off from their supply base in Chattanooga on the other side of the mountains.[50]

On September 9, Sheridan summoned James Card and asked him to find an East Tennessean willing to slip through the Rebel lines in Georgia to learn what Bragg was up to. He would have preferred to send Card, but the Rebels knew him; Card and one of his brothers had been captured that spring while on one of Sheridan's missions. They had escaped from the Chattanooga jail before they could be sentenced for spying.[51]

Card found a Unionist who had been persecuted by Rebel guerrillas and wanted to move to the West. He agreed to locate Bragg's army if Sheridan would buy his livestock to pay for his relocation costs. Sheridan readily consented.

Sheridan's spy found Bragg's army in the Pigeon Mountain area of north Georgia. After infiltrating the Rebel camp, the spy was arrested. He managed to escape somehow, then to slip through the enemy picket line in the dark by crawling on his hands and knees and grunting like a wild hog.

He reached the Union lines on September 12 with the sobering information that Bragg was just twenty miles away and that he intended to fight. Moreover, Lieutenant General James Longstreet's vaunted I Corps was on its way from Virginia to reinforce Bragg.

AFTER GENERAL THOMAS "STONEWALL" Jackson's death at Chancellorsville in May, imperturbable Longstreet had become Robert E. Lee's right hand. Grand strategy was Longstreet's new passion. He rightly believed that the Rebel army could utilize its interior lines of transportation to overwhelm the Yankees at any given point by shifting troops from one theater to another.

Longstreet had persuaded Lee and Confederate president Jefferson Davis to permit him to bring troops from Virginia to Bragg's army. Together, they would drive Rosecrans's army from Chattanooga, and Bragg would then return to the offensive in Tennessee.

On September 8, the day Bragg evacuated Chattanooga, two divisions from Longstreet's I Corps began streaming into Richmond to board worn-out trains for the long trip over rickety tracks to northern Georgia. With Knoxville now in Union hands, the 12,000 troops had to make a much longer journey through southern Virginia and both Carolinas to reach their staging area at Catoosa Station, Georgia.[52]

ALARMED BY MOUNTING EVIDENCE that the Confederates were planning to attack him, Rosecrans issued a flurry of orders to hasten the reconcentration of his three corps. They were spread over fifty-seven miles of heavily wooded hills southeast of Chattanooga, on the lee side of Missionary Ridge.

On September 17, the units had reached supporting distance of one another, and Rosecrans was on the scene. Scouts reported that Confederate troops were just three or four miles distant.

On September 18, a wall of dust arose from the Pigeon Mountain area, moving northward. It was Longstreet's two divisions. Suspecting that the Rebels outnumbered his men—they, in fact, did, 66,000 to 58,000—Rosecrans prepared for a defensive battle.

Flowing through the area where the two armies were forming for battle was the sluggish, tannin-stained Chickamauga Creek, whose Cherokee name has been variously said to mean "bad water," "good country," and "river of death"—the latter becoming the popular translation after what would happen there.[53]

CHAPTER 3

———

Defeat and Victory at Chattanooga

SEPTEMBER–NOVEMBER 1863

With the instinct of military genius [Sheridan] pushed ahead. If others had followed his example we should have had Bragg's army.
—MAJOR GENERAL ULYSSES GRANT DESCRIBING
SHERIDAN'S PURSUIT AFTER MISSIONARY RIDGE[1]

SEPTEMBER 20, 1863–CHICKAMAUGA CREEK, GEORGIA—The blood-red sunrise was portentous, even if lingering smoke from the previous day's fighting was its cause. "This will indeed be a day of blood," predicted Brigadier General James A. Garfield, chief of staff to Major General William Rosecrans, commander of the Army of the Cumberland. Puffy-faced from lack of sleep, Rosecrans rode along the Union lines, encouraging his men.

Phil Sheridan had not slept either. During a meeting of division and corps commanders the night before, there was "much apprehension for the future" because of the large Confederate troop formations in the area. Major General George Thomas, who commanded the XIV Corps, had roused himself from his intermittent naps, whenever Rosecrans addressed him, to say, "I would strengthen the left." The meeting ended about midnight, coffee was brought in, and for reasons unknown

XX Corps commander Major General Alexander McCook felt moved to sing the ballad "The Hebrew Maid."

Afterward, Sheridan had paced for hours, wondering whether he had done everything possible to prepare his men for the coming battle. As the sun poked above the horizon, a Confederate attack was expected momentarily. But none came.[2]

ON SEPTEMBER 19, VETERANS of both armies had remarked on the ferocity of the fighting, although Braxton Bragg described it as "skirmishing." It was far more than that. A division from Thomas's corps on the Union left had started it by fording Chickamauga Creek to engage what it thought was merely an enemy brigade.

The collision exploded into a raging battle pitting four of Thomas's six divisions—half of Rosecrans's army was concentrated in Thomas's sector—against large Rebel forces in the dense woods. The terrific noise made by myriad artillery batteries and thousands of muskets sounded to an Alabama soldier "as if all the fires of earth and hell had been turned loose in one mighty effort to destroy each other." (Decades later, local sawmills would reject logs from Chickamauga because embedded minié balls, grapeshot, and shell fragments fouled the saw teeth.) Amid the furious combat, the soldiers saw an owl fly up, only to be attacked by crows. One infantryman was heard to exclaim, "Moses, what a country! The very birds are fighting!"[3]

The fighting had spread down the line to Thomas Crittenden's XXI Corps in the center and then to McCook's XX Corps on the right. There, at about 4 p.m., Major General John Bell Hood's two divisions from the Army of Northern Virginia struck Jefferson C. Davis's division. Sheridan's timely arrival with two brigades from Lee and Gordon's Mills, south of the battlefield, and the appearance of Thomas Wood's division from Crittenden's corps had stopped Hood's attack. But Sheridan described it as "an ugly fight" in which he had lost a brigade commander, Colonel Luther P. Bradley.

As the Hood fight was ending, Confederate major general Patrick Cleburne's division assaulted the Union left—Thomas's corps. Thomas held, but the sun set on chaotic fighting. When darkness came, the shooting stopped.

Sheridan suggested to Crittenden that they counterattack that night, but Crittenden's men were fought out and in no condition for a night attack. The exhausted Yankees camped without fires and ate dry meals of hardtack and bully beef from their haversacks. The day's fighting was only a prelude.[4]

THE EARLY REBEL ATTACK anticipated for September 20 did not materialize. Lieutenant General Leonidas Polk was at a farmhouse three miles away, reading a newspaper and waiting for his Sunday breakfast, when one of Braxton Bragg's staff officers finally located him. Polk knew neither that there was to be an early-morning attack nor that he was supposed to lead it.

Hours later, at 9:30 a.m., the Rebels struck hard at the Union left, defended by Thomas's massively reinforced XIV Corps. Thomas pleaded for more reinforcements, and Rosecrans sent brigades from Crittenden's corps in the center and Mc-Cook's on the right. Rosecrans and Thomas were certain that the Confederates intended to break the Union left in order to seize the roads behind Thomas and isolate the Army of the Cumberland from Chattanooga.

They were wrong, although their mistake was understandable given that dense woods, smoke, and fog largely hid the armies from one another. With the foliage and smoke, even signaling was problematic. Chickamauga has been justifiably described as "a hidden battle," directed not by army commanders but by field commanders. It became essentially a battle of brigades and regiments—a soldier's fight, waged with rare ferocity.

While Rosecrans and his commanders braced for powerful follow-up attacks on the Union left, Bragg's army instead began probing the Union line from its left to its right, seeking weak spots to exploit. The artillery sounded like "the thunder, as of a thousand anvils," wrote Colonel John Beatty. Bragg's forces found no chinks in Thomas's lines where, by midday, roughly 40,000 of Rosecrans's 58,000 troops were concentrated, leaving the Union center and right thinly manned.

OPPOSITE THE POINT AT which Crittenden's and McCook's corps were joined, and near Sheridan's division, Hood and his commander, Lieutenant General James Longstreet, massed the five divisions of the Army of Northern Virginia's I Corps. The Rebels faced, at most, three scattered Union divisions. Longstreet's men waited for the right moment to strike.

With growing concern, Sheridan watched the steady migration of McCook's and Crittenden's brigades to Thomas's left wing. He recognized that "we were in bad straits" and that Thomas had to be reinforced. But Sheridan questioned the wisdom of shifting troops in the face of a numerically superior enemy.[5]

McCook had just ordered two of Sheridan's three brigades—those commanded by Brigadier General William H. Lytle and the wounded Colonel Bradley's successor, Colonel Nathan Walworth—to join Thomas when Longstreet attacked, his divisions arrayed in a single column to deliver a "clenched-fist blow."[6]

McCook called it "a most furious and impetuous assault in overwhelming numbers." The 16,000 Rebels crashed through a large gap that suddenly yawned in the Union right-center where Brigadier General Thomas Wood had just withdrawn his division to send to Thomas.

With pitch-perfect timing, Longstreet's five attacking divisions struck before the hole left by Wood's division could be filled and just as other units, including Sheridan's two brigades, were shifting to the left. Just thirty minutes earlier or later, and the Rebels might have met better-organized defenders.

Assistant War Secretary Charles Dana, a former journalist assigned to observe Rosecrans's army—some said to spy for War Secretary Edwin Stanton, who despised Rosecrans—had fallen asleep on the grass at Rosecrans's headquarters at the Widow Glenn's cabin behind Wood's division when "the most infernal noise I ever heard" awakened him. Upon sitting up, he observed Rosecrans making the sign of the cross. This alarmed Dana, although Rosecrans, described as "a Jesuit of the highest style of Roman piety," was merely exhibiting his devout Catholicism. Dana, however, concluded, "If the general is crossing himself, we are in a desperate situation."

He then saw for himself that they were indeed in deep trouble. A dense column of gray-clad troops, their bayonets glittering in the hazy sunlight, was quick-stepping toward them. The Rebel column stretched far to the southwest. Wood's division was nowhere to be seen.

Rosecrans and his staff hastily evacuated the cabin when musket balls and shells began to rain down. They rode to higher ground along the eastern flank of Missionary Ridge and halted. There, Rosecrans, who must have felt like he was reliving the first hours of Stones River, watched his right wing break apart. He sent for Sheridan, but Sheridan could not come; "affairs were too critical" for him to leave his command.[7]

Brigadier General Jefferson C. Davis's division and, behind it, Sheridan's third brigade, commanded by Colonel Bernard Laiboldt, were slammed backward as though struck by a flash flood. Under "terrible fire," Sheridan recalled Lytle's and Bradley's brigades, which had begun marching to Thomas, to meet the onslaught. But the intensive gunfire unleashed by Longstreet's assault columns "shivered the two brigades to pieces."[8]

Lytle, a lawyer and well-known lyric poet from Cincinnati, as well as one of the most beloved brigade commanders in the Union army, pulled on his gloves prefatory to leading a counterattack and reportedly said, "If I must die, I will die as a gentleman." He was shot four times and killed. Confederate officers who had known Lytle before the war guarded his body; a Rebel surgeon cut a lock of Lytle's hair and sent it to his sister, along with her brother's notebook and a poem he had composed.[9]

BOTH SHERIDAN'S AND DAVIS'S divisions had been routed. In just forty-five minutes, Longstreet's divisions had crushed the Union right and driven it back one mile. In the hour of stunning defeat, Captain Edwin Parsons of the 24th Wisconsin saw Sheridan "come tearing down in the rear of our line, alone, his hat in hand, and showing in his face the agony he felt at the disaster that had befallen our army there."[10]

As Longstreet turned his columns to strike Thomas's right and Leonidas Polk continued to hammer his front, Longstreet's left column, commanded by General Thomas Hindman, encountered the only serious resistance from the Union right.

Union colonel John T. Wilder had led his cavalry brigade to a hilltop that faced the left side of the charging column. Quickly dismounting, the Yankees opened fire on the Rebels with their Spencer repeating rifles. The lethal volley prompted Hindman's division to veer to its left and attack Wilder's brigade. With sheeting gunfire from their seven-shot carbines, Wilder's men repelled four assaults before the Rebels gave up.[11]

Rosecrans believed that holding the Dry Valley Road, which looped around the rear of his lines, south to north, was essential to his army's survival. It must be kept open so that the routed troops from the right and center could reach McFarland's Gap and Rossville, byways to Chattanooga.

Rosecrans ordered Sheridan and Davis to make a stand on the Dry Valley Road with their divisions. Longstreet had to be prevented from marching up the road and capturing the Union commissary wagons, or capturing Rossville and severing the way to Chattanooga.[12]

ON A LOW RIDGE overlooking the former positions of the army's right and center wings, Sheridan collected his stunned division. Never had he been beaten so badly. Sheridan and Davis began marching up the Dry Valley Road.

Lieutenant Colonel Gates Thruston, the XX Corps chief of staff, encountered the two generals as they marched their men around the army's rear. Sheridan, he wrote, was "furious . . . swearing mad, and no wonder. . . . His splendid fighting qualities and his fine soldiers had not had half a chance. He had lost faith." Thruston offered to find out what Thomas's situation was and to report back to Sheridan and Davis as soon as possible. He rode off.[13]

At last free to report to Rosecrans, Sheridan discovered that he had already left the battlefield. "It is to be regretted that he did not wait till I could join him, for the delay would have permitted him to see that matters were not in quite such bad shape as he supposed," Sheridan later wrote.

Rosecrans had joined the shattered formations making their way back to Chattanooga, where he intended to organize the city's defenses and a "straggler line" to turn back troops retreating from the battlefield. He had planned to send his chief of staff, Garfield, to Chattanooga, but Garfield had convinced Rosecrans to take charge of Chattanooga himself while Garfield went to Thomas.

Rosecrans reached Chattanooga before 4 p.m., as the fighting continued to rage on the other side of Missionary Ridge. His decision to remove himself from the battlefield would be fatal to his military career, while Garfield, who joined Thomas, would see his star rise until, at its zenith in 1881, he became the twentieth president.[14]

THE PHLEGMATIC THOMAS WAS now the ranking officer on the battlefield and, in fact, the only remaining corps commander; McCook and Crittenden had followed Rosecrans to Chattanooga.

Thomas's left wing now constituted fully two-thirds of the army, but with casualties and all the Confederate forces now concentrated against him, he was outnumbered two to one. Atop Horseshoe Ridge and Snodgrass Hill, with the indispensable support of General Gordon Granger's reserve division and battery of three-inch rifles, Thomas threw back attacks by Polk from the east and Longstreet from the south. His courageous stand saved the Army of the Cumberland from destruction and Chattanooga from capture. Thomas deserved his sobriquet: "The Rock of Chickamauga."[15]

Until Thruston reported to him, Thomas had been unaware of the right wing's collapse. Told by Thruston about his encounter with Davis and Sheridan on the Dry Valley Road, Thomas ordered him to have them bring all the troops they could round up. Not daring to attempt a retreat in daylight, Thomas hoped to hold out until dark.

With difficulty, Thruston made his way through the clogged roads to Sheridan and Davis. "We held a hasty conference," Thruston wrote. "Davis ordered a right-about at once, and marched briskly to the front." Sheridan, however, was "still without faith" and continued on to Rossville with his division.

But Sheridan intended to circle back to Thomas from Rossville, believing that Longstreet's corps lay between him and Thomas's embattled divisions on Horseshoe Ridge and Snodgrass Hill. As the day ended, 1,500 men from Sheridan's 3rd Division took positions near Thomas's left in the vicinity of the field hospital at the Cloud House. But by then, the major fighting was over, and Thomas was withdrawing. Sheridan sent his younger brother and aide, Lieutenant Michael Sheridan, to Thomas for instructions. Cover his retreat, Thomas told him.

OUTSIDE ROSSVILLE, SHERIDAN AND Thomas dismounted and sat together on a rail fence watching the endless lines of powder-blackened troops stride by. Both men were downhearted and exhausted; it had been a dreadful day. Neither said much.

As Sheridan rose to go, Thomas asked an aide to fetch a flask of brandy from his saddle holster, and they shared a drink before riding off to their respective commands.

Later, in Rossville, Sheridan lay down under a tree, his saddle serving as a pillow. Some soldiers brewing coffee nearby brought him a tin cup of it and a small piece of hard bread, the first food he had eaten in twenty-four hours. "I was very tired, very hungry, and much discouraged by what had taken place since morning."

Indeed, the Army of the Cumberland had suffered a decisive defeat; more than 16,000 Union soldiers had been killed, wounded, or captured. But the Rebel victory, great though it was, had come at an even higher price: 18,400 casualties. While Chickamauga was the Confederacy's greatest victory, the cream of its Western armies lay dead on the field, and something even more precious had been lost. "The *élan* of the Southern soldier was never seen after Chickamauga," wrote Confederate lieutenant general D. H. Hill. "That brilliant dash which had distinguished him was gone forever."

Bragg did not resume the Confederate offensive the next day, despite the urging of Longstreet and other generals. "How can I?" he reportedly replied when Major General Nathan Bedford Forrest, after observing the disarranged Yankees from atop Missionary Ridge, exhorted him to pursue Rosecrans's army. "Here is two-fifths of my army left on the field, and my artillery without horses," protested Bragg. Afterward, Forrest grumbled to his officers, "What does he fight battles for?" Bragg chose to besiege Chattanooga instead.[16]

CHICKAMAUGA WAS THE NADIR of Sheridan's career as a general. Except for Lytle's gallant counterattack, Sheridan's division had been a nullity, swept aside by Longstreet's onslaught. Sheridan failed to rally his men until after the fighting had moved beyond him, and he arrived too late to aid Thomas.

Some historians have even questioned whether Sheridan reached Cloud House, as well as whether he shared a drink with Thomas, but both events very likely occurred. Sheridan's detractors, irritated by his occasional tendency to gloss over his shortcomings and promote himself, point to his conduct at Chickamauga as evidence that he was overrated as a general.

But Sheridan's performance, even on his worst day of battle, was arguably competent. Despite losing 1,500 of his 4,000 men, Sheridan managed to gather his shattered division and, with part of it, join Thomas. While neither he nor Davis lent material assistance to Thomas, they attempted to return to the battlefield when their commanding general and corps commander did not.

Sheridan's analysis of the battle suggested there was no "well-defined plan of action in the fighting, and this led to so much independence of judgment in construing orders among some of the subordinate generals." Too many people were issuing orders that affected the entire army, he wrote.[17] Colonel Silas Miller, who succeeded Lytle as brigade commander, described the debacle more vividly: the 3rd

Division, he said, had no more chance "than a broken-backed cat in hell without claws . . . with both flanks exposed and receiving fire from three directions."

Sheridan was never officially criticized. Forces beyond his control had sealed his division's fate. Others were deemed negligent, incompetent, and cowardly, but Sheridan's conduct, in fact, received praise in the reports of Rosecrans, McCook, and General in Chief Henry Halleck. "After gallant but fruitless efforts against this rebel torrent," wrote Halleck, "[Sheridan] was compelled to give way, but afterward rallied a considerable portion of his force, and by a circuitous rout, joined General Thomas."[18]

The ax instead fell on the three generals who rode to Chattanooga while Thomas still fought. The eager assassin was Dana, the assistant war secretary and Stanton's eyes and ears. A prolific report writer, Dana was trained in the era's journalistic stock-in-trade of gossip, innuendo, and even slander. He had devoted months to shaping Stanton's impressions of the Army of the Cumberland.

McCook and Crittenden were sacked first. And then, on October 19, Rosecrans was relieved, based partly on Dana's increasingly acid telegrams about his conduct and his men's opinion of him, but largely on Dana's false assertion that Rosecrans intended to evacuate Chattanooga—when Rosecrans was actually trying to secure his supply line so that he could launch a new offensive. Letters by others, including Rosecrans's chief of staff, Garfield, added to the proofs against him and made his downfall inevitable. President Abraham Lincoln remarked that in the weeks after Chickamauga, Rosecrans appeared "confused and stunned, like a duck hit on the head."

Rosecrans's dismissal was delayed because of politics. The Ohio general backed John Brough for governor of his state, and it was important to the Lincoln administration that Brough win. After Brough defeated the Copperhead peace candidate, Clement Vallandigham, Rosecrans was let go.

Falsehoods and electoral politics notwithstanding, the immutable fact remained that Rosecrans had lost the battle and left the field. In the end, it did not really matter which particular accusation brought about his downfall. Stanton, who despised him, wrote that while McCook and Crittenden "made pretty good time away from the fight, Rosecrans beat them both."[19]

Rosecrans's successor was Major General Ulysses Grant, who had become a national hero after capturing Vicksburg and thereby severing Louisiana, Arkansas, and Texas from the rest of the Confederacy. Grant was given broader authority than Rosecrans—command of the Armies of the Cumberland, the Ohio, and the Tennessee under a new Military Division of the Mississippi. Grant now oversaw all Union forces between the Allegheny Mountains and the Mississippi River.

Given the choice of retaining Rosecrans as commander of the Army of the Cumberland or naming Thomas to the position, Grant selected Thomas. Rosecrans was sent to his last command, the Department of the Missouri.

Ambrose Burnside remained commander of the Army of the Ohio, and William Tecumseh Sherman was appointed to command the Army of the Tennessee. The experiment in unified command would inspire subsequent army reorganizations.[20]

TRADITION HAS IT THAT Chattanooga's name derives from an Indian word. It might have been Creek for "rock rising to a point," or it could have come from "Choctaw-nooga," for the Choctaws living along the river, *nooga* being the word for town. Or it might mean "mountains looking at each other." All of these names are apt. Lookout Mountain, the dominant topographical feature, rises 2,300 feet to a point. In fact, mountains surround the city, which lies at the meeting point of the Cumberland Plateau and Appalachian Mountains. The Tennessee River is the town's other principal aspect.[21]

Following their victory at Chickamauga, the Rebels seized the important high ground overlooking the city: Lookout Mountain; Missionary Ridge, rising three hundred feet to the east and seven miles long; and Raccoon Mountain to the west. Long-range cannons were hauled to the summits of these prominences to fire down upon the Yankee camps around Chattanooga. Confederate rifle pits girdled Missionary Ridge, and Lookout Mountain became a fortress.

The Yankees threw up earthworks in the valley. In some places, their pickets were no more than three hundred yards from the Rebel pickets—so close that the army bands dueled with renditions of "Dixie" and "The Star-Spangled Banner." But the Union army, still reeling from its defeat, was unmistakably in a bad spot.

In addition, there was the daunting problem of supplying the army over a rutted, nearly impassable, sixty-mile nightmare of a road from the depot at Bridgeport, Alabama. The road was muddier, four times longer, and ten times more difficult to traverse than the four other potential routes. But land features shielded the road from Rebel artillery fire, while the others were vulnerable to shelling. Even so, Rebels hiding in the coves and valleys along the way ambushed the supply trains with depressing regularity, while the siege guns pounded the city from the mountains, and Rebel sharpshooters picked off Union soldiers. The Army of the Cumberland was soon on half rations.

Drought and the Union army's enormous requirements reduced the scruffy little river city to a wasteland. The trees were cut for fuel and fortifications, and on the branches of the few left standing, the leaves were curled and brown. Dust covered everything; wind moaning through the mountain gaps kicked up blinding dust storms. The crackling gray grass was useless as forage, and so the supply trains had to haul animal feed too. When it finally rained in October, the supply wagons foundered in axle-deep mud, and the soldiers splashed to and from their flooded campsites.[22]

SHERIDAN MADE HIS HEADQUARTERS on the farm of William Crutchfield, a loyal Unionist who reputedly had a fistfight with Jefferson Davis over secession before the war. At first, Sheridan and his men's nerves "were often upset by the whirring of twenty-pounder shells dropped inconsiderately into our camp at untimely hours of the night" from nearby Lookout Mountain. But the shelling caused so few casualties that Sheridan's men soon "responded by jeers and imprecation" whenever a shell landed in the camp. The two armies were so close to one another that the Rebels watched the Yankees turn out for reveille and eat their meager fare, while the Union soldiers studied the Rebel defenses and even spied on Bragg's headquarters on Missionary Ridge.[23]

The food shortage inspired Sheridan, the former commissary officer, to improvise. A company of the 2nd Kentucky Cavalry had attached itself to Sheridan's division without orders, and its commander volunteered for any duty that Sheridan might assign him. Sheridan sent the cavalrymen, guided by his scout and intelligence agent, James Card, to the Sequatchie Valley outside Chattanooga to obtain supplies. By hiding in a cove at the valley's upper end and paying generously for everything, in a few days they had acquired plenty of food and forage, supplementing the scanty rations reaching the division from Bridgeport. "In this way I carried men and animals through our beleaguerment [sic] in pretty fair condition," Sheridan wrote. His officers were so amply supplied, in fact, that they shared their fowl and eggs with other officers' messes.[24]

Still, the siege wore on everyone. Three soldiers who deserted Sheridan's command and headed north were caught, tried, and condemned to death. Sheridan assembled the entire division for the firing squad execution "to make the example effective," he wrote. "It was the saddest spectacle I every witnessed, but there could be no evasion."[25]

On October 23, Grant arrived in Chattanooga on crutches to command the armies of the West. Two weeks earlier in New Orleans, he had dislocated his hip and suffered a head injury when his horse bolted and collided with a carriage during a review prior to his departure for Tennessee (his detractors, with no evidence, whispered that Grant was drunk). At Bridgeport, Rosecrans, on his way out, met with Grant and described a plan made by him and Brigadier General W. F. "Baldy" Smith to open a new supply line between Bridgeport and Chattanooga that would be half the length of the current sixty-mile route, yet safe too. Grant made the plan his.

The daring operation involved more than 14,000 troops from Chattanooga and Bridgeport. Under the Rebel guns on Raccoon and Lookout Mountains, three converging forces—one floating down the river under the brow of Raccoon Mountain—seized Brown's Ferry before dawn on October 27. The troops built pontoon bridges, drove off the Rebels along Raccoon Mountain, and opened a second crossing later in the day at Kelley's Ferry on the west side of the mountain.

The plan worked flawlessly. Three days later, a steamboat reached Kelley's Ferry with 40,000 rations. The new supply route, which crossed the Tennessee River in three places, ended food rationing in Chattanooga. It was christened the "Cracker Line" in recognition of troops' staple food, hardtack crackers.[26]

As supplies now poured into Chattanooga, Major General Joseph Hooker arrived at Bridgeport at the head of 20,000 men from the Army of the Potomac. In mid-November, Major General William Tecumseh Sherman joined Hooker with four divisions, more than 16,000 men, from Mississippi—the core of his new Army of the Tennessee. With the reinforcements, Union forces surpassed 80,000 men. Those who knew Grant were certain they would see action soon.[27]

While Grant's army grew, Bragg's shrank from a peak of 70,000 to about 50,000. Longstreet had left Chattanooga with his I Corps and General Joe Wheeler's cavalry division to drive Major General Ambrose Burnside's army out of Knoxville.

Longstreet and Bragg had been at swords' points since Chickamauga over how to proceed against the Yankees in Chattanooga—Longstreet wanting to take the offensive, Bragg preferring to starve them out. In late October, Confederate president Jefferson Davis visited the army, ostensibly to reconcile the two commanders. Dissatisfaction was also endemic among Bragg's subordinate officers, who were fed up with his habit of squandering hard-fought victories.

It is puzzling that Davis sent Longstreet to Knoxville, weakening Bragg's force at Chattanooga, just as the Union army was adding tens of thousands of troops. Davis might have done it to separate Longstreet and Bragg, or to prevent Burnside from reinforcing Grant, or possibly to win a double victory. Whatever the reason, when Grant learned that Longstreet had gone, he prepared to go on the offensive. In his *Personal Memoirs*, Grant observed that President Davis "had an exalted opinion of his own military genius," sarcastically adding, "On several occasions during the war he came to the relief of the Union army by means of his *superior military genius.*"[28]

November 25, 1863–Missionary Ridge—Thirteen Union divisions numbering about 75,000 troops were either already in motion or poised to assault the towering heights to the south and east of Chattanooga. Arrayed against them were

Braxton Bragg's seven remaining Rebel divisions, with about 43,000 effectives. This was the day that Grant had ordained for ending the siege of the city.

Sheridan's and Wood's divisions were dug in on Orchard Knob, which they had stormed two days earlier. Before them, rising up from the valley floor, was the long silhouette of Missionary Ridge. Sunshine winked off the muskets and cannons of the Rebels in rifle pits at the ridge's base. Between it and the crest was another line of rifle pits, up a steep slope littered with boulders and fallen timber. Atop the ridge were more enemy troops, with cannons that intermittently shelled the two divisions.

The troops on Orchard Knob had been idle all day, as had the Rebel infantrymen on the heights facing them. However, Bragg's headquarters at the Thurman house, directly opposite them on the ridge crest, had been a hive of activity.

Early on November 23, a Confederate deserter had been brought before Sheridan with startling news: Bragg was preparing to fall back into Georgia. This information and other intelligence reaching Union headquarters convinced Grant that he must attack and defeat the Confederates surrounding Chattanooga without delay—before they slipped away to the south.

At 11 a.m. on November 23, Grant ordered Thomas to drive in the Rebel pickets and test the enemy lines to see if they were still held in force. Thomas instructed Major General Gordon Granger to ready his two IV Corps divisions for action. Wood's division would lead the assault, with Sheridan's division supporting it. The objective, Orchard Knob, was a small, lightly timbered hill that jutted one hundred feet above the Chattanooga Valley.

At 1:30 p.m., Grant, Thomas, Granger, Hooker, Assistant War Secretary Charles Dana, and other dignitaries watched from Fort Wood as Sheridan's and Wood's 10,000 men began their steady advance on Orchard Knob. "Flags were flying; the quick earnest steps of thousands beat equal time," wrote Granger's chief of staff, Brigadier General Joseph S. Fullerton. Drums rat-a-tatted, bugles sounded, and officers shouted commands. Ten thousand bayonets flashed like "a flying shower of electric sparks," noted Fullerton.

The Rebels on Orchard Knob left their gun pits to watch the spectacle, believing it was a grand review. When, minutes later, it dawned on them that the Union troops were in fact attacking, they scrambled back to their positions and began firing. After a sharp, short struggle, Sheridan's and Wood's men seized Orchard Knob and an adjacent hill.[29]

The next day, November 24, Sherman reached the north side of Missionary Ridge with his four divisions from Mississippi and attacked Bragg's right flank. A single stubborn division commanded by Patrick Cleburne threw back Sherman's divisions twice.

Hooker's three divisions simultaneously assaulted Lookout Mountain, fighting the "Battle above the Clouds." The 12,000 men crept up the craggy, steep-sided mountain against a Rebel force of 2,400. That night, Bragg, conceding that the mountain was lost, pulled back its defenders and sent them to fortify Missionary Ridge against the Union attack on the center that he expected the next day.

During the morning and the afternoon of November 25, Sherman had resumed his attack on the north side of Missionary Ridge at Tunnel Hill. Major General Oliver O. Howard's two reserve divisions reinforced Sherman. But the result was the same as on the previous day.

When Grant's staff officers, whose field glasses had been trained on the ridge crest, reported seeing Rebels shifting to the north side of the ridge, they feared that a major counterattack was about to be launched against Sherman. Hooker's three divisions were now behind Missionary Ridge, advancing toward Rossville to cut the Rebel supply line. Grant realized that they would not be able to reach Sherman's lines until that night—far too late. To stop the further reinforcement of Sherman's adversary, Grant ordered Thomas to attack the center of Missionary Ridge with his 25,000-man Army of the Cumberland.

IT WAS CONCEIVED AS a limited attack, ending with the capture of the Rebel rifle pits at the base of the ridge—and no more. Its purpose was to freeze the Confederates on the ridgetop until Sherman broke through. Sheridan's and Wood's IV Corps divisions would execute the feint, along with XIV Corps, whose two divisions were led by Brigadier Generals Absalom Baird and Richard Johnson. Six guns fired in quick succession would signal the opening of the assault.[30]

At 3:40 p.m., the high-strung Granger, standing beside Grant and Thomas on Orchard Knob, raised and lowered his arm six times, shouting, "Fire!" each time. The four divisions surged toward Missionary Ridge, ranked north to south: Baird, Wood, Sheridan, and Johnson, with Wood and Sheridan leading. Beside himself with excitement, Granger leaped into a gun emplacement, personally sighted a field piece, and shouted, "Fire!" Visibly irritated, Grant told Granger to concentrate on commanding his troops and let the captain run his battery.

It was the sort of stirring scene that one might read about in accounts of the Napoleonic wars but that was rarely seen during the Civil War, when most battles were either fought in dense woods or spread over many miles. Twenty-five thousand Union troops marched across the floor of a natural amphitheater, watched by tens of thousands of troops from both armies. "With bands playing, flags flying, soldiers cheering and yelling, our men three lines deep in perfect alignment, poured out through the young cottonwood timber," wrote Sylvanus Cadwallader of the *New*

York Herald. Heavy artillery from the Union forts in Chattanooga joined the batteries blazing away from Fort Wood.[31]

Beyond the thin woods, an open plain of four to nine hundred yards, covered
with felled trees, stretched to the foot of Missionary Ridge and the first line of Rebel
rifle pits. Thomas's four divisions, advancing along a two-mile front, ran through
"a most terrible tornado of shot and shell" toward the first line.

Sheridan never doubted that his men would capture the rifle pits, but he was
unsure whether they could then hold them; with Rebels pouring down murderous
fire from a second line of pits and the ridge crest, they might die there. He sent a
staff officer, Captain J. S. Ransom, to ask Granger whether he was only to capture
the lower positions or to press the attack upward.[32]

Without firing a shot, Sheridan's men captured the lower pits with just their
bayonets. Most of the Rebels surrendered, but some of them ran up the mountain.
The Yankees lay flat against the sharply angled ridge as the Rebels fired down on
them with muskets and fifty cannons spewing grapeshot and canister.

As Brigadier General George Wagner's brigade began advancing from the captured positions toward the second line of rifle pits as Ransom and Fullerton returned
with Granger's answer to Sheridan. Ransom stopped to tell Wagner that he and the
rest of Sheridan's division—and all of Thomas's corps, for that matter—must stop
at the lower rifle pits. Wagner ordered his men to return. Many of them were cut
down by Rebel fire when they turned back.[33]

Ransom then informed Sheridan, who was riding through a ditch of entrenchments, flushing out skulkers. But Sheridan's two other brigades were already closing
on the second line of gun pits. Sheridan refused to order "those officers and men
who were so gallantly ascending the hill, step by step, to return." In fact, thousands
of Thomas's foot soldiers, without orders, were forging their way up the steep slope.
Sheridan decided that he could only endorse his men's spontaneous decision to
continue the attack all the way to the top—and so he ordered a charge on the ridge.
His troops erupted in cheers.[34]

When Grant saw the bluecoats swarming toward the ridge crest, he angrily asked
Thomas, "Who ordered those men up the ridge?" Thomas replied, "I don't know.
I did not." Grant then turned to Granger, who said the men had evidently started
up the ridge without orders. "When those fellows get started, all hell can't stop
them," Granger said enthusiastically. Grant sourly remarked that someone would
pay if the attack failed; he issued no further orders.[35]

Granger sent Fullerton and another staff officer, a Captain Avery, to Wood and
Sheridan to ask them whether they had ordered their men up the ridge—and to
proceed with the attack if they thought it could succeed. Sheridan told Avery that
he had issued no such order until his men were already halfway to the crest, adding,

"We are going to take the ridge!" He asked Avery for his flask, waved it at a group of Confederate officers standing in front of Bragg's headquarters on the ridgetop, and shouted, "Here's at you!" As he took a drink, gunners on the ridge depressed two guns and fired on Sheridan and Avery, showering them with dirt. "Ah, that is ungenerous!" Sheridan shouted at them. "I shall take those guns for that!"[36]

It would have been hard work climbing the steep ridge even without musket and cannon fire raining down on the Yankees; the musket balls sounded like "the swarming of bees as they went rushing by." The upper slope, cut by ravines, tilted at a forty-degree angle and was littered with fallen timber and talus.

Spurs projecting from the slope provided some cover. When the Yankees reached the second line of gun pits, sending the retreating Rebels panting up the last yards to the top, the gunfire from the summit faltered. The Rebels feared hitting their own men, and the guns could not be depressed to fire at so steep an angle. The Confederate gunners resorted to rolling short-fused shells and boulders down the hill.[37]

Shouting "Chickamauga! Chickamauga!" the Yankees boiled over the ridgetop in six places at once. Sheridan's men were first, according to Sheridan, Fullerton, and others. Wood's division also claimed the honor. A young soldier from Sheridan's division, Lieutenant Arthur MacArthur Jr. of the 24th Wisconsin, burst over the top crying, "On Wisconsin!" and planted the regimental flag on the Rebel works where everyone could see it.[38]

Charles Dana, watching the spectacle in awe from Orchard Knob, pronounced it "one of the greatest miracles in military history."[39] In just one hour, the Yankees had wrested possession of Missionary Ridge from the Rebels, ending the siege of Chattanooga. The Yankees cheered, shook hands, wept, and waved their caps to urge on their comrades who were still climbing. Sheridan joined in while giddily straddling a captured cannon.

An artillery blast wounded Rienzi seconds after Sheridan dismounted, and a colonel presented him with a gray charger that had belonged to one of Confederate major general John Breckenridge's staff officers. Sheridan named the horse Breckenridge and kept it as a second mount.

Bragg tried to rally his troops and was nearly captured instead. The Rebels bolted down the other side of the ridge. As they ran, many threw away their weapons and blanket rolls.

Confederate battle reports would blame the Rebel defeat on inept leadership by Bragg and Breckenridge. The latter was criticized for dividing his force between the ridge crest and lower gun pits. The men in the pits had been instructed to deliver fire, then rapidly retreat when pressed. But when they ran up the steep hill under fire and reached the ridge crest, they were too exhausted to fight.

Confederate engineers had also mistakenly positioned the upper defensive line on the ridge's geographical crest, which was higher and farther from the edge than the preferred "military crest" would have been. A brigade commander who dug in on the military crest, Brigadier General Arthur Manigault, repelled the attack on his sector.[40]

WHILE THE CELEBRATION CONTINUED on the ridge crest, Sheridan led two of his brigades down the east side of the ridge in pursuit of Bragg's army. Alone among the victors, Sheridan's troops doggedly followed Bragg's retreating army in the hope of capturing his wagon train. Moving quickly without artillery along a road toward Chickamauga Creek, they captured prisoners, guns, and supply wagons during a series of small, sharp clashes with the Rebel rearguard.[41]

On a high hill a mile from Missionary Ridge, Rebel infantry and eight guns made a stand, and as darkness fell, Sheridan's men for the second time that day found themselves clinging to a hillside, with canister and minié balls whizzing by them. As the moon rose behind the hill, Sheridan was treated to "a medallion view of the column . . . as it crossed the moon's disk and attacked the enemy." The Union soldiers drove the Confederates from the hill, capturing two guns and some wagons. It was, Sheridan wrote, "a gallant little fight."[42]

Sheridan rousted Granger from bed at midnight to urge him to throw the rest of IV Corps into the pursuit. Granger told him they had done enough that day. When Sheridan persisted, Granger authorized him to press on to Chickamauga Creek and promised to send troops if Sheridan encountered organized enemy forces. Not encountering significant resistance, but not wishing to continue alone, Sheridan engaged in "a little deception": he had two regiments simulate a firefight. He hoped this would compel Granger to send reinforcements. The ruse didn't work.

The marathon pursuit ended when the Rebels crossed Chickamauga Creek, where Sheridan's men captured more wagons, ammunition, guns, small arms, and prisoners. The Confederates were in such a hurry to get over the creek and frustrate pursuit that they burned a pontoon bridge before all of their troops had crossed.

At 2 a.m., the exhausted Yankees made their camp near Chickamauga Station. Sheridan was frustrated by the Union command's failure to even try to destroy Bragg's retreating army.[43]

GRANT VISITED SHERIDAN'S FORWARD camp later that day. When he learned about the missed opportunity to crush Bragg, he, too, was disappointed. "With the instinct of military genius [Sheridan] pushed ahead. If others had followed his example we should have had Bragg's army," Grant wrote.

Later, Grant's growing dissatisfaction with Granger reached its acme when Granger delayed in starting for Knoxville with a relief expedition to reinforce Burnside. Grant replaced him with Sherman. "I have lost all faith in his energy and capacity to manage an expedition of the importance of this one," Grant wrote General in Chief Henry Halleck.[44]

WHEN SHERIDAN RETURNED TO Missionary Ridge, he found that in his absence, Brigadier General William Hazen's brigade from Wood's division had seized eleven guns that Sheridan had captured on the ridge crest the previous day. Sheridan vehemently protested that the guns were his division's prizes, not Hazen's. He continued to object in his battle report (the guns "were appropriated while I was pushing the enemy on to Chickamauga Station," he indignantly wrote) and in his *Personal Memoirs*, where he scorned "some high officers . . . who were more interested in gleaning that portion of the battle-field over which my command has passed than in destroying a panic-stricken enemy."

Until the late 1880s, Hazen and Sheridan feuded over which of them had reached the top of Missionary Ridge first and who was entitled to the guns. In his 1885 *A Narrative of Military Service*, Hazen devoted fifty-six pages, replete with supporting letters and reports from Union and Confederate officers and soldiers, to the subject. He claimed that his brigade rightfully claimed the guns after reaching the summit of Missionary Ridge before Sheridan. Three years later, in his *Personal Memoirs*, Sheridan dismissed "the absurdity of [Hazen's] deduction" and insisted that the eleven guns were his division's prizes. He then added three pages of excerpts from his subordinates' battle reports to prove that they had captured the guns.[45]

OF THE 6,000 MEN Sheridan led into battle, 1,300 fell wounded or dead on the approaches to Missionary Ridge and on its steep slopes. In his report, Sheridan described their conduct as "more than heroic." His division captured 1,762 Rebels and seventeen artillery pieces—a figure that included the eleven disputed cannons.

In his after-action report, Grant conspicuously praised Sheridan for pursuing Bragg's army all the way to Chickamauga Station. "To Sheridan's prompt movement, the Army of the Cumberland and the nation are indebted for the bulk of the capture of prisoners, artillery and small-arms that day. Except for his prompt pursuit, so much in this way would not have been accomplished."[46]

Grant would not forget that Sheridan relentlessly harried Bragg's retreating army when no other commander did.

CHAPTER 4

Sheridan's Cavalry Corps

APRIL–MAY 1864

Did Sheridan say that? Well, he generally knows what he is talking about. Let him start right out and do it.

—GENERAL ULYSSES GRANT SENDING SHERIDAN
TO FIGHT JEB STUART'S CAVALRY[1]

THE UNION ARMY HAD A SURFEIT OF MAJOR GENERALS but not a single three-star general. The rank of lieutenant general had fallen into disuse after November 1861, when seventy-five-year-old Winfield Scott retired as commanding general. George Washington had been the only permanent US lieutenant general; Scott had held the rank by brevet. On February 26, 1864, Abraham Lincoln signed a law reviving the rank.

The Confederacy boasted more than a dozen lieutenant generals, but Lincoln wanted to appoint just one: Ulysses S. Grant. The Senate swiftly confirmed Lincoln's nomination of Grant. As commander of all Union armies, Grant was now one of the three most powerful men in the Union, along with Lincoln and War Secretary Edwin Stanton.

While Scott had remained in Washington, Grant chose to make his headquarters with the Army of the Potomac in northern Virginia—to be close to the action and to insulate himself from the inevitable second-guessing by Lincoln and Stanton. Major General George Meade, however, remained the Army of the Potomac's titular commander. The army would become Grant's main weapon for crushing the rebellion, and he immediately began readying it for a major campaign.[2]

Grant was a quiet, modest man whose shyness was sometimes misinterpreted as aloofness. In March 1864, Colonel Theodore Lyman of General Meade's staff happened to be in the dining room of the Willard Hotel in Washington when Grant entered with his fourteen-year-old son, Fred. The diners burst into cheers and crowded around the general to shake his hand, but Grant appeared bored by the attention, Lyman wrote. He described him as "rather under middle height, of a spare, strong build; light-brown hair, and short, light-brown beard," with a curved nose set under blue eyes and a square jaw. "His face has three expressions: deep thought; extreme determination; and great simplicity and calmness."[3]

Grant became army commander a week after Brigadier General Hugh Judson Kilpatrick led an unsuccessful raid to rescue Union war prisoners in Richmond. Carried out over the objections of Meade and the Cavalry Corps commander, Major General Alfred Pleasonton, the raid was conceived by the Lincoln administration after the mass escape by Union officers from Libby Prison in Richmond.

The raid's failure tarnished the image of the improving Union cavalry. The 12,000-man Cavalry Corps conducted reconnaissance, escorted officers and wagon trains, and patrolled picket lines, and sometimes it fought Rebel cavalry units.

After Grant's promotion, Pleasonton was transferred to the Division of the Missouri, which was commanded by another Grant exile, Major General William Rosecrans. Kilpatrick was sent to Major General William Sherman's Army of the Tennessee. Grant, Stanton, and Major General Henry Halleck, the army's chief of staff in Washington, began searching for a new cavalry leader.

IN WINFIELD SCOTT'S OPINION, the cavalry had little value; he opposed organizing even regimental-size mounted forces. It was Lincoln who prodded his reluctant generals to create larger units. The early Union cavalry commanders were Old Army mounted officers who lacked experience in leading large formations. They doled out their cavalrymen piecemeal to infantry divisions to use as they saw fit.

Only since early 1863 had the Cavalry Corps existed as a separate command. Its first commander, Major General George Stoneman, lasted until just June 1863, when he was relieved of his command after failing to get into Robert E. Lee's rear as he retreated from Chancellorsville. Stoneman was assigned to run the new Cavalry Bureau, whose job was to equip the Cavalry Corps.

Pleasonton succeeded Stoneman. Under the forty-year-old veteran of the Peninsula Campaign, Antietam, and Chancellorsville, the cavalry fought Jeb Stuart's cavaliers to a draw at Brandy Station, the major all-cavalry battle of the war, and performed solidly at Gettysburg. Pleasonton reorganized the Cavalry Corps into three divisions led by aggressive, battle-tested officers. All this was to the good, but Pleasonton quarreled with Meade. Grant's arrival supplied an excuse to replace him.

Even after the Cavalry Corps became a separate entity, its three divisions rarely operated together and never as an independent strike force. Meade required the Cavalry Corps commander to share quarters with his staff, to better serve the needs of the infantry.[4]

GRANT'S FIRST CHOICE FOR Pleasonton's replacement was Major General William B. Franklin, a classmate of his at West Point who had led troops at Antietam and Fredericksburg. But Franklin had made powerful enemies, chief among them Ambrose Burnside, with whom he had shared blame for the debacle at Fredericksburg in 1862. The poisonous feeling between Franklin and Burnside and their respective allies compelled Grant to drop Franklin. More names were considered and rejected, and then Halleck, during a meeting with Grant and President Lincoln, suggested Philip Sheridan.[5]

Halleck, of course, knew Sheridan from their months together in Mississippi, when Sheridan, before becoming a regimental and brigade commander, had organized Halleck's headquarters campsite. Having no firsthand experience with Sheridan, Stanton and Lincoln took Halleck at his word. "Major General P.H. Sheridan is assigned to command the Cavalry Corps, Army of the Potomac," read the April 4 announcement.[6]

Sheridan had just turned thirty-three. Two years earlier, he was a captain whose highest ambition was to hold a field command. After toiling in the relative obscurity of the western theater as one of dozens of division commanders, he would now move into the bright spotlight trained on the Army of the Potomac. Operating as it did just forty miles from Washington, the army's every move was endlessly scrutinized by the Lincoln administration.

Grant, who would later claim Sheridan was the man he had wanted all along, did not object. While he well remembered Sheridan's aggressiveness at Booneville and Missionary Ridge, at the moment Grant had greater issues to address than the Cavalry Corps; he was busy readying his 120,000-man Army of the Potomac for a major offensive in northern Virginia.

GRANT PLANNED TO ESCALATE the war in the belief that doing so would end it sooner. His strategy called for Union armies in every major theater to attack the

Confederates simultaneously, bringing as many troops to bear on as many points as possible. Lieutenant General James Longstreet had demonstrated at Chicka-mauga that the Rebels could still win battles when permitted to shift troops along their internal lines. Grant's plan would make it difficult, if not impossible, for the Confederates to reinforce one point without placing another in jeopardy.

"The enemy have not got army enough" to reinforce every attacked point, wrote Grant. With the Union's massive superiority in numbers—a half million combat troops, ready for action—Grant believed that at least one field army would be able to break through. Lincoln instantly grasped Grant's point. "As we say out West," said the president, "if a man can't skin, he must hold a leg while somebody else does."

The Army of the Potomac would cross the Rapidan River to engage and destroy Robert E. Lee's Army of Northern Virginia, while Major General Benjamin Butler ascended the James River to threaten Richmond from the southeast. Sherman would march with 120,000 men in three armies on Atlanta; German-born Major General Franz Sigel would advance up the Shenandoah Valley and get on Lee's flank; and Major General Nathaniel Banks would strike at Mobile.

The Lincoln administration and the Union army would discover that Grant's perspective on the importance of winning or losing individual battles sharply dif-fered from his predecessors'. Four of the five previous Union army offensives in northern Virginia had ended in retreat; the fifth, in stalemate.

Grant planned to prosecute his campaign in northern Virginia whether he won battles or lost them. He understood that the war might yet be won if enough irre-placeable Rebel soldiers could be killed or maimed and war's awfulness could be brought into the homes of enough Southern civilians. This was at once a new and an old concept of war: "total war."[7]

LONGSTREET'S DEPARTURE FROM CHATTANOOGA to attack Burnside in Knoxville had prompted Grant to strike at Missionary Ridge and Lookout Moun-tain. After breaking the siege of Chattanooga, Grant had ordered IV Corps—Sheri-dan's and Thomas Wood's divisions—to march to Knoxville to reinforce Major General Ambrose Burnside.

The weary troops were given no time to exchange their ragged clothes and bro-ken shoes or to obtain winter gear, although they would be campaigning in the East Tennessee mountains, where winter had already begun. With four days' rations in their haversacks, they began the hundred-mile march to Knoxville.

Burnside's troops had repulsed Longstreet by the time the relief column reached Knoxville, but Longstreet lingered in the mountains. East of Knoxville, at a cold place improbably named Strawberry Plains, Sheridan's division made its winter camp.[8]

When Longstreet withdrew into Virginia in January, Sheridan's division was then sent to Loudon, southwest of Knoxville, to safeguard labor crews that were rebuilding the railroad between Knoxville and Chattanooga. As Sheridan's men left Strawberry Plains, "a general disgust prevailed" over the seemingly pointless misery they had endured there that winter.

Sheridan took a forty-day furlough—his first extended leave in eleven years and his first break from field command in twenty months. He went home to Somerset and visited Chicago and Milwaukee.[9]

UNBEKNOWNST TO SHERIDAN, WHILE he was on leave in February, his name was in play while Grant and Halleck weighed possible candidates for commander of the Army of the Tennessee. But Major General James B. McPherson got the job.[10] Then, shortly after Sheridan returned from his furlough, he received a telegram from Halleck: "Lieutenant-General Grant directs that Major-General Sheridan immediately repair to Washington and report to the Adjutant-General of the Army."[11]

Sheridan did not know why he was being summoned, but he was certain the telegram meant "a severing of my relations" with his division. Finding the idea of a formal leave-taking from his men unbearable, Sheridan resolved to depart without saying good-bye. "I feared to trust my emotions," he wrote.

When he boarded the train at the Loudon station, however, he discovered that his division had assembled on the hillsides to see him off. Many of these soldiers had served with him at Perryville, Stones River, Chickamauga, and Missionary Ridge. "They amply repaid all my care and anxiety, courageously and readily meeting all demands in every emergency that arose," he wrote.

As the train left for Chattanooga, Sheridan's men waved good-bye to him.[12]

SHERIDAN LEARNED FROM MAJOR General George Thomas when he reached Chattanooga that he had been appointed commander of the Cavalry Corps of the Army of the Potomac—the largest cavalry force in the Union army. The news was daunting. "The information staggered me at first," Sheridan wrote. "I felt loth [*sic*] to undergo the trials of the new position."

This was understandable. He knew scarcely anyone in Washington; he had no political connections in the Lincoln administration, or in the Army of the Potomac for that matter. Moreover, he knew little about the army's previous operations in Virginia. These negative factors notwithstanding, "there was no help for it, so after reflecting on the matter a little I concluded to make the best of the situation."[13]

For Phil Sheridan, who believed in careful preparation and energetic execution, this meant more than adjusting mentally to his new role. He studied maps of Virginia and the Army of the Potomac's history, and he learned what he could about the men with whom he would serve. And in Major James Forsyth of the 18th US Infantry he found someone to tutor him in the ways of the Army of the Potomac. Not only was Forsyth Sheridan's friend and his former adjutant at Chickamauga, but he had also served in the Army of the Potomac during the Peninsula and Antietam campaigns. Sheridan named Forsyth as his chief of staff.

Sheridan also brought with him two aides-de-camp from Tennessee: his younger brother Michael and First Lieutenant Thomas Moore. Needing an advisor with cavalry experience, he chose Captain Frederick Newhall of the 6th Pennsylvania Cavalry to be his senior aide-de-camp.[14]

SHERIDAN'S FIRST VISIT TO Washington was dizzying. "I was an entire stranger, and I cannot now recall that I met a single individual whom I had ever before known." Sheridan, Forsyth, and Moore checked into the Willard Hotel, where Union officers stayed when returning to duty in Virginia after furloughs. At the War Department, Halleck briefed Sheridan on his new duties, described the military situation in Virginia, and introduced Sheridan to War Secretary Edwin Stanton. Stanton looked Sheridan up and down with open skepticism. "I could feel that Mr. Stanton was eyeing me closely and searchingly, endeavoring to form some estimate of one about whom he knew absolutely nothing," Sheridan wrote, certain that Stanton had never heard of him until his appointment to the Cavalry Corps.

Under Stanton's searching gaze, Sheridan uncomfortably felt every deficiency, real or imagined, in his education, his character, and even his appearance. He was a youthful-looking thirty-three years old, stood five-foot-five, and weighed a "thin almost to emaciation" 115 pounds. Sheridan was nearly tongue-tied during the interview. "If I had ever possessed any self-assertion in manner or speech, it certainly vanished in the presence of the imperious Secretary, whose name at the time was the synonym of all that was cold and formal."

Sheridan never learned what Stanton really thought of him that day. After they became better acquainted and Stanton warmed to him, Sheridan concluded that the secretary's reputation for coldness was "more mythical than real."[15]

When Sheridan met Lincoln, the president offered both hands in greeting. Lincoln said the cavalry had not yet lived up to its potential. He repeated an old joke from the war's early years: "Who ever saw a dead cavalryman?" Sheridan refused to read any hidden meaning into the jest.[16]

Afterward, a War Department official remarked to Grant, "The officer you brought on from the West is rather a little fellow to handle your cavalry." Grant replied, "You will find him big enough for the purpose before we get through with him."[17]

On April 5, Sheridan left Washington on an army train bound for the Army of the Potomac's camps in northern Virginia. He reached the Cavalry Corps headquarters at Brandy Station that night.

INITIALLY, THE CAVALRY CORPS was as unimpressed with Sheridan as the wags at the War Department. After getting a look at him, a young Wisconsin officer concluded there were probably officers in the ranks who could do a better job. Some of the veterans watched with interest as Sheridan prepared to mount his horse. "We wondered how he was going to do it," said one of them, "and expected to see him shin up his long saber."[18]

After formally reviewing his corps, Sheridan remarked that it "presented a fine appearance," while noting that the horses were thin and looked worn. He learned that the cavalry had been constantly employed, even when the army was in winter camp. It scouted, hunted guerrillas, guarded firewood details and cattle herds, escorted officers, and rode the sixty-mile picket line around the Army of the Potomac for three days at a time. On the picket line, the mounted troops usually encountered only enemy infantry; the Rebel cavalry was excused from picketing. Parades, reviews, inspections, classes, and regular drill occupied the cavalrymen much of the rest of the time.[19]

Sheridan's senior aide-de-camp, Captain Newhall, conducted a closer inspection of the 1st and 3rd Divisions and was dismayed by their weapons and clothing. Their arms were inferior—mostly single-shot Joslyn and Smith carbines. Some of the men had only sidearms. Their clothing was "used-up," their horses desperately needed rest, and the camps were badly located and policed. Newhall concluded that between the two divisions, 5,000 men might be combat ready. Sheridan later found identical conditions in the 2nd Division.[20]

Sheridan sought an interview with General Meade. Their conversation began with the condition of the Cavalry Corps but then proceeded to the cavalry's mission and duties. Sheridan and Meade discovered that they disagreed sharply.

It is unclear when Sheridan conceived his ideas on the strategic use of mounted troops. It might have happened when he was a cavalry commander in Mississippi. Perhaps he formulated them between his appointment and arrival at Brandy Station, or after reviewing his corps and reflecting on the poor condition of its mounts. Whatever their provenance, Sheridan now bluntly articulated his ideas to Meade.

Dispersing the cavalry for its current manifold duties was "burdensome and wasteful," he said, and needlessly hard on horses. "In name only was it a corps at all," and in actuality it was just a subordinate arm of the infantry. The cavalry, Sheridan asserted, should be employed as a concentrated, independent force to fight and destroy the enemy's cavalry.

Sheridan's notions challenged the Union army's doctrine of placing the cavalry at the infantry's disposal. The Confederate cavalry, he noted, often operated autonomously, and with success. Jeb Stuart was revered in the South, but the Union army had no one comparable.

"My proposition seemed to stagger General Meade not a little," wrote Sheridan. Meade wanted to know who would protect the wagon trains and artillery reserve. Sheridan replied that the trains and artillery would not need guarding against Rebel cavalry raids if the Union Cavalry Corps were unleashed against the enemy cavalry.

"With a mass of ten thousand mounted men . . . I could make it so lively for the enemy's cavalry that . . . the flanks and rear of the Army of the Potomac would require little or no defense," Sheridan told Meade. The infantry could provide what protection might be needed. After defeating the Rebel cavalry in combat, he said, the Cavalry Corps would play havoc with Confederate communications and supply lines.

Sheridan's proposals only annoyed Meade and would later lead to trouble between them. Yet, when Sheridan on April 19 formally requested that his men's picket lines be shortened, Meade surprised him by relieving the corps of nearly all picket duty. The horses' condition immediately improved.

Sheridan remained fixated on winning for the Cavalry Corps "the same privileges and responsibilities that attached to the other corps—conditions that never actually existed before."[21]

As his corps refitted for the upcoming offensive, Sheridan met individually with his division and brigade commanders. When he sat down with Brigadier General George Armstrong Custer, commander of the 1st Brigade of the 1st Division, the men established an instant rapport. "I remained . . . last night and to-day until nearly 4 o'clock. . . . Major-General Sheridan impressed me very favorably," Custer wrote to his wife, Libbie. Both men of action, Sheridan and Custer would remain friends and comrades until Custer's death.[22]

On paper, the Cavalry Corps's three divisions and eight horse artillery batteries totaled 35,000 men in thirty-one regiments. In reality, Sheridan could field 12,500 fully equipped veteran cavalrymen and 863 gunners.[23]

Division commanders Alfred Torbert, David Gregg, and James Wilson were critical to any success that the corps might win. Sheridan had personally chosen only Torbert, successor to the late Major General John Buford, who had selected the battleground at Gettysburg that had proved so advantageous to the Union.

Sheridan's choice of Torbert, an 1855 West Point graduate with impressive mutton chops, was somewhat puzzling, because Torbert had never commanded cavalry. But he had competently led the 1st New Jersey Infantry and later a brigade of VI

Corps through the Peninsula Campaign, Second Manassas, South Mountain, Antietam, Fredericksburg, Chancellorsville, and Gettysburg. Sheridan probably gave Torbert command of the 1st Division because of his combat experience and familiarity with Virginia.[24]

Sheridan was lucky to have Gregg, the full-bearded, basset-eyed incumbent 2nd Division commander. Modest and popular, Gregg had led a mounted brigade at Fredericksburg and the 2nd Division at Chancellorsville, Brandy Station, and Gettysburg.[25]

Wilson, just twenty-six years old, had never led troops. He was Grant's choice to replace Kilpatrick, whom Grant had transferred to Sherman's army. An engineering officer, Wilson had served with distinction on Grant's staff during the Vicksburg and Chattanooga campaigns, and he had briefly directed the Cavalry Bureau. There, his lasting contribution was designating the Spencer repeating rifle as the cavalry's standard-issue weapon.

Christopher Spencer's innovative weapon was a "force-multiplier" and one of the great technological advances of the Civil War. While essentially a single-shot rifle, the Spencer's tube magazine, inserted into the butt stock, enabled a cavalryman to fire seven shots successively, ejecting the fired cartridge and chambering a new round by working the lever action. By replacing empty tube magazines with preloaded ones, a trooper might fire twenty-one rounds in one minute—the time in which a skilled infantryman might fire a musket four times. A cavalryman's cartridge box might contain up to a dozen preloaded firing tubes.

Brigadier General Horace Porter, one of Grant's staff officers, once overheard a Rebel prisoner remark about the Spencer, "You can load it up on Sunday and fire it off all the rest o' the week." While no match for the Rebels' Enfield musket at long range, at distances under one hundred yards, the Spencer endowed dismounted cavalrymen with enormous firepower.[26]

The Spencer was well suited to Sheridan's evolving ideas about the cavalry as a highly mobile unit able to reach critical points quickly. Upon dismounting, it could unleash overwhelming firepower. While the cavalry still fought enemy horsemen with sabers and pistols on horseback, in late 1863, both armies had begun using dismounted cavalry as skirmishers and sometimes to support infantry. Sheridan wanted the cavalry to break away from the infantry's supervision altogether and to operate independently, whether on horseback or dismounted.[27]

MAY 4, 1864–THE WILDERNESS, VIRGINIA—At midnight, the death-haunted landscape appeared as a dark, featureless mass looming over the Rapidan River's south bank. Sheridan's cavalrymen efficiently secured the Ely and Germanna fords,

six miles apart and a few miles west of where the Rapidan merged with the Rappa-
hannock. Engineers began laying down wood-canvass pontoon bridges for the vast
army that followed—120,000 men and 50,000 mules and horses.[28]

Waiting on the river's north bank behind the cavalry and engineers, and winding
northward for miles, was the Army of the Potomac, with its infantrymen and gunners,
artillery batteries, and endless wagon trains. The march to Richmond had begun.

While elements of Torbert's division guarded the crossings and the army wagon
trains north of the river, Sheridan's two other divisions rode south. Wilson's marched
in advance of Major General Gouverneur Warren's V Corps, and Gregg's division
traveled ahead of Major General Winfield Scott Hancock's II Corps. They rode
down roads that tunneled through the living mountain of vegetation known simply
as "the Wilderness." The Rapidan described the north rim of the province of bogs
and jungle growth whose one hundred square miles could easily swallow up an
army without leaving a trace. The dense second-growth woods, brakes, and tangled
undergrowth—underlain by innumerable knolls and ravines—muffled the noise
made by thousands of hooves and clinking harnesses.

Because of the terrain and Meade's orders, Sheridan knew his cavalrymen would
be limited in their operations. "There would be little opportunity for mounted
troops to acquit themselves well in a region so thickly wooded, and traversed by so
many almost parallel streams."

He, like Grant, believed that if General Robert E. Lee's Army of Northern Virginia did strike the Yankees, it would be here or at the river crossings, where they
were most vulnerable. If the army emerged from the claustrophobic perpetual twilight of the Wilderness, the relatively open areas beyond would provide maneuver-
ing room. As the dawn of May 4 approached and Sheridan's cavalrymen rode down
the narrow, snaking dirt roads with trees and vines arching overhead, they tensed
to receive the expected blow, but none fell.[29]

THERE WAS SKIRMISHING ON May 4 but no major fighting. Lee, whose army had
been in winter quarters near Orange Courthouse southwest of the Wilderness, permitted Grant to cross the Rapidan unmolested as he waited for Longstreet's 12,000
men to reach him. But Lee did not plan to let Grant emerge from the Wilderness
unscathed. The woods and underbrush would not just hide Lee's movements; they
would conceal the fact that when Longstreet's troops arrived, Lee's army would
number just 65,000, little more than half of Grant's force.

In this inhospitable wild tangle, almost exactly a year earlier, at Chancellorsville,
Lee and the late Stonewall Jackson had beaten the much larger Army of the Potomac under Major General Joe Hooker, with whom many of the troops now
marching with Grant had served. As they made their camps on this night, there

was little levity and no singing. Near the charred ruins of the Chancellor mansion, the soldiers found human skulls and "skeletons in rotted blue" washed by spring rains from shallow graves.[30]

ON MAY 5, THE battle exploded. Near the junction of Brock Road and Orange Court House Turnpike at Wilderness Tavern, Warren's V Corps crashed into Confederate lieutenant general Richard Ewell's II Corps. Even with Major General John Sedgwick's VI Corps assisting, Warren was unable to break Ewell's lines. At the end of the day, casualties from both armies littered the paths and burning fields.

The story was much the same when Confederate lieutenant general A. P. Hill's III Corps attacked Wilson's cavalry division on the Orange Plank Road three miles to the south. Sheridan sent Gregg to assist Wilson. Together, with the help of their fast-firing Spencer carbines, they slowed Hill's advance until Hancock's II Corps infantrymen got into position. The two corps battered one another throughout the day.[31]

The armies resumed the carnage on May 6. Hancock attacked with half of Grant's army down the Orange Plank Road, with Sheridan's Cavalry Corps guarding Hancock's left flank and rear against repeated Rebel attacks by Major General Fitzhugh Lee's cavalry. Two brigades from Torbert's division, led by Custer and Colonel Thomas Devin, dismounted and, blazing away with their Spencer carbines, drove Fitzhugh Lee from the field. One of Custer's officers described it as "sulky, stubborn, bulldog fighting, entirely opposed to the brilliant methods by which Custer had gained his reputation, dismounted lines of skirmishers pressing grimly forward through tangled woods, firing at each other like lines of infantry."

Later in the day, Longstreet's corps reached the battlefield, and Lee immediately sent it up the Orange Plank Road along a belt three-fourths of a mile wide. Bursting shells set the woods afire, and the screams of wounded men burning alive rent the air. Longstreet was severely wounded by his own men. At the day's end, neither army had gained a decisive advantage.

On May 7, as the adversaries waited for one another to make the first move, Jeb Stuart sent Fitzhugh Lee's and Major General Wade Hampton's cavalry divisions to capture the crossroads at Todd's Tavern. Gregg's division and Brigadier General Wesley Merritt's Reserve Brigade battled them there. It was "an exceedingly severe and, at times, fluctuating fight," wrote Sheridan. The Union cavalrymen finally drove the Rebels nearly all the way to Spotsylvania Court House.

Sheridan was proud of his cavalry's performance during the two-day battle, while acknowledging that its outcome "had not been all that was desired."[32]

GRANT PRONOUNCED IT A victory; the Army of the Potomac had crossed the Rapidan and had held its own. The facts pointed to another conclusion: the Yankees had lost 17,500 men, compared with 11,000 Confederate casualties, and the Union forces, despite their enormous numerical superiority, had been unable to dislodge the Rebels. Still, the Army of Northern Virginia, with its proud tradition of winning battles in that state, had been unable to destroy the Army of the Potomac in the Wilderness, a terrain hostile to the Yankees' advantages in men and firepower. The Confederates had wounded Grant's army, but the Yankees were not beaten.

As the morning of May 7 advanced with neither side launching a major attack, the Union troops gloomily pondered the prospect of yet another retreat. They would surely withdraw across the Rapidan, they believed, just as they had always done whenever Lee had licked them in northern Virginia. And following in the train of their retreat would be the appointment of a new commander with a new scheme for defeating Lee and capturing Richmond.

Orders went out to the Union divisions to prepare for a night march. In low spirits, the Yankees shouldered their packs. At dusk, they moved out.

But they soon realized that something was different this time. They were marching south, not north. They began to cheer and sing. "That night we were happy," one soldier wrote.[33]

Lee knew that Grant would not withdraw, and he divined his next objective: Spotsylvania Court House. The macabre dance of the armies of Grant and Lee had begun.

No one in blue or gray slept that night. Dust hung over the moonlit roads, choked with columns of soldiers, the Yankees marching southeast to envelope Lee's army, the Rebels racing to thwart the movement. The creak of wagons and wheeled artillery and the tramp-tramp of thousands of troops and horses coalesced into an ominous rumble that set the silvery air trembling like an angry bass chord.

As the Union infantrymen crowded Brock Road, which connected Wilderness Tavern and Spotsylvania Court House to the southeast, Sheridan made a bold plan. Hoping to prove the Cavalry Corps's worth as an independent arm of the Army of the Potomac, Sheridan planned to capture Spotsylvania and the three nearby bridges over the unfordable Po River before either army got there. But he consulted neither Meade nor Grant beforehand.

At 1 a.m., he ordered Wilson's division, operating near Sheridan's headquarters, to ride immediately to Spotsylvania Court House and to capture Snell's Bridge three miles to the south. Torbert's division, commanded by Wesley Merritt in Torbert's absence, and Gregg's division were awaiting orders at Todd's Tavern on Brock Road, midway between Wilderness Tavern and Spotsylvania Court House. Sheridan sent them instructions to capture Corbin's Bridge, six miles up the Po from Spotsylvania. While Gregg remained at the bridge to bar the enemy, Merritt's division would ride three miles downstream and seize the Blockhouse Bridge. With all three bridges in

Union hands, Lee's army would be unable to reach Spotsylvania Court House, and Grant's army could then occupy the town.

Wilson's troopers rode into Spotsylvania and expelled Brigadier General Thomas Rosser's cavalry brigade, sent ahead by Lee. The Union cavalry division had made a splendid beginning in seizing the strategic town. Had everything else gone according to Sheridan's plan, the Army of the Potomac would have occupied Spotsylvania Court House without the bloodletting for which the town is now remembered.

The Confederate infantry, too, was marching through the night toward the town, on a woodland road being hewed by pioneers. The Rebels hoped to interpose themselves between Spotsylvania and the Yankees advancing toward it on Brock Road.

MEADE WAS WITH THE leading regiments of Gouverneur Warren's V Corps when they arrived at Todd's Tavern at about 1 a.m. He was annoyed to find Sheridan's two cavalry divisions at the crossing—and in the path of the infantry. The cavalrymen were momentarily without orders, because Sheridan's instructions to seize the Po bridges had not yet reached them.

Not informed of Sheridan's plan, Meade ordered the two cavalry divisions to move out ahead of Warren's corps and sent a courier to inform Sheridan of what he had done. In the darkness, Warren's infantrymen and Sheridan's troopers became hopelessly tangled up on Brock Road. Grant's plan to steal a march on Lee to Spotsylvania began to unravel as the advance slowed to a maddening crawl.[34]

AS THE EASTERN SKY turned gunmetal gray, Wilson and his 4,000 veteran cavalrymen, still at Spotsylvania Court House, anxiously watched Brock Road for signs of the infantry bluecoats approaching from the northwest. But the column was still two or more miles away. It had been delayed at least an hour, maybe two, by the colossal traffic jam of men, wagons, horses, apoplectic teamsters, and bellowing officers. And there was no sign of Gregg's or Merritt's divisions either.

Leading the march toward Spotsylvania, Sheridan's troopers were facing a new problem: dismounted Rebel cavalrymen shooting at them from the northern approaches to the town. Stopping to return fire, Gregg's and Merritt's divisions encountered Fitzhugh Lee's two cavalry brigades, entrenched behind piled fence rails in the middle of the road. The Rebels had crossed the Po River at Blockhouse Bridge—the bridge that Sheridan had wanted Merritt to occupy but that instead remained wide open.

Moreover, thousands of Rebel infantrymen were near Fitzhugh Lee's embattled cavalrymen. Working through the night, Confederate pioneers had cut a five-mile road through the woods west of Todd's Tavern. I Corps, led by General Richard

Anderson in the place of the wounded Longstreet, had stopped for a quick breakfast just a mile from Fitzhugh Lee.

As Fitzhugh Lee's men held off Sheridan's cavalrymen, couriers raced to exhort the Rebel infantry to please hurry up. Behind the attacking Union cavalry, Fitzhugh Lee now knew, were dense formations of Yankee infantry, against which he would stand little chance if the Rebel infantry did not reach him in time.

The courier's message spurred Anderson's infantrymen to pack up their cooking gear hastily and set out at a quick march. When they heard heavy firing coming from the Brock Road, they broke into a run.

WITH RISING ANGER, SHERIDAN read the message informing him that Meade had ordered Gregg and Merritt to march down Brock Road ahead of Warren's corps—frustrating his plan to seize the two bridges. He was also just learning about the Rebel cavalry blocking the road to Spotsylvania.

Sheridan realized that he must immediately recall Wilson from Spotsylvania before the Confederates trapped him there. Sending a courier by way of the Fredericksburg Road, Sheridan ordered Wilson, whose division had been the only one to carry out Sheridan's plan, to withdraw. Confederate infantry, however, were already driving Wilson out of Spotsylvania.

Grant had lost his chance to seize the strategic town without a battle. In Sheridan's *Personal Memoirs*, written more than twenty years later, his disappointment over Meade's inadvertent frustration of his plan to seize the three bridges remains palpable: "Had Gregg and Merritt been permitted to proceed as they were originally instructed, it is doubtful whether the battles fought at Spotsylvania would have occurred." Instead, the Confederates' approach to the town was "entirely unobstructed, while three divisions of cavalry remained practically ineffective by reason of disjointed and irregular instructions."[35]

SHERIDAN JOINED THE DEVELOPING battle north of Spotsylvania. Warren complained to him that the cavalry was blocking his infantry columns. Sheridan removed his divisions from Brock Road to open the way for Warren's corps to attack.

Warren's men were advancing steadily on Fitzhugh Lee's barricade when Anderson's foot soldiers dashed up Brock Road, flung themselves down breathlessly beside Lee's dismounted cavalry behind the piled fence rails, and unleashed a devastating fire on the bluecoats when they were just sixty yards away. Warren's infantrymen recoiled.[36]

Meade was livid. He knew that, by just a minute or two, he had lost the race to occupy Spotsylvania Court House. And it was the fault of Sheridan's Cavalry Corps,

which had clogged Brock Road all night and then had obstructed Warren when his
V Corps might have easily overrun Fitzhugh Lee before the arrival of the Confederate infantry. Meade summoned Sheridan to his headquarters.

The ensuing donnybrook was arguably the most portentous event in the Cavalry
Corps's history and possibly in Sheridan's career. This day had been coming since
Sheridan took command of the Cavalry Corps and began agitating to make the
cavalry an independent strike force rather than a handmaiden of the infantry.[37]

When Sheridan appeared, wrote Colonel Horace Porter, a Grant aide-de-camp
who witnessed the tempest, Meade "went at him hammer and tongs, accusing him
of blunders, and charging him with not making a proper disposition of his troops,
and letting the cavalry block the advance of the infantry." Sheridan, with his notoriously hot Irish temper, retorted that Meade had caused the problems by counter-
manding his orders. Because of Meade's interference, Sheridan charged, the troops
had gotten mixed up on Brock Road, and Wilson's division had been exposed to
great danger.

The men were shouting at one another. Sheridan burst out, "[I] could whip
[Jeb] Stuart if [you] would only let me, but since [you] insisted on giving the cavalry
directions without consulting or even notifying me, [you] could henceforth command the Cavalry Corp himself"; Sheridan would not issue another command. At
that, he stormed out of Meade's tent.

Outraged by Sheridan's insubordination, Meade stalked over to Grant's headquarters, where he heatedly recounted the argument. Observing Meade's and
Grant's respective demeanors, Porter noted, "The excitement of the one was in singular contrast with the calmness of the other." When Meade repeated what Sheridan
had said about whipping Stuart if given the chance, Grant replied, "Did Sheridan
say that? Well, he generally knows what he is talking about. Let him start right out
and do it."[38]

Grant's reaction undoubtedly disappointed Meade, who was weary of Sheridan's
stubborn insistence on a larger role for his Cavalry Corps. But Meade understood
that he had lost this battle and that Grant had taken Sheridan's side. An hour later,
Sheridan received his orders:

General Sheridan, Commanding Cavalry Corps:

The major general commanding [Meade] directs you to immediately concentrate your available mounted force, and with your ammunition trains and
such supply trains as are filled (exclusive of ambulances) proceed against the
enemy's cavalry, and when your supplies are exhausted, proceed via New

Market and Green Bay to Haxall's Landing on the James River, there communicating with General Butler, procuring supplies and return to this army. Your dismounted men will be left with the train here.

A.A. Humphreys,
Major-General, Chief-of-Staff[39]

For the first time in its history, the Union Cavalry Corps was setting out to pick a fight with the Rebel cavalry.

CHAPTER 5

Killing Jeb Stuart

MAY–JULY 1864

Sheridan was more than magnetic. He was electric.
—J. W. MILLER OF THE *Cincinnati Commercial*[1]

AT FIRST LIGHT ON MAY 9, the Cavalry Corps began riding down the Telegraph Road connecting Fredericksburg and Richmond. Assembled in its entirety as it was on this day, the Cavalry Corps was impressive: 9,800 troopers rode four abreast, followed by thirty-two guns, forage for the horses and mules, and wagons loaded with food and ammunition. The column stretched thirteen miles.

In freeing Philip Sheridan to ride around the Rebel army's right flank—to draw out and defeat Jeb Stuart, ravage Robert E. Lee's supply line, and threaten Richmond—Ulysses Grant was throwing the dice. The cavalry's departure would leave the Army of the Potomac practically bereft of mounted reconnaissance troops, a potentially disastrous situation with the two armies locked in a bloody battle at Spotsylvania Court House. Yet, if Sheridan's corps did whip Stuart's vaunted cavalry, destroy Lee's supply depots, and sow panic in Richmond, the expedition would have been well worth the risk. Moreover, it would give Grant a terrible new weapon to wield in his total war against the Confederacy.

The Cavalry Corps traveled at a regal, four-mile-an-hour pace that projected power and not deception. Colonel James Kidd of the 6th Michigan Cavalry, who

73

had participated in General Hugh Judson Kilpatrick's raid on Richmond two months earlier, was struck by the difference between Kilpatrick's galloping ride and the Cavalry Corps's measured gait. "Sheridan went out with the utmost deliberation, looking for trouble—seeking it—and desiring before every other thing to fight Stuart and fight him on his native heath."

At this point in the war, Jeb Stuart's invincibility was all but accepted fact within the Army of the Potomac. But Sheridan was confident that his powerful Cavalry Corps would reveal Stuart's vulnerabilities. "We will give him a fair, square fight; we are strong, and I know we can beat him, and in view of my recent representations to General Meade I shall expect nothing but success," he told his three division commanders, David Gregg, James Wilson, and Wesley Merritt, as he laid out his plan.

Its boldness surprised them. Previous cavalry raids had been little more than "a hurried ride through the enemy's country," Sheridan observed, "without purpose of fighting more than enough to escape in case of molestation, and here and there to destroy a bridge." This raid would be radically different—no less than "a cavalry duel behind Lee's lines, in his own country."[2]

It was a mild day, and the weather was calm. The long column stirred up clouds of dust that soon coated men and horses with a gray patina. Kidd observed that the march's leisurely pace was not taxing and had a calming effect that buoyed everyone's confidence.[3]

Leaving the Telegraph Road at the Ta River to follow a road that angled to the southwest, the Union cavalrymen neared Chilesbur and the North Anna River. A Rebel cavalry brigade attacked the rear of the column. The Cavalry Corps's stately raid had at last aroused the interest of the Rebel cavalry—as Sheridan had expected. Sheridan dispatched Brigadier General Henry Davies's brigade to fight a rearguard action, while the rest of the corps proceeded toward Richmond.

Jeb Stuart had sent the brigade to slow the column's progress so that he could interpose the rest of his cavalry between Sheridan and the Confederate capital. Sheridan had every intention of letting Stuart do just that; the more enemy cavalrymen that attempted to block his path, the more there would be to destroy.

STURDILY BUILT AND ABOVE average height, James Ewell Brown "Jeb" Stuart was given the tongue-in-cheek nickname of "Beauty" by his West Point classmates because of his high forehead and blunt features. Before the war, he chased Plains Indians with the 1st US Cavalry at Fort Leavenworth, Kansas, and once was shot by a Cheyenne warrior in the chest; his sternum deflected the pistol ball, and he recovered.

At Fort Leavenworth, he met Flora Cooke, the riding, shooting, guitar-playing daughter of Lieutenant Colonel Phillip St. George Cooke, and they married in 1855. Four years later, at Harper's Ferry, Stuart signaled his former West Point instructor, Colonel Robert E. Lee, to launch the attack on John Brown's insurgents when they refused to surrender. Stuart kept Brown's Bowie knife as a souvenir.[4]

When the war began, Stuart, a loyal Virginian descended from generations of Virginians, resigned his US Army commission and joined the Confederacy. Lee assigned him to General Thomas "Stonewall" Jackson's division with the rank of lieutenant colonel, and he led a cavalry charge at First Manassas. In September 1861, Stuart was promoted to brigadier general. Soon after that, he was commanding the Army of Northern Virginia's cavalry.

Full-bearded and ruddy-faced, Stuart was robust, energetic, and ebullient to the point of refusing to acknowledge defeats or personal shortcomings. He was famously vain, dressing like a knight-errant from medieval times—tall cavalry boots, golden spurs, gauntlet gloves, gray coat buttoned to the chin, French saber, red-lined cape, yellow sash, and a feather in his hat. He surrounded himself with musicians and loved to sing.[5]

Stuart burst upon the consciousness of ordinary Southerners in 1862 when, during Major General George McClellan's Peninsula Campaign, he led a Rebel brigade in a ride completely around McClellan's army—figuratively counting coup on the Yankee invaders. As daring raid followed daring raid, Stuart's reputation grew to nearly mythic proportions, and even his enemies grudgingly acknowledged his aura of seeming invincibility.

But there were failures, too, notably at Gettysburg. While Lee's army fought arguably the war's pivotal battle, Stuart was off raiding. His absence had left Lee virtually blind, and his single contribution to the battle, on its third day, was his failed cavalry attack during Major General George Pickett's disastrous charge up Cemetery Ridge.

While the Union cavalry stumbled, failed, learned, improved, and eventually flourished during 1863 and 1864, Stuart continued to operate much as he always had.

SHERIDAN'S TROOPERS REACHED THE North Anna River just before dusk on May 9. In the sky to the west, they saw a large smoke plume. It was coming from

Beaver Dam Station on the Virginia Central Railroad, which connected the mountains and northern Virginia. Lee had established an advance supply depot at the station in case he was forced to fall back to the North Anna. When news reached them that Yankee cavalry were nearby, the Rebel guards had set fire to the depot's enormous stockpile: 1 million rations of meat and more than 500,000 bread rations.

Brigadier General George Custer's Wolverine Brigade rode toward the smoke. Custer had risen fast and traveled far since graduating last in West Point's Class of 1861, having barely avoided expulsion for demerits. Custer's daredevil feats during the Peninsula Campaign won him a place on George McClellan's staff and, with McClellan's removal, he had moved to Alfred Pleasonton's staff.

After distinguishing himself at Brandy Station and Aldie, twenty-three-year-old Lieutenant Custer was promoted directly to brigadier general. On the third day of fighting at Gettysburg, Custer's cavalry brigade had driven Jeb Stuart from the field. With his reddish-blond ringlets, handlebar moustache, bright red necktie, black velvet jacket, gold braid and stars, and broad-brimmed hat, Custer was in many ways a mirror image of Stuart.

On the way to Beaver Dam Station, Custer's brigade drove off enemy guards escorting four hundred Union prisoners and liberated the captives, who were on their way to prisons in Richmond from the fighting in the Wilderness and at Spotsylvania Court House.

Arriving at the station, the troopers seized two locomotives and three trains with one hundred cars laden with supplies for Lee's army. After the Yankee cavalrymen helped themselves to all the bacon, flour, meal, sugar, molasses, liquor, and medical supplies they could carry, they burned the rest—several million dollars' worth, Custer reported—as well as the station.

The cavalrymen fired artillery shells through the locomotives' boilers, while lightning sizzled, thunder boomed, and rain poured down. The orgy of destruction surpassed that of any Union cavalry raid in three years of war. The next morning, Custer's men added to it by tearing up ten miles of railroad track and telegraph lines, disrupting communications between Richmond and Lee's army.[6]

Jeb Stuart had left half of his 9,000-man corps behind at Spotsylvania Court House; he was unsure whether Sheridan meant to proceed from Beaver Dam Station to Richmond or to turn back and hit Lee's rear at Spotsylvania and Stuart was hedging his bets. Reaching the smoking ruins of Beaver Dam Station, he redoubled his efforts to thrust his cavalrymen between Sheridan and Richmond. Breaking off his harassment of Sheridan's rearguard, Stuart and his three brigades began tracing a long eastward loop around Sheridan, whose corps rode unmolested during the day of May 10. That night, while Sheridan's cavalrymen camped peacefully on the south bank of the South Anna River at Ground Squirrel Bridge, Stuart's men rode on, straining to get ahead of the Yankee troopers.[7]

MAY 11, 1864–YELLOW TAVERN—Stuart's cavaliers rode all night. Learning that Union cavalrymen had burned a locomotive and its train and torn up railroad tracks at Ashland, he was still unsure of Sheridan's intentions. Once more, as he had on the first day of the pursuit, Stuart divided his force, sending a detachment to hang on the Cavalry Corps's rear.

With his 3,000 remaining men, Stuart arrived ahead of Sheridan at a derelict hostelry known as Yellow Tavern. He sent an aide to Richmond with a message for Lieutenant General Braxton Bragg, who now commanded the city's defenses, informing him of his disposition. "My men and horses are tired, hungry, and jaded, but *all right*," he wrote.[8]

Armed with single-shot muzzleloaders, Stuart and his troopers stood between Sheridan's 10,000 men and the Rebel capital, just six miles down the Brook Turnpike. It had taken hard riding to interject his force between the Yankees and the Confederacy's greatest prize, but the South's "Beau Sabreur" was used to hard riding—and accustomed to overcoming long odds such as those he now faced.[9]

The day before, near Beaver Dam Station, Stuart had visited his wife, Flora, who, with their children, was staying at the home of Edmund Fontaine. They spoke quietly in the yard, Stuart never dismounting, and then they kissed and said their good-byes. Stuart was uncharacteristically silent for a time as he rode on. Then, he turned to one of his staff officers, Major Reid Venable, and told him that he had never expected to survive the war.[10]

AT YELLOW TAVERN, STUART's brigades dismounted and took positions on a bluff that paralleled the Cavalry Corps's route back to the Telegraph Road from Beaver Dam Station. The fact that they were dismounted, possibly because the men and horses were worn out from riding all night, meant that one in four of Stuart's troopers was relegated to the job of holding the horses—and was out of the fight. Thus, Stuart had fewer than 2,500 effectives, and having ceded mobility, he would necessarily fight a defensive battle.[11]

Sheridan personally scouted the ground. Major Kidd said that his demeanor was "calm, unruffled" as he made his battle plan, and he wasted no time in putting it into action.

Merritt's division attacked Stuart's right, was repulsed, attacked again, and drove the Rebels eastward. The Confederates counterattacked, and there were more charges and countercharges. At about 2 p.m., after three hours of fighting, there was a lull while Sheridan waited for more of his regiments to come up. He studied the ground and decided now to attack Stuart's left.

Sheridan threw Merritt's and Wilson's divisions and one of Gregg's brigades into a battle line and rode along it waving his black hat and shouting encouragement. At about 4 p.m., Custer's Wolverine Brigade led the assault, with Custer and the 1st Michigan charging on horseback while the brigade's other three regiments advanced on foot.[12]

When the attack came, Stuart was roving the left side of his position on horseback, exhorting his 1st Virginia Cavalry. The proud, storied regiment threw back Custer's first attack. On their next assault, the Wolverines overran Stuart's entire left wing, while the rest of the Cavalry Corps scattered the center and right. Stuart's cavalry broke into small pieces. Thousands of bluecoats, their repeating carbines spraying the Rebels with lead, rode through and around the heavily outnumbered Rebels and their slow-firing muzzleloaders.[13]

STUART, AT THE FRONT of his broken line, tried desperately to rally his men, firing his pistol into Custer's swarming Wolverines. Then, a dismounted Union trooper, John A. Huff, a forty-eight-year-old private and former top marksman with Berdan's Sharpshooters, shot Stuart from ten or fifteen feet away with a .44-caliber pistol.

Stuart clasped his right side. His hat fell off, and he wobbled on his horse. "Oh, the general! The general!" his men cried as Stuart's horse jerked violently. An aide moved him to a calmer horse, but Stuart could not sit up and so was placed on the ground and leaned against a tree. He ordered all of his men back to the line. An ambulance arrived, along with Major General Fitzhugh Lee, and Stuart relinquished to him command of the cavalry, saying, "Go ahead, old fellow: I know you'll do what is right."

From the ambulance taking him to Richmond, Stuart saw his men leaving the field. "Go back! Go back! I would rather die than be whipped!" he shouted. It was Stuart's destiny to suffer both fates. His cavaliers withdrew toward Ashland. Sheridan had a clear road to Richmond.[14]

AS THE MOMENTOUS DAY—momentous because Stuart's celebrated cavalry had been decisively defeated and the South's great cavalry hero mortally wounded—drew to a close, Sheridan's troopers entered the outskirts of Richmond, driving off a small force of defenders and penetrating the capital's outer defenses. From the city center, just three miles away, they could hear church bells tolling the alarm that the enemy was at the gates. Sheridan might have been tempted to ride into the city, and his men undoubtedly would have followed him. They might even have briefly occupied Richmond—but certainly not for long, for Sheridan knew that nearby Rebel infantry brigades would react quickly.[15]

Between the capital's outer and middle defenses was a road that Sheridan believed would lead to the Mechanicsville Pike and thence to Fair Oaks, where he planned to make his camp northeast of Richmond. The weather suddenly turned, and wind and rain lashed the bluecoats. They made their wounded as comfortable as possible—the corps had suffered 625 casualties.

Having come closer to the Confederate Capitol and Jefferson Davis's White House than any other Union force, the Cavalry Corps turned away to the north as midnight approached and began to ride toward the Chickahominy River.[16] Anticipating this move, the Rebels had booby-trapped the road with trip-wired shells, which began going off when the horses' hooves struck the wires in the dark. The explosions killed several horses, wounded a few men, and brought the column to a halt.

Highly irritated by the enemy's skullduggery, Sheridan ordered twenty-five prisoners brought up. In the pitch darkness, the Confederates were made to get down on their knees and crawl ahead of Sheridan's men, groping for the trip wires. When they found the wires, they had to follow them gingerly to the shells and disarm them. The nerve-wracking work prompted one prisoner to blurt out that a nearby resident had planted many of the shells.

The troopers invaded the resident's house, capturing him and his family. The disarmed shells were placed in his basement, and after the cavalry had ridden on, the Yankees rearmed some of the shells and placed trip wires across the road. If pursuing Rebels struck the wires, the man's home would be blown to bits.[17]

DURING THIS SEEMINGLY ENDLESS, black, rainy night, thousands of Richmond's militia and regular Confederate infantry commanded by Bragg and President Jefferson Davis were coming after Sheridan's troopers. The Yankees had smashed Jeb Stuart's supposedly invincible cavalry just north of their capital and mortally wounded Stuart, one of the Confederacy's most revered military leaders. And Sheridan's men had sent a real shiver of fear coursing through the capital. The Rebels now wanted revenge.

To reach safety, it was imperative that the Cavalry Corps cross the Chickahominy River north of Richmond. But when Sheridan's men reached the Mechanicsville Road bridge, Fitzhugh Lee and the remnants of Stuart's cavalry were already there, behind fieldworks and barring their way. With the Richmond troops nipping at their heels and the defended river in front of them, the Cavalry Corps was in an extremely dangerous situation.

Rather than try to force a crossing of the barricaded bridge under fire, Sheridan sent a brigade upstream to scout Meadow Bridge. The scouts reported back that the Rebels had burned the main bridge, but the railroad trestle was intact. Moreover, fewer Rebels guarded Meadow Bridge than the Mechanicsville bridge.

They would cross at Meadow Bridge then. Sheridan dispatched Merritt's division to find planking to place between the trestle rails so that horses, artillery, and the supply train could cross. As the rain pelted down, Sheridan declared that they must "make the crossing at all hazards."

From the Chickahominy's north bank, the Rebels swept the bridge with cannon and musket fire, slowing the work of Merritt's men. Under fire the entire time, they struggled to retrofit the bridge in the rainy darkness while precariously balanced dozens of feet above the rushing river water.

Suddenly, the Rebel force from Richmond, personally led by Bragg, launched a full-scale attack on Sheridan's rear. Wilson's division was driven back toward the river.

Sheridan was everywhere, exhorting his men. The Rebels, he told them, "are green recruits just from Richmond. There's not a veteran among them. . . . We have got to whip them. We can do it and we will."

The Rebels' brief advantage evaporated when they marched into killing artillery fire from Sheridan's field batteries and when Gregg's division, hidden in a brushy ravine, rose up and unleashed withering fire from its repeating carbines. Simultaneously, Wilson rallied some of his retreating men, who turned and counterattacked Bragg's right flank, breaking it. The bloodied Confederate infantry recoiled and withdrew behind Richmond's outer defenses, forfeiting its chance to destroy Sheridan's cavalry between the capital and the river.

Three of Merritt's dismounted regiments waded across the Chickahominy to drive off the Confederates firing on the bridge but were hurled back. As the Rebel artillery raked the river and bridge with grapeshot and canister and small arms fire stabbed at them from the wet, black woods, Merritt's men stubbornly continued working on the bridge.

After Merritt's regiments were repulsed, two dismounted regiments from the Wolverine Brigade braved the gauntlet of enemy fire and crossed the bridge on the railroad ties. They attacked the Rebels and drove them back to their breastworks. The Wolverines kept them pinned down there for two to three hours, until the bridge builders had completed their work.

When the bridge was ready for use, Merritt's division and seven other regiments formed a line and drove the Confederates from their breastworks. Having beaten all comers, the Cavalry Corps made its camp at Walnut Grove and Gaines Mill, where it rested and collected its wounded.

"My command is in fine spirits with its success," Sheridan reported to Grant. The enemy's cavalry "was very badly whipped." He bullishly added, "If I could be permitted to cross the James River and go southward, I could almost ruin the Confederacy."[18]

SHERIDAN DID NOT YET know it, but the Confederacy was mourning Stuart's death. He had died during the evening of May 12 at his brother-in-law's home in Richmond. During his last hours, Stuart had sung his favorite hymn, "Rock of Ages," with his minister and friends and conversed with Jefferson Davis, who visited him that morning. Stuart told Davis that he was willing to die "if God and my country think I have fulfilled my destiny and done my duty." Stuart's wife, Flora, informed that her husband had been badly wounded, set out for Richmond but arrived too late.

Upon learning of his cavalry chief's death, Robert E. Lee put his hands over his face and retired to his tent. Later, he told one of Stuart's staff officers, "I can scarcely think of him without weeping." Stuart's successors led the Rebel cavalry with surpassing competence but none with Stuart's swashbuckling brio.[19]

SHERIDAN'S TROOPERS RECROSSED THE Chickahominy at Bottom's Bridge, southeast of Richmond, and rode to Haxall's Landing on the James River, where Major General Benjamin Butler's medical officers treated the Cavalry Corps's wounded, and Sheridan's troops obtained food, clothing, and supplies. On June 24, sixteen days after the raid began, Sheridan and his triumphant cavalrymen rejoined the Army of the Potomac, having inflicted on the Rebel cavalry "the most thorough defeat that had yet befallen them in Virginia."

Grant was pleased with the results and amused when he laid eyes on some of Sheridan's officers wearing new naval uniforms obtained at Haxall's Landing. "Hallooo, Sheridan, have you captured the navy?" Grant asked. In a letter to Major General Ambrose Burnside, Grant recounted the material losses inflicted by the cavalry, which had also "whipped Stuards [*sic*] Cavalry and had carried the Outer works at Richmond besides whipping the infantry sent out to drive him away."

Yellow Tavern ended the Southern cavalry's nearly unbroken record of superiority. While the Union cavalry had faced just two of Stuart's six brigades at Yellow Tavern, it had fought with complete self-assurance. The unintended result of Sheridan's quarrel with George Meade was the Cavalry Corps's realization of its full potential.

During Sheridan's absence, the Army of the Potomac had fought one of the most savage battles of the war at Spotsylvania Court House on May 12. At the end of the day, there was no winner, only a torn battleground drenched in the blood of 6,800

Union casualties and 5,000 Confederate killed and wounded. Fighting continued fitfully over the next week up and down the Rebel line without a decisive outcome.

The combatants finally disengaged on May 21. Since it had crossed the Rapidan seventeen days earlier, Grant's army had lost a staggering 36,000 killed, wounded, or captured to Lee's more than 20,000 casualties. But Grant gave no thought to quitting.[20]

THE ARMY OF THE Potomac resumed its march toward Richmond, with Sheridan's Cavalry Corps leading the way over the pontoon bridges spanning the Pamunkey River at Hanovertown Ford. During the three weeks since the Army of the Potomac had forded the Rapidan and entered the Wilderness, it had scarcely paused in its drive toward the Confederate capital. Grant hoped to break through Lee's army somewhere northeast of Richmond. If the Rebels deflected him further to the south, he would be confronted with Richmond's formidable permanent defenses at the Chickahominy River and the inevitability of a prolonged siege.

Just as determined to force the issue was Lee. "We must destroy this army of Grant's before he gets to the James River. If he gets there, it will become a siege, and then it will be a mere question of time," Lee wrote to Lieutenant General Jubal Early.[21]

Riding ahead of Grant's army as it marched southwest to threaten Richmond, Gregg's cavalry division entered the tiny hamlet of Haw's Shop on May 28. Waiting behind barricades were the cavalry divisions of Major Generals Wade Hampton and Fitzhugh Lee and a brigade of South Carolina mounted troops armed with long-range Enfield rifle-muskets. Many regarded Hampton as the Army of Northern Virginia's ablest surviving cavalry leader and the likely heir to Jeb Stuart's mantle. Reputed to be the richest man in the South, Hampton was Stuart's antithesis in matters of style, both personal and sartorial; he was modest and dressed plainly. Robert E. Lee had not yet anointed a successor to Stuart, and for the moment he was dividing the command between his nephew and Hampton.

Ordered to hold Haw's Shop until the Rebel army could cover all of the approaches to Richmond, the five Confederate cavalry brigades drove back Gregg's two brigades with cannon and small arms fire. Just as determined to capture Haw's Shop, Sheridan sent Custer's Wolverine Brigade to reinforce Gregg. Custer's men assaulted the South Carolina brigade, which proved the "most stubborn foe" the Michigan regiments had ever faced, according to Major James Kidd. "The sound of their bullets sweeping the undergrowth was like that of hot flames crackling through dry timber." Ten minutes after Kidd's 6th Michigan Cavalry went into action, eighteen of his troopers lay dead.

Sheridan described the battle as being "of the severest character." When it ended indecisively more than five hours later, the two hundred men of the 1st Pennsylvania Cavalry had fired 18,000 rounds from their Spencer rifles.[22]

BOTH COMBATANTS WITHDREW, AND Sheridan pushed his pickets toward the crossroads town of Cold Harbor—its name a British appellation for an inn without hot food. Kidd wrote that a glance at a map explained the town's importance: there were "roads radiating from it in all directions."

Lee also recognized Cold Harbor's significance and sent his nephew's cavalry division to hold the crossroads until Major General Robert Hoke's infantry division could get there. On May 30, Fitzhugh Lee's men built fence-rail breastworks just outside the town and waited for the Yankees.[23]

Alfred Torbert, recently returned to duty after an illness, reached Cold Harbor on May 31 with his 1st Division. It attacked Fitzhugh Lee's left while simultaneously assaulting his front, with Custer leading a saber charge. The Confederates repulsed the attacks but abandoned their breastworks upon receiving reports of approaching Union infantry—which were actually miles away. Sheridan rode into the town with Torbert's division, and a brigade of Gregg's division joined him later.[24]

Any pride that Sheridan might have taken in capturing the town vanished when he learned that Confederate infantry brigades were coming his way. He decided that he should withdraw. "My isolated position . . . made me a little uneasy," he wrote. To Meade and Grant, he wrote, "With the heavy odds against me here, I do not think it prudent to hold on."[25] Grant and Meade, however, believed that Cold Harbor was too important strategically to be abandoned. Ordered to hold the town, Sheridan's 5,500 troopers occupied the breastworks from which, hours earlier, they had driven Fitzhugh Lee's men.

At daylight on June 1, units from two Rebel infantry divisions commanded by Major General Joseph Kershaw struck Sheridan's troopers. Sheridan's cavalrymen beat back two Confederate assaults, waiting both times until the attacking Rebels were within the range of their Spencer repeaters before opening up. They held on until late morning, when Major General Horatio Wright's VI Corps reached Cold Harbor. "Never were reinforcements more cordially welcomed," wrote Kidd, adding that it was the beginning of the enduring bond between the Cavalry Corps and VI Corps.[26]

AFTER LOSING 7,000 MEN in a calamitous frontal assault at Cold Harbor on June 3, then 3,000 more over the ensuing two days, Grant stopped trying to break Lee's lines northeast of Richmond. On June 7, the Army of the Potomac prepared to

swing eastward again, prefatory to crossing the James River and either menacing
Richmond or attacking Petersburg—or both.

Grant sent the Cavalry Corps on a destroying mission west of Richmond in the
hope of drawing off the Army of Northern Virginia's cavalry so that Grant's army
might cross the James River unopposed. Sheridan would lead two divisions—
roughly 5,500 cavalrymen and four horse artillery batteries—to Charlottesville,
leaving Brigadier General James Wilson's 3rd Division with Grant.

Sheridan was ordered to destroy the Rivanna River railroad bridge at Charlottesville and to rendezvous there with Brigadier General David Hunter's 20,000
troops from the Department of West Virginia. Together, Sheridan and Hunter
were to then wreck the James River canal and tear up the Virginia Central Railroad
all the way to Staunton. This would effectively sever Lee's supply line to the
Shenandoah Valley. "It is desirable that every rail . . . should be so bent and twisted
as to make it impossible to repair the road without supplying new rails," Sheridan's
orders said.

In the months ahead, Grant would continue to harp on destroying the railroad
and canal. While attacking the Rebel armies at a half dozen points was the core of
his strategy, crippling the Confederate transportation system was another element.
Down the James River canal and Virginia Central Railroad to Richmond flowed
food, clothing, and weapons from the Shenandoah Valley and from Lynchburg, a
major supply depot. Grant believed that shutting off these conduits would weaken
Lee's forces and bring hardship to the doorsteps of Richmond's citizens.

After finishing their rampage, Hunter and Sheridan were to rejoin the Army of
the Potomac. While Grant's instructions did not spell out the mission's object of
drawing the Rebel cavalry away from Richmond, Sheridan asserted, "The diversion
of the enemy's cavalry from the south side of the Chickahominy was [the raid's]
main purpose."[27]

TRAVELING AT THE WALKING pace favored by Sheridan, the Cavalry Corps rode
north of Richmond and then turned west, following the north bank of the North
Anna River. The troopers soon noticed that Confederate soldiers were shadowing
them. Major General John Breckenridge's corps, sent by Lee to thwart Hunter in
the Shenandoah Valley, kept Sheridan under observation until Wade Hampton and
Fitzhugh Lee could catch up.

Following the railroad west from Richmond, Hampton's division and three batteries joined Breckenridge's infantry. Not far behind was Fitzhugh Lee, who had
farther to travel. Breckenridge continued marching west to confront Hunter, while
Hampton's and Lee's cavalrymen took responsibility for Sheridan's two divisions.

The Cavalry Corps crossed to the North Anna's south bank and camped on a road to Trevilian Station on the Virginia Central Railroad, ten miles east of Gordonsville and twenty-eight miles from Charlottesville. Hampton's division was close by. Fitzhugh Lee's division was several miles away, at Louisa Court House.[28]

SHERIDAN HAD NOW LED the Cavalry Corps for two months, through battles major and minor. His hard-bitten cavalrymen had taken their measure of "Little Phil," as some of them had begun calling him. They liked the fact that he was blunt, open, and unpretentious, equally at ease speaking with privates and generals. Captain Henry A. DuBois, the Cavalry Corps's assistant medical director, wrote that when they first met, Sheridan talked freely to him and DuBois's tent mate, Dr. Morris Asche, drawing out their opinions about the army and sharing his own views. DuBois wrote,

> He wore the uniform of a major general, but there was no constraint in his manner in talking to us, although our rank was but that of captains—nor on the other hand did we feel any reserve towards him on account of his rank. . . . He came into the tent an utter stranger and in less than an hour both of us not only believed in him but felt an affection for him. . . . I thought this very strange—this love at first sight, and without apparent reason. . . . Soon, however, I found that others felt much as I did—that we had a personal ownership in him, that he would at all times acknowledge, and this without any feeling of superiority."

The soldiers in the ranks felt the same way, observed DuBois, "much as they would towards a brother in whom they had unlimited confidence and whose interests were also theirs."

Sheridan's men also noted his careful operational planning and his interest in topography and intelligence from scouts and spies—all integral to a battle plan's success. "There was an alertness, evinced rather in look than in movement," Kidd observed. "Nothing escaped his eye, which was brilliant and searching and, at the same time emitted flashes of kindly good nature." During combat, Sheridan, like Grant, smoked cigars incessantly, "a constant cloud enveloping him in his busiest moments."

Normally reserved and restrained, he habitually concealed his emotions, except in battle, when he was "clear to the front," exhorting his men, wrote Captain Edwin Parsons. At those times, he was altogether aggressive and ruthless and became enraged when he witnessed "stupidity, cowardice, incompetence, and panic." Then, wrote newspaper correspondent James Taylor, "strange, novel, picturesque oaths, made up on the spot, would burst from him spontaneously."[29]

In a profile of Sheridan, J. W. Miller of the *Cincinnati Commercial* wrote, "Sheridan was more than magnetic. He was electric." Sheridan's men were just beginning to appreciate their commander's tremendous abilities.[30]

JUNE 11, 1864–TREVILIAN STATION—It was a clear day that held the promise of sweltering heat. The Cavalry Corps was in the saddle, marching toward Trevilian Station, where it would begin wrecking the Virginia Central Railroad.

Sheridan's men had not ridden far before they collided with Wade Hampton's cavalry. During the night, Hampton's division had interposed itself between Sheridan and the station. Severe fighting spread up and down the line.

Hampton and Fitzhugh Lee's plan called for Hampton to drive in Sheridan's front, while Lee struck Sheridan's flank. They would then pin the Cavalry Corps against the North Anna River and destroy it.

Sheridan and Hampton had fought before, at Haw's Shop, Hampton's first action since suffering severe head wounds at Gettysburg. The diminutive Irishman from Ohio and the strapping, six-foot South Carolina aristocrat were about to wage one of the largest all-cavalry battles of the war.

Wherever they found themselves, Sheridan and his staff habitually winkled out every nearby logging trace, wagon road, and footpath on their maps. Their attention to topographic arcana now paid off: they discovered a road that swung around Hampton's right flank and then angled toward Trevilian Station.

Sheridan ordered Custer's brigade down the road in the hope of turning Hampton's flank. While Hampton and Sheridan fought it out and Fitzhugh Lee rode to his planned rendezvous with Hampton, the Wolverine Brigade, unseen, tiptoed around Hampton's right flank.

But the meandering road did not bring the brigade close to Hampton's flank but instead veered around it and deposited the Wolverines in Hampton's rear, near Trevilian Station. To their delight, the Michigan troopers spotted Hampton's wagons parked on a nearby knoll. "They went through our center like a thunderbolt," wrote a Rebel officer assigned to guard the wagon train. Custer's brigade quickly scooped up eight hundred prisoners, 1,500 horses, six caissons, forty ambulances, and fifty army wagons. The Wolverines couldn't believe their great luck.[31]

They could not savor it for long though. Learning of this development, Hampton detached Brigadier General Thomas Rosser's brigade from his heavily engaged division. Rosser, a former West Point classmate and friend of Custer's, struck the Wolverine Brigade from the west, driving it eastward.

The Rebels recovered everything that Custer's men had seized, plus Custer's black cook, Eliza, nicknamed by his men the "Queen of Sheba." Eliza managed to escape with Custer's personal valise but not Custer's wife Libbie's love letters, which later appeared in Richmond newspapers.

Soon after Rosser's attack, Fitzhugh Lee's division, galloping in from Louisa Court House, hit Custer from the east. The Wolverine Brigade was surrounded.

CUSTER'S DISMOUNTED MEN FANNED out in a circle around their artillery in an open, grassy area to fend off the attackers, who outnumbered the Yankees three to one. Custer rode among them, shouting encouragement, as Rebel minié balls plucked at his coat. The Confederates repeatedly attacked the circle. They captured one of Custer's guns; Custer personally led a saber attack and retrieved it. The Wolverines fought for their very lives.[32]

Through their field glasses, Sheridan's staff officers caught glimpses of Custer's fight in the open grassland. When his headquarters flag was no longer visible, they feared the worst.

Sheridan and his staff led attacks on both of Hampton's flanks and flung Torbert's division at the Rebel center, hoping to break through and relieve the beleaguered Wolverines. Captain George Sanford of the 1st US Cavalry wrote that Sheridan acted on his men "like an electric shock . . . an immediate and positive stimulus to battle."[33]

THE ALL-OUT ASSAULT DROVE Hampton's division backward—into Custer's position. Trevilian Station again fell into Union hands. During the melee, the Yankees took five hundred Rebel prisoners. Gregg's division pushed Fitzhugh Lee eastward, and Torbert pursued Hampton's division west of Trevilian Station.

Sheridan rode up to Custer and asked him if the Confederates had captured his headquarters flag. "Not by a damned sight!" Custer exclaimed, removing it from inside his shirt, where he had secreted it after his color sergeant was killed. "There it is!" Custer's stand—not his last—cost his brigade 416 casualties.[34]

HAMPTON AND LEE RENDEZVOUSED west of Trevilian Station and began digging entrenchments to block Sheridan from marching on Charlottesville. The Cavalry Corps went into camp for the night.

From Rebel prisoners Sheridan learned that General Hunter was not on his way to Charlottesville but marching to Lynchburg, "away from instead of toward me, thus making the junction of our commands beyond all reasonable probability." Moreover, Breckenridge's infantry division was reportedly lingering in the Charlottesville vicinity, and there were reports that Lieutenant General Richard Ewell's corps—led by Jubal Early because Ewell was disabled by illness—was coming west from Richmond to engage Hunter.

The Cavalry Corps's five hundred wounded and five hundred prisoners were problematic, and it had enough ammunition for just one big battle. Sheridan believed his troopers would have to fight more than one to reach Charlottesville, with Hampton, Lee, and Breckenridge barring the way—and with Hunter's 20,000 men beyond supporting range.[35]

After pondering these stark facts, Sheridan elected to end the mission and turn back. It was a disappointment, but the risks appeared to outweigh the potential rewards. By pressing on alone to Charlottesville, where he would likely face enemy cavalry and infantry in great numbers, he would risk destroying his Cavalry Corps—for the purpose of wrecking bridges, canals, and railroad tracks. One might imagine the Cavalry Corps, on the run with its ammunition gone, having to leave its wounded behind.

A "return by leisurely marches," as Sheridan described his new plan to Grant, might yet accomplish the goal of keeping the Rebel cavalry occupied—and continue to deprive Lee's army of its "eyes"—while the Army of the Potomac crossed the James. Moreover, Sheridan would be able to bring out his wounded and preserve his divisions to fight another day.

On June 12, Sheridan ordered Gregg's division to rip up the rails between Trevilian Station and Louisa Court House to the east. He sent Torbert's division west toward Gordonsville and Charlottesville to secure Mallory's Ford, where Sheridan planned to cross the North Anna and take a shorter route back to Grant's army.

Two miles west of Trevilian Station, Torbert's division ran into Hampton's dismounted cavalrymen, who were dug in along a railroad embankment, with dense woods all around. As the two sides began fighting, Fitzhugh Lee's division joined Hampton. Torbert attacked repeatedly—seven times in all, the last attempts made with the aid of one of Gregg's brigades. But the Yankees were unable to dislodge the Rebel cavalry.

Rather than expend his remaining ammunition fighting another battle, Sheridan chose to recross the North Anna at Carpenter's Ford, the way that he had come. After a day's rest, the Cavalry Corps began the long march back to Grant's army. Hampton's and Lee's divisions shadowed the Cavalry Corps from the river's south bank. Sheridan left behind ninety of his men who were too badly wounded to travel, as well as the wounded Rebels in his care.[36]

Sheridan had not rendezvoused with Hunter or destroyed any of the bridges, canals, and railroad tracks between Charlottesville and the Shenandoah Valley. Southern newspapers pronounced Trevilian Station a Confederate victory, and Robert E. Lee sent congratulations to Hampton. Yet Sheridan's expedition had diverted the Rebel cavalry for three weeks during its march to and from Trevilian Station. Lacking his "eyes," Lee lost track of Grant's army for two critical days, and the 100,000-man Army of the Potomac safely crossed the James River between June 14 and 17. With the Yankees now east and southeast of Petersburg and Richmond, the siege that Lee had dreaded was about to become a reality.[37]

THE INTENSE SUMMER HEAT and two weeks without rain made the return march over roads "deep with dust" a cheerless slog for man and beast. The Cavalry Corps's destination, the supply depot at White House on the Pamunkey River, lay one hundred miles distant. The column moved slowly—ten miles per day on average, with frequent halts—because its Rebel prisoners were afoot and the hundreds of wounded required dressing changes and refreshment. The disabled rode in old buggies, family carriages, and carts—anything on wheels that could move in all conditions. "The suffering was intense," wrote Sheridan, "but our means for mitigating their distress were limited." He was impressed by the wounded men's stoic forbearance. "The fortitude and cheerfulness of the poor fellows under such conditions were remarkable, for no word of complaint was heard."[38]

The Cavalry Corps lived off the land. The bitter residents disparagingly called the foragers "Sheridan's Robbers," a sobriquet some of the men embraced. They stripped the country and its inhabitants of everything useful, although the booty was sometimes pitiable, or worse. Guerrillas pounced on stray foragers and hanged them, mutilating their bodies.

The worn-out, overheated horses collapsed in the dust and were shot by the cavalrymen at a dismaying rate of about a dozen per mile—an estimate some historians have deemed too conservative. Surgeon Elias W. H. Beck wrote to his wife, "So terrible to see every time a poor horse would give out by sheer exhaustion—out with the pistol & shoot him—break up the saddle & walk on." The cavalrymen replaced their mounts with horses taken from Virginia civilians, further poisoning the people's feelings toward them.[39]

In addition to the wounded and the Rebel prisoners, another group also joined the Cavalry Corps column: 2,000 blacks, most of them runaway slaves. The men, women, and children had first appeared near Trevilian Station with bundles containing all their worldly goods. On Sheridan's march east, their numbers grew daily.[40]

The procession passed through the Spotsylvania battlefield, where the marchers did not see another living person. They shuddered at the macabre, revolting sights everywhere: putrefying bodies, charred corpses, ghastly mass graves partially excavated by scavengers. Everywhere were splintered trees and wrecked buildings. The soldiers were relieved to put the scenes of desolation behind them.

ON JUNE 20, THE Cavalry Corps crossed the Pamunkey River to White House Landing, where the men found plentiful food and new clothing. New, unwelcome orders awaited Sheridan: to break up the supply depot and escort the wagon train southward across the peninsula to the Army of the Potomac.[41] Sheridan grumbled that the train "ought never to have been left to the cavalry to escort, after a fatiguing expedition of three weeks." The depot's stockpiles filled nine hundred wagons.

Sheridan's two divisions began shepherding the ponderous cavalcade across the peninsula. The weary Union troopers scrupulously guarded the long line of wagons against Hampton's and Fitzhugh Lee's cavalrymen, hovering like wolves on its flanks, looking for openings.

With his instinct for roads and terrain, Sheridan believed there had to be a short cut to the Chickahominy River that would get the supply train to its destination more quickly. He told his staff he was certain that a road connected New Kent Court House to a crossing called Providence Forge. But none appeared on the army's maps, and local citizens solemnly averred that none existed.

"There *was* a road, *must* be a road," Sheridan insisted. Stubbornly pointing the supply train in the direction where he believed the road should be, he sent Brigadier General George Getty of VI Corps and a staff officer to locate it. Amazingly, they found a wood road just where Sheridan had said it must be; it led directly to the Chickahominy.[42]

South of the river, Lee's and Hampton's divisions attacked the wagon train on June 24 near Samaria Church—St. Mary's Church on Union maps. Gregg's men, serving as the wagon train's rearguard, managed to repel three attacks and hold off the Rebel cavalry for two hours, at a cost of 357 Yankees killed, wounded, or captured. The Rebels were delayed long enough for the train to get clear.

Blocked by the enemy from crossing the James River pontoon bridge at the stipulated place near Malvern Hill, Sheridan led the column southeastward through Charles City Court House. Ferries met the procession on the north river bank and transported the wagons and Sheridan's corps to the south bank.[43]

WHILE THE CAVALRY CORPS's 1st and 2nd Divisions were crossing to the south bank, James Wilson's 3rd Division, which had remained with Grant's army these past three weeks, was riding into trouble. Certain that Fitzhugh Lee's and Hampton's cavalry divisions would stick with Sheridan, Grant had sent Wilson and Brigadier General August Kautz's small cavalry division from the Army of the James on a long, daring raid nearly one hundred miles around the south of Petersburg. At the place where the Southside Railroad intersected the Richmond & Danville Railroad thirty miles southwest of Petersburg, Wilson and Kautz were to destroy the railroads as far as possible in both directions. This would prevent supplies from the Carolinas and Georgia from reaching Petersburg and Richmond.

Even as the 6,000 cavalrymen set out on June 22, two days before Sheridan reached the James, Meade had misgivings. They might fend off General William H. F. "Rooney" Lee's cavalry division, but what if Fitzhugh Lee and Hampton returned and joined Rooney Lee against Wilson and Kautz?

Wilson's expedition reached the railroad junction unmolested. The bluecoats were wrecking mills, burning crops, driving off the slave labor, and ripping up the tracks when Rooney Lee attacked them. Then, to Wilson's dismay, the divisions of Fitzhugh Lee and Hampton also appeared. Suddenly, the Union cavalry was in trouble, outnumbered and one hundred miles from Grant's army.

Wilson and Kautz made a dash for safety, with the Rebel cavalry snapping at their flanks. At Ream's Station on the Nottoway River, the three Rebel cavalry divisions, aided by two infantry brigades with artillery, hemmed the Union raiders and inflicted heavy casualties. Wilson burned his supply trains, abandoned his artillery, and broke out, in the process becoming separated from Kautz.

On June 30, Grant and Meade, alerted to Wilson's danger, sent Sheridan on a rescue mission, but Wilson appeared the next day without his help. Wilson's division returned from its nine-day raid without its artillery and wagon train or the services of 1,445 men who had been killed, wounded, or captured—fully one-fourth of its force. Yet all of the mission's objectives had been achieved: the Union cavalry had struck a blow in Confederate-controlled territory, it had entirely disarranged the early summer harvest, and the damage inflicted on the railroad tracks halted northbound rail traffic into Petersburg for nine weeks.[44]

FOR THE FIRST TIME in fifty days, Sheridan's men had time to rest and refit. "In the campaign we were almost always on the march, night and day, often unable to care properly for our wounded, and obliged to bury our dead where they fell," wrote Sheridan. Camped at Light House Point, the Cavalry Corps was idle from July 2 to 26.

Fifteen hundred replacement horses arrived from the Cavalry Bureau's Washington corrals. But the Cavalry Corps had lost so many horses that even with these remounts, some cavalrymen remained afoot and had to be reassigned to infantry units.

It had been the most successful period in the Cavalry Corps's history. Sheridan's men were the equals, if not the betters, of the vaunted Confederate cavalry that had embarrassed the armies of McClellan, John Pope, Ambrose Burnside, and Joseph Hooker. Time, better resources, and improved leadership had immensely benefited the Union cavalry, while time and losses had eroded the Rebel cavalry's once unquestioned superiority.

In the Wilderness, the Union cavalry had flexed its muscles; at Yellow Tavern it had delivered a shattering blow to Jeb Stuart's legendary cavalry and deprived the Confederacy of its great cavalry leader. At Haw's Shop and Cold Harbor, Sheridan's dismounted troopers had grittily flung back Rebel attacks and driven the enemy from the field. It had lured the Confederate cavalry to Trevilian Station so Grant could cross the James without interference and had there fought to a bloody draw. The spectral procession that arrived at White House Landing, encumbered by wounded and in large part dismounted, bespoke the high cost that the Trevilian raid had exacted on Sheridan's legion.

But as Sheridan, Grant, Abraham Lincoln, and William Sherman well knew, the Cavalry Corps's losses in men and horses could be made good relatively quickly, while the Confederacy, with its vanishing pool of available soldiers, struggled to find replacements—and sometimes did not. Attrition had begun to enforce its iron law on the South.

One replacement agreeable to both Robert E. Lee and Jefferson Davis was Wade Hampton as the new commander of the Army of Northern Virginia's Cavalry Corps. Hampton's conduct at Trevilian Station and his harrying of Wilson's division outside Petersburg had convinced them he was a worthy successor to Jeb Stuart.

THE UNION ARMY'S OVERLAND Campaign ended on June 16, when a planned lightning attack on Petersburg instead unfolded with maddening slowness and was easily repelled. Casualties during the "Forty Days" were the highest ever recorded on US soil—more than 60,000 Union soldiers killed, wounded, and captured, while the Rebels sustained more than 30,000 casualties. After all the bloodletting, peace remained elusive. Grant, however, had correctly observed after the Battle of the Wilderness that his men "had passed through the 'beginning of the end.'"[45]

CHAPTER 6

———

The Shenandoah Valley

AUGUST–SEPTEMBER 1864

Follow him to the death.
—GRANT'S INSTRUCTIONS TO SHERIDAN REGARDING
CONFEDERATE LIEUTENANT GENERAL JUBAL EARLY[1]

UNION ARMY HEADQUARTERS, CITY POINT, VIRGINIA—Since May 4, Philip Sheridan's horsemen had fought and raided from the Wilderness to the James and from Haw's Shop to Trevilian Station. Thus, Sheridan was surprised when Ulysses Grant summoned him to his headquarters cabin on July 31 to tell him that he was being sent to an entirely new arena—the Shenandoah Valley, the graveyard of so many Union hopes and generals' careers.

Sheridan was expected to harry and destroy Confederate lieutenant general Jubal Early's Army of the Valley. Early's army had recently swept the Valley clean of Union troops before marching into Maryland, throwing a scare into Washington, DC, and burning Chambersburg, Pennsylvania. The North was in an uproar.

This was certainly not the first time the 125-mile-long Valley, a dagger aimed at the capital and the rich farmlands of Maryland and Pennsylvania, had proved to be the Union's Achilles' heel—and a drain on its resources. From the first days of the war, Confederates had launched raids and major offensives across the Potomac River into the North from the Shenandoah. The Valley also gave the Rebels a sanctuary from which to strike at two vital Union transportation links: the Chesapeake & Ohio Canal and the B&O Railroad, the lifeline from Washington to the Midwest.

The Yankees had a dismal record of stopping the armies of Joseph Johnston, Stonewall Jackson, Richard Ewell, James Longstreet, and now Early from using the Valley to counterbalance Union offensives in northern Virginia. The record was replete with Union generals who had failed in the Valley: Robert Patterson, John C. Fremont, James Shields, Nathaniel Banks (driven by Jackson from the Valley in just three days) and, recently, David Hunter and Franz Sigel.

Grant believed the situation could be retrieved with a reorganized military hierarchy and a new, aggressive commander. The Valley fell under four military departments, none with overall responsibility. For months, Grant had wanted to combine the departments into a single division, but the Lincoln administration—not wanting to risk alienating anyone with a close election looming—had demurred.

But Early's alarming sally from the Valley had radically altered the circumstances. President Abraham Lincoln and War Secretary Edwin Stanton now supported Grant's plan to create a Middle Military Division. It would absorb the former departments of Washington, the Susquehanna, Maryland, and West Virginia; the Shenandoah Valley would be its focus. As the question of who would command the Cavalry Corps had produced disunity in March, so too, in July, did the subject of who would lead this new division.[2]

EARLY'S TRANSFORMATION INTO THE terror of the Shenandoah occurred rapidly and unexpectedly. One of three corps commanders in the Army of Northern Virginia, "Old Jube" had taken command of Stonewall Jackson's former command, II Corps, when Ewell became incapacitated at Cold Harbor. On June 12, Robert E. Lee ordered Early to march with his three infantry divisions and two artillery batteries to the Shenandoah Valley and destroy Hunter's army. Once Hunter was removed from the picture, Early would be free to operate against Washington and Baltimore.[3]

Rather than meeting Sheridan in Charlottesville as planned, Hunter had proceeded directly south from Staunton toward Lynchburg. At Piedmont, his men defeated Confederate brigadier general William "Grumble" Jones's outnumbered force, and Jones was killed.

Grant had directed Hunter to make the Valley "a desert as high up as possible," but Hunter was in too much of a hurry. At Lexington, however, his men paused long enough to burn down the home of Virginia governor John Letcher, as well as the Virginia Military Institute—the source of so many Confederate leaders. The

Yankees looted Washington College and stole its statue of George Washington. These symbolic gestures rankled with the Confederates; Early called them "outrages."

From Lexington, Hunter continued south to Lynchburg. The southwestern Virginia city was a long-coveted Union objective, serving the Confederacy as a railroad hub, manufacturing center, and Rebel food and supply depot.

On June 17, Hunter's 18,000 men reached Lynchburg's outskirts to find Major General John Breckenridge's division blocking the Yankees' path. Although probably numbering no more than 4,000, the Rebel force was large enough to fill the cautious Hunter with trepidation; he stopped for the night to contemplate the situation. By the next morning, it had gotten worse: Early and 5,000 men had arrived by train during the night.

Hunter attacked, and Breckenridge's and Early's veterans flung him back. Believing he was outnumbered when he in fact enjoyed a two-to-one advantage, Hunter marched away into the Allegheny Mountains and thence into West Virginia, with Early's army following him. Hunter's army was out of the war for weeks; it did not reach Charleston, West Virginia, until July 2.[4]

With Hunter removed from the Shenandoah Valley, Lee and his staff recognized a rare strategic opportunity: Early could strike at Washington. The threat would compel Grant to shuttle reinforcements from his army outside Petersburg to the capital. If Grant were significantly weakened, Lee might counterattack. Moreover, Lincoln's reelection prospects would be harmed by the specter of the enemy at Washington's gates after three years of war. If Lincoln were defeated, his successor might negotiate a peace with the Confederacy that would leave it intact. The Confederate command liked the possibilities presented by a march on Washington by Early.

Early ended his pursuit of Hunter after three or four days and returned to Lynchburg, where he combined his II Corps with Breckenridge's division to form the Army of the Valley. Before the army began its descent upon the largely undefended lower Shenandoah and Washington, Early led his 14,000 men through Lexington to honor the dead hero Stonewall Jackson. As a band played a dirge, Jackson's former corps marched past its captain's grave with heads uncovered and arms reversed. From their homage march, the men drew the inspiration to withstand the rigors of the coming campaign.[5]

General Franz Sigel, derisively called "the Flying Dutchman" by the Confederates, still commanded Union troops in the lower Valley, despite Major General Henry Halleck's attempt to have him sacked after his defeat at New Market in May. Halleck had written Grant, "He will do nothing but run. He never did anything else." True to form, when Early approached Martinsburg, West Virginia, Sigel fled before the Army of the Valley's 10,000 infantry and 4,000 cavalry and artillery, barricading himself on the heights at Harper's Ferry.

Early crossed the Potomac, entered Frederick, Maryland, and at the Monocacy River crushed a small, cobbled Union force of 7,000 under Major General Lew Wallace, the future author of *Ben Hur*. In defeat, however, Wallace's men served the crucial purpose of delaying Early's reaching Washington by one day. On July 11, the Army of the Valley stood before Washington's outer defenses at Fort Stevens, less than ten miles from the Capitol Building. Panic spread through the city.

Early's tired, dusty army, reduced to 10,000 effectives by the long march's rigors, surveyed the massive fortress and its intimidating gun ports, ditches, palisades, and abatis. Then, in the distance, the Rebels observed columns of blue-clad soldiers marching out of the city toward the fort. With their field glasses, the Confederates were able to identify the Union troops by their insignia; they belonged to Horatio Wright's veteran VI Corps—two divisions rushed to Washington from Petersburg. Scouts then reported that the rest of the VI Corps as well as XIX Corps were also en route. Early prudently called off an attack that he had planned for dawn on July 12.[6]

Wright invited the president to Fort Stevens that day to watch one of his brigades launch an assault on the Rebels, who lingered outside the fort all day, sniping at the Yankees inside. Lincoln, who liked to see his army in action, readily accepted. When the attack began, the president stood on the parapet, all six feet, four inches of him, with his stovepipe hat adding another eight inches and presenting a profile familiar to millions.

Rebel bullets spattered around Lincoln, knocking down an officer standing three feet away. "Get down, you damn fool, before you get shot!" someone shouted. Amused by the rebuke, Lincoln complied. The warning shout had come from twenty-three-year-old Captain Oliver Wendell Holmes Jr., the future US Supreme Court justice.[7]

Assistant War Secretary Charles Dana watched the proceedings with consternation. He telegraphed Grant that while Early's army had been prevented from entering Washington, he was certain there would be no pursuit of him. "There is no head to the whole, and it seems indispensable that you should at once appoint one. Hunter will be the ranking officer if he ever gets up, but he will not do."

Dana's July 12 message might have revived in Grant's mind the idea of a unified command under a dynamic leader to remove the ubiquitous Rebel threat from the Shenandoah. The public frustration with the enemy eruptions from the Valley was reflected in the *New York Times's* cutting summation: "The old story again—the back door, by way of the Shenandoah Valley, has been left invitingly open."[8]

THAT NIGHT, EARLY WITHDREW from Washington and returned to the lower Shenandoah Valley. At Kernstown on July 24, Early sent Major General George

Crook's West Virginians flying back into West Virginia with 1,185 casualties. Crook had disregarded warnings from his subordinate commanders about Early; after the battle, he blamed his subordinates for the defeat.

On July 20, Crook's cavalry, under Brigadier General William Averell, had defeated Stephen Dodson Ramseur's division, left by Early at Winchester, and then occupied the town. With Crook's defeat, it was now Early's turn to reoccupy Winchester, whose citizens had become almost blasé about the frequent changes. One of Hunter's staff officers observed that since July 1861, when Union major general Robert Patterson's army had abandoned the Valley, "annually since that date, we have been driven out. Here we are in 1864 in the same position."[9]

Early learned that in his absence Hunter had returned to the Valley from West Virginia and burned the homes of prominent Virginians, among them state senator Andrew Hunter; Alexander Boteler, a former member of the US and Confederate congresses; and Edmond Lee, a relative of Robert E. Lee. Hunter's actions were retaliation for the recent burning in Maryland by Early's men of the homes of Postmaster General Montgomery Blair and Maryland governor A. W. Bradford—which had been retribution for the Lexington outrages.

The new incendiary attacks on Southern civilians filled Early with cold rage. "I now came to the conclusion that we had stood this mode of warfare long enough, and that it was time to open the eyes of the people of the North to its enormity, by an example in the way of retaliation," he wrote. His chosen target was Chambersburg, Pennsylvania.

On July 30, two Rebel cavalry brigades rode into Chambersburg and demanded $100,000 in gold and $500,000 in currency as compensation for the destruction of Southern homes. It was a reprise of Jeb Stuart's October 1862 raid on the city, which had netted his raiders nothing because the bank funds had been removed. This time, though, the Confederates warned that if the $600,000 were not paid, they would burn Chambersburg to the ground. The townspeople defiantly replied that they were unafraid of whatever the Rebels might do. The raiders promptly lit fires that destroyed most of the town of 3,000 people.

This act, following Early's shocking appearance outside Washington, pushed the Lincoln administration to agree to Grant's proposed shake-up of the Shenandoah Valley command.[10]

SHERIDAN WAS GRANT'S THIRD choice to command the new Middle Military Division. Grant again proposed Major General William Franklin, his former West Point classmate. But Stanton and Lincoln, as they had when Grant nominated

Franklin for the Cavalry Corps, vetoed his choice; Franklin's clash with Ambrose Burnside at Fredericksburg had not been forgotten in the War Department. "General Franklin would not give satisfaction," Halleck told Grant, reminding him that Lincoln had wanted to put Franklin on trial for negligence and disobeying orders.[11]

Grant's second recommendation was George Meade, commander of the Army of the Potomac. "With General Meade in command . . . I would have every confidence that all the troops within the military division would be used to the very best advantage," Grant wrote to Lincoln. If Meade were appointed, Grant proposed that Major General Winfield Scott Hancock be given Meade's present command.[12]

When Meade learned that Sheridan was on his way to Washington to command the new army, he demanded to know why he had not been accepted; Grant had promised him the position. Grant told him that Lincoln feared the public might misconstrue Meade's selection to mean the administration disapproved of his management of the Army of the Potomac. "I believe Grant is honest and would not deceive me, but I think there is something more than is acknowledged," Meade wrote to his wife.[13]

War Secretary Stanton believed that Sheridan, at the age of thirty-three, was "too young" to command an army. To allay Stanton's concerns, Grant proposed that General Hunter, a robust sixty-two years old, become the division's titular commander and administrator, while Sheridan led the troops in the field. General William Sherman, campaigning in Georgia, applauded Sheridan's appointment. "He will worry Early to death," Sherman told Grant. "Let us give those southern fellows all the fighting they want, and when they are tired we can tell them we are just warming to the work."

On August 5, Sheridan met with Lincoln and Stanton in Washington. Lincoln told Sheridan that since Grant had "ploughed around" his and Stanton's reservations about Sheridan's appointment by selecting him to command the "boys in the field," they now "hoped for the best." Stanton did not speak during their meeting with Lincoln, but when he and Sheridan left the White House, he freely discussed what he expected Sheridan to accomplish and warned him that failure would have not only military but major political consequences. It went without saying that Lincoln's reelection hung in the balance.

The next day, at the Union camp outside Frederick, Maryland, Hunter met with Grant, and the shared command arrangement ended before it began. Probably recognizing that it would prove too cumbersome when decisions must be made quickly, Hunter graciously bowed out. Sheridan should be able to communicate directly with army headquarters and not through an intermediary, said Hunter, adding that he also suspected that Halleck questioned his fitness for such an important command.

At their meeting hours later, Grant informed Sheridan that he was now the sole commander of the new Middle Military Division. Grant handed Sheridan the instructions he had prepared for Hunter, ordering him to concentrate his forces at Harper's Ferry. If the Rebels have moved north of the Potomac, the instructions said, cut them off and attack their rear; if they have gone south of the river, push them up the Shenandoah Valley. "Follow him [Early] to the death," Grant wrote, while driving Confederate partisans operating in the area from their homes.

Grant raised one additional issue of surpassing importance. He ordered Sheridan to destroy the Army of Northern Virginia's primary source of food—the Shenandoah Valley's grains, produce, and livestock. As he pushed Early's army southward, Sheridan must ensure "that nothing should be left to invite the enemy to return. Take all provisions, forage, and stock wanted for the use of your command. Such as cannot be consumed, destroy." Civilian homes must be spared, "but the people should be informed that so long as an army can subsist among them recurrences of these raids can be expected."

Grant told Halleck that he had instructed Sheridan to relentlessly harry Early's army. "Wherever the enemy goes let our troops go also. Once started up the Valley they ought to be followed until we get possession of the Virginia Central Railroad."

Lincoln, who had seen too many generals arrive with great fanfare and depart under a cloud, insisted that Grant personally oversee the operation that he had described. The president invited Grant to look over recent dispatches from the War Department "and discover, if you can, that there is any idea in the head of any one here of . . . or of 'following him to the death' in any direction. I repeat to you it will neither be done nor attempted, unless you watch it every day and hour and force it."

Lincoln was telling Grant to communicate directly with Sheridan, bypassing the War Department, which sometimes rewrote orders before sending them on.[14]

SHERIDAN'S NEW ARMY OF the Shenandoah, wrote Grant's biographer, William McFeely, was an "elite corps"—no green troops, no laggards. The army totaled nearly 40,000 men, the largest Union army force ever assembled in the Valley. There were three divisions of VI Corps under Major General Horatio Wright; a division of the XIX Corps, commanded by Brigadier General William Emory; Major General George Crook's West Virginia Army, along with a cavalry division under Brigadier General William Averell; and, from the Cavalry Corps, the 1st and 3rd Divisions, commanded, respectively, by Brigadier Generals Alfred Torbert and James Wilson. Brigadier General David Gregg's 2nd Division had remained with the Army of the Potomac.

Thirty thousand of the men were taken from Grant's Army of the Potomac. This surely pleased Robert E. Lee, who had counted on Early's raids forcing just such a drawdown of Union forces outside of Richmond and Petersburg. While it would not assure victory, it would buy Lee more time to counteract Grant.

THE CAVALRY CORPS HAD been idle during most of July, but during the last week of the month, the 1st and 2nd Divisions, cooperating with Major General Winfield Scott Hancock's II Corps, had threatened Richmond. It was a massive feint designed to lure most of Lee's army north of the James River and east of Richmond, thinning Petersburg's defenses so that Grant could attack that city. To reinforce the illusion that Richmond was the real target, Sheridan had marched his divisions back and forth over a bridge—muffling the nighttime return crossing by spreading hay and recrossing in broad daylight in full view of the Rebels—in order to create the impression of a troop buildup. The deception worked: Lee transferred all but three infantry divisions and one cavalry division north of the James to defend Richmond from the anticipated attack.

On July 27 at Darbytown outside Richmond, Sheridan's dismounted troopers repelled a combined Rebel cavalry and infantry attack as the last preparations were being made for the surprise attack at Petersburg. The assault would be preceded by the detonation of 320 kegs of gunpowder in a mine secretly dug beneath the Confederate works.

On July 30, the gunpowder kegs were ignited, killing hundreds of Confederate soldiers. But instead of pouring into Petersburg, the attacking Union troops careered into the enormous crater made by the bomb. The Rebels, after recovering from the shock of the blast, ringed the crater's rim and slaughtered the Yankees trapped in the crater. The armies settled in for a long siege.[15]

THE TROOPS THAT GRANT sent from eastern Virginia to rid the Shenandoah Valley of enemy units and sustenance welcomed the change of scene. They gladly left behind the hot, war-wasted lowland countryside for the cooler Shenandoah and its well-kept farms, scarcely touched by the war—at least, so far. Henry Lewis of the 6th Michigan Cavalry wrote, "To say we are pleased with our change of base would be too dull an expression—we are more than pleased." George Stevens, a surgeon with the 77th New York Infantry in VI Corps, wrote, "The air was delightfully cool and refreshing, and it seemed as though each particular breath was laden with health and strength." Before the troops stretched miles of orchards, fields of grain, and overflowing barns. It was indeed a land of plenty.[16]

Sheridan was a new, unknown quantity for everyone except Torbert's and Wilson's men. During their first weeks under his command, the West Virginians and the VI and XIX Corps infantrymen watched him closely to form an impression of what kind of leader he would be. With his high cheekbones and almond-shaped eyes, he bore a striking resemblance to a Cossack chief. His men noticed the large bump on his head behind the ears that made nearly every hat a bad fit; he found a small-brimmed civilian porkpie hat that stayed on his head.

"Nothing superfluous about him, square-shouldered, muscular, wiry to the last degree," noted Lieutenant Colonel Frederick Newhall, Sheridan's adjutant general, "and as nearly insensible to hardship and fatigue as is consistent with humanity." Stevens observed that the men appreciated Sheridan's visibility. "Wherever we went he was with the column, inhaling the dust, leaving the road for the teams, never a day or two days behind the rest of the army, but always riding by the side of the men." The men also liked the simplicity of Sheridan's headquarters, with its single wall tent and three other, smaller tents, as compared to that of the Army of the Potomac, where "more than eighty six-mule teams were required to haul the baggage for the head-quarters of the army."[17]

SINCE HIS JUNIOR OFFICER days in Oregon and Mississippi, Sheridan had been a devoted student of topography. Now, he had the great fortune to have as his chief engineering officer twenty-two-year-old Lieutenant John Meigs, son of Montgomery Meigs, the Union army's quartermaster general. Young Meigs, who had graduated at the top of his 1863 West Point class, was one of the army's foremost topographical experts. He had made a study of the Shenandoah's roads, landmarks, and river and stream crossings. Just as Stonewall Jackson had had the renowned cartographer Jedediah Hotchkiss as his topographical engineer, Sheridan had Meigs.

In a rundown hotel in Harper's Ferry, Meigs began tutoring Sheridan in the Valley's land features. Determined not to fail as so many of his predecessors had, Sheridan buckled down and learned what Meigs had to teach. "It has always come rather easy to learn the geography of a new section, and its important topographical features as well; the region in which I was to operate would soon be well fixed in my mind," Sheridan wrote.[18]

From Harper's Ferry at its north end, where the Shenandoah River empties into the Potomac, the Valley rises 110 miles to the southwest, all the way to Staunton. Bordering it on the east are the Blue Ridge Mountains and, on the west, the Alleghenies. At its widest near Martinsburg, West Virginia, where its breadth measures forty-five miles, the Valley narrows to twenty-five miles as one travels southward on the numerous good roads. At Strasburg, forty miles south of Harper's Ferry, the broad brow of Massanutten Mountain divides the Valley into two valleys: the Luray Valley to the east and the Shenandoah to the west.

Sixteen families from York, Pennsylvania, first settled the Valley in 1732, and Quakers later followed them there. Unlike eastern Virginia's farmlands, where excessive tobacco cultivation had exhausted the soil in places, the Shenandoah, comparatively cool and temperate with soil resting on limestone beds, remained robust, producing fruit and grain and forage for the area's abundant livestock. While the Northern and Southern armies had waged war up and down the Valley, its inhabitants had largely escaped the ravages visited upon wide swaths of eastern Virginia.[19]

From Meigs and his maps Sheridan learned that the armies operating in the Shenandoah were highly vulnerable to flank attacks through the many gaps that honeycombed the Blue Ridge Mountains: Snicker's, Ashby's, Manassas, Chester, Thornton's, Swift Run, Brown's, and Rockfish. Through these gaps Rebel reinforcements from Richmond might enter the Valley after riding up the Virginia Central Railroad to Gordonsville.[20]

FOR HIS LAST ACT as West Virginia Department commander, Hunter had concentrated his troops at Halltown, near the Potomac River. Early reacted by recalling his detached units from the north side of the river, fearing that they might be cut off.[21]

In mid-August, Brigadier General George Custer reported the approach of about 8,000 Rebel troops toward Front Royal—reinforcements sent by Robert E. Lee to Early when he learned of the Yankee troop buildup. The new arrivals were Major General Joseph Kershaw's infantry division and Fitzhugh Lee's cavalry division, both commanded by Lieutenant General Richard Anderson. Torbert's division attacked the reinforcements and captured two battle flags before withdrawing.

Sheridan deliberately left unguarded some nearby Potomac River crossings, inviting Early to cross into Maryland so that Sheridan could attack his rear, prevent him from recrossing, and destroy his army. But Early was too savvy to fall for the ploy.[22]

On August 25, Early feinted toward Maryland in the hope of drawing out some of Sheridan's troops and pinning them against the Potomac River. Torbert took the bait and ran into Confederate infantry and cavalry. The Rebel force backed up Custer's Wolverine Brigade against the Potomac. Only by skillfully leapfrogging his regiments across the river under fire was Custer able to wriggle out of the tight spot.

Early's army abandoned its positions at Charlestown, south of Halltown, and pulled back to Winchester. Sheridan's troops occupied the former Rebel positions. The armies maneuvered for the next three weeks, with Opequon Creek near Winchester serving as the unofficial dividing line between them.[23]

HEEDING STANTON'S WARNING TO not risk battle until he was certain that he would win, Sheridan proceeded cautiously. "I could not afford to risk a disaster," he wrote. He moved his seven divisions like chess pieces in the lower Valley, attempting to position them to deliver a crushing blow against Early's army, while also guarding against Rebel raids into Maryland and Pennsylvania. But Early proved as adept at this game as Sheridan.

The Union and Confederate cavalry skirmished almost daily, but weeks passed without a decisive battle. Brigadier General Wesley Merritt believed the clashes between Union cavalry and Rebel infantry served an important purpose. "They gave the cavalry increased confidence, and made the enemy correspondingly doubtful even of the ability of its infantry, in anything like equal numbers, to contend against our cavalry in the open fields of the Valley."

From the Northern public, "mutterings of dissatisfaction" reached Sheridan from many quarters, with some critics calling for his removal. Convinced that "the best course was to bide my time," Sheridan waited for "an opportunity under such conditions that I could not well fail of success."[24]

IN JUBAL EARLY, SHERIDAN faced a wily opponent who had excelled as a division commander but had little experience in leading an independent command. Self-reliant, aggressive, cool under fire, and with a knack for strategy, Early, forty-seven years old, was full-bearded and tall, although somewhat stooped from arthritis. In 1837, he had graduated eighteenth in his West Point class of fifty, and he later fought in the Mexican War. When the Civil War began, Early, a lawyer in private practice, had represented Unionist Franklin County at the Virginia Secession Convention. The clamor for states' rights had drowned out his arguments against secession. When Virginia seceded, Early, loyal to his state no matter what, became commander of the 24th Virginia Infantry.

He had capably led infantry divisions at Antietam, Fredericksburg, Chancellorsville, Gettysburg, and the Wilderness. Sarcastic, abrupt, and profane, Early was unpopular with his subordinates. And while he was unquestionably courageous, he lacked the quality of self-assurance, or perhaps greatness, that inspired Jackson and Lee—and, later, Sheridan, Grant, and Sherman—to act boldly when presented with unexpected opportunities.

Early's Army of the Valley never exceeded 20,000 men; therefore, when confronting Sheridan's army, it was usually outnumbered by two to one or more. But all of Early's troops were lean, weathered veterans of nearly every battle in the East since 1861. With the arrival of Kershaw's infantry division and Fitzhugh Lee's cavalry division, Early commanded five infantry divisions, two cavalry divisions, and five artillery battalions, including some horse artillery. His II Corps included the proud remnants of the Stonewall Brigade, the legendary "foot cavalry" that had run roughshod over Union armies in the Valley during 1861 and 1862. The survivors of those campaigns knew the locations of the region's most obscure footpaths, its secret valleys, and its most defensible and vulnerable points.[25]

AUGUST BECAME SEPTEMBER, AND Sheridan's infantry remained largely idle. He kept his cavalry active, though, maintaining a six-mile interval between the two lines. Sheridan wrote that he "wished to control this ground" so that when he went on the offensive, the Rebels could not easily observe his preparations.

But no preparations were under way. Stanton and Halleck had warned Sheridan not to risk a defeat, and Grant had cautioned him to remain on the defensive until Early sent away some of his troops. Sheridan waited and watched.[26]

Early, satisfied that he had accomplished his object of threatening the North and tying up a large Yankee force, was scornful of Sheridan's inaction. "The commander opposed to me was without enterprise, and possessed an excessive caution which amounted to timidity," Early wrote. "If it was his policy to produce the impression that his force was too weak to fight me, he did not succeed, but if it was to convince me that he was not an able or energetic commander, his strategy was a complete success."

Early's men began calling Sheridan's army "Harper's Weekly" for its frequent withdrawals to its breastworks in the north end of the Valley near Harper's Ferry.[27]

ON SEPTEMBER 3, GENERAL Richard Anderson, needed by Lee in Richmond, began marching south from Winchester with Kershaw's infantry division and Fitzhugh Lee's cavalry. Reaching Berryville, the Rebels turned east toward Ashby's Gap through the Blue Ridge Mountains.

The Confederates were unpleasantly surprised when, rather than passing through the mountains, they encountered Major General George Crook's West Virginia army, now known as VIII Corps. Sheridan had shifted troops from Charlestown to lines northeast of Winchester to better guard the lower mountain gaps and the approaches to the B&O Railroad.

"A bitter little fight" erupted when Anderson collided with VIII Corps, with the result that Crook's troops threw back the Confederates. Anderson retraced his steps to Winchester, intending to wait for a more favorable time to leave the Valley and join Lee.[28]

SHERIDAN'S BROTHER MICHAEL, AN aide-de-camp on Sheridan's staff, was a man of action like his big brother. Another Sheridan brother, John, was a different sort: nearsighted, shy, and bookish. He happened to be serving with the Army of the Shenandoah as a one-hundred-day volunteer with an Ohio infantry regiment when he became ill. His two brothers rallied around him, with Michael making sure that

John received all the medications he needed and procuring "delicacies" to speed his recovery.[29]

AS SEPTEMBER ADVANCED, THE cavalries of Sheridan and Early tirelessly marched, countermarched, and skirmished, seeking to gain an advantage by maneuver. An expert on the Union cavalry, Stephen Z. Starr, compared the armies' relatively bloodless movements during these weeks to "the elaborate choreographed evolutions of eighteenth-century warfare."

But Sheridan was doing more than marking time until he might attack Early with an assurance of victory; he was acclimating his infantry and cavalry to joint operations.[30] Their objective would be not just victory but the complete destruction of the enemy's fighting capabilities. When the time came to give battle, Sheridan intended to utilize his mounted troops' superior speed and mobility to cut off the enemy's avenues of retreat and force him into pockets where combined infantry and cavalry might annihilate him.

He had broken new ground in the Army of the Potomac by utilizing the Cavalry Corps as an independent strike force. Now, in the Shenandoah Valley, he was on the verge of another innovation: integrating the cavalry's operations with the infantry's. This was as revolutionary a concept as would be the use of tanks and aircraft in the twentieth century to support fighting men on the ground.

Sheridan's dynamic twining of infantry and cavalry would prove extremely useful to the pioneers of mechanized warfare during the 1930s. But Sheridan's early attempts to effect the most basic combinations of these two arms would run up against frustrating human limitations.

CHAPTER 7

Triumph at Winchester

SEPTEMBER 1864

We just sent them a whirling through Winchester, and we are after them tomorrow. This army behaved splendidly.
—SHERIDAN BATTLE REPORT[1]

THE YOUNG QUAKER SCHOOLTEACHER was lecturing a roomful of girls when she was interrupted by a knock on the door of her Winchester classroom on September 16. When she opened the door, an older black man stood before her. Was she Rebecca Wright? he asked. Yes, she answered.

There were more questions until the stranger had satisfied himself that she was indeed the Miss Wright who lived in the Wright family home on Fort Hill in Winchester—the same Miss Wright who two months earlier had made the acquaintance of Major General George Crook during Crook's brief occupation of Winchester. Wright was all of that, and a Union sympathizer, which was what had brought Thomas Laws to her door.

Laws, who lived between the Union and Rebel lines near Berryville, had obtained a pass from Confederate lieutenant general Jubal Early that permitted him to travel through the Rebel lines and into Winchester to sell vegetables. But he hadn't come to sell vegetables to Wright; today, he was acting as a messenger for Major General Phil Sheridan.

After Wright had invited Laws inside, he removed some tinfoil secreted beneath his tongue and opened it to reveal a piece of tissue paper. The small pellet would have been easy to swallow if Rebel pickets had decided to search Laws; they hadn't. The message said,

15 SEPTEMBER 1864

I learn from Maj. Gen. Crook that you are a loyal lady and still love the old flag. Can you inform me of the position of Early and his forces, the number of divisions in his army, and the strength of any or all of them, and his probable or reported intentions? Have any more troops arrived from Richmond or are any more coming or reported to be coming?

I am, very respectfully, your most obedient servant,

P.H. Sheridan,
Major General Commanding.

P.S. You can trust the bearer.[2]

Wright told Laws to return at 3 p.m. She then sought her mother's advice about whether to aid Sheridan. Her father was unavailable for consultation—he was in Richmond's infamous Libby Prison, where Union officers were held captive. Wright's mother encouraged her to assist the Yankee general.

Coincidentally, the previous day a convalescing Confederate officer had visited the Wright home and spoken unrestrainedly about the movements and strength of the Army of the Valley. When Laws returned, Wright handed him the compressed pellet of foil, now containing her reply to Sheridan:

SEPTEMBER 16TH, 1864.

I have no communication whatever with the rebels, but will tell thee what I know. The division of Gen. Kershaw, and [Major Winfred] Cutshaw's artillery, twelve guns and men, Gen. Anderson commanding, has been sent away, and no more troops are expected, as they cannot be spared from Richmond. I do not know how the troops are situated, but the force is much smaller than represented. I will take pleasure hereafter in learning all I can of their strength and position, and the bearer may call again.

X.X.X.X.[3]

Wright's note confirmed the reports of Richard Anderson's departure that had reached the Union camp over the past several days. It freed Sheridan to act at last—for Joseph Kershaw's departure gave Sheridan a lopsided advantage, with more than 40,000 Union troops to Early's 18,000.

Sheridan began making a battle plan. He would not act upon it until Anderson had marched too far away to come to Early's assistance when Sheridan attacked.[4]

LATE THAT NIGHT, SHERIDAN received a message from Ulysses Grant. The general in chief was ten miles away in Charles Town, West Virginia, and he wanted Sheridan to meet him there.

Weeks earlier, President Abraham Lincoln had emphasized to Grant that he must personally oversee the Shenandoah Valley campaign because, he feared, "it will neither be done nor attempted, unless you watch it every day and hour and force it." Since then, Grant had closely monitored the operations in the Valley. Throughout August and September, he peppered Sheridan with telegrams every two or three days. They included his observations and thoughts, as well as gleaned intelligence—often incorrect—on the movement of Rebel units to and from the Shenandoah.

On August 21, Grant had told Sheridan that if his operations near Petersburg were successful, Confederate troops would probably be withdrawn from the Valley to reinforce Robert E. Lee. On August 25 and 26, Grant was certain that Fitzhugh Lee's cavalry was being recalled from the Valley to southern Virginia; it wasn't. On August 29, he reported that Major General John Breckenridge had been sent from the Valley to West Virginia—to which Sheridan exasperatedly replied, "There is not one word of truth in the report. . . . It is a copperhead report. I saw his corps at the crossing of Opequon Creek this evening." On September 1, Grant passed along a rumor, also false, that Early's army had been ordered to Richmond.

On September 8, Grant suggested that Sheridan reinforce his army with troops from Washington, "if you want to attack Early." But the next day, Grant advised against an assault: "I would not have you make an attack with the advantages against you, but would prefer just the course you seem to be pursuing: that is pressing closely upon the enemy and when he moves, follow him up, being ready at all times to pounce upon him if he detaches any considerable force."[5]

Lincoln's reelection prospects had received an enormous boost on September 3, when the electrifying news of William Sherman's capture of Atlanta had reached Washington. But Atlanta's fall alone might not necessarily secure Lincoln a second term. George McClellan, the Democratic Party's presidential nominee and a former Union Army major general, had a large following of dissidents: those demanding immediate peace and others who were disheartened by Early's menacing of Washington, Grant's stalemate at Petersburg, and this war without apparent end.

On September 12, Lincoln, pressured by the growing number of Northern critics derogating the seemingly inert Army of the Shenandoah, penned a note to Grant:

> Sheridan and Early are facing each other at a dead lock. Could we not pick up a regiment here and there, to the number of say ten thousand men, and quietly, but suddenly concentrate them at Sheridan's camp and enable him to make a strike? This is but a suggestion.

Grant replied to the president the next day: "It has been my intention for a week back to start to-morrow, or the day following, to see Sheridan and arrange what was necessary to enable him to start Early out of the valley. It seems to me it can be successfully done."[6]

ON SEPTEMBER 17, SHERIDAN rode to Charles Town and met with Grant. Captain John De Forest of the 12th Connecticut was strolling nearby when a sergeant pointed out two "undersized men, rather squarely built." They were walking together and talking quietly. Grant, "blond and sandy-bearded," listened as Sheridan spoke "in a low silvery voice . . . his elbows pressed to his sides, but gesturing slightly with his fingers. The sergeant gazed silently at Grant for a moment, then said to De Forest, 'I hate to see that old cuss around. When that old cuss is around there's sure to be a big fight on hand.'"[7]

By now, Sheridan had a thorough working knowledge of the area's topography and good maps. He drew one out of a side pocket and proceeded to show Grant the locations of roads, streams, and the camps of the two armies.

Since receiving Wright's note, Sheridan and his staff had been working intensively on a plan to attack Early's four remaining divisions east of Winchester and not only to defeat but to destroy them by blocking their escape up the Valley Turnpike. Sheridan spread out his map and explained to Grant how he proposed to "whip them."

Before leaving City Point, Grant had drawn up an attack plan of his own for Sheridan. "But, seeing that [Sheridan] was so clear and so positive in his views and so confident of success, I said nothing about this and did not take it out of my pocket," Grant later wrote.[8]

Impressed by Sheridan's plan and his contagious enthusiasm, Grant ordered him to attack on Tuesday, September 20. Sheridan replied that if Grant approved, he wished to launch the assault on September 19.

"Go in," Grant told Sheridan. The general in chief departed the next day.[9]

In the Shenandoah Valley, possibly just Harper's Ferry held greater strategic importance than Winchester—both as a springboard for invasions north and south and as a stronghold from which to repel those invasions. Coveted because it was a crossroads city of 4,400, as well as a railroad and mercantile center, Winchester had changed hands more than seventy times during the war—once, a dizzying thirteen times in one day. There had been a dozen full-fledged occupations. Battles had been fought up and down Main Street. Winchester's homes and buildings had been looted, burned, and made to serve as hostels, military headquarters, and hospitals.

The Confederate army had won the two major battles fought at Winchester in 1862 and 1863. The first time, Stonewall Jackson's army had beaten Major General Nathaniel Banks's forces and driven him completely out of the Shenandoah; a year later, Richard Ewell had expelled a Union occupying force prefatory to Robert E. Lee's Gettysburg invasion.

On September 18 Sheridan and his commanders completed their plan to eject Early from Winchester and destroy his army.

Scouts reported that Early had left Winchester with two infantry divisions for Martinsburg, across the border in West Virginia, evidently in the hope of gaining a strategic advantage. Sheridan exulted at this opportunity: if he moved quickly, he might defeat the two divisions remaining in the Winchester area while Early and his two other divisions were beyond supporting distance. There was no time to waste. The assault was scheduled to begin at 3 a.m. on Monday, September 19.[10]

Although Sheridan did not know it, his window for attacking Early's army while it was so divided was swiftly closing. When Early reached Martinsburg, he learned at the telegraph office that Grant and Sheridan had been seen in Charles Town the previous day. Instantly recognizing that the meeting likely portended an imminent attack, Early ordered his two division commanders, Major Generals John Gordon and Robert Rodes, to turn their troops around and return immediately to Winchester.

Early was worried, and with good reason. On a plateau a mile and a half east of Winchester was Major General Stephen Ramseur's unsupported infantry division. Its 2,000 men blocked the Berryville Turnpike, which descended a narrow canyon as it proceeded eastward, connecting Winchester and Berryville. Early knew that Ramseur's troops would stand little chance against Sheridan's seven divisions at Berryville.[11]

At Stephenson's Depot, five miles north of Ramseur's troops, was Early's fourth infantry division, commanded by Major General Gabriel Wharton. Early alerted Wharton to be ready to reinforce Ramseur quickly if necessary.[12]

SEPTEMBER 19, 1864—WINCHESTER, VIRGINIA—SHERIDAN's plan called for his divisions in Berryville to march west up the Berryville Turnpike and envelope and destroy Ramseur's division just east of Winchester, while two cavalry divisions simultaneously converged from the north on the Rebels.

After crossing Opequon Creek in the predawn darkness, Brigadier General James Wilson's 3rd Cavalry Division rode into a narrow canyon, closely bordered by steep, densely wooded hills. Behind Wilson came VI and XIX Corps and their more than 25,000 infantrymen. Crook's smaller VIII Corps remained at the foot of the defile, with orders to later cut off Ramseur's avenue of retreat.

Ramseur's division was entrenched in fields of ripe corn at the head of the canyon. As Wilson and the infantry divisions advanced on Ramseur from the east, approaching from the north were the Army of West Virginia's cavalry, renamed the 2nd Division and commanded by Brigadier General William Averell, and Wesley Merritt's 1st Division—Alfred Torbert now commanding all of Sheridan's cavalry.

While Wilson, Crook, Merritt, and Averell swarmed around Ramseur's flanks and rear, VI and XIX Corps would attack him head-on. Had everything gone according plan, Ramseur's division, outnumbered twenty to one, would not have stood a chance.

WILSON's 3,500 CAVALRYMEN PASSED up the canyon quickly and drove in Ramseur's pickets. Dismounting, they took up positions to shield the infantrymen marching behind them.

A major problem developed in the canyon. Inexplicably, Major General Horatio Wright, the commander of VI Corps, had decided to bring along his ammunition train. It was a huge mistake. The long line of lumbering, mule-drawn wagons clogged the narrow canyon, blocking the path of XIX Corps.

The lightning strike at Ramseur bogged down. Six hours were lost getting the army through the three-mile-long canyon. The jam was broken only when Sheridan, angrily and with great profanity, ordered Wright's train run into the ditches.

By then it was 11 a.m., and the divisions of Rodes, Gordon, and Wharton were joining Ramseur's infantrymen, who had held their ground against Wilson's dismounted troopers. The fresh Confederate divisions rushed into positions to Ramseur's left and rear and pitched into the fighting that now raged along a ninety-degree arc from the Berryville Pike east of Winchester to the Martinsburg Pike on the city's north side.

NOW FACING EARLY's REUNITED army rather than just Ramseur's division, Sheridan had to improvise a new plan, and he wasted no time in doing so. Placing VI and XIX Corps in a line facing the Confederate positions, at about noon Sheridan ordered the infantrymen to advance on Early's fully reassembled army of more than 12,000 men. The attack faltered, a gap developed between VI and XIX Corps, and Gordon's and Rodes's two divisions charged into the gap.

During the intensive fighting, Rodes fell mortally wounded, and Sheridan lost Brigadier General David Russell, commander of the 1st Division of VI Corps, as he tried to stop the Rebel counterattack. Russell had been Sheridan's captain in the old 4th Infantry in Oregon, and Sheridan mourned his death. "He was my captain and friend," he wrote.[13]

The 1st and 2nd Cavalry Divisions attacked from the north, driving Fitzhugh Lee's cavalry before them. Sheridan summoned the cavalrymen to help execute the next phase of his new plan, a "half wheel" to the left by the entire army. Crook's corps, brought up from the foot of Berryville Canyon and placed to the right of XIX Corps, would lead the movement. If the plan worked, the Rebels' left flank would be shattered and Early's army driven from the field.

Sheridan sent word to Wilson, southeast of Winchester, to ride to the Valley Turnpike and block Early's retreat if possible. Under Sheridan's original plan to envelop Ramseur's division with a combination of infantry and cavalry, Crook's 8,000 men were supposed to have aided Wilson in barring Ramseur's flight. However, with Crook leading the main attack, Wilson, with just 3,500 men, was now expected to block the retreat of Early's entire army.[14]

Sheridan rode along the VI and XIX Corps lines, periodically stopping to lean forward and address his men. His eyes burning with intensity, he told them, "Kill every son of a bitch!"

At one point, a shell screeched through the air, plowed into the ground beneath Rienzi, and exploded. Sheridan emerged from the smoke and dust and remarked, "Damn close, but we'll lick hell out of them yet!" The men cheered wildly.

Sheridan galloped up to Brigadier General Cuvier Grover, who commanded a division of XIX Corps, and said, "Now is the time to go in."

The infantry divisions advanced across a field toward the Confederate positions, "a rare opportunity to witness the precision with which the attack was taken up from right to left," Sheridan wrote. As Crook's infantrymen began their "half wheel" to the left, Sheridan ordered his five cavalry brigades to charge the Confederates' flank and get in the rear of Early's army. The open ground, Sheridan noted, "offered an opportunity such as seldom had been presented during the war for a mounted attack."[15]

The 7,000 horsemen formed three lines. Then, the dense, half-mile-wide phalanx of horses and men rumbled toward the left and rear of the Rebel infantry. Brigadier General George Custer, commanding one of the brigades, wrote that as bands played inspiring martial music, the advancing formation "presented in the sunlight one moving mass of glittering sabers. This, combined with the various and bright-colored banners and battle-flags, intermingled here and there with the plain blue uniforms of the troops, furnished one of the most inspiring as well as imposing scenes of martial grandeur ever witnessed upon a battle-field."

The rare sight of a massive cavalry charge transfixed soldiers in both armies. "I never saw such a sight in my life as that of the tremendous force," a Virginian later said. "Guidons fluttered and sabers glistened," wrote Major James Kidd, who led the 6th Michigan Cavalry. Captain John De Forest, who was advancing on the Rebel line with XIX Corps, described "a faraway, dark line of eager horsemen— fleeting over a broad grey slope of land, and dashing into a swarm of refugees."

The Rebels launched a preemptive attack against the charging cavalry, but it caused the Yankees to pause only momentarily. Early's small army was outnumbered and without hope of reinforcement.

The Confederate left flank drew back as Crook's VIII Corps crashed between Wharton's and Gordon's divisions and as VI Corps broke Rodes's division and pushed back Ramseur. Confederate colonel George S. Patton, grandfather of the legendary World War II general, was mortally wounded while futilely urging his Patton's Brigade to withstand the cavalry's onslaught.

Hearing the Union cavalry firing in its rear, Early's army retreated, hurtling through Winchester. John Gordon's wife, Fanny, who was staying in Winchester, exhorted the Rebels from a friend's front porch to turn back. A short time later, with shells and musket balls dropping around her, Fanny Gordon fled the city in her carriage with her six-year-old son and two wounded Rebel officers.

KIDD WAS IMPRESSED BY Sheridan's inspired use of cavalry and infantry in support of one another. It was, he said, "the first time that proper use of [the cavalry] had been made in a great battle during the war." Indeed, in his first major battle as an independent commander, Sheridan had sent Early's combat veterans reeling from the one-two punch of a combined cavalry charge and infantry attack.

Colonel Rutherford B. Hayes, who began the battle as brigade commander in VIII Corps and ended it commanding a division, was equally impressed. "Sheridan's cavalry is splendid. It is the most like the right thing that I have seen during the war." Custer clapped one of his officers on the shoulder and said, "Major, this is the bulliest day since Christ was born!"

Slowed by rough terrain, a determined Rebel rearguard, and then darkness, Wilson's 3rd Division was unable to block the Valley Turnpike, and Early's army escaped to fight another day. Still, Jubal Early, who had recently thrown Washington into a panic, had been decisively beaten in the arena that he had lately so dominated.

At the Third Battle of Winchester, Sheridan's army reversed the train of major defeats that had dogged Union armies in the Shenandoah Valley since Stonewall Jackson's heyday.[16]

THE ARMY OF THE Shenandoah poured into Winchester, and Crook took Sheridan to Rebecca Wright's home. The schoolteacher heard "sabers clanking against the porch" and found a group of Union officers waiting outside. She welcomed them with handshakes, and when they came inside, Sheridan told her it was "entirely on information [Wright] had sent him that he had fought the battle." He promised never to forget her "courage and patriotism."[17]

Sheridan sat down at Wright's desk and composed his battle report. He later sent a telegram to Grant announcing the great victory. His army had captured 2,500 to 3,000 prisoners, five artillery pieces, and nine battle flags. It had sustained 4,500 casualties, and Sheridan estimated Early's total dead and wounded to be comparable. In their hasty retreat to the south, toward Fisher's Hill, the Rebels had left behind 3,000 wounded. "We just sent them a whirling through Winchester, and we are after them tomorrow. The army behaved splendidly," Sheridan wrote.

Grant replied the next day: "I have just received the news of your great victory and ordered each of the Armies here to fire a salute of one hundred guns in honor of it at 7 a.m. tomorrow morning.—If practicable push your success and make all you can of it." Grant's bland congratulatory note did not begin to convey his exultation—and relief—over the victory. It was, wrote Brigadier General Horace Porter of Grant's staff, no less than "an entire vindication of Grant's judgment" in bringing Sheridan to the Shenandoah Valley despite the doubts of Lincoln and Edwin Stanton.

The president and war secretary telegraphed Sheridan their own laudatory messages; their previous reservations about him were gone. Stanton made Sheridan's temporary appointment as commander of the Middle Military Division a permanent one. He also promoted Sheridan to brigadier general in the regular army, making his general rank permanent and not brevet. Lincoln simply wrote, "God bless you all, officers and men. Strongly inclined to come up and see you."[18]

In his report to Robert E. Lee, Early wrote that he "had already defeated the enemy's infantry, and could have continued to do so, but the enemy's very great superiority in cavalry and the comparative inefficiency of ours turned the scale against us."[19]

SHERIDAN'S TROOPS BROKE OFF their pursuit of Early during the early evening of September 19. The next day, the army marched to Strasburg, fifteen miles to the south, where the Shenandoah Valley split into two smaller valleys: the Luray on the east side of Massanutten Mountain and the Shenandoah on the west side. Early was five miles beyond Strasburg in the western valley, in strongly fortified positions on Fisher's Hill.

Fisher's Hill, three and a half miles wide, commanded the western valley's northern approaches. The jagged ridge extended west from Massanutten Mountain to Little North Mountain, a spur of the Alleghenies. Rising from the bed of Tumbling Run Creek, it appeared invulnerable to direct attack from the north. Assault troops would have to cross Tumbling Run under artillery fire and then charge uphill into the breastworks that the Confederates had erected on the ridge crest. Still possessing most of their guns and more than 12,000 men, Early was confident that his army could repulse any Yankee attack on Fisher's Hill.[20]

But a novel attack plan had suggested itself to George Crook. His VIII Corps would stealthily march during the night to the dense woods and ravines on Little North Mountain. The next day, while VI and XIX Corps ostentatiously prepared for an advance toward Tumbling Run, engaging the Confederates' full attention, VIII Corps would work its way under the forest canopy to the east face of Little North Mountain, from which it could strike the left and rear of Early's entrenched army.

THROUGH THE NIGHT OF September 20 into the morning of September 21, VIII Corps crossed Cedar Creek, reaching a stand of timber. Concealed from the Rebels manning the signal station on Three Top Mountain, part of Massanutten Mountain, VIII Corps spent nearly all of September 22 edging into position on Little North Mountain, while VI Corps diverted the Confederates' attention.

Sheridan had added another dimension to the plan. His two cardinal rules were always to act offensively and to follow up any advantage to the utmost—lessons that he had learned in Dennis Hart Mahan's "Science of War" seminar at West Point. In other words, never let a beaten enemy escape—as Early had at Winchester. Sheridan was determined this time to trap and destroy the Rebel army. He sent Torbert with two cavalry divisions to block Early's southward retreat.

At 4 p.m. on September 22, Crook's corps suddenly emerged from the forest in two parallel columns behind the Rebel breastworks. Led by Averell's 2nd Cavalry Division and Colonel Rutherford Hayes's infantry division, VIII Corps swung left, merging with an advancing VI Corps division. With surprising speed, they rolled up Early's battle lines.

It was a rout, plain and simple. This time, Early lost twenty guns and 1,100 prisoners. Confederate major general John Gordon wrote, "To all experienced soldiers the whole story is told in one word—'flanked.'"[21]

Sheridan pronounced Fisher's Hill "a most signal victory" in his telegram to Grant that night. Grant quickly replied, "Keep on and your work will cause the fall of Richmond."[22]

In a letter to his uncle, Hayes expressed great pride in Crook's clever plan that had so efficiently cracked Early's defenses. "General Crook is the brains of this army," Hayes wrote. "Intellectually, [Sheridan] is not General Crook's equal," although Hayes acknowledged that Sheridan was "a whole-souled, brave man."[23]

TORBERT, WITH HIS 1ST and 3rd Divisions, had started up the Luray Valley on September 20 with the intention of getting behind Early and blocking his retreat when Fisher's Hill was attacked. Torbert planned to cross back into the main Shenandoah Valley at New Market, thirty miles south of Fisher's Hill. Before the cavalrymen reached New Market, however, they encountered Rebel horsemen, half as many as Torbert's, barring their way. Unnerving the Rebels by blowing 250 bugles in the fog, Wilson's 3rd Division initially drove Confederate brigadier general William Wickham's division six miles. But when Wickham regrouped and repelled an attack by Custer's brigade, Torbert timidly withdrew to Front Royal. Early's army retreated from Fisher's Hill unimpeded.[24]

Averell, too, had been singularly unaggressive in his pursuit of Early after rolling up his lines on Fisher's Hill. His 2nd Division had broken off the pursuit after seven miles and gone into camp for the night, letting the VI and XIX Corps infantry do the chasing for fifteen miles.[25]

The next day, Colonel Thomas Devin's cavalry brigade was fighting the Rebel rearguard at Mount Jackson, awaiting Averell's arrival. Averell got there late, after Devin's brigade had forced the Rebels to retreat. Sheridan reprimanded Averell for his tardiness and gave him explicit orders to do "actual fighting, with necessary casualties, before you retire." Instead, Averell made camp for the night.

Sheridan was "astonished and chagrined" when he learned that his cavalry had failed to pursue or trap Early. "My disappointment was extreme," he wrote. Torbert had made "little or no attempt" to dislodge Wickham and "ought to have made a fight." Sheridan ordered him to redouble his efforts to get behind Early before he got away.

Averell's conduct, however, was not only disappointing but actionable, Sheridan believed. On September 1, Grant, already concerned about Averell's lack of aggressiveness, had authorized Sheridan to dismiss him if it became necessary. Sheridan now did so, citing his "growing indifference." Averell responded by complaining that Sheridan had sought a pretext for his removal since choosing Torbert to be his cavalry commander, rather than Averell, who was Torbert's senior.[26]

Twenty-four-year-old Brigadier General George Custer initially became the new commander of Averell's 2nd Division. But a week later, when James Wilson was appointed to command Major General William Sherman's cavalry in Georgia, Custer was given Wilson's 3rd Division. Colonel William Powell of the 2nd West Virginia Cavalry took over Averell's former division.

The 3rd Division's brilliant, colorful new leader would transform it during the war's closing months into the army's most illustrious cavalry unit: Custer's Division. Custer, like many of Sheridan's other lieutenants—Wilson, Merritt, Crook, and later Ranald McKenzie—possessed the winning traits that Sheridan so prized: physical courage, audacity, energy, a knack for improvisation, and relentlessness. They would help shape the postwar army.[27]

JUBAL EARLY WITHDREW UP the Valley fifty miles to Port Republic. Grant proposed that Sheridan chase him through the Blue Ridge passes to Charlottesville and Gordonsville, where he could wreck the James River canal and the Virginia Central Railroad while advancing toward Richmond.

Sounding uncharacteristically cautious, Sheridan objected. "It is no easy matter to pass these mountain gaps & attack Charlottesville, hauling supplies through difficult passes fourteen miles in length & with a line of communication from 135 to 145 miles in length," he wrote. Moreover, if he marched on Charlottesville, he said, he must detach Crook's VIII Corps to protect the B&O and Orange & Alexander Railroads. That would leave him with too few troops to complete his mission.[28]

He instead proposed marching north down the Valley, burning barns and crops and destroying livestock, then traveling by train and boat to join the Army of the Potomac at Petersburg. Disliking Sheridan's plan, Grant nonetheless left the final decision in his hands. Sheridan issued orders to withdraw down the Valley to Strasburg.[29]

THE TWO DEFEATS, COMING just three days apart, had left Early feeling depressed and frustrated. Sheridan had prevailed despite his manifest failures, Early believed. He had bogged down his army in Berryville Canyon, and his superb cavalry had been unable to cut off Early's retreat and destroy his army. "I have always thought that instead of being promoted, Sheridan ought to have been cashiered," Early later wrote.[30]

In his report to Robert E. Lee, Early said that his men were exhausted, and many lacked shoes. He offered a halfhearted apology. "I deeply regret the present state of things, and I assure [you] everything in my power has been done to avert it. The enemy's force is very much larger than mine, being three or four to one."

Early should in fact have been proud of his little army's outsized accomplishments: striking terror into the Union capital, compelling the Yankees to divert more than 40,000 troops to the Shenandoah Valley, and keeping them guessing for months as to his intentions. But rather than spare a kind word for the herculean efforts made by Early and his Army of the Valley—the Southern public at the moment was clamoring for Early's head—Lee replied with studied coolness: "I have such confidence in the men and officers that I am sure all will unite in the defense of the country."

Lee promised to send back Kershaw's infantry division and a small cavalry brigade commanded by Brigadier General Thomas Rosser. He advised Early to hold Sheridan in check until he could concentrate his forces and then "strike him with all your strength. . . . We are obliged to fight against great odds. A kind Providence will yet overrule everything for our good."[31]

CHAPTER 8

Burning the Valley

AUGUST–NOVEMBER 1864

*The Union army came up the Valley sweeping everything before
them like a hurricane; there was nothing left for man or beast from
the horse down to the chicken.*
—SHENANDOAH VALLEY RESIDENT[1]

PHILIP SHERIDAN SURVEYED HIS AWFUL HANDIWORK with satisfaction. Plumes
of black smoke smudged the Shenandoah Valley's fairytale landscape of rolling green
hills and brooks. In places, yellow flames could be seen shooting from a barn's gam-
brel roof or racing through a grain field. Distance muted the crackle of burning
fires, the crash of barns and outbuildings collapsing in heaps of charred timbers,
and the cries of women and children as the bluecoats shot down their livestock.

Ulysses Grant had ordered the destruction in his initial instructions to Sheridan.
"Nothing should be left to invite the enemy to return," Grant wrote.[2]

On August 17, two weeks after his appointment, Sheridan first acted on this di-
rective—when Grant specifically ordered him to burn Loudoun County, the sanctuary of Lieutenant Colonel John Mosby. Mosby's mounted partisans, with
maddening regularity, swooped down on Union wagon trains, bushwhacked Yankee
couriers and scouts, and then melted back into the populace. Mosby's Rangers had
recently attacked one of Sheridan's wagon trains, burning forty wagons, and seizing

430 mules, thirty-six horses, and two hundred head of cattle. "Where any of Mosby's men are caught with nothing to designate what they are, hang them without trial," Grant instructed Sheridan.

Grant also wanted Sheridan's cavalry to round up the families of Mosby's men and imprison them at Fort McHenry "or some other secure place, as hostages for the good conduct of Mosby and his men"—in other words, he was to establish a Union concentration camp. This never happened; nor did Grant's suggestion that Sheridan's men seize all of Loudoun County's men under the age of fifty. "If not already soldiers they will be made so the moment the rebel army gets hold of them," Grant had written in explaining this draconian proposal.[3]

Sheridan had ordered Brigadier General Alfred Torbert to deploy his cavalry divisions along a line running southeast from Winchester. Fields and farm buildings were to be burned, livestock destroyed, and slaves set free. "No houses will be burned, and officers in charge of this delicate but necessary duty must inform the people that the object is to make this valley untenable for the raiding parties of the rebel army," said Sheridan's orders.[4]

Many Union cavalrymen loathed this duty; they had not gone to war to destroy the life's work of noncombatants. "It was a phase of warfare we had not seen before," wrote a Pennsylvania cavalryman, "and though we admitted its necessity, we could not but sympathize with the sufferers."

From a hill, Matthela Harrison counted fifty fires. "The sky was lurid and but for the green trees one might have imagined the shades of Hades had descended suddenly," she wrote. "Large families of children were left without one cow."[5] A Richmond newspaper reported that the Yankees burned all the wheat, oats, and hay. "They drove before them every horse, cow, sheep, hog, calf and living animal from the country. What the people are to do, God only knows."[6]

There followed a six-week hiatus in "the Burning"—the inhabitants' bitter shorthand for the ruthless purging of the Valley—while Sheridan and Jubal Early contended militarily. When it resumed in late September and October, its scope was greatly enlarged.

THE BURNING WAS A refinement of an old form of war making—during the 1920s, the Italian Fascists began calling it "total war," and the appellation stuck. It was an older, crueler warfare that made fewer distinctions than Grant and Sheridan did between soldiers and civilians. Throughout history, examples abound: Rome burning Carthage to the ground during the Third Punic War; Timur's horsemen making pyramids of human skulls during their scorched-earth campaigns of the fourteenth century.

In modern Europe during the Enlightenment, the pendulum swung the other way. Professional armies fought gentlemanly, choreographed battles that generally excluded noncombatants, except in calculated acts of reprisal—for example, the British army's burning of Washington in retaliation for the Americans' burning of York, Upper Canada's capital. From 1861 through 1864, the Union and Confederate armies had carefully targeted one another, except when battles were fought in cities.

But even Francis Lieber in his 157-article *Code for the Government of Armies in the Field*, written at Major General Henry Halleck's request, had deemed it permissible for Yankee soldiers to seize and destroy Rebel civilian property under certain circumstances. Any citizen of a hostile territory was by definition "an enemy" and might be "subjected to the hardships of war," the code said. There was wiggle room everywhere. Article 22 stated that unarmed civilians were to be "spared in person, property, and honor as much as the exigencies of war will admit." One of the code's rare unqualified assertions on the subject of noncombatant civilians stated, "Private citizens are no longer murdered, enslaved, or carried off to distant parts."[7]

All of that notwithstanding, for the first time an American army—Phil Sheridan's—was deliberately, systematically destroying an enemy's capacity to fight by targeting its food supply and crushing the fighting spirit of its civilians. With the Lincoln administration's approval, Grant had quietly shelved the three-year-old "gentleman's war" in order to expose the Southern people to hardship and personal loss.

SHERIDAN HAD BEEN RIPE for conversion. "I do not hold war to mean simply that lines of men shall engage each other in battle," he wrote. "This is but a duel, in which one combatant seeks the other's life; war means much more, and is far worse than this. . . . Death is popularly considered the maximum punishment in war, but it is not; reduction to poverty brings prayers for peace more surely and more quickly than does the destruction of human life."[8*]

Abraham Lincoln, William Sherman, Grant, and Sheridan shared the belief that prosecuting a total war was the shortest path to peace. By 1864, it appeared to them the only viable path. The Union faced the Manichean choices of union and emancipation or Southern independence and slavery—with no middle ground. Referring to Jefferson Davis, Lincoln wrote in his December 1864 message to Congress, "He cannot voluntarily reaccept the Union; we cannot voluntarily yield it. Between him

---

* Historian James McPherson observed that during the war's early years, Sheridan, Grant, and Major General William Sherman had all served in Missouri, a hotbed of retributive partisan warfare. Because of their exposure to this kind of no-holds-barred fighting, he suggested, they had fewer inhibitions against enacting harsh measures in Virginia and Georgia. See James M. McPherson, "From Limited War to Total War in America," in *On the Road to Total War: The American Civil War and the German Wars of Unification, 1861–1871*, ed. Stig Förster and Jörg Nagler (Cambridge: Cambridge University Press, 1997), 302.

and us the issue is distinct, simple, and inflexible. It is an issue which can only be tried by war, and decided by victory. If we yield, we are beaten; if the Southern people fail·him, he is beaten."[9]

The drift toward total war began in 1863, when Lincoln exhorted his Eastern commanders to focus on destroying Robert E. Lee's army and not on geographical gains, which could be fleeting. A year later, Grant became the first to put this policy into practice by prosecuting the bloody Overland Campaign and by suspending prisoner exchanges, denying the tens of thousands of veteran Confederacy troops.

But killing Confederate soldiers on battlefields and locking up enemy captives indefinitely were slow agents of victory, Grant and Lincoln soon recognized; the war's awfulness must also be carried to the doorsteps of Southern civilians, whose defiance kept the Confederacy alive. This was not just a war of armies; it was a war of cultures, to be fought to the death. Moreover, Lincoln and Grant, like Sherman and Sheridan, also believed that the advent in the South of guerrilla warfare justified their jettisoning the old rules.[10] Reasoning within their severe Hobbesian universe, they concluded that by systematically targeting civilian property—unprecedented on the North American continent (except toward Native Americans)—they might psychologically break the enemy, thereby shortening the war and saving lives.

And so Lincoln and Grant chose to sow ruin throughout the enemy homeland, wrecking the South's war industries, despoiling its farmlands, and bringing hunger into the homes of its people. This new guiding principle was never set down as policy, but its outlines were clearly visible in the actions of Sheridan and Sherman. The two would later bring this kind of warfare to a wicked apotheosis on the Great Plains when they wiped out villages of Indian warriors, women, and children in order to stop depredations against white settlers.

As HE READIED THE Army of the Tennessee to march from Atlanta to the sea, Sherman told Grant, "I can make the march, and make Georgia howl." The march would deliver a powerful psychological blow, demonstrating to the Southern people that the Confederacy no longer could protect them from the enemy. As he later explained to General Henry Halleck, "We are not only fighting hostile armies, but a hostile people, and must make old and young, rich and poor, feel the hard hand of war, as well as their organized armies."[11]

More outspoken than Grant and Sheridan on the subject of total war, Sherman was also the first to prosecute it. During the February 1864 Meridian, Mississippi, campaigning, Sherman's troops wrecked railroads, terrorized citizens, destroyed property, cleared out guerrillas, and lived off the land. After the Vicksburg campaign, his men burned homes and villages near Memphis that were believed to harbor guerrillas. "Our duty is not to build up; it is rather to destroy both the rebel army and whatever of wealth or property it has founded its boasted strength upon," he wrote.[12]

Sherman's bombardment of Atlanta in August 1864 provoked strenuous objections from Confederate lieutenant general John Bell Hood for its "studied and injurious cruelty." Sherman replied, "War is cruelty, and you cannot refine it; and those who brought war into our country deserve all the curses and maledictions a people can pour out. . . . You might as well appeal against the thunderstorm as against these terrible hardships of war."[13] After Atlanta fell on September 2, Sherman forcibly depopulated the city of all civilians not in essential government jobs. A total of 705 adults, 860 children, and seventy-nine slaves were expelled.

Newspapers throughout the South condemned Sherman's callousness. Sherman justified his conduct as an expedient to remove potential guerrillas from his new base of operations. In his view, guerrillas violated the accepted norms of warfare and must be mercilessly suppressed wherever they were found.

Confederate civilians were enemies, too, Sherman believed. "I am not willing to have Atlanta encumbered by the families of our enemies," he told Halleck. "I want it a pure Gibraltar." Sherman, brilliant and sometimes erratic, had a gift for distilling his beliefs into crisp aphorisms.

In October 1864, as Sherman's men began methodically burning depots, shops, factories, foundries, and most of the Atlanta's business district prefatory to leaving on their three-hundred-mile march, the general shared some of his dark musings on warfare with Sheridan. "The problem of this war consists in the awful fact that the present class of men who rule the South must be killed outright rather than in the conquest of territory, so that hard, bull-dog fighting, and a great deal of it, yet remains to be done." Later, as he led his 62,000-man army across eastern Georgia to the sea, with smoke billowing into the sky in its wake, Sherman explained to Major General George Thomas, "I propose to demonstrate the vulnerability of the South and make its inhabitants feel that war and individual ruin are synonymous terms."[14]

SHERIDAN'S VICTORIES AT WINCHESTER and Fisher's Hill in September had wholly reversed the situation in the Shenandoah Valley. As recently as July, Early's army had controlled the upper Potomac River and menaced Washington. Sheridan had sent Early backpedaling sixty miles. As Grant wrote in his congratulatory telegram after Fisher's Hill, "It wipes out much of the stain upon our arms by previous disasters in that locality."

But Sheridan had not destroyed Early's army. Although hopelessly outnumbered—even more so after Sheridan received 5,000 reinforcements—the Army of the Valley yet remained a dangerous weapon, especially with the return of Major

General Joseph Kershaw's division and the arrival of Brigadier General Thomas Rosser, commanding the Laurel Brigade. The brigade's 7th Virginia Cavalry Regiment had covered itself with glory during Stonewall Jackson's 1862 campaign, and Valley residents hoped that it would once more distinguish itself against Sheridan.[15]

Early, however, could not count on receiving many more men from Robert E. Lee, straitjacketed by the Army of the Potomac's siege at Petersburg. Tethered to the Petersburg-Richmond area and receiving few replacements for the men lost during the Union Army's Overland Campaign, Lee was unable either to prevent Sherman from rampaging through Georgia or to send Early more than token reinforcements. Grant's siege liberated Sherman and Sheridan to wage campaigns of destruction without Lee's interference.[16]

REBEL PARTISANS STEPPED UP the pressure while Early regrouped. They laid ambushes and struck without warning, often at night, pillaging supply trains and bushwhacking and killing Union soldiers caught out alone on the roads. The murders of their comrades stoked a hunger for vengeance among Sheridan's men.

From the time Sheridan received Grant's August 17 order to visit destruction upon Loudoun County, he had also quietly carried out another, more sinister program: the cold-blooded killing of guerrillas, wherever he encountered them. "Mosby has annoyed me and captured a few wagons. We hung one and shot six of his men yesterday," he reported. On August 19, Sheridan informed Grant, "Guerrillas give me great annoyance, but I am quietly disposing of numbers of them." Three days later, he wrote to Grant, "We have disposed of quite a number of Mosby's men."[17]

The thorn in Sheridan's side was John Mosby, commander of the 43rd Battalion, Virginia Cavalry, the partisan ranger unit better known as Mosby's Rangers that had grown to regimental size. In 1864, Mosby was thirty years old; Douglas Southall Freeman describes him in *Lee's Lieutenants* as gaunt, thin-lipped, and "stoop-necked," with a "satirical smile" and "strange, roving eyes." Before the war, Mosby, like Early, had been a lawyer who opposed Virginia's secession. When the fighting began, Mosby became a scout for Jeb Stuart, and in 1863 he was given command of the Rangers. The "Gray Ghost"—so nicknamed for his uncanny ability to elude pursuers and melt into the countryside—and his three hundred men were heroes to the Valley's loyal Confederates and to people across the large swath of northern Virginia known as Mosby's Confederacy.

While Mosby's Rangers were the best-known partisans, other bands were led by Harry Gilmer, James Kincheloe, John McNeill, Charles T. O'Ferrall, and Robert White. Even taken together, the various Confederate ranger forays did not materially interfere with the campaigns of Sheridan or Grant. Still they were a needling reminder that the invading Yankees did not completely control the territory they occupied.[18]

ON AUGUST 18, LIEUTENANT Colonel William Chapman, Mosby's second in command, killed a 5th Michigan Cavalry vedette who fired on Chapman when he demanded the Yankee's surrender. Assuming that partisans had ambushed the trooper, George Custer ordered the 5th Michigan to burn homes near where the shooting had occurred. When Chapman and his men, still in the area, observed thirty Union cavalrymen burning homes, they attacked. A few of the troopers escaped, but twenty-five were trapped and forced to surrender. Under orders to kill home burners, Mosby's Rangers shot all twenty-five prisoners and left their bodies on the ground. The headline of the *New York Times* account of the killings read, "Massacre by Mosby—Rebel Treachery—Cowardly Cruelty."[19]

ON SEPTEMBER 23, A band of Mosby's Rangers led by Captain Samuel Chapman pounced on a Union ambulance train outside Front Royal. Too late, they spotted a brigade from Brigadier General Wesley Merritt's 1st Cavalry Division nearby; Merritt's men came to the train's rescue. As the partisans raced toward Chester Gap, a small Union detachment led by Lieutenant Charles McMaster tried to block their escape. In the melee, McMaster fell to the ground, riddled with bullets, and was trampled by the partisans' horses during their flight.

When Union cavalrymen found McMaster's body, they concluded that he was killed after he had surrendered. In retribution, the Yankees shot four partisan captives and hanged two others on a hill overlooking Front Royal. A placard was draped over one of the hanged men. It read, "This will be the fate of Mosby and all his men."[20]

PARTISANS SWEPT DOWN ON an ambulance escorted by Union cavalry behind Union lines. When the shooting stopped, VI Corps quartermaster Cornelius Tolles and Dr. Emil Ohlenschlager, the corps' medical director, had been mortally wounded. In reprisal, some of Colonel William Powell's 2nd Cavalry Division troopers hanged a Mosby Ranger, Absalom Willis, with a placard reading, "Hanged by the neck in retaliation for the murder of a U.S. soldier."

Powell announced that henceforth two partisans would be shot or hanged for every Union soldier killed, and "if two is not sufficient I will increase it to 22 to one." Not long after that, Mosby and his men derailed and burned a train on the B&O Railroad and robbed a group of Union paymasters of $168,000 in cash.[21]

LIEUTENANT JOHN MEIGS WAS the Army of the Shenandoah's chief engineering officer and one of the Union army's most talented mapmakers. During Sheridan's first days in the Valley, Meigs had tutored him in the area's topography; he had since become one of Sheridan's favorite subordinate officers.

It had rained all day on October 3. Meigs and two orderlies had spent the daylight hours in rain slickers, mapping the Harrisonburg area and plotting the Army of the Shenandoah's positions so that Sheridan could move his men quickly. At dusk, while riding on a public road between Dayton and Harrisonburg on their way to camp, they overtook three mounted men dressed in blue uniforms. Believing the riders to be comrades, Meigs and his companions joined them. The strangers, however, were Rebel scouts from Brigadier General William Wickham's cavalry brigade.

Accounts differ over what happened next, but the outcome was clear: when the gun smoke cleared, Meigs lay dead in the muddy road, and one of his companions had been taken prisoner. The third surveyor managed to escape. He raced to Sheridan's headquarters to report that the Rebels had killed Meigs without warning as he cried, "Don't shoot me!"

Sheridan believed the surveyor's account, true or not. Not only had he lost his prized topographer, who had become somewhat like a son to the bachelor general, but the shooting had occurred a mere mile and a half from headquarters and inside Union lines—suggesting to Sheridan that the Confederates had been visiting their homes in the area. Sheridan vowed to "teach a lesson to these abettors of the foul deed—a lesson they would never forget." The next day, he ordered all the homes within five miles burned to the ground.

Anticipating just this eventuality, the Rebels had released their prisoner on the condition that he tell Sheridan what had actually happened. According to the Confederate scouts, they had gotten the drop on Meigs and his assistants. The two survivors had thrown up their hands, but Meigs had fired a pistol from beneath his slicker, wounding Private George Martin in the groin. Martin's companions had then shot Meigs.[22]

The burn area included the town of Dayton, which erupted in frenzied activity when residents were told what was planned. Some of the women threw their arms around the necks of the Yankees, begging for mercy. Although required to carry out Sheridan's order, some soldiers helped citizens remove their possessions from their homes. Before long, Dayton's main street was jammed with wagons piled high with furniture and clothing—all streaming out of the village.

But before Dayton could be consigned to the flames, Sheridan—persuaded either by the released prisoner's report or, according to another account, by the pleadings of his subordinate officers—rescinded the burn order. Instead, he ordered buildings burned near the site where Meigs was shot and the arrest as war prisoners of all able-bodied men in the area. But the Yankees' hatred of the Rebel partisans and their protectors continued to boil.[23]

FLUNG BACK BY EARLY'S troops near Waynesboro, to which the Rebels had withdrawn after Fisher's Hill, Torbert's cavalrymen on September 29 began driving off livestock and burning crops and farm buildings in the rich farmland between Staunton and Waynesboro. They killed livestock and put barns, mills, and foundries to the torch. A young schoolteacher wrote with bitter sarcasm, "Truly the great? [*sic*] General Sheridan has achieved a wonderful victory over the helpless women and children of the Valley of Virginia." At the same time, a *New York Herald* reporter triumphantly wrote, "We destroyed enough wheat to subsist the whole rebel army for a year to come."[24]

But this was only a foretaste of the widespread destruction that commenced on the day that Torbert's cavalry reached Harrisonburg, with the memory of Meigs's murder still fresh.

LIKE A FISHERMAN'S NET, the cavalry spread out behind Sheridan's infantrymen on October 6 as they marched down the Valley toward Winchester. One of the bleakest chapters of the war now began.

The cavalrymen drove off all livestock and destroyed crops, barns, and outbuildings in their path, at last fulfilling Grant's August 26 instructions to the letter. "If the war is to last another year," he had written, "we want the Shenandoah Valley to remain a barren waste."[25] The Union cavalrymen had endured too many bush-whackings to "shrink from the duty," Wesley Merritt wrote. Rebel partisans and highwaymen, he said, "had committed numerous murders and wanton acts of cruelty on all parties weaker than themselves. Officers and men had been murdered in cold blood on the roads."

The invaders "came up the Valley sweeping everything before them like a hurricane," wrote one resident. "There was nothing left for man or beast from the horse down to the chicken." Taking burning brands from victims' fireplaces, the Yankees set fire to their barns, mills, and outbuildings. A newspaper correspondent wrote, "The atmosphere, from horizon to horizon, has been black with the smoke of a hundred conflagrations, and at night a gleam brighter and more lurid than sunset has shot from every verge. . . . The completeness of the devastation is awful."

Spared ruin were the homesteads of Dunkards and Mennonites. They were loyal to the Union, as were members of those sects everywhere, because of their unbending hatred of slavery. But many of them wanted to leave the Valley and asked for Sheridan's assistance; they feared that if they remained, the Rebels would return and draft them into the Confederate army. Peter Hartman, one of the supplicants, described Sheridan as "the most savage looking man I ever saw" but approvingly observed that he gave each of them a horse from the army's herd.[26]

Sheridan watched the methodical destruction with approval. "As we marched along the many columns of smoke from burning stacks, and mills filled with grain, indicated that the adjacent country was fast losing the features which hitherto had made it a great magazine of stores for the Confederate armies," he wrote.[27] Like Grant and Sherman, he believed that by obliterating the Confederate granary, destroying the fighting spirit of its people, and crippling the Confederacy's ability to recover, they would end the war sooner and save lives. "There is more mercy in destroying supplies than in killing their young men. . . . If I had a barn full of wheat and a son, I would much sooner lose the barn and wheat than my son," Sheridan wrote. Until the end of his life, Sheridan remained convinced that this was the right choice.[28]

Not all the combat veterans obeyed the orders to burn and destroy. Lacking a taste for vandalism, some of them applied the torch sparingly. A detachment from the 2nd Ohio Cavalry left many barns standing in its area of operation, and other units, too, made less than a clean sweep.

Some of those who most distinguished themselves on the battlefield made the poorest incendiaries. Yet, most of the Union troopers did their job, disagreeable as they may have found it. They worked fast. One officer blew a whistle when it was time for his men to move on to the next farm.

Some residents fought back. One man shot and killed a Union officer and threw the man's body into his burning barn. Another farmer stood on a haystack and fired steadily at a column of Yankees until they riddled him with bullets.[29]

MAJOR JAMES KIDD OF the 6th Michigan Cavalry had painstakingly labored to get some grain mills in the area up and running, and they were producing flour for Kidd's cavalrymen when Merritt ordered them burned. "The wheels were not stopped but the torch was applied and the crackling of flames intermingled with the rumbling of the stones made a mournful requiem," wrote Kidd. Women and children pleaded with the soldiers for some flour before the mills were burned, but they received none.

As Kidd and his men watched, the flames spread beyond the mills and threatened homes. "Women with children in their arms stood in the street and gazed frantically upon the threatened ruin of their homes, while the tears rained down their cheeks." Kidd ordered his men to prevent the homes from burning. The homes were saved.[30]

Custer's men executed a civilian found in the woods with a rifle. They killed him even after a merchant told them the man was developmentally disabled. Afterward, the merchant warned Custer with remarkable prescience, "You will have to sleep in a bloody grave for this."[31]

At the end of the second day of the scorched-earth march, Sheridan was able to report to Grant from Woodstock,

In moving back to this point the whole country from the Blue Ridge to the North Mountain has been made untenable for a rebel army. I have destroyed over two thousand barns filled with wheat, hay & farming implements, over seventy mills filled with flour & wheat, have driven in front of the army over 4,000 head of stock and have killed & issued to the troops not less than 3,000 sheep. . . . Tomorrow I will continue the destruction of wheat, forage Etc., down to Fisher's Hill. When this is completed the valley from Winchester up to Staunton, 92 miles, will have but little in it for man or beast.[32]

Loyal Confederate citizens bitterly denounced the systematic ruin of the Valley. Mrs. Hugh Lee of Winchester wrote in her diary, "Sheridan-Sheridan, what demon of destruction has possessed you? God grant that you may meet with a righteous compensation."

The *Richmond Whig* urged reprisals. "They chose to substitute the torch for the sword. We may so use their own weapon as to make them repent." The *Whig* proposed burning a Northern city in retaliation. "It is a game at which we can beat them. New York is worth twenty Richmonds."[33]

The calculated destruction had an immediate impact on Early's army. He reported to Lee on October 9 that because nearly everything in his area of operation had gone up in smoke, "I will have to rely on Augusta [Georgia] for my supplies, and they are not abundant there." Until those supplies arrived, the Rebels were reduced to picking corn in the countryside and bartering labor for food. "Our mess is shucking corn for a farmer who will pay us for our services in flour," wrote Confederate Private Creed Davis in his diary.[34]

BRIGADIER GENERAL THOMAS ROSSER'S Laurel Brigade trailed Sheridan's army as the Yankees burned and destroyed. Rosser, twenty-seven, was a West Point classmate and friend of George Custer. Until he was severely wounded in 1862, Rosser was an artillery officer and best known for having shot down a Union observation balloon. Returning to duty, he was given command of a cavalry regiment and quickly made a reputation for daring attacks, much like his former classmate.

His proud cavalrymen wore laurel sprigs in their hats, just as members of Custer's Wolverine Brigade had adopted the red cravat as its signature, in imitation of their leader. At Trevilian Station, Rosser was wounded again while leading his brigade against Custer's. The friends were fated to soon meet in battle once more.[35]

The Valley's Confederate loyalists anointed Rosser the "Savior of the Valley" before his men had even fired a shot—so desperate were they to believe that Sheridan might yet be driven off and their farmsteads preserved. Early demonstrated his confidence in Rosser by giving him Fitzhugh Lee's two brigades while Lee recovered from wounds suffered at Winchester. With his division of 3,000 men, Rosser skirmished with Sheridan's rearguard—Custer's division—near Brock's Gap on October 6, the day "the Burning" commenced. Operating nearby, but independently, was Early's other cavalry division, commanded by Brigadier General Lunsford Lomax. The two divisions reported separately to Early and had little contact with one another.[36]

On October 7, the thick smoke from the smoldering fields and barns so cloaked both armies that Rosser fell upon Sheridan's rear before either side was even aware of the other's presence. Inspired by their "hatred of the wretches" destroying their food supply, the Rebels scattered Sheridan's cavalrymen and pursued them for miles. Rosser's division continued to follow the Union army north toward Strasburg. When his men bivouacked on October 8, a Union cavalry force was camped nearby, on the other side of Tom's Brook.[37]

SHERIDAN HAD BECOME INCREASINGLY exasperated with Rosser's terrier-like rushes on his rear. During the night of October 8, Sheridan's impatience boiled over, and the fiery general stalked off in search of Torbert, his cavalry commander, to prod him into acting "to open the enemy's eyes in earnest."

He stormed into Torbert's headquarters just as Torbert and his staff were finishing a turkey dinner. Captain George Sanford, a Torbert aide, wrote that Sheridan angrily burst out, "If you ain't sitting here stuffing yourselves, general, staff and all, while the Rebels are riding into our camp! Having a party, while Rosser is carrying off your guns! Got on your nice clothes and clean shirts! Torbert, mount quicker than hell will scorch a feather! I want you to go out there in the morning and whip that Rebel cavalry or get whipped yourself!"[38]

Until this was done, Sheridan continued, the infantry would not march another mile. He announced that he would ride at daybreak the next morning to the summit of Round Top Mountain to watch Torbert give Rosser his "drubbing." To Grant, Sheridan wrote, "I deemed it best to make this delay of one day here and settle this new cavalry general."[39]

AS THE SUN POKED above the hills on October 9, Custer's 3rd Division faced Rosser's troopers at Tom's Brook Crossing. Custer rode along his line, making sure his brigades were ready for battle. Then, turning toward where Rosser was watching through his field glasses, Custer raised his hat and made a deep bow to his old West Point friend. The men of both armies cheered loudly. It was one of many such instances of Custer's chivalry in battle.

Bugles blared, and Custer's men began to advance. One of Rosser's brigades suddenly burst into the middle of the bluecoats, stopping their forward movement. Custer's seasoned veterans regrouped and renewed their assault. Simultaneously, Merritt's 1st Division fell upon Lomax's two brigades nearby on the Valley Turnpike.

It was open country, ideal for an old-fashioned cavalry fight on horseback with sabers and pistols—as well as for artillery. From Round Top Mountain, Sheridan intently watched the charges and countercharges.

Two hours into the battle, Rosser's flanks collapsed, and Merritt and Custer mounted a great concerted charge along the entire front. The Rebel cavalry, outnumbered two to one, buckled and sagged. Then there was, as Sheridan triumphantly noted, "a general smash-up of the entire Confederate line." A *Philadelphia Inquirer* reporter who witnessed the battle wrote, "It was a square cavalry fight in which the enemy was routed beyond my power to describe."[40]

The rout became a "wild stampede." Some Rebel cavalrymen stopped along the way to offer brief, but futile, resistance before continuing their flight—past Woodstock, all the way to Mount Jackson, twenty miles away. Sheridan's men nicknamed the rollicking pursuit the "Woodstock Races."

The Yankees captured eleven guns, all of the Rebel cavalry's wagons and ambulances, and three hundred prisoners. Sheridan reported that some of the guns had never been fired and were stamped "Tredegar Works," the name of the Richmond foundry where they were made. In one of the captured wagons, the men found an ambrotype of Libbie Custer that had been lost at Trevilian Station.[41]

The ignominious flight of the Rebel cavalry was an embarrassment to Rosser, Lomax, Early, and everyone involved. George Neese, a gunner in the horse artillery, wrote, "The shameful way that our cavalry . . . fought, bled, and died a-running rearward was enough to make its old commander, General J.E.B. Stuart, weep in his grave."[42]

The Laurel Brigade had never lost a battle until Tom's Brook, and the men were "all very sore about it." Rosser complained that Early should not have pressured him to attack a larger force without infantry and that the disjointed command structure prevented him from directly communicating with Lomax.[43]

"This is very distressing to me," Early wrote in his report to Robert E. Lee. His cavalry, he said, was outnumbered and poorly equipped compared with the Yankees' mounted troops. "It would be better if they could all be put into the infantry; but if that were tried, I am afraid they would all run off."[44]

MOSBY SOUGHT ROBERT E. Lee's permission to avenge the executions of Willis and the six men at Front Royal. He mistakenly believed that Custer had ordered the Front Royal executions, when Merritt and Torbert had done so. "It is my purpose to hang an equal number of Custer's men whenever I capture them," Mosby told Lee. After consulting with the Confederate War Department, Lee authorized Mosby to carry out the revenge killings.

From a prison warehouse in Rectortown, twenty-seven Union captives, some of them Custer's men, were marched to the banks of a creek and ordered to draw slips of paper from a hat. Twenty of them drew blanks; seven drew numbered slips that condemned them to death. Those seven were taken to a place near Custer's headquarters. Three were hanged, two were shot but lived, and two were permitted to escape by guards who had no stomach for cold-blooded executions. Pinned to one corpse was a note reading, "These men have been hung in retaliation for an equal number of Colonel Mosby's men hung by order of General Custer, at Front Royal, Measure for Measure."[45]

In his letter informing Sheridan of the executions, Mosby extended an olive branch with one hand while grasping a sword with the other. "Hereafter, any prisoners falling into my hands will be treated with the kindness due to their condition, unless some act of barbarity shall compel me, reluctantly, to adopt a line of policy repugnant to humanity." There is no record of any reply by Sheridan, and his *Personal Memoirs* do not mention Mosby's personal letter. However, no reprisals were made for Mosby's executions of the Yankee prisoners. The cycle of revenge killings began to wind down, although Sheridan had not yet finished his business with Mosby.[46]

HAVING ROUTED THE "SAVIOR of the Valley" at Tom's Brook, Sheridan's army resumed its march down the Shenandoah. On October 10, it crossed Cedar Creek and camped on its north bank, south of Middletown—all except Major General Horatio Wright's VI Corps and William Powell's 2nd Cavalry Division.

Powell's troopers embarked on a raid toward Charlottesville and Gordonsville, while VI Corps marched into Middletown and then turned east toward Front Royal. Sheridan informed Grant on October 12 that Wright's men were on their way to Alexandria, Virginia, and would thence travel by steamship to Petersburg to join Grant's army. "I believe that a rebel advance down the valley will not take place," he wrote.

But the next day, Early's army unexpectedly appeared at Strasburg, just a few miles from Cedar Creek, and shelled XIX Corps's camp. Two brigades from Crook's VIII Corps forded Cedar Creek to assay the Rebels' strength. Kershaw's division provided the answer by driving them back to their camp during a one-hour fight.

Fearing that Early intended to attack now that VI Corps had left, Sheridan recalled the corps to Cedar Creek and laid plans for an assault on Early. When Early abruptly withdrew his army to Fisher's Hill, however, Sheridan canceled the attack.

Powell's two brigades rode south toward Gordonsville but turned back thirty-five miles short of their objective without engaging the Rebel cavalry in the area. The raid accomplished nothing.

Sheridan's actions during the weeks after Fisher's Hill mystified Confederate major general John Gordon. "Why did he halt or hesitate, why turn to the torch in the hope of starving his enemy, instead of beating him in resolute battle?" Gordon wondered. "Why did General Sheridan hesitate to hurl his inspirited and overwhelming army on us?"

Sheridan had not taken the fight to Early, so Early intended to bring it to Sheridan. As the Army of the Valley settled into its old rifle pits on Fisher's Hill, Brigadier General Stephen Dodson Ramseur wrote to his brother-in-law, "We are all called on to show that we are made of the true metal. Let us be brave, cheerful, and truthful. Remembering that Might is not Right."[47]

OCTOBER 18, 1864–THREE TOP MOUNTAIN, OVERLOOKING CEDAR CREEK— Such a bold plan of attack had rarely been hazarded. Confederate major general John Gordon and Jedediah Hotchkiss, the Confederate army's foremost topographer, had excitedly sketched its bare outlines while descending Three Top Mountain, the northernmost part of Massanutten Mountain. Three Top overlooked Strasburg, Front Royal, and, most importantly, Phil Sheridan's Army of the Shenandoah, whose encampment was spread over the ridges and low plateaus that rippled northwestward from Cedar Creek and the Shenandoah River's North Fork.

At the request of Jubal Early, whose arthritis prevented him from joining them, Gordon, Hotchkiss, Brigadier General Clement Evans, and Gordon's chief of staff, Major Robert Hunter, had surmounted boulders and steep cliffs to reach the summit of Three Top, the location of the Confederate signal station. It was a fine autumn day, and through their field glasses, the men had a superb view of the bluecoat camps, their breastworks, pickets, and vedettes. Gordon was able to count the Yankees' guns. "I could see distinctly the three colors of trimmings on the jackets respectively of infantry, artillery, and cavalry," he wrote. Hotchkiss drew a map of it all.

The difficult descent and the ride back to Fisher's Hill gave Hotchkiss and Gordon time to discuss an intriguing idea: a surprise attack. Having beat the Rebels at Winchester, Fisher's Hill, and Tom's Brook, the last thing Sheridan's army would expect was an attack by Early's battered army—especially since it had just withdrawn to Fisher's Hill from positions close to Cedar Creek. When the survey party returned to Fisher's Hill, Early summoned all of his generals to a meeting.[48]

John Gordon had spent his boyhood in northern Georgia near Chickamauga Creek on land appropriated from Cherokee chief John Ross after his forced exile on the Trail of Tears. Smart and articulate, Gordon became a lawyer. When the war broke out, he joined a mountaineer regiment. Although Gordon had no military training, he was fearless, aggressive, and a natural leader. He rose rapidly through the Confederate army's ranks.

Gordon had fought at First Manassas, in the Seven Days battles, then at Antietam (where he was wounded several times), Gettysburg, the Wilderness, and Spotsylvania

Court House before coming to the Valley with Early as a brigadier general and division commander. When Early was promoted to lieutenant general and named commander of the Army of the Valley, Gordon assumed leadership of Early's II Corps.

At the council of generals, Gordon argued for an immediate attack. Early needed little persuading; Sheridan's wholesale devastation of the Valley's fields, barns, mills, and livestock had destroyed Early's larder; his men were hungry. "I was now compelled to move back for want of provisions and forage, or attack the enemy in his position with the hope of driving him from it, and I determined to attack . . . by surprise if I could," Early wrote.[49]

From Three Top Mountain, Gordon had concluded that the Union left flank—anchored by George Crook's VIII Corps—was the Army of the Shenandoah's most vulnerable point. Opposite Crook, directly across Cedar Creek and the North Fork of the Shenandoah River, was the sheer northern face of double-domed Massanutten Mountain. With the mountain crowding against the waterways near Crook, it appeared a highly unlikely attack route. Sheridan and his generals would expect the Confederates to target the more accessible Union right flank, not its left. This was exactly why Early should attack Crook, Gordon believed.

Achieving surprise would be tricky. The Rebels must secretly bring a large assault force to the wagon road wedged between the base of Massanutten Mountain and the river. Gordon believed this was possible. He was convinced that if such an attack could be properly executed and pressed to completion, "the destruction of Sheridan's army was inevitable."

Gordon's plan was a brilliant gamble—and one that Early was willing to take. If the attack broke Sheridan's army, Early might once more threaten Washington, as he had three months earlier, and stampede Northern voters into rejecting Abraham Lincoln in the coming election. Lincoln's successor might agree to a negotiated peace with the Confederacy.[50]

WHEN EARLY HAD SUDDENLY reappeared at Strasburg, Sheridan had recalled VI Corps, after first starting the 15,000 men to Grant at Petersburg. But then Early had withdrawn to Fisher's Hill, and the threat had seemingly receded.

On October 12, War Secretary Edwin Stanton requested that Sheridan come to Washington to consult with him before Stanton sailed to City Point for discussions with Grant.[51] Major General Henry Halleck, the army's chief of staff, followed Stanton's message with a telegram reporting that no new Rebel reinforcements had been sent from Richmond to Early, although he peevishly added that he had "very little confidence in the information collected at [Grant's] headquarters. If you can leave your command with safety, come to Washington as I wish to give you the views of the authorities here," Halleck wrote.[52]

The outstanding issue was Grant's and Sheridan's standing disagreement over the Army of the Shenandoah's next move. Sheridan wished to man a strong defensive line in the northern Valley and to send most of his army to Grant. But Grant persisted in prodding—but never ordering—Sheridan to march on Charlottesville and Gordonsville in order to destroy the Virginia Central Railroad and James River canal, then to advance on Richmond from the west. He had repeatedly proposed this movement since August. Each time, Sheridan had demurred.[53]

Grant's plan was undoubtedly sound strategy, for if Sheridan succeeded, he would threaten Richmond and Petersburg from the west while Grant kept up pressure from the southeast. Richmond might fall, and with it the Confederacy. But Sheridan, unwilling to risk ceding the Valley to Early, balked.

CHAPTER 9

Miracle at Cedar Creek

OCTOBER 1864

Such a scene as his presence produced and such emotions as it
awoke cannot be realized but once in a century . . . a pressure of
emotion beyond description.

—MAJOR ALDACE WALKER DESCRIBING SHERIDAN'S
RETURN TO CEDAR CREEK AFTER THE REBEL ATTACK[1]

PHILIP SHERIDAN DEPARTED FOR WASHINGTON the evening of October 15 to consult with War Secretary Edwin Stanton and Major General Henry Halleck. Sheridan's cavalry commander, Major General Alfred Torbert, and some cavalry units accompanied him from his headquarters at the Belle Grove mansion near Cedar Creek. At Front Royal, Torbert planned to join Colonel William Powell's two brigades for a major cavalry expedition to Charlottesville and Gordonsville, while Sheridan continued to Washington.

But Sheridan had no sooner reached Front Royal than a courier galloped up with a note from Major General Horatio Wright, the VI Corps commander whom Sheridan had left in charge in his absence. Union signal officers, Wright reported, had intercepted a message that was being relayed by semaphore from the Rebel signal station on Three Top Mountain:

To Lieutenant-General Early:

Be ready to move as soon as my forces join you, and we will crush Sheridan.

Longstreet, Lieutenant-General.

Wright's accompanying note expressed his concern that the Confederates were planning to attack. With a strong cavalry force, Jubal Early might turn his right flank, he wrote, and "give us a great deal of trouble. I shall hold on here until the enemy's movements are developed, and shall only fear an attack on my right."[2]

Sheridan was highly skeptical. He believed the message was a canard "and hardly worth attention." *[1] But if it happened to be true that James Longstreet—whom Sheridan, perhaps remembering Chickamauga, regarded as "one of the ablest of the Confederate generals"—was on his way, Wright would need every available man. Sheridan postponed the Gordonsville raid and sent Torbert and his cavalrymen back to Wright, keeping one regiment to escort him and his staff officers to the railroad that would take them to Washington.

"The cavalry is all ordered back to you; make your position strong," he counseled Wright. "If the enemy should make an advance, I know you will defeat him. Look well to your ground and be well prepared." He promised to return in two days, if not sooner.[3]

CEDAR CREEK RISES IN the foothills of the Allegheny Mountains and crosses the Shenandoah Valley. Meadow Brook, at the bottom of a deep ravine, empties into Cedar Creek three-fourths of a mile west of the Valley Turnpike; two miles north of the turnpike bridge is Middletown. Cedar Creek continues eastward through Strasburg, where it is thirty yards wide, shallow, and fast. About a mile east of Strasburg, it joins the North Fork of the Shenandoah River and sweeps around the base of Massanutten Mountain.

East of the Valley Turnpike, Cedar Creek's banks are sharp and steep. Rippling northwestward from the creek is a series of densely wooded ridges and plateaus. Here the Army of the Shenandoah rested in idle watchfulness along a five-mile line.

"Cedar Creek was a good place for water, but a bad place for a fight," observed a Massachusetts soldier. "Very crooked, fordable, but with steep banks difficult for

---

* In 1890, Early admitted in a letter to Richard Bache Irwin, author of *History of the Nineteenth Army Corps*, that he had written the message and sent it under an older code that the Rebels knew the Yankees had broken, certain that Union Signal Corps personnel were watching. His object was to discourage Sheridan from sending troops to Petersburg. See Richard Bache Irwin, *History of the Nineteenth Corps* (New York and London: G. P. Putnam's Sons, 1892), 407.

artillery or wagons," except at the fords where ramps had been carved out, noted Major James Kidd of the 6th Michigan Cavalry. The Yankees would discover that the folded, grooved terrain was difficult ground on which to maneuver.[4]

MAJOR GENERAL JOHN GORDON's plan of attack would certainly achieve over-whelming surprise—if it in fact worked. Nothing so audacious had been attempted during the war: a dawn attack, its preparations cloaked in secrecy, by 18,000 men against a wholly unsuspecting enemy numbering up to 40,000, after an all-night march that included fording two rivers. If Gordon's plan succeeded, it would not only turn upside down the balance of power in the Valley but might well be the war's most glittering triumph.

In the Union camps north of Cedar Creek, October 18 ended with a striking crimson sunset. Trumpeters from the 1st Connecticut Cavalry played "Home Sweet Home" and "The Girl I Left Behind Me." The 2nd Ohio Cavalry glee club sang favorites around the campfire, including "Lorena."[5]

Shortly after 8 p.m., the 9,000 infantrymen of Gordon's II Corps—three divi-sions led by Major Generals Stephen Dodson Ramseur and John Pegram and Brigadier General Clement Evans (commanding the late Robert Rodes's division)—crossed the Valley Turnpike near Fisher's Hill. In near-complete silence, forbidden to carry any equipment that rattled, the men forded the North Fork of the Shenan-doah River. The cold water and the piercing nighttime chill of October in the mountains were sharply unpleasant, but without complaint the ragged, sinewy Rebels marched all night to their staging area. Under the waning gibbous moon, they followed a narrow footpath to the base of Massanutten Mountain and a wagon road along the south bank of Cedar Creek.

Gordon had taken the precaution of posting guides at every fork along the route and at every creek ford to point the way for the Rebel foot soldiers. The men spoke in whispers when they spoke at all. A hundred yards or so beyond where Cedar Creek joined the Shenandoah River, the Confederates halted. They waited for the cold gleam of daybreak and the signal to cross the Shenandoah a second time and begin the assault.

CROSSING THE TURNPIKE BEHIND Gordon's corps, Major General Joseph Ker-shaw's 3,000-man division skirted the northwestern bank of the Shenandoah River and halted on the south bank of Cedar Creek upstream from Gordon. On a ridge a mile to the north slumbered Colonel Joseph Thoburn's forward-posted division of George Crook's VIII Corps.

Early had direct command of Kershaw's and Brigadier General Gabriel Whar-ton's divisions. Wharton's men, with Brigadier General Lunsford Lomax's cavalry, quietly waited north of Strasburg, ready to lunge northward up the Valley Turnpike.

Across the Cedar Creek bridge and along the road was Major General William Emory's XIX Corps, between VIII Corps on the Union left and VI Corps on the right.

At the same time, Thomas Rosser was poised to lead two cavalry brigades against Wesley Merritt's and George Custer's mounted divisions on the Union far right. It was a feint, designed to trick the Yankees into bracing for an all-out attack on their right flank, while the Rebels delivered a paralyzing blow to the Union left.

It was a complex plan meshing four assault groups—and four objectives to be struck simultaneously miles apart. Early and Gordon were also flouting two cardinal rules of offensive warfare: attackers should outnumber defenders, and one should never divide his army in the face of the enemy. In a few hours, they would learn if their shoot-the-moon gamble had paid off.

By 4:30 a.m. on October 19—the eighty-third anniversary of Lieutenant General Lord Cornwallis's surrender at Yorktown—everyone was in place. And then something unplanned occurred: a swaddling fog reduced visibility to the length of one's arm and muffled and distorted sound. The conditions favored surprise and confusion.

In the murky half light, Rebel officers turned away from the river to strike a match and check their watches as the minutes ticked down to the moment of attack. "The whole situation was unspeakably impressive," wrote Gordon. "Everything conspired to make the conditions both thrilling and weird."[6]

CROOK'S MOUNTED PICKETS, ASTRIDE horses standing in the river shallows with water churning around their hooves, heard Gordon's men moving in the fog, despite the Rebels' precautions against making noise. They dutifully reported the movement to headquarters. Crook placed his command on alert but sent no one out to investigate. "Not a private in the army, and hardly an officer . . . believed that the often-beaten and badly-beaten Early would venture an attack," wrote Frank Flinn of the 38th Massachusetts Infantry.[7]

At 5:30 a.m., Colonel William Payne's small Rebel cavalry brigade, pistols blazing, suddenly materialized before Union vedettes in the swirling river fog. The Yankees, from Powell's division, took to their heels. The attack was the signal for Gordon's divisions, poised to cross the Shenandoah at Bowman's Ford, to plunge in. To the west, Kershaw's division splashed across Cedar Creek, and Wharton's men began marching down the Valley Pike toward the Cedar Creek bridge. The Army of the Valley had launched its attack.[8]

THE SHENANDOAH RIVER WAS chest deep and freezing. Gordon's men emerged from the waters at Bowman's Ford gasping from cold and shivering in their soaked clothing. Their officers wasted no time in sending them jogging northward up a farm road. Without complaint, in fact grateful to be able to generate body heat to counter the effects of the freezing river water, II Corps rapidly covered a mile and a half.

When they were well behind and east of Thoburn's forward division—and within striking distance of the rest of Crook's VIII Corps near the Army of the Shenandoah's headquarters at Belle Grove mansion—they stopped, wheeled left, and waited silently. A few hundred yards to the west, but invisible in the fog, were two Union divisions, 7,500 men total, under Colonels J. Howard Kitching and Rutherford Hayes, the future nineteenth president. Gordon hoped to destroy them both and to make Sheridan his prisoner.[9]

Captain John De Forest, a XIX Corps staff officer, was in the saddle early to send off a reconnaissance in force to Fisher's Hill when he heard, coming from Crook's corps to his left, "a shrill prolonged wail of musketry . . . followed by scream on scream of the Rebel Yell." It was Kershaw's South Carolinians attacking Thoburn's division.

In less than five minutes—before many of the Yankees had time to get dressed— the Rebels were inside Thoburn's breastworks. "The men sprang from their tents, and fled without boots or clothing save what they had worn through the night," wrote Major Aldace Walker of the 11th Vermont Infantry, who witnessed the flight. "The very tents were pulled off from some as they lay in their blankets." A few managed to reach their breastworks without orders, ready to fight, but they were instantly flanked and taken in reverse. The Rebels captured seven guns before they could be fired.[10]

A few minutes later, Gordon's II Corps advanced in solid lines without skirmishers against Kitching's and Hayes's divisions. The Yankees' first awareness of the Rebels' presence dawned when Gordon's seven brigades emerged from the fog bank, running and shrieking their high-pitched foxhunter's yell. The bluecoats fell back in confusion. Some were trapped in a ravine and shot by the Rebels. "It looked like murder to kill them huddled up there," a Confederate soldier wrote.[11]

In just thirty minutes, Crook's "Buzzards"—the 9,000 men of VIII Corps—had been utterly routed. These were the same veteran troops who had spearheaded the triumphant attack at Fisher's Hill. Major Walker understood their panic. "A night surprise, total and terrific, is too trying for the morale of the best troops in the world to survive."[12]

Hayes's horse was shot out from under him as he vainly attempted to stem the onslaught; Hayes landed hard on the ground and was badly bruised. An aide lent Hayes his horse, and a short time later he was struck in the head with a spent minié ball, "a slight shock"—and his second battle wound of the war. The morning was a sobering turn of events for Hayes, who had recently enjoyed a period of good fortune. The Ohio lawyer had learned that he had been nominated in absentia for Congress and that his wife had given birth to a boy, their second. At Fisher's Hill, Hayes's division had led the decisive attack. Today, however, it was hurriedly retreating.[13]

THE COURAGEOUS ACTIONS OF a few bought precious time for their VIII Corps comrades to escape safely. Two batteries under Captain Henry DuPont, Crook's artillery commander, whose family business supplied the Union army with nearly half its gunpowder, held off Kershaw's Rebels for a short time. Some officers—including Wright, the VI Corps commander, bleeding profusely from a minié ball wound to the chin—rallied 1,500 of Crook's soldiers and made a stand between Belle Grove and the Valley Turnpike. They held off Gordon's columns for thirty minutes, enabling most of the army's wagon train to ride away to Middletown.[14]

The armies groped for one another through the miasmic fog, now considerably thicker with the addition of billowing clouds of gun smoke. At the attack's outset, the Confederates had had the distinct advantage of knowing where they were with respect to the enemy. But with everyone now in motion, they became nearly as disoriented as the Yankees. Directional momentum and their carefully drawn attack plan, however, yet favored the Confederates over the fumbling Yankees.[15]

FIFTEEN MINUTES PAST SUNRISE, and one hour into the battle, Kershaw's and Wharton's divisions, as well as Evans's division from II Corps, were converging on Major General William Emory's XIX Corps along a curved axis extending from the south to the northeast. Emory's two divisions were under arms and behind their breastworks. The heavy musketry and yelling on Thoburn's knoll a mile to the south had first awakened them to their danger. The sound from the subsequent fight at Belle Grove mansion had been noticeably closer, just a half mile to the east. Then, swarms of fleeing soldiers had streamed past. Now the gunfire had fallen off, but Emory's men could see gun flashes flickering through the fog—like lightning from an approaching storm.

Emory sent Colonel Stephen Thomas and three regiments straight into the juggernaut's path. In a densely wooded area, Thomas's brigade collided with Evans's division. They fought with clubbed muskets, bayonets, and bare hands—"more like demons than human beings," a Union soldier wrote. One-third of Thomas's infantrymen were killed or wounded in ten minutes; the 8th Vermont lost 106 of its 175 men. They "fought like tigers," Captain S. E. Howard proudly wrote of the Vermonters. The columns of Evans, Kershaw, and Wharton marched on. Minutes later, they slammed into XIX Corps's breastworks.[16]

Captain De Forest and other XIX Corps officers had tried to rally the remnants of Crook's three broken divisions as they drifted rearward "with curious deliberation . . . not in the least wild with fright, but discreetly seeking the best cover, slipping through hollows and woods, halting for rest and discourse behind buildings." The beaten men steadfastly ignored the officers' pleas to stop and fight, wrote Howard. "The chief trouble with them seems to be that they have got out of their places in the military machine," De Forest observed.[17]

VIII Corps's disintegration had placed the Rebels in positions overlooking the XIX Corps camp, transforming it "from a fortress into a slaughter pen." The Rebels drove Emory's troops from their breastworks in a frenzy of hand-to-hand fighting, blasted them with musket fire on the open ground, and drove the two divisions, brigade by brigade, from their positions. It was over in thirty minutes.

XIX Corps fell back in orderly fashion, retreating 1,000 yards at a time, turning and firing. The troops slid down the steep-sided banks of Meadow Creek, scaled the opposite bank, and threw up fieldworks on VI Corps's left flank. XIX Corps's path of retreat was clearly delineated by the profusion of men's bodies, horse carcasses, and blood, "in splashes . . . and zigzag trails," more than De Forest had ever seen before on a battlefield. "The firm limestone would not receive it, and there was no pitying summer grass to hide it."[18]

It was just 7:30 a.m., and Early's assault troops had swept away two of Sheridan's three infantry corps. Five Union divisions, or nearly 20,000 men, had astonishingly been wiped from the battlefield by a smaller Rebel force. Early's gamble had succeeded brilliantly.

VI Corps's three divisions were the Army of the Shenandoah's last hope of stemming the Confederate blitz. Early's army pounded two of them backward—those of Colonel J. Warren Keifer and Brigadier General Frank Wheaton. They joined the stream of refugees from VIII and XIX Corps.

That left just one intact Union infantry division south of Middletown: Major General George Getty's. When he saw that Wheaton's and Keifer's divisions were retreating and that the Rebel divisions of Ramseur, Wharton, and Pegram were closing in on him, Getty looked around for a better position.

Several hundred yards to the rear lay a crescent-shaped hill—the Middletown cemetery. "In perfect order," Getty's three brigades withdrew to the field of granite headstones and markers, while stolidly ignoring the "universal confusion and dismay . . . crowds of officers and men, some shod and some barefoot, many of them coatless and hatless . . . all rushing wildly to the rear; oaths and blows alike powerless to halt them; a cavalry regiment stretched across the field, unable to stem the torrent. . . . It was a sight that might have demoralized the Old Guard of the first Napoleon."[19]

Minutes after positioning his men in strong, horseshoe-shaped works in the cemetery, Getty glimpsed Pegram's 1,700-man division advancing in solid lines through the thinning fog. He ordered his 4,000 men to hold their fire until the Rebels running up the slope toward them were thirty yards away. The eruption of musketry sent Pegram's troops reeling backward. Getty's division instantly counterattacked, driving the Rebels across Meadow Brook. Early ordered a second assault by Pegram and a third by Wharton's division. All of the attacks failed to dislodge Getty.

Getty's stand was the first time that Sheridan's troops had stopped the Rebels that morning. The gritty fight in the cemetery had also distracted Early from marching up the Valley Turnpike and severing the Union army's path of retreat. About an hour after it deployed in the cemetery, Getty's division began an orderly withdrawal as Rebel gunners began zeroing in on them.[20]

THE IRASCIBLE, ARTHRITIS-TORMENTED EARLY, who had suffered defeat upon defeat over the past month, experienced an exquisite moment of exhilaration as he and his staff neared Middletown. For once, everything was going Early's way. Even the fog was now lifting, as though sensing that the Rebels no longer needed it.

Captain S. V. Southall, a staff officer, watched Early's face become "radiant with joy" upon receiving another piece of good news. Early suddenly exclaimed, "The sun of Middletown! The sun of Middletown!" remembering Napoleon Bonaparte's famous cry at Austerlitz in 1805 when the sun emerged during his army's climactic attack on the Russo-Austrian forces.[21]

Getty's stand had given Horatio Wright time to send 7,500 cavalrymen and five horse artillery batteries to the Valley Turnpike north of Middletown to take up defensive positions. After Getty withdrew from the cemetery and Early's men resumed marching up the turnpike, they encountered Merritt's and Custer's cavalry divisions. Each approach by the Rebels was met by a torrent of gunfire from the Yankees' Spencer repeaters.

From Middletown, Early studied the Yankee cavalry, which potentially threatened his right flank, and the cemetery hill where Getty's division had repulsed three attacks. Gordon had just directed Colonel Thomas H. Carter, the chief artillery officer, to open fire on Getty's division—ultimately driving it off. Gordon intended to pursue Getty and VI Corps northward and destroy them.

Early rode up to Gordon. "Well, Gordon," he said, "this is glory enough for one day."

In his *Reminiscences of the Civil War*, Gordon wrote that he replied, "It is very well so far, general; but we have one more blow to strike, and then there will not be left an organized company of infantry in Sheridan's army." He told Early that he had sent Carter's artillery to bombard VI Corps.

Early responded, "No use in that; they will all go directly."

Gordon told Early that VI Corps would not go unless driven from the field.

"Yes, it will go too, directly," Early responded.

Gordon was stunned. "My heart went into my boots," he wrote. Gordon envisioned consequences as fatal as those attending the Confederates' failure to seize the high ground at Gettysburg on the first day or the hesitation to assault Ulysses Grant's exposed flank in the Wilderness. "If one more heavy blow had been delivered with unhesitating energy, with Jacksonian confidence and vigor, and with the combined power of every heavy gun and every exultant soldier of Early's army, the battle would have ended in one of the most complete and inexpensive victories ever won in war," wrote Gordon.[22]

Thomas Rosser, the Confederate cavalry commander whom Custer had chastened ten days earlier, also ran up against Early's inflexibility. Rosser asked Early to permit his two brigades to break off their ineffectual skirmishing with the enemy cavalry on the Union right so that he could charge down the Valley Turnpike behind Gordon's corps. Early rejected Rosser's proposal. "I could have done great execution upon their broken ranks," Rosser wrote. Instead, his 1,700 men played an insignificant role in the battle.[23]

Early would later explain in his report to Robert E. Lee that "so many of our men had stopped in the camp to plunder (in which I am sorry to say that officers participated), the country was so open, and the enemy's cavalry so strong, that I did not deem it prudent to press farther. . . . I determined, therefore, to content myself with trying to hold the advantages I had gained until all my troops had come up and the captured property was secured."[24]

It was 10 a.m. when Jubal Early decided to break off the attack. His exhausted men, who had been marching and fighting without food since eight o'clock the previous night, had not eaten a square meal in weeks. Their clothing was ragged, and hundreds of them were barefoot. It is questionable whether they could have rallied for one last assault.

Not having to, they fell upon the Yankees' amply supplied camps like wolves, snatching up shoes, hats, trousers, blankets, pots, pans, and tent cloths. "The world will never know the extreme poverty of the Confederate soldier at this time," wrote Sergeant John Worsham of the 21st Virginia Infantry. Laden with plunder, they rejoined their units and stretched out to rest, savoring their loot and their great victory.[25]

DURING HIS JOURNEY TO Washington, Sheridan worried about his army at Cedar Creek. It was impossible not to, after reading the intercepted Confederate message purportedly signed by Longstreet—canard or not—and after Early's sudden reappearance at Fisher's Hill. Sheridan believed he had acted prudently by recalling VI Corps and sending Torbert's two cavalry divisions back to Wright from Front Royal. But he wondered whether he should have even gone to Washington. He wondered whether the Rebels were planning a surprise.

Upon reaching the capital at 8 a.m. on October 17, Sheridan went directly to the War Department. Before he met with War Secretary Stanton and Army Chief of Staff Halleck, Sheridan requested that a special train be readied to take him back to Virginia at noon. He wished to complete his business at the War Department as speedily as possible. Perhaps he had a premonition of disaster; his *Personal Memoirs* don't say.[26]

Stanton and Halleck endorsed Sheridan's plan to send most of his army to Grant at Petersburg and to build a defensive line across the northern Valley. Two engineering officers—one of them Colonel George Thom, who had employed Sheridan in corduroying roads in Mississippi in 1862—were detailed to accompany him back to the Shenandoah and to assist in designing the defenses. His business in Washington completed, Sheridan left on the special train from Union Station at noon. By dusk, Sheridan's party was in Martinsburg, West Virginia, where it spent the night.

The next morning, October 18, Sheridan, with a three-hundred-man cavalry escort, set out on horseback for Winchester. But the two engineers from Washington—one of them overweight and the other "correspondingly light"—were unaccustomed to traveling by horseback, and it took the party most of the day to cover the twenty-eight miles to their destination. Before nightfall, Sheridan and the engineer officers surveyed the Winchester countryside for likely defensive positions.

A courier from General Wright at Cedar Creek reported to Sheridan that all was quiet. That night, he visited a friend, Aaron Griffith, and slept in the home of a local tobacco merchant, Lloyd Logan, who lived across the street from Griffith.[27]

JUST BEFORE 6 A.M. on October 19, Colonel Oliver Edwards, in charge of a VI Corps brigade on duty in Winchester, awakened Sheridan to report artillery fire coming from Cedar Creek. Sheridan was unconcerned; Wright's report from the previous night had said that XIX Corps was sending out a reconnaissance that morning. But Sheridan rose and dressed, anxious to return to his army.

Sheridan requested that the grooms saddle Rienzi, his towering black warhorse from Mississippi. After a quick breakfast, he and his escort left the Logan house. When, as they rode through Winchester, some townswomen mocked him and his escort by shaking their skirts at them, Sheridan worried that something might have happened to his army. At the edge of town, the sound of firing was louder, and he stopped to listen. Riding to the top of a ridge, Sheridan saw his worst nightmare: his army in panicked retreat.

With Major George Forsyth, Captain Joseph O'Keefe, and a dozen troopers, Sheridan rode on toward Cedar Creek, shouting at the retreating soldiers that he encountered to turn back. Having broken a rowel on one of his spurs, he asked Forsyth to cut him a switch to urge on Rienzi. He lightly struck his horse's shoulder with the stick, and Rienzi at once broke into "that long swinging gallop, almost a run, which he seemed to maintain so easily and so endlessly—a most distressing gait for those who had to follow far."

As they rode toward Cedar Creek, Forsyth closely watched Sheridan's face to try to fathom what he was thinking. When the turnpike, jammed with wagons and men, became impassable, they left it and galloped over the fields.

Sheridan was debating whether to reform his army in new lines to his rear, somewhere outside Winchester, or to strike back hard. Every atom of his being urged a counterstroke. He reasoned that his men had confidence in him because of the army's success in the Valley so far. Previously, he had always responded "at the slightest sign of trouble or distress" and had succeeded in turning temporary setbacks into stirring victories.

It did not take Sheridan long to reach his momentous decision. "I felt that I ought to try now to restore their broken ranks, or, failing in that, share their fate because of what they had done hitherto." Forsyth watched Sheridan's face harden with resolution, "as though carved in stone, and the same dull red glint I had seen in his piercing black eyes when, on other occasions, the battle was going against us, was there now." As Sheridan's party rode on, an infantry colonel they encountered declared, "We're whipped," to which Sheridan retorted, "You are, but the army isn't."[28]

At every point along the way to the front lines, Sheridan conducted a running exhortatory with the stragglers, as they continued to applaud him furiously. "About face, boys! We are going back to our camps. We are going to lick them out of their boots!" "Boys, turn back! Face the other way! I am going to sleep in that camp tonight or in hell!"[29]

THE SIGHT OF THE fiery little man on the big black horse sent an electric charge through the shell-shocked army. Frank Flinn's 38th Massachusetts Infantry of XIX Corps had just taken a new position when, from the rear, he heard "a faint cheer. Louder and louder, nearer and nearer it came."[30] Major Walker of the 11th Vermont was astounded when he heard cheering behind him on the Valley Turnpike, coming from "the stragglers and hospital bummers, and the gun-less artillerymen . . . as though a victory had been won."[31]

Sheridan met Major William McKinley, the future twenty-fifth president, who was on Crook's staff, and McKinley began spreading the news among the VIII Corps refugees that Sheridan had returned. Sheridan rode past XIX Corps, shouting to the men to turn around, but he didn't stop, "desiring to get to the extreme front."

The extreme front was Getty's division of VI Corps. Sheridan reached it at 10 a.m., about the time Early stopped his attack. After pulling out of the Middletown cemetery, Getty's men had occupied positions on high ground a mile or two to the rear, on Old Forge Road near Meadow Creek. Torbert's two cavalry divisions were nearby, holding Early's army in check on the Valley Pike. "This division and the cavalry were the only troops in the presence of and resisting the enemy," Sheridan wrote.

Torbert galloped up to Sheridan, exclaiming, "My God! I am glad you've come." Sheridan jumped Rienzi over Getty's fence-rail fieldworks, rode to the hillcrest, removed his hat, and waved it at the troops. The men rose up from behind the barricade and roared their approval.[32] "Such a scene as his presence produced and such emotions as it awoke cannot be realized but once in a century . . . a pressure of emotion beyond description," wrote Major Walker of Sheridan's greeting by VI Corps. "No more doubt or chance for doubt existed; we were safe, perfectly and unconditionally safe, and every man knew it."[33]

Riding to the rear of Getty's division, Sheridan was surprised when suddenly "a line of regimental flags rose up out of the ground, it seemed to welcome me"—the colors of Crook's routed regiments. The color guard was composed of officers, among them Colonel Rutherford Hayes. Sheridan crossed a small valley, dismounted on the opposite crest, and there established his headquarters.[34]

Major Hazard Stevens, a Getty staff officer, wrote that the pall of desolation hanging over the division staff instantly lifted with Sheridan's return. "Hope and confidence returned at a bound. . . . Now we all burned to attack the enemy, to drive him back, to retrieve our honor, and sleep in our camps that night. And every man knew that Sheridan would do it."[35]

GENERALS CROOK, TORBERT, EMORY, and Wright gathered at Sheridan's new headquarters. Sheridan embraced his old West Point roommate, Crook. "What are you doing way back here?" he asked him. "Well, we've done the best we could," Wright wearily replied, the bloodstained bandages on his chin attesting to the fight he had made. Emory said XIX Corps was ready to cover the army's retreat. Sheridan instantly disabused them of that notion.

"Retreat hell!" he told his generals. "We'll be back in our camps tonight!"

Sheridan began to put into action his plan to re-form his dispersed Army of the Shenandoah into a dangerous offensive weapon that he would unleash upon Early's triumphant but now idle troops. Praising the tenacious stand made that morning by Getty's division, Sheridan declared that his army would "fight on Getty's line."[36]

WHEATON'S AND BRIGADIER GENERAL James B. Ricketts's VI Corps divisions were placed to the right of Getty, and XIX Corps were positioned to their right. Sheridan sent Custer's cavalry division back to the extreme right, beyond XIX Corps. The cavalry brigade of Colonel Charles Russell Lowell Jr.—the ninth-generation, Harvard-educated scion of the famous Massachusetts Lowells and nephew of poet James Russell Lowell—was placed to Getty's left, along with Crook's shattered VIII Corps, whenever it could be reassembled, and Merritt's cavalry division.[37]

Throughout the late morning and noon hour, Sheridan personally supervised the arrangement of his divisions on the ridges north of Middletown, while periodically riding to a commanding height to see what the Rebels were up to. Shortly before 1 p.m., he detected unmistakable signs that the Confederates were preparing to attack. Major George Forsyth suggested that Sheridan ride along his army's battle lines so that all of the troops would know that he had reassumed command. Major McKinley further recommended that he remove his coat and hat so that he would be readily identifiable.

At first, Sheridan modestly declined. But then, hat in hand, he rode the length of his army's battle line, stopping before each unit to transmit to the men his fierce belief that they could retrieve victory from apparent defeat. "We'll whip 'em like hell before night!" he told them again and again. "We'll raise them out of their boots before the day is over!"

Never before had Sheridan's personal magnetism exerted as powerful an influence as it did on this day. His mere presence, cementing the special bond Sheridan had formed with his men during their previous victories over Early, produced an electric, if not magical, effect—an "all-conquering energy," wrote Major Walker; "an immediate stimulus to battle," said Captain George B. Sanford of the 1st US Cavalry.

Sheridan wrote that he was received with "heartiness," but the reception was in fact tumultuous.[38] "The men went wild," wrote Reverend James Ewer of the 3rd Massachusetts Cavalry. "Cheer after cheer broke forth, and rolled from regiment to regiment as he passed along." Officers pressed in to shake Sheridan's hand. A soldier in the 114th New York Infantry said the men were thrown into "a perfect frenzy of enthusiasm." "The presence of a master spirit was at once felt," wrote a soldier of the 38th Massachusetts. "Instantly all thought of merely defeating an attack upon us ended," wrote Lieutenant Colonel Moses Granger of the 122nd Ohio Infantry. "In its stead was a conviction that we were to attack and defeat them that very afternoon."[39]

Before that happened, the Rebels attacked again, although it was more of a probe than an assault. From Massanutten Mountain, the Confederate Signal Corps, watching the Yankees re-form their ranks, had been reporting these developments to Early and Gordon. Wishing to test the enemy lines, Early told Gordon not to press if he found them too strong.

At 1 p.m., the Yankees heard a "low, rustling murmur" in the dense woods in front of XIX Corps, and then "a long gray line stretching away through the woods" began advancing on the waiting Union infantrymen. With small arms fire alone, Emory's men easily flung back the Rebel thrust. It was so limited in scope and brief that many of Sheridan's troops were unaware that it had even happened. But the repulse restored the Yankees' confidence. Now, they enjoyed not only numerical superiority but a psychological advantage too. Early decided not to attack again.

"That's good! That's good!" Sheridan exclaimed when Captain John De Forest gave him the news from Emory. "Thank God for that! Now then, tell General Emory if they attack him again to go after them, and to follow them up, and to sock it to them, and to give them the devil. We'll get the tightest twist on them yet that you ever saw. We'll have all those camps and cannon back again."[40]

FOR MORE THAN TWO hours, nothing happened. Sheridan knew that he now held the initiative, and the aggressor's role suited him fine. He could afford to wait for stragglers from the rear to rejoin his "thin ranks," with Crook's badly dispersed corps especially needed on the left. As the hours passed, the Yankee divisions grew steadily stronger as more bluecoats returned to the front. While he waited, Sheridan told his infantrymen to lie down—to rest and eat and to make smaller targets for the Confederate sharpshooters sniping at them.

He ordered Merritt to raid a Rebel battery and bring back prisoners. The fear that Longstreet's I Corps had either joined Early, or was on its way, continued to nag him. But Merritt's prisoners said Longstreet was not coming.

Just when Sheridan was satisfied that he could launch his counteroffensive, a new report reached him that Longstreet was marching from Front Royal to strike his rear in Winchester. He sent a courier to Powell, whose 2nd Cavalry Division was hanging on the Union far left, near Front Royal. Longstreet wasn't there, Powell said.[41]

Sheridan was now free to execute his plan of attack, which resembled his revised Winchester strategy: simultaneous assaults on Early's center and left, with XIX Corps on the Union right then swinging to the left like a door closing on the Valley Turnpike. Custer would lead a cavalry charge on the Rebel left to get behind Early and block his retreat.[42]

Orders reached the Union troops to get ready to attack. The infantrymen retied their shoes, drew their woolen socks over their trouser bottoms, rebuckled and tightened their waist belts, rearranged their haversacks and canteens, and pulled down the visors of their forage caps to shield their eyes. Seasoned veterans that they were, they took meticulous pains to ensure that their weapons were in perfect working order. "There rang from one end of the line to the other the rattle of ramrods and snapping of gun locks as each man tested for himself the condition of his rifle," wrote Major George Forsyth. When they were satisfied that their weapons were battle worthy, they grounded their arms and stood at ease, "grimly gazing straight toward the front."[43]

BEFORE SHERIDAN'S ARMY STRETCHED a broad depression cleaved by two ravines and a creek. A hill fringed with woods rose to the south. Dug in there were the Rebels, whose unease grew with each passing hour. The messages from Massanutten Mountain had increased in urgency as the afternoon progressed.

Gordon became alarmed when a "long gap" appeared on the left side of the Confederate lines. Then Rosser reported that Union infantry and cavalry were gathering in front of the gap; if they attacked, the Confederate army's left and rear would be placed in extreme jeopardy.

Gordon sent one staff officer after another to Early to apprise him of the problem. When he received "no satisfactory answer," Gordon rode to Early to entreat him personally to reinforce the left, where every commander foresaw impending disaster. Early told him to move a gun battery to the left and stretch out his lines. By the time Gordon returned to his corps, columns of blue-clad infantry were rushing through the gap.[44]

JUST BEFORE 4 P.M., the blare of two hundred bugles echoed across the accordion ridges, the artillery opened a thunderous fire, and 25,000 Union infantrymen began advancing across the shallow depression toward the entrenched Rebels. Before XIX Corps stepped off, Sheridan had instructed General Emory's brigades on the far right to wait until they saw Custer descending the hills. "And then, by God, I want you to *push* the rebels!" he said, standing up in his stirrups and thrusting both arms forward. To Emory, Sheridan emphasized that the attack must be made boldly and energetically, "and I want you to see to it, General."

When Sheridan had gone, Captain De Forest said aloud, "If we beat them now, it will be magnificent." Emory replied, "And we are very likely to do it; they will be so far from expecting us." A soldier was heard to say, "We may as well whip them tonight; if we don't, we shall have to do it tomorrow. Sheridan will get it out of us some time."[45]

A Rebel brigade suddenly raked XIX Corps's right flank with enfilading fire. Without breaking stride, Brigadier General James McMillan wheeled his division to the right and attacked the Confederate enfilades, cutting them off from the main Rebel force and driving them to the west.

The moment was ripe for Custer's cavalry to deliver a powerful follow-up blow that would end the Rebel flanking attack and roll up the Rebel left and rear. While his cavalrymen formed for the attack, Custer, who had not seen Sheridan since his return, impulsively galloped up to him, flung his arms around his neck, and kissed him. With the counterattack only minutes under way and Custer's counterstroke brooking no delay, Sheridan was irritated by Custer's extravagant gesture.

Moments later, however, when Sheridan saw Custer's men sweeping toward Cedar Creek, while taking large numbers of prisoners, "I forgave his delay," he wrote. Sheridan ordered Crook and Merritt to assail the Rebel right, and he then personally joined the attack. The men saw his two-starred pennant snapping above the front and center of the army, "literally leading it to victory."[46]

Custer's 4,000 riders passed like a dark shadow over the Middletown meadows, the drumming of their horses' hooves insinuating its way into the awareness of combatants from both armies. To Gordon, it was "a dull, heavy swelling sound like the roaring of a distant cyclone, the omen of additional disaster." The sound signaled to XIX Corps that it was time to make its leftward half turn. Cavalry and infantry together struck the left side of Early's army with tremendous force.

With shocking suddenness, the Confederate army crumbled, and then broke. By the time Gordon reached his corps, after his consultation with Early, it was too late. The Yankees were rolling up his flank "like a scroll. Regiment after regiment, brigade after brigade, in rapid succession was crushed and, like hard clots of clay under a pelting rain, the superb commands crumbled to pieces," Gordon wrote.

Gordon attempted to make a stand on the Valley Pike, but Custer's cavalry overwhelmed his men. And then the last of Early's regiments broke and fled in panic into the twilight, "running as fast as a herd of wild, stampeded cattle," a Rebel soldier wrote. Discarded packs and weapons marked the path of their retreat. A Confederate soldier remembered Early shouting angrily at his routed men, "Run, run, goddamn you, they will get you!"[47]

As the Rebels raced for their old gun pits on Fisher's Hill, with Sheridan's cavalry in full pursuit, Custer's men hemmed Gordon and his staff on three sides. On the fourth side was a cliff. "The alternatives were the precipice or Yankee prison," wrote Gordon. He chose the precipice, plunging down it in the dark. Alone, he rode through the fields, seeking out his fellow Rebels, while avoiding the Yankees.[48]

MAJOR GENERAL STEPHEN DODSON Ramseur's division of Gordon's corps, fighting from behind a stone wall, was one of the stubborn holdouts. But Ramseur's veteran North Carolinians and Virginians broke, too, when the twenty-seven-year-old major general, the youngest in the Confederate army, was shot through both lungs. He still wore on his breast the white flower he had pinned there that morning to celebrate the news of his daughter's birth. As he was sped in an ambulance wagon toward Fisher's Hill, Merritt's cavalrymen swooped down on the train in the dark with flashing sabers, capturing prisoners, cannons, wagons, and ambulances, one of them bearing Ramseur.[49]

The Yankees took Ramseur to the Belle Grove plantation—it had again become Sheridan's headquarters—where doctors pronounced his wound fatal and prescribed all the laudanum that he could handle. As Ramseur lay on his deathbed in the library, a parade of old acquaintances from West Point and the Old Army paid their last respects, including Sheridan, Custer, Merritt, and Captain Henry DuPont. Ramseur died the next morning. At his request, his enemies sent a lock of his hair to his widow.[50]

Another deeply felt loss, but on the Union side, was Charles Russell Lowell Jr., the popular, boyish-looking twenty-nine-year-old colonel. Wounded during the Confederates' morning attack, Lowell had continued to lead his cavalry brigade, despite being in great pain. During the Yankee counterattack, however, a sharpshooter shot him in the chest. Like Ramseur, Lowell lived until the next morning, succumbing after having dictated letters to his wife and friends.[51]

At Belle Grove plantation, Sheridan and his top officers were celebrating their great victory around a blazing bonfire in the front yard when Custer galloped up to them at about 9 p.m. He leaped off his horse, grabbed Sheridan around the waist, and lifted him high. "By God, Phil!" he exclaimed. "We've cleaned them out of their guns and got ours back!" During the counterattack, Custer's men had captured the lion's share of the forty-eight guns taken—among them cannons seized that morning by the Rebels from Union batteries. One was a long, black rifle cannon—a replacement gun on which a wag at Tredegar Works in Richmond had presciently printed "Respectfully consigned to General Sheridan through General Early."

As Sheridan had promised, his infantry corps returned to their camps that night. They discovered that the Confederates had stolen their food, tents, and blankets and, during their looting frenzy, stripped naked many of the Union dead. The hungry victors slept under the stars, "among dead comrades and dead enemies."[52]

Sheridan sent Grant a brief report that night, followed by more detailed accounts over the next two days. "We have again been favored by a great victory—a victory won from disaster by the gallantry of our officers and men. . . . The accident of the morning turned to our advantage as much as though the whole movement had been planned."

Early's army was at Mount Jackson, twenty-five miles past Fisher's Hill, and it was still retreating. "The road and country was covered with small arms, thrown away by the flying rebels, and other debris," Sheridan told Grant, adding that "persons who left the Rebel army at Mount Jackson report it broken up and demoralized worse than it ever has been."[53]

Upon learning of the victory, Major General George Meade wrote to Grant, "To achieve such results after having met the reverse he describes, is one of the most brilliant feats of the war." Grant ordered a one-hundred-gun salute by his armies in Virginia and wrote to War Secretary Stanton, "Turning what bid fare [*sic*] to be a disaster into glorious victory stamps Sheridan what I have always thought of him, one of the ablest of Generals."[54]

In a span of twelve hours, both armies at Cedar Creek had experienced the extremes of triumph and disaster as no other army had or would during the Civil War. The battle cost Sheridan's army nearly 6,000 casualties, twice Early's losses.[55]

SHERIDAN HAD MADE THE unlikely victory possible. Lieutenant Colonel Thomas Wildes of VIII Corps observed that the Yankees triumphed "without receiving any reinforcements, save one man—Sheridan."[56]

The rare "eleventh-hour victory" transformed Sheridan into one of the nation's best-known military leaders literally overnight. In Washington, DC, citizens paraded by torchlight through the White House grounds in homage to Sheridan and his men. Standing at an open window under the White House portico, President Abraham Lincoln proposed three cheers for Sheridan, adding, "While we are at it we may as well consider how fortunate it was for the secesh that Sheridan was a very little man. If he had been a large man, there is no knowing what he would have done with them!"[57]

Ten days later, Shakespearean actor Thomas Murdoch read Thomas Buchanan Read's new poem, "Sheridan's Ride," for the first time at Pikes Opera House in Cincinnati. It was an instant sensation—as was Rienzi, portrayed as a nearly mythic steed that, "like a barque fed with furnace ire,/Swept on, with his wild eye full of fire." When horse and rider reached their destination, Rienzi "seemed to the whole great army to say:/'I have brought you Sheridan all the way/From Winchester down to save the day.'"

"Sheridan's Ride" was widely reprinted in newspapers across the North. Read, who was also an accomplished artist, later made an oil painting depicting the famous ride. Thirty thousand people viewed the painting during the first month of its exhibition at the Philadelphia Academy of Fine Arts.[58]

CEDAR CREEK SILENCED THOSE who still doubted, after General William Sherman's capture of Atlanta and Sheridan's victories at Winchester and Fisher's Hill, that President Lincoln would be reelected. As recently as August, Lincoln had glumly predicted that voters, weary of a war seemingly without end, would probably vote him out of office, replacing him with someone who would negotiate a peace with the South. But the battlefield triumphs of September and October had reaffirmed the electorate's faith in Lincoln's pursuit of total victory. He ultimately won 212 electoral votes to 21 for the Democratic candidate—Lincoln's former commanding general George McClellan.[59]

The president's congratulatory note to Sheridan conveyed his relief and gratitude. "I tender to you and your brave army the thanks of the nation, and my own personal admiration and gratitude, for the month's operations in the Shenandoah Valley; and especially for your splendid work of October 19, 1864."

Late during the night following the battle, Sheridan awoke in his tent to find Assistant War Secretary Charles A. Dana standing beside his bed with a letter from the war secretary. Dana had traveled to Cedar Creek from Washington to deliver it personally. "In the presence of a few sleepy aides-de-camp and of my own tired escort, I presented to Sheridan his commission as major general of the regular army," wrote Dana, adding that the groggy Sheridan said little but appeared satisfied with the promotion.

Two and a half years earlier, Sheridan was an unknown captain in Mississippi, commanding a cavalry regiment. He was now the fourth-ranking officer in the army, behind only Grant, Sherman, and Meade.

Sheridan obtained brevet major general promotions for Wright, Merritt, and Custer. Custer and the men who captured five Rebel battle flags at Cedar Creek were given the honor of carrying them and eight others to the War Department in Washington. They were loudly cheered when they rode up Pennsylvania Avenue in an omnibus with a flag protruding from each window.

After his midnight promotion, Sheridan and Dana rode the next morning through the Army of the Shenandoah. "I was struck, in riding through the lines, by the universal demonstration of personal affection for Sheridan," Dana wrote. "Everybody seemed personally to be attached to him. He was like the most popular man after an election—the whole force everywhere honored him."

When Dana asked Sheridan about it, Sheridan replied, "My practice has always been to fight in the front rank. It is the right thing to do. . . . [The men] know that when the hard pinch comes I am exposed just as much as any of them."[60]

"THE YANKEES GOT WHIPPED and we got scared," Early remarked to some of his officers after Cedar Creek.

There was some truth in Early's terse assessment, but the blame for his army's third defeat in a month was heaped on him alone by Southern citizens, government officials, and writers for the South's leading newspapers. They vilified Early as incompetent and inefficient and unfairly accused of him being a drunkard and a coward. His many critics either did not know, or had conveniently forgotten, that Early, with an army of fewer than 20,000 men, for months had tied up 40,000 elite Union combat troops sent from Petersburg, limiting Grant's movements there. But as the Confederacy's hopes for victory waned, the demand for scapegoats waxed.

Early's generals were some of his harshest critics. Gordon, who had urged Early to sustain the attacks on VI Corps, believed that if "we had concentrated our fire and assaults . . . they would have destroyed the Sixth Corps hours before Sheridan reached the field." He disputed Early's assertion that combat soldiers had stopped to loot, noting that an army chaplain had told him that the plundering was done by disabled troops following the army. Rosser, the cavalry commander, said that Early "had no idea of managing cavalry and had very little respect for its efficiency and a low estimate of its value. Yet, after all, it was the cavalry that destroyed him." Brigadier General Clement Evans wrote in his diary, "The victory is due to the plan and management of Gordon, the defeat is due to Early. When shall we be relieved of his heavy incubus? . . . It was Early's miserable generalship which lost the battle."[61]

In his report to Robert E. Lee, Early confessed, "The rout was as thorough and disgraceful as ever happened to our army. The state of things was distressing and mortifying beyond measure."[62] Early blamed the debacle on the small size of his cavalry force and his troops' "bad conduct"—their ransacking of the Yankee camps and failure to withstand the Yankee counterattack. His officers should have stopped the pillaging, but they had not. "The truth is, we have very few field or company officers worth anything," Early sourly wrote. Even when Sheridan counterattacked, his army would have yet prevailed "if my directions had been strictly complied with, and my troops had awaited my orders to retire." Almost pathetically, Early wrote that he had "labored faithfully to gain success, and I have not failed to expose my person and to set an example to my men." He offered to "surrender [his] command into other hands" if Lee believed it would serve the army's best interests.[63]

For all its blame laying and self-pity, Early's report never mentioned the singular decision, made by him alone, that had lost the battle: his failure to press the attack late in the morning. But Early knew in his heart that he should not have stopped. When he handed his report to topographer Jedediah Hotchkiss to carry to Richmond, he instructed Hotchkiss to not tell Lee that "we ought to have advanced in the morning at Middletown," admitting that "we ought to have done so."[64]

SHERIDAN'S TRIUMPH EARNED HIM not only accolades from Lincoln and Grant but also the respect and friendship of Sherman, the other member of the triumvirate that would win the war. In a letter to his father-in-law, former Ohio senator Thomas Ewing, Sherman wrote, "Sheridan, as you rightly say, the poor Irish boy of Perry County, is making his mark. . . . Sheridan is like Grant, a persevering terrier dog and won't be shaken off. He too, is honest, modest, plucky and smart enough."[65]

Sherman also wrote a letter to Sheridan. "You have youth and vigor, and this single event has given you a hold upon an army that gives you a future better than older men can hope for. . . . I shall expect you on any and all occasions to make bloody results."[66]

Cedar Creek concluded Sheridan's campaign against Early's army. When it began in August, he wrote, "we found our enemy boastful and confident, unwilling to acknowledge that the soldiers of the Union were their equal. . . . When it closed . . . this impression had been removed from his mind."[67]

CHAPTER 10

The End of Jubal Early's Army

NOVEMBER 1864–MARCH 1865

*I now saw that everything was lost. . . . I rode aside into the woods,
and in that way escaped capture.*

—CONFEDERATE LIEUTENANT GENERAL JUBAL EARLY,
AFTER THE BATTLE OF WAYNESBORO[1]

ON NOVEMBER 28, 1864, Wesley Merritt's 1st Cavalry Division crossed the Blue
Ridge Mountains at Ashby's Gap and, like destroying angels, swooped down on
the farmland to the east. It was another punitive raid on "Mosby's Confederacy"—
Loudoun County, the homeland of Lieutenant Colonel John Mosby's 43rd Battalion Partisan Rangers. Philip Sheridan had written to Major General Henry Halleck
two days earlier, "I will soon commence on Loudoun County, and let them know
there is a God in Israel. . . . Those who live at home, in peace and plenty, want the
duello part of this war to go on; but when they have to bear their burden by loss of
property and comforts they will cry for peace."[2]

Since Cedar Creek, the Rangers and other Confederate partisans and bushwhackers had continued to waylay couriers, ambush small Union detachments, and pillage
and burn wagon trains. As a result, large cavalry escorts were required to ensure the

delivery of supplies. Urged by Ulysses Grant to devastate the countryside "so that it will not support Mosby's gang," Sheridan was acting decisively.[3]

While the burning of the upper Valley in October had targeted the Confederacy's breadbasket, this mission of destruction took aim, for the second time since mid-August, on Mosby's support base. Sheridan ordered Merritt to burn all barns and mills, to drive off all livestock, and to "clear the country of forage and subsistence" that Mosby might use.[4] While the raid was under way, Sheridan told Brigadier General John Stevenson, who was in command at Harper's Ferry, "Should complaints come in from the citizens of Loudoun County tell them that they have furnished too many meals to guerrillas to expect much sympathy."[5]

For four days, Merritt's 4,000 cavalrymen desolated the countryside and filled the sky with black smoke. They spared the Unionist Quakers when they could, but no one else, slogging through slush, sleet, and snow to carry out their grim task. When the mission ended, Merritt's men had driven off or destroyed 3,000 to 4,000 sheep, 5,000 to 6,000 cattle, and nearly 1,000 hogs. They seized between five and seven hundred horses. A forage depot and several hundred tons of hay were destroyed, along with barns, stables, smokehouses, and corncribs. Losses totaled millions of dollars.

Despite these impressive numbers, Merritt was not entirely satisfied with the raid's results. "It was found next to impossible to come in contact with any guerrillas," he wrote. The "Gray Ghost" and his men were famously able to seemingly materialize and vanish at will, baffling pursuit and all attempts to entrap them. Nor had the scorched-earth raid caused the farmers and townspeople whose property was destroyed to repent their support of Mosby's men and turn against them.

Still, Merritt's riders had so denuded Loudoun County of food and forage that Mosby was compelled to quit it. With Robert E. Lee's permission, he divided his command, sending half of his men to northeastern Virginia.[6]

IN THE WEEKS FOLLOWING Cedar Creek, the Army of the Shenandoah had busied itself with small-bore operations such as these. Jubal Early's army had withdrawn nearly to Staunton, and it was being parceled out for Robert E. Lee's defense of Petersburg and Richmond. And so Sheridan had immersed himself in the pursuit of the Rebel partisans and guerrillas, in building a spy network composed of secret loyalists, and forming a credible intelligence-gathering unit: Major Henry K. Young's sixty scouts, who roved the countryside, often dressed in Rebel uniforms to obtain information more easily from loyal Confederate citizens.

Sheridan paid the scouts bonuses for information, after first cross-examining them to satisfy himself that they were telling the truth. Young, too, sometimes secretly trailed his men to ensure the veracity of their reports. Lieutenant Colonel Frederick Newhall, Sheridan's adjutant general, wrote that Young's men "were much more afraid of the general and of the major than they were of the enemy."[7]

From his spy network, Sheridan learned that guerrilla leader Major Harry Gilmore was in Harrisonburg, thirty miles north of Staunton. He sent two of Young's scouts to shadow him. A few days later, they reported that Gilmore was staying in a house outside Moorefield, West Virginia, ninety miles southwest of Winchester. Two other scouts dispatched to Moorefield learned that Gilmore was planning to welcome twenty new recruits coming from Maryland. The scouts obtained detailed information about Gilmore's men, their numbers, and where they were camped.

In February 1865, Sheridan launched a daring effort to capture Gilmore. Young and twenty of his scouts set out for Moorefield, with three hundred Union cavalrymen following, fifteen miles to their rear. Young and his scouts galloped into Gilmore's camp, claiming to be the Maryland recruits and warning that Yankee troopers were after them. As Gilmore's men prepared to face the enemy horsemen, others led Young to Gilmore's room, where the guerrilla leader was in bed, asleep. Before Gilmore could snatch up the pistols that he kept under his pillow, he had become Young's prisoner.[8]

Days later, the Rebels struck back, seizing Generals George Crook and Benjamin Kelley while they slept at Crook's hotel headquarters in Cumberland, Maryland. Crook and Kelley were spirited to Richmond and later exchanged.[9]

LEE AND GRANT RECALLED units from the Shenandoah Valley to Petersburg. Major General Joseph Kershaw's division left on November 15. Two weeks later, VI Corps marched away to join Grant, followed by a division from Crook's VIII Corps; Crook's other division went to Cumberland, where Rebels captured Crook.

Confederate major general John Gordon's II Corps departed in mid-December. As he left the Shenandoah for the last time, Gordon described the blighted landscape: "Heaps of ashes, of half-melted iron axles and bent tires, were the melancholy remains of burnt barns and farm-wagons. . . . Stone and brick chimneys [stood] alone in the midst of charred trees which had once shaded the porches of luxurious and happy homes."

Gordon's departure left Early, as he went into winter quarters at Staunton, with just Brigadier General Gabriel Wharton's infantry division and Thomas Rosser's and Lunsford Lomax's small cavalry brigades. Sheridan, with an infantry division from XIX Corps and Alfred Torbert's three cavalry divisions, went into winter camp near Winchester.[10]

The War Department passed along information from West Virginia officials that Rosser was planning a cavalry attack on the B&O Railroad in that state. Rosser was not in West Virginia, Sheridan replied. He went on to say that if he reacted to the "always alarming" reports emanating from West Virginia, "I certainly would have my hands full," and gratuitously added that West Virginia's authorities were "stupid in their duties and actions."

War Secretary Edwin Stanton tartly pointed out that his department had forwarded the information to Sheridan in the belief that "such information might be useful and desired by you, as it is by other commanders who are your seniors." In the future, added Stanton by way of chastisement, he would expect such correspondence "to be received with the respect due the Department of which you are a subordinate."[11]

GRANT HAD LONG NAGGED Sheridan to destroy the Virginia Central Railroad near Gordonsville, thereby severing the Rebel supply line between western Virginia and Richmond. In December, Sheridan sent Torbert's cavalry divisions over the Blue Ridge Mountains to carry out Grant's orders. Torbert led Wesley Merritt's and William Powell's divisions through Chester Gap, while George Custer's division rode up the Valley toward Staunton.

The Confederates had the Union cavalry under surveillance from the moment it left camp and thwarted Torbert's raid at every turn. Rosser, in partial payback for Tom's Brook, surprised Custer's troopers in their camp near Lacy Springs before reveille in a sleet storm and drove them from their bivouac, capturing prisoners, horses, and equipment. Lomax turned Torbert away from Gordonsville. During the ride back to Winchester, Merritt's and Powell's divisions destroyed forage and cattle but suffered greatly from frostbite.[12]

IN THE VALLEY, HUNGER was abroad everywhere; the Yankees had destroyed the farmers' crops, burned their barns, and run off their livestock.

While Sheridan had pitilessly carried out the total-war policy that had caused this state of affairs, he also revealed a compassionate streak. On Christmas Day 1864, Sheridan sought the War Department's permission to share his rations with the Valley's citizens. Halleck refused to grant it. "While the men of Virginia are either serving in the rebel ranks, or as bushwhackers are waylaying or murdering our soldiers, our Government must decline to support their wives and children," he wrote.

Later in the winter, however, the government relented and sent emergency rations by train to Winchester. After the war, a claims commission awarded compensation to Union loyalists whose property Sheridan's army had destroyed.[13]

IN FEBRUARY 1865, GRANT once more ordered Sheridan to destroy the Virginia Central Railroad and the James River canal—and to then capture Lynchburg, the Confederates' southwestern Virginia arsenal. Afterward, circumstances dictating, Grant said, Sheridan either could march to North Carolina and join General William Sherman or return to Winchester.[14]

After balking for months at Grant's wishes for just such an expedition, Sheridan now obeyed without objection. He recognized that no more major fighting would occur in the Shenandoah Valley and that the war would soon be over. He did not want to miss its final act.

It is debatable whether Sheridan ever seriously considered marching to Lynchburg. He clearly did not intend to join Sherman, believing that the war's very last battles would be fought in southern Virginia. Grant, as he lately was wont to do with Sheridan, had laid out possible options, leaving it to Sheridan to decide how to proceed.

Sheridan knew that few Rebels remained to stop him from marching on Gordonsville. His female spy network in the southern Shenandoah Valley had informed him of the steady drain of men from Early's army in Staunton, leaving him with just 2,000 troops. One of his spies was a letter carrier who permitted Sheridan's scouts to read the mail that she couriered between the Valley and Baltimore. Another woman, who visited the Rebel camps often, had agreed to aid Sheridan on the condition that he obtain her husband's release from a Union war prison. Her information was so valuable that Sheridan also gave her money to set up her husband as a tinsmith in Baltimore.[15]

MARCH 2, 1865–WAYNESBORO, VIRGINIA—Pouring rain cloaked Sheridan's men and horses in a special kind of misery as they rode east from Staunton toward Waynesboro, ten miles away. "The by-roads were miry beyond description, rain having fallen incessantly since we left Winchester," Sheridan wrote, "men and horses growing almost unrecognizable from the mud covering them from head to foot."[16]

With Torbert disabled by a flare-up of a spinal abscess, Merritt was in command of the 9,000-man Cavalry Corps when it rode out of Winchester, four abreast, for the last time on February 27. Sheridan had elected not even to attempt to recall Torbert, who "had disappointed me" after Fisher's Hill and during his failed raid on Gordonsville in December. When he did return to duty, Torbert would command the remnants of the Army of the Shenandoah scattered across the lower Valley. His war was over.

"It was a grand sight," a witness wrote of the cavalry's departure from Winchester. The horse's equipage, she said, "shone like gold." The long column of mounted troops quickly lost its spit and polish, however, in the rain and mud.[17]

TWO AVOWEDLY DISAFFECTED REBELS who had offered Sheridan their services had turned out to be Confederate spies, which Sheridan had discovered after sending them on phony missions and having Young's scouts follow them. Surprisingly adroit at counterintelligence work, Sheridan had kept the spies in play, feeding them false information to take back to the Confederates. Near Staunton, he supplied them with one last fiction: that he planned to hold a fox hunt. His purpose was to lull the Rebels into thinking that his army planned to remain in Staunton.

After Young's scouts watched the spies pass on the information to the Rebels, they arrested the men. The pair later escaped from their guards in Baltimore while en route to the Union prison at Fort Warren; they were never seen again. In his *Personal Memoirs*, Sheridan speculated that the men might have been involved in the conspiracy to assassinate President Abraham Lincoln.[18]

Of course, there was no fox hunt, and Early was not fooled anyway. He collected Wharton's skeletal division of 1,500 infantrymen, Rosser's 500 troopers, and some artillery, and they marched to Waynesboro to await Sheridan. Early made a point of telling people in Staunton that he intended to fight Sheridan there.[19]

THE 4,500 MEN OF Custer's division led the way to Waynesboro, proudly displaying their red ties, formerly the signature attire of his Wolverine Brigade.

The responsibilities of the twenty-five-year-old "boy general" had grown during his seven months in Sheridan's Shenandoah army, and he had become one of Sheridan's most dependable combat leaders. He had tipped the scales at Winchester, Cedar Creek, and Tom's Brook. Just days earlier, during the march up the Valley to Staunton, he had boldly swum two regiments over the North Fork of the Shenandoah River to flank his old friend Rosser when Rosser had tried to bar Custer's crossing.

On this miserable day, Custer would display to stunning effect the battle skills that he had mastered in the Valley.

EARLY HAD PLACED HIS small force and cannons on a commanding ridge north-west of Waynesboro. Nestled in a bend of the South River, the high ground over-looked the town and the Staunton Pike. But Custer instantly perceived the Confederate position's major vulnerability: Early's left flank was anchored not on the river but on a patch of woods—woods that might be infiltrated to turn his flank.

Custer implemented a simple tactical plan. While he kept Early occupied on his main front, three regiments slipped into the woods on Early's left. When gunfire erupting in the woods signaled that the regiments had made contact with the Rebels, the rest of the division attacked frontally.

The shattering twin assaults sent the Rebels into panicked flight—which took them into the clutches of Union cavalrymen who had cut off the Confederates' re-treat. "I now saw that everything was lost. . . . I rode aside into the woods, and in that way escaped capture," wrote Early, who got away with his staff, Wharton, and fifteen or twenty others. Custer captured 1,600 of Early's 2,000 men, along with eleven guns, seventeen battle flags, ambulances and wagons, and Early's headquar-ters wagon with all of his army's records.

Early's Army of the Valley no longer existed, and the road to Charlottesville lay wide open to Sheridan's cavalry.[20]

THE NEXT DAY, A delegation of Charlottesville leaders awaited Custer on the town's outskirts. "With medieval ceremony," they handed over the keys to all the public buildings and the University of Virginia. When Custer learned that townspeople feared the Yankees might destroy the historic campus designed by Thomas Jefferson, he ringed it with a provost guard to keep everyone away.[21]

WHILE HIS CAVALRY WRECKED the James River canal and tore up the Virginia Central Railroad, Sheridan sought a place to cross the James. He had concluded that Lynchburg was too heavily defended and instead had decided to cross the river, march on Appomattox Court House, and destroy the Southside Railroad, the Rebels' crucial lifeline to Petersburg and Richmond. But the Confederates had burned the bridges, and the James River was too swollen by the heavy rains to ford. Moreover, the army did not have enough pontoon bridges for a river crossing. Sheri-dan could not reach Appomattox Court House.

Sheridan had a clear path eastward along the James's north bank, though. Neither enemy troops nor natural barriers would stand in the way of his army riding east-ward, skirting Richmond's northern and eastern approaches, and joining Grant outside Petersburg. "I was master of the whole country north of the James as far down as Goochland, hence the destruction of these arteries of supply could be easily compassed, and feeling that the war was nearing its end, I desired my cavalry to be in at the death," he wrote.

On March 9, the army rode east, destroying locks, dams, and boats on the James River and wrecking tracks and rails on the Virginia Central Railroad. Sheridan sent a message to Grant requesting that rations and forage be sent to White House, along with a pontoon bridge so that he could cross the Pamunkey River there.[22]

At Frederick's Hall Station, Custer captured the telegraph office and found an unsent message from Early to Lee revealing that Early planned to attack Sheridan with two hundred cavalrymen. Two hours later, Custer's cavalrymen scattered Early's ambush party, capturing most of them. Early and a half dozen Confederates—the last remnant of the army that had threatened Washington the previous July—escaped to Richmond.

Early was ill, and he went home to Lynchburg, where a letter waiting for him from Lee informed him that he was relieved of his command. "Your reverses . . . have, I fear, impaired your influence both with the people and the soldiers," Lee wrote, but he added that he still believed in his downtrodden general.[23]

IT RAINED DAY AND night as Sheridan's cavalrymen rode east. The roads were "wellnigh bottomless," horses staggered from fatigue, and troopers nodded off in the saddle. "But all hearts were jubilant," wrote Captain Harlan Lloyd, "and soldiers were never known in better spirits than we were." "Every one was buoyed up by the cheering thought that we should soon take part in the final struggle of the war," Sheridan wrote.[24]

At White House on March 19, Sheridan wired a request for twenty-five forges to make replacements for his horses' shoes, worn out by the nearly two-hundred-mile march over rough roads and through mud. Farriers reported 2,000 cases of "hoof rot."

A week later, the cavalry crossed the James River on a bridge below Dutch Gap Canal, as President Lincoln, Grant, and Sheridan watched from the steamer *Mary Martin*; Lincoln was paying an extended visit to Grant's City Point headquarters. Sheridan's men once more made their camp on the James's south bank.[25]

One of the earliest known photographs of Philip Sheridan, depicted here as a second lieutenant fresh from the U.S. Military Academy. *Library of Congress*

Sheridan with some of his Civil War cavalry commanders, from left: James Forsyth, Sheridan's chief of staff; David Gregg; Sheridan; Wesley Merritt; Alfred Torbert; and James Wilson. *Library of Congress*

President Abraham Lincoln
National Archives

War Secretary Edwin Stanton
National Archives

Major General William T. Sherman
National Archives

George Armstrong Custer
National Archives

Major General William Rosecrans
National Archives

Confederate general Jubal A. Early
Library of Congress

General Robert E. Lee
National Archives

Photo of captured Confederate
soldiers after the battle at Five Forks
on April 1, 1865. *Library of Congress*

During the Civil War, Sheridan wore a flat-brimmed hat, one of the few that he was able to keep on his oddly shaped head. *Library of Congress*

A popular illustration of Philip Sheridan during his famous ride to rally his troops at Cedar Creek. Note his starred, swallow-tail pennant. *Library of Congress*

Major General Phil Sheridan in his field tent during the Civil War. *Massachusetts Commandery Military Order of the Loyal Legion and the U.S. Army Military History Institute*

Sheridan pictured with his Cavalry Corps commanders during the Civil War's final weeks. Left to right: Sheridan; James Forsyth, Sheridan's chief of staff; Wesley Merritt; Thomas Devin; and George Custer
Massachusetts Commandery Military Order of the Loyal Legion and the U.S. Army Military History Institute

Sheridan and these men, photographed during the last months of the Civil War, became the Army's leading commanders during the Plains Indians wars. Left to right: Wesley Merritt; Sheridan; George Crook; James Forsyth, Sheridan's chief of staff; and George Custer. *Library of Congress*

Ulysses Grant regarded Ranald Mackenzie as the Union Army's most promising young officer at the conclusion of the Civil War. He became one of Phil Sheridan's indispensable commanders on the Great Plains. *Library of Congress*

The army and the railroads were partners in settling the West during the post–Civil War years. In this photo, Generals Phil Sheridan, Ulysses Grant, and William T. Sherman have just met at Fort Sanders, Wyoming, in July 1868 with Union Pacific Railroad officials to discuss the intercontinental railroad. At far left is Sidney Dillon, a Union Pacific director and future president. Sheridan is next to him. Grant is in the straw hat behind the fence, and Sherman is standing next to the steps, beside the girl. The large man on the right is Major General William Harney, and beside him, perched on the fence, is Thomas Durant, Union Pacific vice president. *Library of Congress*

James Taylor's "The Attack at Dawn" dramatically illustrates the Seventh Cavalry's attack on Black Kettle's Cheyenne winter camp on the Washita River on November 27, 1868. The troopers killed at least 103 Indians, and took 53 women and children captive, at a loss of 21 killed. *Library of Congress*

Commercial hunters slaughtered millions of buffalo on the Great Plains. Sheridan, Sherman, and Grant applauded the buffalos' extermination, believing it would force the Plains Indians to accept reservation life. *National Archives*

Pile of bones at the place where Lieutenant Colonel George Custer and his command were killed in June 1876 near the Little Bighorn River by Northern Cheyenne and Sioux Indians. *National Archives*

Chiricahua Apaches on their way to exile in Florida at a railroad siding in Texas. Geronimo is third from left in the bottom row. *National Archives*

Sitting Bull, chief of the Oglala Sioux, was the last holdout among the Northern Plains Indians. *Library of Congress*

Members of Sheridan's 1883 presidential expedition to Yellowstone National Park. President Chester Arthur is seated at the center, with Lieutenant General Philip Sheridan to his right. Standing at left is Michael Sheridan. *Library of Congress*

This photograph was taken at the Sheridan family vacation home in Nonquitt, Massachusetts, in 1887, one year before Sheridan's death. Left to right in the rear: Mrs. Michael Sheridan, Michael Sheridan, Irene Rucker Sheridan, and Philip Sheridan. Philip and Irene Sheridan's four children are in the foreground, left to right: Irene, Philip Jr., Louisa, and Mary. *Illinois Historical Society*

Sheridan, Sherman, and Grant appeared together on a commemorative stamp in 1937, one of a series honoring army and navy heroes.

Lieutenant General Ulysses S. Grant
National Archives

Lieutenant General Philip
Sheridan in middle age
Library of Congress

CHAPTER II

Waterloo for the Confederacy

MARCH–APRIL 1865

I have never in my life taken a command into battle, and had the slightest desire to come out alive unless I won.
— PHIL SHERIDAN AFTER FIVE FORKS[1]

UNION ARMY HEADQUARTERS, CITY POINT, VIRGINIA—In late March 1865, Philip Sheridan returned to the place outside Petersburg where his journey to national greatness had begun so inauspiciously seven months earlier. Here, in August 1864, General Ulysses Grant had informed him that he would command a new army in the Shenandoah Valley.

Sheridan's mastery of subsequent events had radically altered his status in the Union army. In August 1864, he had been Grant's third choice to command the Army of the Shenandoah. President Abraham Lincoln and the War Department had questioned whether he was up to the job; War Secretary Edwin Stanton had thought him "too young," and Lincoln had thought him short.

Having seen more fizzle than sizzle in his war leaders, Lincoln had many other reasons to doubt Sheridan. He had pointedly told Grant that the destruction of Jubal Early's army "[would] neither be done nor attempted, unless you watch it every day and force it." Among the top military hierarchy, only General William Sherman had been enthusiastic about Sheridan. "He will worry Early to death," Sherman had predicted.

Sheridan had wiped the Shenandoah clean of Rebel armies and destroyed its crops and livestock, at once breaking up the Confederacy's conduit to the North and ravaging its breadbasket. His stunning victories—Cedar Creek, particularly—had, with Sherman's conquest of Georgia, helped reelect Lincoln. The people of the North now believed that victory was near and that the Confederacy was doomed.

Consequently, Sheridan was received at City Point on March 26, 1865, with extremely gratifying marks of pleasure and respect by President Lincoln and General Grant, who were there with their wives. Three weeks earlier, Lincoln, his lined face and sunken cheeks—he had recently lost thirty pounds—making him look older than his fifty-six years, had been sworn into office for a second term at the US Capitol in Washington. "Fondly do we hope, fervently do we pray, that this mighty scourge of war may speedily pass away," he had said.

Sheridan found the president "dejected, giving no indication of his usual means of diversion, by which (his quaint stories) I had often heard he could find relief from his cares." The president, however, displayed his fondness for Sheridan when he reportedly said, "When this peculiar war began I thought a cavalryman should be at least six feet four inches high, but I have changed my mind. Five feet four will do in a pinch."

WHEN SHERIDAN MET PRIVATELY with Grant to discuss military matters, Grant bestowed a signal mark of the army's soaring faith in Sheridan. His Cavalry Corps would operate as an independent command—in other words, as the equal of the Army of the Potomac and the Army of the James. He would report directly to Grant and not through George Meade, the Army of the Potomac's commander. With this promotion, Grant, who in person was mild, quiet, and confrontation averse, both neatly rewarded Sheridan's exemplary service and preempted any disruptive clashes between Meade and Sheridan.

Grant had unbounded confidence in Sheridan, and he did not wish to damage their excellent relationship. His intimates knew that he admired Sheridan as a man who "would fight—always" and as "incomparably the greatest general our civil war produced." Sheridan, in the words of one observer, had now become "the left-hand man of Grant the left-handed." The Rebels had begun referring to him as "Sheridan the inevitable."[2]

Sheridan's status assured, there remained the question of what role he would play, and herein lay a major problem. Still on the table was Grant's expectation—proposed by Sherman but unacceptable to Sheridan—that he lead the Cavalry

Corps into North Carolina, replace the erratic Hugh Judson "Kill Cavalry" Kilpatrick as Sherman's cavalry chief, and support Sherman's infantrymen as they marched north to join Grant in Virginia.

Sheridan would have none of it, and in forcefully articulating his objections, he cast his arguments in a light that he knew would appeal strongly to Grant. If he left Grant to join Sherman, Sheridan argued, the Army of the Potomac would remain stalemated before Petersburg, just as it had been these past nine months. Consequently, it would be Sherman's army, with Sheridan's cavalry in support, and not Grant's that would finally tip the scales against Robert E. Lee, driving him from Petersburg and receiving an unfair share of the credit for ending the war. But if Sheridan remained with Grant, together they could beat Lee before Sherman reached Virginia.[3]

Grant ended the discussion by suddenly reversing himself and telling Sheridan that he had intended all along for Sheridan to remain at Petersburg. The order to march to North Carolina had only been a "blind"—to deceive peace advocates in Washington. If Grant's planned operation against Lee's right flank failed, the peace group would make a case for negotiations. However, if the maneuver were seen simply as an attempt to close the gap with Sherman, there would be no ground for criticism. Viewed objectively, Grant's explanation strains credulity.

The upshot was that Grant wished to keep Sheridan close at hand, according to Colonel Adam Badeau, a Grant aide who witnessed the conversation. "I mean to end this business here," Grant said. Sheridan slapped his leg and replied, "That's what I like to hear you say. Let us end the business here." During their conversation, wrote Badeau, "the two natures struck fire from each other in the contact."[4]

SHERMAN LEFT HIS ARMY in North Carolina to confer with Lincoln and Grant at City Point. At army headquarters, Sherman lobbied Grant to send Sheridan's Cavalry Corps to North Carolina.

Sheridan was with his men at their camp near the James River when he learned that Sherman was with Grant. Fearing that Grant would change his mind again and send him south, he boarded a military train to City Point. He didn't reach headquarters until nearly midnight—the locomotive jumped the rickety tracks, causing a long delay—but when he got there, Sherman and Grant were still discussing strategy.

As aggressively forthright as Sheridan, Sherman instantly proposed to Sheridan that he join his army; Sheridan just as vigorously argued against the plan. "My uneasiness made me somewhat too earnest, I fear," Sheridan confessed, "but Grant soon mollified me" by reassuring Sheridan that the Cavalry Corps would remain with Grant.

Sherman did not give up easily. Early the next morning, he entered the sleeping Sheridan's tent and renewed his arguments. Sheridan remained unmoved; he intended to stay with the Army of the Potomac.[5]

THE COMBATANTS FACED ONE another across a thirty-seven-mile-long maze of Rebel trenches and breastworks sprawling across Petersburg's eastern and southern approaches. Filth and a scarcity of food had spawned appalling conditions. The cold winter weather, along with the rats, disease, and short rations in the trenches, had carved gaps in the Confederate ranks due to disability and desertion; of the 57,000 troops listed on unit rosters, no more than 35,000 were present.

After a midnight meeting with Robert E. Lee in late March, Major General John Gordon wrote that Lee recognized that his army was starving and must soon evacuate Petersburg and attempt to join Lieutenant General Joseph Johnston's army in North Carolina. But horses were dying at such a rate that the army would be unable to move half of its artillery, ammunition, and supply trains during a breakout. The alarming situation had fostered "a deep and sincere religious feeling" in Lee's army; whenever they could, the Confederates held prayer meetings.

Well they might. At least 125,000 Union troops—perhaps as many as 150,000—were arrayed against them. They were well fed, generously supplied, and growing stronger by the week. And with the arrival of spring, active operations would soon resume after a long winter of probing, indecisive actions.[6]

The siege had begun in June 1864, and little had changed since the bungled mine explosion and calamitous Union attack of July 30. A peace conference held on February 3 aboard a steamer anchored off Hampton Roads had yielded no agreement. The Confederates had continued to insist on independence, while Lincoln and Secretary of State William Seward had not budged from demanding full restoration of the Union.[7]

On March 25, the day after Lincoln arrived at City Point, Gordon, whose II Corps had rolled up Sheridan's army at Cedar Creek at dawn on October 19, attacked the Union right flank at Fort Stedman. Lee had carefully planned the attack, hoping to puncture the Union lines so that he could send troops to Johnston in North Carolina.

Gordon's assault achieved complete surprise initially. His men drove the Yankees from the fort and threw the Union right flank into disarray. But Major General John Parke's IX Corps quickly closed the gap with infantry and a punishing artillery barrage that repulsed the Confederates with more than 4,000 killed, wounded, or captured, compared with 1,000 Union losses. Lee's gamble had only weakened his army.[8]

Lincoln had sailed to City Point to nudge things forward, as had become his habit after years of enduring generals who were seemingly loath to take the offensive. But Grant, the antithesis of inertia, had shown the president his plan to force the Rebels from their citadel so that he could destroy them and end the war. He and his generals were cleared for action on March 29.

GRANT PLANNED TO SHIFT his army westward to compel Lee to further stretch his defensive lines and perhaps tempt him to send troops out of Petersburg to attack the Yankees. To achieve the latter, he would dangle Sheridan's cavalry as bait. Lee's response to these movements could offer new opportunities for Grant's army to break his lines.

V and II Corps would march westward on March 29 to Dinwiddie Court House along with Sheridan's three mounted divisions. "Push round the enemy if you can and get onto his right rear," Grant's orders to Sheridan said, and "force him out if possible." If the Rebels left their fortifications to attack Sheridan's 9,000 troopers, he was to "move in with your entire force in your own way," the orders continued, while the two infantry corps marched on the enemy's rear. But if the Rebels remained in their fortifications, the Cavalry Corps would seize or destroy the last viable supply routes into Petersburg and Richmond: the Southside and Danville Railroads and the Boydton Plank Road, which passed through Dinwiddie Court House.[9]

The plan looked better on paper than it did on March 29, when the tens of thousands of soldiers, horses, wagons, and artillery caissons ventured onto the atrocious roads south of Petersburg. Winter frosts and spring rains had transformed them into "almost bottomless" morasses—forcing the column into adjoining fields that were even worse, pitted with "bogs and quicksands."

"In the face of these discouragements we floundered on, however," wrote Sheridan. Two of his cavalry divisions—commanded by Brigadier General Thomas Devin and, in a new role, Major General George Crook, recently liberated from captivity—managed by day's end to reach Dinwiddie and the Boydton Plank Road, thirteen miles south of Petersburg. George Custer's division lagged with the wagon train, which proceeded at a crawl from mudhole to mudhole, with the men sometimes having to unload and lift the wagons out of thigh-deep liquid mud.[10]

That night, torrential rain lashed southern Virginia. It poured down without letup for the next thirty-six hours. Brigadier General Horace Porter of Grant's staff wrote that by daylight on March 30, the roads were "sheets of water." Pioneer units corduroyed the roads with logs and fence rails, but the wagons still sank two feet into the mire. It took fifty-six hours for a train of six hundred wagons, aided by 1,000 pioneers, to travel five miles.

"By evening of the 30th," wrote Porter, "whole fields had become quicksand, in which the troops waded in mud above their ankles, horses sank to their bellies, and wagons threatened to disappear altogether." The wagon train inched along with the help of men who, using rails and poles, repeatedly lifted the wheels from the mud-holes, "the atmosphere blue with the Curses issuing from men and officers alike." In an attempt at levity, soldiers called out to passing officers, "I say, fetch along the pontoons" and "When are the gunboats coming up?"[11]

Dinwiddie Court House, where Sheridan's mounted troops were to offer them-selves as bait, lay near the junction of five roads that included the critical Boydton Plank supply road and the Courthouse Road, which ran north to another important crossroads at Five Forks. Sheridan and most of his staff stayed in the town's ram-shackle hotel and tavern, the temporary lodgings of two young women who had fled Charleston for Petersburg and thence made their way to Dinwiddie. They asked the Yankees to fight their battle someplace where the women would not have to witness the carnage. The officers promised not to bring "red war to the doorstep of the Dinwiddie Hotel."

As the rain poured down, the women made coffee for the Union officers, who gathered around the out-of-tune piano and belted out popular songs, munching berries. Later, they wrapped themselves in their cloaks and slept on the wood floor, using "chairs for pillows."[12]

ON THE NIGHT OF March 30, Sheridan received a troubling dispatch from Grant, who had made his field headquarters in a waterlogged cornfield at Gravelly Run. "The heavy rains of today will make it impossible for us to do much until it dries up a little or we get roads around our rear repaired." Grant instructed Sheridan to hold his position and send unneeded cavalry back to the Union right for hay and grain.[13]

The message acted on Sheridan like a fire bell; suspending operations was out of the question. Sheridan did not bother writing a response but called for his gray horse, Breckenridge. Plunging almost to its knees in mud at each step, Breckenridge carried Sheridan through the rainy night to Grant's headquarters. He was deter-mined to change his commander's mind and prevent him from making "a serious mistake."

At Gravelly Run, Sheridan found Grant's staff officers gathered around a fire. He stuck his head into Grant's tent, where Grant and his chief of staff, General John Rawlins, were discussing Grant's decision. Sheridan overheard Grant say gloomily, "Well, Rawlins, I think you had better take command."

Sheridan beat a hasty retreat, and Grant's staff officers gathered around him, quizzing him about the situation on the left. According to Porter, who was there, Sheridan cheerfully described what he proposed to do: "I can drive in the whole cavalry force of the enemy with ease, and if an infantry force is added to my command, I can strike out for Lee's right, and either crush it or force him to so weaken his entrenched lines that our troops in front of them can break through and march into Petersburg."

Another officer asked him where he would obtain forage for his horses if the rain continued. "I'll haul it out, if I have to set every man in the command to corduroying roads, and corduroy every mile of them from the railroad to Dinwiddie.

"I tell you, I'm ready to strike out tomorrow and go to smashing things," he said, pacing up and down, Porter wrote, "like a hound in [*sic*] the leash."

Sheridan's fighting talk buoyed Grant's staff officers. "We told him that this was the kind of talk we liked to hear," wrote Porter, and they suggested that Grant should hear it too. One of them informed Grant that Sheridan had made some interesting remarks, and Grant invited him into the tent. When the other officers attempted to follow Sheridan inside, Grant told them that he wanted to have a private conversation.

Sheridan got right to the point, urging Grant not to stop the operation. His cavalry was already in motion, Sheridan said. If the suspension took effect, Grant would "surely be ridiculed," he said, reminding him of the scorn heaped upon Ambrose Burnside and his army when Burnside called off his "mud march" offensive in January 1863—and soon afterward was relieved of command.

Sheridan sensed that Grant was wavering and that he might have acted in haste after listening to a host of complaints about the impossibility of moving trains through the mud. He encouraged Grant to stick to his battle plan. "It needed little argument to convince him," Sheridan wrote. His arguments and cheerful demeanor restored Grant's confidence.

"We will go on," Grant told Sheridan and rescinded his order. Later, Grant wrote that "the spirit of confidence with which [Sheridan] was imbued" had inspired him, and "I determined to make a movement at once."

Sheridan requested the services of VI Corps, his favorite infantry unit from the Army of the Shenandoah, for his movement on Five Forks. No, said Grant, VI Corps was needed on the right. Five Forks would have to be taken with cavalry alone.

As he was leaving, Sheridan encountered the V Corps commander, Major General Gouverneur Warren, who, evidently disheartened by the rainy weather, began "speaking rather despondently of the outlook." Sheridan was not favorably impressed.[14]

WHILE SHERIDAN WAS PERSUADING Grant to countermand his suspension of the offensive, Rebel forces were massing between Dinwiddie Court House and Five Forks. Lee's scouts had observed Grant's slip-slide to the left. To thwart the obvious attempt to flank his right, Lee had created a task force with all of his available cavalry, five infantry brigades scattered throughout the Richmond-Petersburg area, and some artillery batteries. The 11,000 men were all that Lee could spare without seriously weakening his defenses.

In the same miserly spirit, Lee begrudged the task force any of his first-rate generals from the Petersburg lines. Instead, he assigned the command to Major General George Pickett, the war's embittered doyen of futility. Since his division's suicidal attack at Gettysburg, Pickett had served in relatively quiet sectors. Now, with midnight about to toll for the Confederacy, the job of foiling possibly the war's decisive flanking movement had fallen to the jaded career officer.

Under Pickett's command were 5,500 cavalrymen from the divisions of William H. F. "Rooney" Lee and Fitzhugh Lee—Robert E. Lee's son and nephew, respectively—and Thomas Rosser. Absent was Wade Hampton, inheritor of Jeb Stuart's mantle, who had gone to South Carolina with a division of dismounted cavalrymen to find fresh horses. The 5,000 infantrymen belonged to five brigades, three from Pickett's division and two from Major General Bushrod Johnson's division. About five hundred artillerymen completed the contingent.

Half starved, rail thin, and many of them barefoot, the Rebels hardly seemed a match for Sheridan's well-equipped troopers and two nearby infantry corps—comprising more than 40,000 Union troops.[15]

THE RAIN STOPPED DURING the night, and a brilliant spring day dawned on March 31. Neither Sheridan nor Pickett had an opportunity to enjoy it.

Major Henry Young's scouts reported enemy troops massing at Five Forks. Sheridan sent Brigadier General Wesley Merritt toward the crossroads with Devin's division and a brigade from Crook's division—in all, about 4,000 troopers. Pickett's troops attacked and drove Crook's and Devin's cavalrymen back over the muddy fields toward Dinwiddie.

Sheridan reacted by launching a counterattack that stopped Pickett before he could reach the rear of nearby V Corps. Rallying his milling cavalrymen, Sheridan led them to new defensive positions on the Courthouse Road a few miles north of Dinwiddie. Sheridan's dismounted troopers slowed Pickett's advance while falling back to a succession of barricades.

All day long, Sheridan and Pickett battled, with first one side and then the other gaining temporary advantage, but with the Rebels steadily driving back Sheridan's cavalrymen. Weirdly, Union bands on a nearby hill serenaded the combatants "with gay and patriotic airs" as they slaughtered one another. Horace Porter of Grant's staff encountered a band "playing 'Nellie Bly' as cheerfully as if furnishing music for a country picnic" as bullets whistled by and exploding shells sprayed shrapnel.

Sheridan summoned Custer's division from its thankless duty of prodding the Cavalry Corps's wagon train through endless quagmires. Custer responded with his customary "vim," wrote Sheridan's adjutant-general, Lieutenant Colonel Frederick Newhall. While a brigade of Crook's division held off the Rebels, Custer's men threw up breastworks of rails on a hill and brought up the field artillery—just in time to repel an enemy lunge toward Dinwiddie.

Sheridan ordered new fieldworks thrown up just three-quarters of a mile north of Dinwiddie. Here he would make his stand defending the crossroads.

"All was life, activity, and industry," as the men dug in, wrote Major Henry Tremain of Crook's staff. "Sheridan seemed to have infused his own indomitable spirit among his subordinates. . . . If the enemy could not be conquered today at least he must be overawed."

In short order, the Yankees repelled a cavalry attack, and Sheridan, confident that "we were now in good shape," believed his men could drive away whatever the Confederates threw at him.[16]

It wasn't long in coming. Just before sunset, Pickett's infantrymen emerged from the woods.

Sheridan, Merritt, Custer, and Sheridan's staff officers rode along the barricades, encouraging the men. "Our enthusiastic reception showed that they were determined to stay," Sheridan wrote.

The advancing Rebels soldiers showed their appreciation by firing on Sheridan's party with their far-ranging muskets, emptying several saddles and wounding a *New York Herald* correspondent. "Mud and bullets flew," wrote Newhall. Meanwhile, Sheridan's troopers lay behind the barricades, holding their fire until the Confederates entered the killing range of their Spencer rifles.

As Custer galloped away from Sheridan's side, he was summoned back by shouts. "General! General!" Sheridan called. "You understand? I want you to *give* it to them!" Custer replied, "Yes, yes, I'll give it to them," before riding to his men.

The waiting Yankees were impressed by the Rebel infantrymen's "air of abandon, a sort of devil-may-care swing in their long stride as they advanced over the field, that was rather disheartening to men that did not want to get shot," wrote Merritt.

"Then they opened," Sheridan wrote, "Custer's repeating rifles pouring out such a shower of lead that nothing could stand up against it." The repeaters were "puffing out their cartridges like Roman candles," Newhall observed.

The Rebels retreated to the woods but did not withdraw toward Five Forks. The two veteran forces stubbornly fought on, neither willing to give way. Pickett's determined infantrymen pushed Sheridan's troopers backward, almost to the courthouse in Dinwiddie, but they did not break through.[17]

BELIEVING THAT PICKETT WOULD remain on the field and resume his attempt to capture Dinwiddie the next morning, Sheridan saw "a rare opportunity," as did Grant when he received Sheridan's report: Lee's men had ventured outside Petersburg's defenses and were now vulnerable to attack. "If I am cut off from the Army of the Potomac, [Pickett's force] is cut off from Lee's army, and not a man in it ought ever be allowed to get back to Lee," Sheridan told Porter. "We at last have drawn the enemy's infantry out of its fortifications, and this is our chance to attack it."

Sheridan sent Porter to Grant to request VI Corps once more. VI Corps was too far away to assist Sheridan, Grant told Porter. He telegraphed his aide's report to Major General George Meade. The possibilities excited Meade, who recommended that V Corps move quickly to "smash up" Pickett's rear. Grant agreed. Warren's corps was to report to Sheridan, along with Brigadier General Ranald Mackenzie's 1,000 cavalrymen from the Army of the James. Sent at 10:05 p.m., Grant's message to Sheridan added that V Corps ought to reach him by midnight.

There being no sign of Warren's men at midnight, or at 3 a.m. on April 1, Sheridan began to doubt that V Corps would arrive at Dinwiddie in time to be of any use. Sleepless and chafing at the delay, Sheridan sent a message to Warren, whom he believed to be behind the Rebels and practically on their flank. "I will hold on here. Possibly they may attack Custer at daylight; if so, attack instantly and in full force; attack at daylight anyhow."[18]

At daybreak, as fog hugged the ground, a division from Warren's V Corps, commanded by Major General Romeyn Ayres, reached Sheridan. Hoping that during the night Warren's other two divisions had gotten behind the Rebels, Sheridan ordered Devin's and Custer's divisions forward. The Yankee cavalrymen discovered that Pickett's men were already falling back toward Five Forks. Sheridan, however, continued to believe that Warren's two other divisions would attack Pickett's rear at any moment.

But there was no attack, because the rest of V Corps was miles away. When he received Grant's order, Warren had immediately sent Ayres's division to Sheridan. Warren's other two divisions, under Major Generals Charles Griffin and Samuel Crawford, did not reach Pickett's left rear until 7 a.m.—when the Rebels had already gotten past them and were streaming into Five Forks.[19]

WHILE SHERIDAN'S CAVALRYMEN WERE struggling to stop Pickett's task force from overrunning them and capturing Dinwiddie on March 31, V Corps was having an even worse day. Leading the Army of the Potomac's march westward toward the right flank of Lee's Petersburg defenses, Warren's corps tried to seize White Oak Road, one of the highways that met at Five Forks.

Confederate major general Bushrod Johnson's division was ready for him and launched a furious attack—under the eyes of Robert E. Lee, who had come from Petersburg to watch—that broke two of Warren's three divisions, commanded by Ayres and Crawford.

Shocked by the sight of his corps in full retreat, Warren had seized the colors of a Pennsylvania regiment and, aided by his staff officers, rallied them behind his only intact division, Griffin's. Griffin held, and with the aid of II Corps, regained the ground lost earlier in the day. Johnson's Rebels ran out of steam and withdrew. Warren made his camp at the place where the fighting stopped, five miles east of Five Forks—near the left rear of Pickett's force.

That night, Grant, in a note to Meade, questioned Warren's management of his troops that day. "I don't understand why Warren permitted his corps to be fought in detail when Ayres pushed forward. He should have sent other troops to their support."[20]

Grant had been dissatisfied with what he perceived to be Warren's dilatoriness since Spotsylvania Court House, when he had instructed Meade, "If Warren fails to attack promptly, send Humphreys to command his corps and relieve him." It hadn't been necessary. In his *Personal Memoirs*, Grant said that while Warren was intelligent and perceptive, he anticipated every conceivable threat and prepared to meet them all.[21]

No one doubted Warren's intelligence and peculiar genius. At sixteen, he had entered the US Military Academy, graduating second in the Class of 1850. During the decade before the war, Warren became one of the army's top cartographers; among his accomplishments was a map conflating all the transcontinental railroad surveys.

Warren's talent for identifying key terrain features may have saved the Union army at Gettysburg, where, as chief engineer for the Army of the Potomac, he recognized the tactical importance of Little Round Top and rushed troops there minutes before the Rebels arrived. Meade rewarded him with temporary command of II Corps when Winfield Scott Hancock was wounded, then gave him permanent command of V Corps during the Overland Campaign.[22]

APRIL 1, 1865–FIVE FORKS—Grant assigned Porter to ride with Sheridan all day, ordering him to send Grant updates every half hour or so. This April Fool's Day promised to be a memorable one, with Sheridan and Warren seemingly poised like millstones to crush Pickett's army between them. If all went according to plan, Lee would have no choice but to abandon Petersburg.

Porter met Sheridan at about 11 a.m. Sheridan had slept little but was sharp and active. The Rebels had withdrawn to their entrenchments at Five Forks, he told Porter, irritably adding that two of Warren's divisions had finally reached the area, though not Warren himself, who had been expected since midnight but had stopped to rebuild a bridge. As if on cue, Warren rode up a few minutes later and reported to Sheridan.

Never one to waste time lamenting a lost opportunity, Sheridan sketched a new battle plan in the dirt with his saber. While Sheridan's dismounted cavalrymen blazed away at the Rebel front line with their Spencer repeaters and harried the Confederate right flank, Warren would move his corps into position near Pickett's left flank. When Warren's men were ready, V Corps and the Cavalry Corps would both attack. If the plan worked, Pickett's force would be trapped and destroyed.[23]

Sheridan urged Warren to move quickly. But Warren lived up to his reputation for acting at his own deliberate pace. He further annoyed Sheridan by sending his staff officers to inform his division commanders of the battle plan rather than seeing to the task personally—as Sheridan would have done. Warren rode off.[24]

After observing Warren's conduct the day before on White Oak Road, Grant, too, was beset by fresh doubts about his general. About an hour after Sheridan and Warren met, Lieutenant Colonel Orville Babcock of Grant's staff—later, President Grant's private secretary—rode up to Sheridan with a remarkable message from the general in chief. Sheridan was authorized to relieve Warren if, said Grant, V Corps would be better served by one of its division commanders. Sheridan remarked that he hoped he would not have to take that action.[25]

When three hours passed without any gunfire coming from the Rebel left signifying that V Corps was attacking, Sheridan rode out to find Warren. The head of Warren's column was just then appearing at Gravelly Run Church, a half mile from the Confederate left flank—and just two miles from its starting point. Sheridan found Warren sitting under a tree making a sketch in the dirt. "I was disappointed that more of the corps was not already up," Sheridan wrote, "and as the precious minutes went by without any apparent effort to hurry the troops on to the field, this disappointment grew into disgust."

Sheridan told Warren that his cavalrymen might run out of ammunition before Warren's men attacked. He added that "the sun would go down before the battle could be begun," giving Lee time to send troops from Petersburg, just three miles away, to strike Sheridan's rear. Warren displayed "decided apathy," Sheridan angrily observed, "and he remarked with indifference that 'Bobby Lee was always getting people into trouble.'"

It took every ounce of self-restraint for Sheridan to refrain from giving Warren a tongue-lashing. But he did break protocol by complaining to his staff that Warren, fearing defeat, evidently did not want to fight.[26]

Sheridan's staff officers watched Warren's show of coolness with raised eyebrows. "We remarked to each other that there would be a deuce of a row if the Fifth Corps was not ready to move out soon," Newhall wrote.[27]

More time passed. Porter watched Sheridan's impatience grow. "He made every possible appeal for promptness, dismounted from his horse, paced up and down, struck the clenched fist of one hand against the palm of the other, and fretted like a caged tiger," wrote Porter. At one point Sheridan exclaimed, "This battle must be fought and won before the sun goes down." At 4 p.m., V Corps was finally ready.

"HOLD FIVE FORKS AT all hazards," read Lee's orders to Pickett. "Protect road to Ford's Depot and prevent Union forces from striking the Southside Railroad." Pickett's five infantry brigades were bookended by the two Lees' dismounted cavalrymen and supported by ten guns. Pickett was as ready to meet a Union attack as he would ever be.

But as the hours passed without a Yankee assault on his entrenchments, Pickett became convinced that there would be no attack that day. Fitzhugh Lee thought the same, believing that the Dinwiddie fight had disrupted Sheridan's plans. And so Pickett and Fitzhugh Lee decided to go to a shad bake.[28]

Major General Thomas Rosser had invited Pickett and Lee to his camp a mile and a half north of Five Forks at Hatcher's Run, where Rosser's cavalry division was in reserve. The shad were running, and Rosser had caught a mess of them on the Nottoway River with a borrowed seine. At 2 p.m. the officers sat down to feast on the shad prepared by Rosser's commissary officer and to imbibe some of Rosser's choice spirits.

Couriers brought Pickett updates from Five Forks, where no attack had yet occurred but where enemy movements appeared to be pointing toward one. Pickett, however, elected to remain at the shad bake. Sergeant J. B. Flippin, carrying a message from Colonel Thomas Munford to Fitzhugh Lee, found Pickett and Lee sitting under a tent fly with a bottle of whiskey or brandy. Pickett instructed Flippin to tell Munford "to do the best [he] could."[29]

About 4 p.m., Pickett handed one of Rosser's couriers a note to carry to Five Forks. The messenger was still in sight when bluecoats suddenly appeared and captured him. Then, a line of Union infantry emerged from the woods and crossed the road. The party was over.[30]

WARREN'S 12,000 MEN IN three divisions—his effective force down 3,000 from three days earlier—advanced on Pickett's left flank in double and triple battle lines. The 1,000 cavalrymen from the Army of the James led by Mackenzie, who was as lethally aggressive as Sheridan and Custer, roved V Corps's right flank and scattered Brigadier General William Roberts's Rebel cavalry brigade on White Oak Road.

A shower of artillery fire and the zip-zip of musket balls greeted Ayres's Yankee infantrymen as they advanced on the Rebels' upturned left flank through dense woods laced by ravines. To Ayres's right, Crawford's division neared the Confederate rear, where it was to make a sharp left turn after crossing White Oak Road, remaining in contact with Ayres's right. Behind the two divisions was Griffin's division in reserve. Crawford's division, however, mistakenly pushed several hundred yards past White Oak Road before wheeling left. A gap opened up between his men and Ayres's.

When they heard V Corps go into action, 7,000 of Sheridan's dismounted cavalrymen rose up and launched their frontal assault. Ayres's regiments charged into a swarm of Rebels, whose musketry shredded the Yankees' ranks. Not fully recovered from their drubbing by Bushrod Johnson's Rebels the previous day, Ayres's men began to waver.

Fearing that the attack might stall, Sheridan snatched up his two-starred, swallow-tailed standard and rode into the midst of Ayres's flagging division, swinging his clenched fist and shouting, "Smash 'em! Smash 'em!" He rode along the front of the lines, encouraging each regiment. Rebels poured gunfire into the attackers from an angle in their earthworks.

The Rebels turned their firepower on Sheridan and his escort. A ball pierced Sheridan's flag. A color sergeant went down, dead. A quartermaster was wounded, and staff officers tumbled to the ground when their horses were shot. "Come on, men!" Porter heard Sheridan cry. "Go at 'em with a will! Move on at a clean jump, or you'll not catch one of them!"[31]

In the woods, Sheridan encountered Brigadier General Joshua Chamberlain, whose brigade of Griffin's division had stormed Bushrod Johnson's positions the day before when Johnson routed Ayres's and Crawford's divisions. Chamberlain had been sent from Griffin's reserve division to plug the gap between Ayres and Crawford.

Sheridan was pleased to see Chamberlain leading his men. "By God, that's what I want to see—general officers at the front!" Sheridan exclaimed to the hero of Little Round Top, who was in great pain from recent battle wounds. Sheridan told Chamberlain to take charge of all the infantrymen scattered throughout the area and to fill the space between Ayres and Crawford. Chamberlain rode among the men, firing them up.[32]

Porter saw a man struck in the neck by a bullet fall to the ground, blood spurting from his jugular. "I'm killed!" he yelled. Sheridan rode up and said, "You're not hurt a bit! Pick up your gun, man, and move right on to the front." Incredibly, his words inspired the soldier to snatch up his musket. He rushed forward a dozen steps before falling dead.[33]

Sheridan spurred Rienzi over the angled earthworks on the Rebel left and landed amid a group of startled Confederates, who threw down their muskets in surrender. They asked Sheridan where they should go.

He pointed to the rear. "Get right along now," Sheridan said. "Drop your guns; you'll never need them any more. You'll all be safe over there. Are there any more of you? We want every one of you fellows."

Along Pickett's front line, Devin's and Custer's cavalrymen poured over the Rebel earthworks and seized the enemy's guns.

Pickett's task force crumbled and broke, although some Rebels valiantly attempted to re-form on Ford's Road to bar the Yankees from going around Robert E. Lee's right flank and entering Petersburg. Correspondent Alfred Townsend of the *New York Herald* described the desperate charge of a shattered Rebel regiment that came on "like the surge from the fog, depleted, but determined." Repulsed and forced into a hollow square, the Confederates fought until most of them fell. The survivors fled.

Custer's and Devin's men rounded up prisoners on the front line, as Ayres's troops collected captives on the Confederate left flank. Griffin, Crawford, and Mackenzie tried to intercept the retreating Rebels flowing westward through the woods.

More than 5,000 Confederates were captured, on top of Pickett's losses of several hundred killed or wounded. Just half of Lee's task force escaped. As the "drones of silent 'Johnnies'" were led into captivity, the jubilant Yankees badgered them with shouts and catcalls.

Sheridan's dissatisfaction with Warren now reached its acme. Sheridan had rallied Ayres's division of Warren's corps when it lost heart, and he had ordered Chamberlain's brigade of Griffin's division to fill a gap, but nowhere had he seen Warren. Was he even in the battle? Sheridan wondered. Two staff officers sent by Sheridan to tell Warren to collar the wayward Crawford and send him to Ayres's aid could not find him. Sheridan had to instead bring up the rest of Griffin's reserve division.

Warren, however, had chased after Crawford's division when he saw that it had gone off course and had managed to turn it and attack the Rebel rear. During the fight, Warren's horse was shot, and two officers near him were killed. Crawford's division rolled over a Rebel brigade and captured hundreds of Confederates as they streamed west.

Warren sent Colonel H. C. Bankhead, his inspector general, to inform Sheridan of his whereabouts and to tell him that Crawford's division had gotten between Pickett and Petersburg. But by then, Sheridan was livid.

"By God, sir, tell General Warren he wasn't in that fight!" Sheridan exploded to Bankhead. The shocked colonel asked Sheridan if he could write down what he had just said. "Take it down, sir!" Sheridan snapped. "Tell him by God he was not at the front."

A short time later, Sheridan informed Warren that he was relieved from duty and that he must report to Grant's headquarters for new orders. Sheridan appointed Griffin to command V Corps.

Warren rode to Sheridan's headquarters to request that Sheridan reconsider his decision. Sheridan retorted, "Reconsider? Hell! I don't reconsider my determinations."[34]

IN HIS BATTLE REPORT, Sheridan asserted that Warren "did not exert himself to get up his corps as rapidly as he might have done, and his manner gave me the impression that he wished the sun to go down before dispositions for the attack could be completed." This was unfair; Warren might have been slow in joining Sheridan and getting into position, but he never exhibited an unwillingness to fight.

Warren also "did not exert himself to inspire" Ayres's division when it appeared to lose heart, claimed Sheridan. Warren said that his presence was never requested, and that he thought it best to remain where couriers from all of his divisions could easily find him. For his part, Grant was "very sorry" that Warren had to be relieved and "regretted still more that [he] had not long before taken occasion to assign him to another field of duty."[35]

During the years that followed, when Grant was commanding general and then president, Warren's requests for a court of inquiry were routinely denied. The question of whether Sheridan was justified in dismissing Warren, a man with an otherwise unblemished record, remained unanswered. No longer deemed a fit combat leader, Warren returned to the Army Corps of Engineers, where he built bridges and wrote prolifically. Finally, in 1879, Warren got his hearing.

After sifting through shelves of testimony and depositions, the military court in November 1882 exonerated Warren of the principal charge against him—that he had neglected his duties at Five Forks. But the court also found that he had not managed his command effectively, either at Five Forks or during the White Oak Road battle the previous day. The verdict satisfied no one. Warren had died three months before the findings' release. And Sheridan grumpily described the findings as "more in the nature of apologies than in the annunciation of the facts as shown in the evidence."[36]

JOSHUA CHAMBERLAIN, WHO HAD never served with Sheridan before Five Forks, wrote, "We had had a taste of his style of fighting, and we liked it. . . . Sheridan does not entrench. He pushes on, carrying his flank and rear with him—rushing, flashing, smashing. . . . He shows the power of a commander—inspiring both confidence and fear."[37]

After the battle Porter told Sheridan that he had exposed himself more than Porter believed a corps commander should—to which Sheridan replied, "I have never in my life taken a command into battle, and had the slightest desire to come out alive unless I won."[38]

Exhausted by the day's fighting, Sheridan stretched out on the ground before a fire, his head propped on a saddle. Sylvanus Cadwallader of the *New York Herald* sat beside him, writing his newspaper report of the battle—with Sheridan's editorial assistance.

When Porter rode off to Grant's headquarters, he observed that along the clogged roads, corduroyed in places with captured muskets, "everybody was riotous over the victory." Arriving at Grant's headquarters, Porter discovered that Grant and his staff had not yet learned of Sheridan's great triumph.

Grant and most of his staff were sitting before a blazing fire when Porter began shouting that Pickett had been beaten. Everyone "but the imperturbable general-in-chief" began exclaiming with joy. "For some minutes there was a bewildering state of excitement, and officers fell to grasping hands, shouting and hugging each other like schoolboys. It meant the beginning of the end, the reaching of the 'last ditch,'" Porter happily noted.

Forgetting army etiquette, Porter clapped Grant on the back, "to his no little astonishment." Grant disappeared into his tent and began writing out dispatches. He emerged to announce that he had just issued orders for an immediate all-out assault on Petersburg.

Grant's chief of staff, General John Rawlins, sat down and penned these words to his wife: "The hero of the Shenandoah stands affront of all on the Appomattox [River]. His personal gallantry and great genius have secured us a great success today." Sheridan's "great generalship" at Dinwiddie, Grant wrote, where he stubbornly fought Pickett with dismounted cavalry instead of retreating, had made the victory at Five Forks possible.

Five Forks has been justifiably nicknamed "the Waterloo of the Confederacy." Sheridan shattered Pickett's task force, rendering Petersburg and Richmond indefensible. The nine-month stalemate was ended. In a finger snap, the Union army again crackled with optimism and determination. Five Forks, wrote Porter, "pointed to peace and home."[39]

CHAPTER 12

The Race to Appomattox

APRIL 1865

Damn them, I wish they had held out an hour longer and I would have whipped hell out of them.
—SHERIDAN REACTING TO THE TRUCE AT APPOMATTOX
COURT HOUSE[1]

PHILIP SHERIDAN'S TROOPERS SEVERED the Southside Railroad, a vital escape route for Robert E. Lee's besieged troops in Petersburg. From the Confederate citadel ten miles to the northeast, the distant thump of cannon fire and the roar of musketry reached the cavalrymen's ears. At 4:45 a.m. on April 2, four Union army corps had launched an all-out attack on the city.

The triumphant Cavalry Corps cheered lustily whenever their fierce-looking leader rode along the column. Lieutenant Colonel Frederick Newhall noted that he had rarely seen such zeal for a commander "since the old enthusiastic days."[2] One and all, the men recognized the momentousness of Five Forks, and Sheridan's integral role in it.

Not only was Five Forks the first unmistakable Union military victory over Lee's army since Ulysses Grant took command a year earlier, but it made Lee's continued occupation of Petersburg impossible. Grant had hoped that by sending Sheridan to threaten Lee's right flank, he would compel Lee either to attack him or to abandon Petersburg. In fact, Sheridan's movement had accomplished both objects. The collapse of Petersburg's southwestern defenses and Grant's all-out attack meant that the Confederates had to abandon the city immediately or be destroyed.[3]

AT HIS HEADQUARTERS AT the Turnbull House on Edge Hill, Lee heard the thunder of his impending doom. He had seen this coming since the previous summer, when he had failed to stop Grant from reaching the James River. To Jubal Early, he had presciently written, "If he gets [to the James], it will become a siege, and then it will be a mere question of time."

The gaunt veterans still loyal to the Southern cause had fought for years, and many of them had been wounded at least once. But Petersburg's miserable trenches, the drenching rains, the semistarvation rations, and the very stasis of a siege had driven their morale to its lowest point. Desertions had spiked to one hundred or more a day—with groups of neighbors and relatives sometimes slipping away together. There were probably no more than 35,000 effectives at Petersburg on April 2, when the Union troops massed outside the city launched their onslaught.

Lee recognized that time had finally run out for Petersburg and the Confederate capital, Richmond, and that both cities must be evacuated.[4]

VIGOROUS, DISCIPLINED, AND PROACTIVE, Lee rarely indulged his dark fears about his unraveling army. Penned up these nine months at Petersburg, he almost welcomed preparing for the likelihood of a retreat, because it at least promised movement, on which Lee thrived.

Planning had begun in February. The army's objective would be Danville, a Rebel supply depot 140 miles to the southwest, followed by a union with General Joseph Johnston's 20,000-man Army of Tennessee in North Carolina. Lee's last hope was that his and Johnston's combined armies might crush William Sherman, then return to Virginia to drive out Grant.

The time to leave Petersburg was at hand. Lee ordered the withdrawal to begin at dusk—if his army could hang on for that long. Lee sent a telegram that reached President Jefferson Davis as he was attending Sunday services at St. Paul's Episcopal Church.

As Davis read Lee's message, nearby worshippers saw him blanch. Leave Richmond immediately, the telegram said. That night, a train filled with Confederate government officials, boxes of government files, and more than $500,000 in gold and silver crossed the James River, headed south. Smoke and flames began to fill the sky behind them.[5]

The next day, April 3, black Union troops from Major General Godfrey Weitzel's XXV Corps entered Richmond as its quailing citizens braced themselves for rapine, looting, and murder. Instead, Weitzel's men put out the fires set by the retreating Rebels—although not before the conflagration had destroyed tobacco warehouses, foundries, gunboats, the armory, and most of the downtown business district.

EARLY ON APRIL 2, 60,000 Union troops smashed six miles of A. P. Hill's III Corps lines. Horatio Wright's VI Corps infantrymen were the first to breach Petersburg's defenses. Suddenly there were bluecoats in the woods and fields near the city. III Corps losses included Hill, shot dead during a confrontation with Union Troops.

As night fell, the Confederate army marched out of Petersburg. Burning buildings lighted the way along the muddy roads to Pocahontas Bridge over the Appomattox River. The thirty-mile-long train included tens of thousands of thin, gray-uniformed troops, as well as 4,000 gaunt horses and mules pulling 1,000 supply and ammunition wagons and more than two hundred guns. They pressed on through the night for Amelia Court House, one hundred railroad miles from Danville and North Carolina.

Amelia Court House, forty miles from both Petersburg and Richmond, would be the rendezvous point for Lieutenant General Richard Ewell's mixed units of Richmond reserves, marines, and artillerists; Lieutenant General James Longstreet's I Corps from the far left; and Lee's Petersburg troops. Lee had ordered 350,000 rations to be sent to Amelia from Greensboro, Lynchburg, and Danville. The prospect of plentiful food kept the hungry Rebels marching all that night and the next day.[6]

THE YANKEES TRAILED LEE's army by a full day—except for George Custer's cavalry division, which harried the Rebels' left rear sporadically throughout April 3 in the hope of provoking the Confederates to stop and fight. During a clash at Namozine Church, Custer's men captured 1,200 Rebels. Sheridan informed Grant that a Yankee prisoner who was recaptured by Union troops reported "not one in five of the rebels have arms in their hands."

With the Richmond & Danville Railroad still open to the south, Lee planned to resupply at Amelia and then to transport supplies and food by rail as he marched south to Danville. By shifting his operational base there from Richmond, Lee would shorten his own supply lines and lengthen Grant's.

BUT WHEN THE CONFEDERATES reached Amelia Court House on April 4, the promised rations were not there. Instead of food, the Rebels found boxcars filled with caissons, crates of ammunition, and harnesses. What happened to Lee's order and the rations has never been explained.

Lee sent foragers throughout the boggy countryside to find food. The need for it was now so acute as to eclipse military priorities. He was waiting, too, for Ewell, whose troops had been delayed in crossing the Appomattox River.

Lee's one-day lead over his pursuers evaporated as his foragers gathered what scanty supplies they could for the 45,000 Rebel soldiers gathering at Amelia from Petersburg and Richmond. "The delay was fatal," Lee later acknowledged, "and could not be retrieved."[7]

THE DELAY WAS A godsend for Sheridan, whose Cavalry Corps, hot on Lee's trail, was gobbling up Rebel stragglers. Grant updated President Abraham Lincoln at City Point: "I have not yet heard from Sheridan, but I have an abiding faith that he is in the right place at the right time."

When Sheridan surfaced on April 3, Grant informed him that the Rebels were converging on Amelia Court House. "The first object of the present movement will be to intercept Lee's army, and the second to secure Burkeville," he wrote. Burkeville Junction was on the Richmond & Danville Railroad line twenty miles southwest of Amelia.

Sheridan sent George Crook's and Wesley Merritt's cavalrymen ahead to Jetersville, midway between Burkeville and Amelia, with V Corps right behind them. If the Yankees reached Jetersville before Lee, the Confederates would have to find another way to Danville or continue traveling west to Lynchburg.[8]

The Cavalry Corps arrived at Jetersville on April 4 to find that the Confederate army had not yet been there. And then pickets arrested a man with two copies of a telegram from Lee's army ordering 300,000 rations to be sent to Burkeville Junction. The telegraph lines were down at Amelia, and the man was under orders to send the telegram to Danville and Lynchburg from the first working telegraph station.

Sheridan exulted at the stroke of good fortune; the telegram not only apprised him of Lee's location and approximate troop strength but suggested that the Rebels were "short of provisions." Two of Major Henry Young's scouts, disguised as Confederate troopers, set out toward Danville and Lynchburg with instructions to send the telegrams to the intended recipients.

Sheridan planned to appropriate the provisions for his own men. During their rapid march, the Cavalry Corps and V Corps had outrun the supply trains and were "hard up for rations." The infantrymen, who had covered twenty miles in the warm, hazy weather, had resorted to shooting cattle in the fields for their dinners.[9]

On April 5, Lee sent cavalry scouts toward Burkeville Station. If the way was clear, he intended to march to Burkeville and collect the 300,000 rations he had requested from Danville and Lynchburg.[10] But when his scouts informed him that Union cavalrymen were at Jetersville and V Corps was digging in nearby, Lee decided to march west to Farmville, twenty miles away. From Farmville, the Confederates might yet turn southeast, slip behind the Yankees at Jetersville, and reach Burkeville Junction.

Brigadier General Henry Davies's cavalry brigade from Crook's division, scouting near Amelia Court House, spotted Lee's army on the march. Lee was traveling west, not south, Davies reported to Sheridan.[11]

Major General George Meade, prostrated by nerves and indigestion and riding in an ambulance, arrived at Jetersville with II Corps and VI Corps. Meade ordered Sheridan to ready his cavalry, as well as II, V, and VI Corps, to march on Amelia Court House.

Sheridan pointed out that Lee had already started for Farmville—and that the army should fast-march straight west and place itself in Lee's path rather than "make our pursuit a stern-chase." Unimpressed by Sheridan's plan, Meade ordered him to wait until the rest of the Army of the Potomac reached Jetersville.

Sheridan fumed at the delay, which he was certain would allow Lee to escape. He sent a telegram to Grant, who was traveling behind the army, and included the contents of a captured letter written by a Confederate staff officer, Colonel William Taylor, to his mother in Michlenburg, to "give you [Grant] an idea of the condition of the enemy." Taylor's letter began with the words "Our army is ruined, I fear."

Sheridan then got to the gist of what he really wanted to tell Grant: "I wish you were here yourself," he wrote. "I feel confident of capturing the Army of Northern Virginia if we exert ourselves. I see no escape for Lee."[12]

As he hoped they would, Sheridan's words brought Grant to Jetersville. Just before midnight, Grant, his staff, and Sylvanus Cadwallader of the *New York Herald* burst into Sheridan's headquarters, a small log cabin in the middle of a tobacco field, rousting Sheridan from his sleeping place on the floor upstairs.

Sheridan scrambled down the ladder, spread out his maps, and eagerly showed Grant where the Union army was located and where he believed Lee was headed. Sheridan declared that if Meade would make a night march, "then not a man of Lee's army would escape." Cadwallader said Sheridan was emphatic, enthusiastic, "and not a little profane in expressing his opinions."

Grant listened with an expression of "quiet enjoyment" and mildly told Sheridan that he must not expect too much too soon. Sheridan sputtered that not a single regiment would escape "and reiterated the opinion many times." The two generals then went to see Meade in his tent.

Grant explained to the Army of the Potomac commander that "we did not want to follow the enemy; we wanted to get ahead of him" and that Meade's plan "would

allow the enemy to escape." Meade changed his orders. The infantry would march
north to Amelia Court House as planned, but Sheridan's cavalrymen would ride
west, shadowing Lee's army and watching for opportunities to attack or head off
the enemy column.

Brigadier General Joshua Chamberlain wrote that, from that moment forward,
"Meade was no longer in reality commander of the Army of the Potomac, but only
the vanishing simulacrum of it." Grant and Sheridan were directing the chase.[13]

EWELL'S CORPS FROM RICHMOND had no sooner reached Amelia Court House
on April 5 than Lee issued the order to march. It was late in the day, but Lee could
not afford to wait; his men were hungry, and 80,000 rations in railroad cars from
Lynchburg awaited them at Farmville. The Confederates would have to march all
night—and Ewell's just-arrived troops would get no rest. "This was the most cruel
marching order the commanders had given the men in four years of fighting," wrote
Confederate army historian Douglas Southall Freeman.

Longstreet's I Corps, which had absorbed the late A. P. Hill's III Corps, was in
the lead, followed by Richard Anderson's IV Corps, containing the remnants of
George Pickett's and Bushrod Johnson's divisions. Then came Ewell's Reserve Corps,
made up of the Richmond defense forces, the marines, and the reserves. It was followed by the wagon train. John Gordon's II Corps formed the rearguard.

The Rebel column stretched for many miles down the dark, muddy road,
clogged with horses, mules, and wagons. The bone-weary, gaunt troops were forced
to travel at an agonizing "inchworm pace," taking a few steps and then standing
and waiting; they often covered no more than a mile in one hour. Straggling and
desertions reached epidemic proportions. The shrinking Army of Northern Virginia
dwindled further.[14]

As they pursued Lee to Farmville, Joshua Chamberlain's two brigades of New
Englanders and Pennsylvanians came upon a stretch of low ground where the mud
was axle deep. The area was strewn with abandoned wagons "stuck fast in the
mire—the trembling mules still harnessed to the wrecks; horses starved and over-
tasked, but still saddled and packed, turned loose by their masters." Chamberlain
also saw a place where some of Sheridan's cavalrymen had "burst across the flying
column and left a black and withered track behind [them] like the lightning's path"
of burned wagons and supplies.[15]

THE "BLACK DAY OF the Army of Northern Virginia," as it became known in the
South, began with Meade's infantrymen reaching Amelia Court House in a morning drizzle on April 6. As Sheridan had tried to tell Meade, Lee was gone. "I did
not permit my cavalry to participate in Meade's useless advance," Sheridan wrote,
a touch smugly.

The Cavalry Corps was riding directly west from Jetersville, parallel to Lee's army. Sheridan ordered his commanders to launch flank attacks to slow the Confederates so that Meade's infantry could overtake them. Grant's army, Sheridan believed, must stop the Rebels from reaching Lynchburg, fifty miles beyond Farmville.[16]

Grant moved VI Corps from the army's right side to its left—so that it could operate with Sheridan's cavalry, "with which they had formerly served so harmoniously and so efficiently in the valley of Virginia." Sheridan once more commanded Wright's crack corps, whose stand at Cedar Creek had presaged a spectacular victory. Grant's extraordinary action—unprecedented amid a hot pursuit of the enemy—signified his unbounded faith in Sheridan's judgment and abilities.[17]

That morning, Major General Edward O. C. Ord, commander of the Army of the James, had sent a small brigade of six hundred infantry and cavalry to burn a railroad bridge, known as High Bridge, over the Appomattox River before Lee's army could get there. If Colonel Theodore Read's brigade succeeded, part of Lee's army might be pinned on the south bank and destroyed before it could cross on the smaller bridges nearby.

But the task force reached the bridge just as Longstreet's corps appeared. Believing that the Yankees were the vanguard of a much larger column, the Rebels dug in.

Read valiantly drew up his little brigade in a line, made an inspirational speech, and led it in repeated, albeit futile, attacks on the Rebels—against odds of twenty to one or more.

Most of Read's men were killed or wounded. Read perished in a dramatic pistol duel with a Confederate cavalry commander, Brigadier General James Dearing, who died two weeks later of wounds inflicted by Read. The Yankee survivors surrendered. Grant wrote of this seemingly minor action, "This gallant band of six hundred" delayed Lee's column and "no doubt saved to us the trains following."[18]

SHERIDAN'S TROOPERS SHADOWED LEE's column to Sailor's Creek, a picturesque stream in the Virginia Piedmont country between Amelia Court House and Farmville. The wooded hills, fields, farms, and creeks were charmingly bucolic, but Sailor's Creek would become a byword for disaster for the exhausted Rebels.

A gap had opened between Longstreet's corps and Anderson's corps to its rear. Behind Anderson marched Ewell's corps, followed by the wagon train and then Gordon's corps. Unaware that it had become separated from the rest of the army, Longstreet's corps marched on, and the gap widened. Anderson neglected to inform Longstreet of the breach.[19]

Earlier, Sheridan had messaged Grant: "I think that now is the time to attack them with all your infantry." The Rebels had marched all night and were in bad shape, he wrote. "They are reported to have begged provisions of the people of the country all along the road as they passed." Grant assured Sheridan that "the Sixth Corps will go in with a vim any place you may dictate."[20]

Sheridan's Cavalry Corps struck where the interval between Longstreet's corps and Anderson's was greatest. Throwing itself across the road, Crook's cavalry division, supported on the right by Thomas Devin's and Custer's troopers, attacked Anderson's infantrymen. Sheridan sent a message to Horatio Wright to bring VI Corps into action as fast as his men could run.[21]

Ewell reacted to the looming disaster by alertly sending the vulnerable supply train on a side road to the northwest. But he failed to tell Gordon, whose corps was behind the wagons, to remain with Ewell and not to march after the train. And so Gordon followed the wagons as they veered off the main road, with Major General Andrew Humphrey's II Corps on his heels. Anderson's and Ewell's communication lapses had broken Lee's army into three segments, setting the stage for its ruin.[22]

As the Cavalry Corps poured into the gap, Anderson's divisions, led by Major Generals Joseph Kershaw and George W. Custis Lee, Robert E. Lee's oldest son, threw up fence-rail breastworks and fought back.[23]

Behind Anderson, Ewell was just discovering that Gordon was gone and that his scratch corps was now the rearguard. Ewell placed his men on a ridge paralleling Sailor's Creek and faced northeast. Within minutes, the hill on the creek's other side teemed with bluecoats; two divisions from VI Corps had arrived.[24]

Exactly how many Rebels remained in the Army of Northern Virginia after its all-night march cannot be known with certainty, but an educated guess would be no more than 30,000. Possibly 15,000 of them were now under attack by three Union corps whose numbers exceeded 45,000. While Gordon fought a running battle with Humphrey's II Corps, Anderson and Ewell were trapped between Sheridan's three cavalry divisions and Wright's two infantry divisions.

VI Corps's lead regiments splashed across Sailor's Creek and charged the ridge where Ewell's infantrymen lay in the grass to present smaller targets for Wright's fulminating batteries. As one, the Rebels rose to discharge volleys of musket fire into the oncoming Yankees, driving them back across the creek. "The water in the creek was dancing over the dropping bullets," wrote Sheridan aide Frederick Newhall. "A good many men were falling."

VI Corps charged again, in greater numbers. And then, to everyone's amazement, a small Richmond brigade of Confederate marines and Georgia artillerymen, clad in scarlet-trimmed uniforms made for the parade ground, furiously counterattacked. They forced the Union infantrymen back over the creek—"with an élan which has never been surpassed," wrote the awed Newhall—and defiantly planted the Stars and Bars at the water's edge. "I was never more astonished," wrote Wright, the commander of VI Corps. The valorous display ended when the gallant marines and cannoneers were smashed to pieces by Yankee musket and artillery fire.[25]

Custer's and Devin's cavalry divisions squeezed Anderson's beleaguered corps front and rear, while Crook battered its midsection. Some of the most intensive fighting of the war took place here. "The enemy fought with desperation to escape capture, and we, bent on his destruction, were no less eager and determined," wrote Sheridan.[26]

"Never mind your flanks!" Sheridan shouted when he saw troopers dismounting. "Go through them! They're demoralized as hell!"[27]

Anderson's divisions broke, but there was nowhere to go. Somehow, Anderson escaped with two brigades. Then, the Cavalry Corps struck Ewell's infantry from behind as VI Corps swarmed up the ridge in his front. With the tigerish ferocity of men who have lost all hope, the Confederates fought with clubbed muskets, bayonets, and fists until their dead lay in dense windrows, but they had no chance against the thousands of bluecoats all around them. Ewell surrendered.[28]

It was a tour de force by Sheridan, who had brilliantly coordinated the operations of large cavalry and infantry forces in a running fight over unfamiliar terrain to trap and destroy two Confederate corps. His months-long apprenticeship in combined operations in the Shenandoah Valley had prepared him for this apotheosis of tactical mastery. No other Union general could have accomplished what Sheridan had done.

ON A NEARBY HILL, Lee sat astride his horse Traveller with the rearguard of Longstreet's corps and surveyed the wreckage of nearly half his army: 8,000 men from Ewell's and Anderson's corps had been made prisoners. Gordon had largely eluded the clutches of II Corps but had lost three hundred wagons, four guns, and another 1,700 men to captivity.

"My God! Has the army been dissolved?" Lee reportedly exclaimed as dazed survivors streamed up the hill toward him. Not dissolved, but a third of it was gone.

Among the nearly 10,000 prisoners were half a dozen generals, including Ewell, Kershaw, and Custis Lee. That night, Union officers shared their fire with the captive Rebel officers. Ewell, sitting on the ground, silently hugged his knees in "utter despondency."[29]

Sheridan informed Grant that the Cavalry Corps and VI Corps had "routed them handsomely" and continued to pursue Lee. "If the thing is pressed I think that Lee will surrender," he wrote.[30] When Grant passed Sheridan's message to Lincoln at City Point, the president telegraphed Grant, "Let the thing be pressed."[31]

LEE'S ARMY WAS RAPIDLY disintegrating under the Union army's hammer blows. A broad swath of discarded Confederate ammunition and weapons, and dead and dying horses, marked the dying Rebel army's passage. After stopping to examine a dead Rebel soldier in the road, Lieutenant Edward Tobie noted that he had "every appearance of having died from hunger and exhaustion."[32] "Horses and mules dead or dying in the mud," wrote a Confederate artilleryman. "The constant marching and fighting without sleep or food are rapidly thinning the ranks of this grand old army."[33]

While Crook's division kept Lee under observation, Sheridan swung southwest of Farmville with Custer's and Devin's divisions. The Cavalry Corps traveled at the "long slinging walk" acquired during the corps's many campaigns. Lieutenant Colonel Newhall marveled that 10,000 cavalrymen, who a year earlier had alternated between straggling and galloping on their marches, could now travel from daybreak to dark without a single regiment altering its gait.

On April 7, Sheridan and his two cavalry divisions reached the hamlet of Prince Edward Court House, which lay ten miles from Farmville. If Lee suddenly pivoted and marched south, hoping to reach Danville, Sheridan's cavalry could block the Confederates' path.[34]

AFTER DISPOSING OF READ'S brigade, Longstreet's I Corps crossed the Appomattox River, intent on reaching the 80,000 rations awaiting them at Farmville. The Rebels set fire to the Appomattox bridges, but Crook's cavalry division, snapping at their heels, managed to save one of them. The Yankee troopers got over the river and overtook the Rebels.

Like a cornered wolf, Longstreet's infantry counterattacked Crook's mounted troops, forcing Colonel J. Irvin Gregg's brigade back across the Appomattox and capturing Gregg. At Farmville, the Confederates collected their two days' rations, but they could not rest with the Yankees pressing them.[35]

When the report of Crook's fight reached Sheridan, he knew that Lee's destination was Lynchburg, not Danville, and he made a new plan. Much like at Sailor's Creek, Sheridan intended to pin Longstreet's and Gordon's corps between his cavalrymen and infantrymen. He would "throw [his] cavalry again across his [Lee's] path, and hold him till the infantry could overtake him."

Late on April 7, Sheridan ordered Crook to bring his division to Prospect Station to join the rest of the Cavalry Corps. Together they would ride to Appomattox Station in the hope of getting in front of Lee.[36]

THAT NIGHT, GRANT CALLED upon Lee to surrender. "The result of the last week must convince you of the hopelessness of further resistance," Grant wrote. The message reached Lee northwest of Farmville, where the weary Rebels had halted after a daylong slog over muddy roads, harassed by Crook's cavalry. Without comment, Lee handed the note to Longstreet, who returned it, saying only, "Not yet."

Lee wrote to Grant that he disagreed with Grant's analysis of his army's plight, but he asked what terms Grant was offering. Grant replied that Lee's men must lay down their arms until exchanged. To Sheridan, Grant expressed optimism early on April 8 that "Lee will surrender today. . . . We will push him until terms are agreed upon."

As Grant was writing those words during the predawn hours of April 8, Lee tried to steal a march on the Yankees to Appomattox Station. There he hoped to obtain the rations that he had requested from Lynchburg. Sheridan and Lee were racing for the same destination.[37]

SINCE LEE'S ARMY HAD left Amelia Court House, the Rebels had been harried and attacked, receiving little rest or sustenance. Saturday, April 8, a warm, springlike day, was their first respite. For once, the ragged men in gray had both ample rations—thanks to the shipment at Farmville—and relative peace and quiet.

While these unexpected gifts improved the Rebels' morale, the mass desertions and straggling continued. Moreover, Sailor's Creek had severely eroded their staunch belief that the Army of Northern Virginia would somehow survive. Defeatism had begun spreading through the army, even infecting Lee's lieutenants.

Brigadier General William Pendleton, Lee's artillery chief, West Point contemporary, and good friend, was nominated by a group of high-ranking Confederate officers to urge surrender. As Lee rested under a pine tree, Pendleton stated his case; Lee rejected the proposition. Instead, he consolidated his battered, depleted army. Richard Anderson, George Pickett, and Bushrod Johnson were relieved of their commands, which no longer existed. Lee told them they were free to go home if they wished.

The remnants of the Army of Northern Virginia marched on, keeping the Appomattox River between them and the Yankees. Lee's path to Appomattox Station was longer than Sheridan's southerly route. From Farmville, Lee's men would have to travel thirty-nine miles, but Sheridan, just thirty.[38]

SHERIDAN AND HIS STAFF rode up to a home where a middle-aged Southern gentleman, dressed in a swallowtail coat, vest, pantaloons, and morocco slippers, was seated in a chair on the piazza. Sheridan dismounted, sat on a step, lit a fresh cigar, and asked the man if Lee's troops had passed by. The man replied with a little speech about why his loyalty to the Confederacy prohibited him from answering.

Sheridan whistled softly, unrolled a map, and asked the uncooperative citizen how far away Buffalo Creek was. The man said he did not know. Sheridan replied exasperatedly, "The devil you don't!" He asked the Rebel how long he had lived there. All his life, the man said.

"Very well, sir, it's time you did know," Sheridan said. He summoned a captain. "Put this gentleman in charge of a guard, and when we move, walk him down to

Buffalo Creek and show it to him." The man shot Sheridan "a savage glare" as he began the five-mile hike to Buffalo Creek in his slippers.[39]

SHERIDAN LISTENED TO HIS scout's report with satisfaction. The Confederate telegram that his men had intercepted three days earlier, ordering 300,000 rations—and which Sheridan's scouts had transmitted—had borne fruit. Supply trains were rolling from Lynchburg toward Appomattox Station, five miles southwest of Appomattox Court House. Sheridan instructed Custer's division to tear up the tracks west of Appomattox Station after the trains passed so that they could not make a dash back to Lynchburg when they discovered that Yankees, not Rebels, were at the depot.[40]

One of Major Young's scouts in Confederate gray met the trains—there were four of them—and led the engineers to a place east of the station. Custer's men seized the trains and the depot, while other troopers tore up the tracks behind the trains. Union locomotive engineers took charge of the four trains, whose freight cars bulged with supplies carefully selected by Lynchburg quartermasters to succor Lee's army.

Troops set fire to one of the trains, while the other three became the playthings of the engineers. Sheridan irritably observed that they "amused themselves by running the trains to and fro, creating much confusion, and keeping up such an unearthly screeching with the whistles that I was on the point of ordering the cars burned." When an advance unit of Lee's army arrived to claim the supplies, the engineers drove the trains eastward, beyond the Rebels' reach.[41]

The arriving Confederate infantry and cavalry immediately pitched into Custer's cavalrymen, and they fought a chaotic battle in the woods that continued for the rest of the day. At one point, Custer's men nearly captured the Rebel artillery chief, Pendleton, who hours earlier had urged Lee to surrender. Devin's cavalry division helped Custer's men finally drive away the Rebels about 9 p.m.[42]

In a note to Major General John Gibbon of XXIV Corps of the Army of the James, Sheridan reported the capture of 1,000 prisoners, as well as thirty guns and 150 to 200 wagons that were evidently to have been sent back to Lynchburg on the trains bringing the supplies. Sheridan pointedly added, "If it is possible to push on your troops we may have handsome results in the morning."[43]

Sheridan's goal since Five Forks now lay within his grasp: the Cavalry Corps was poised to close off Lee's final escape route to Lynchburg. The Army of Northern Virginia had reached the end of its tether.[44]

THE NIGHT OF APRIL 8 was an anxious one for both armies, which were camped just a few miles from one another near Appomattox Court House. Saturday evening's lurid red sunset seemed to portend a climactic battle on Palm Sunday morning.

Sheridan's corps had stopped between Appomattox Station and Appomattox Court House. Lee's army camped east of the village; Major General Thomas Rosser stayed in town at the home of a friend, Wilmer McLean. Meade's II and VI Corps were bivouacked to the east of Lee's troops. Another 35,000 Union infantrymen were marching through the night from the south and southwest to join Sheridan at Appomattox Station.

It was a night for making plans: Sheridan, for preventing Lee from reaching Lynchburg; Lee, for breaking through. "I did not sleep at all, nor did anybody else, the entire command being up all night long," wrote Sheridan, who stayed in a small frame house just south of Appomattox Station. A member of his staff wrote that "everybody was jubilant" and too excited to sleep because of rumors that Lee was going to surrender.[45]

Sheridan's great concern was that Gibbon's XXIV Corps—which was doggedly following the Cavalry Corps along with a brigade of black troops from XXV Corps and with V Corps right behind it—would not arrive before Lee's tatterdemalion army tried to break through to Lynchburg. Sheridan knew that without infantry support, the Cavalry Corps alone could not stop the Confederates. As he worriedly paced the floor, Sheridan might have felt that he was reliving the tortuous hours before Five Forks, when he awaited V Corps's arrival.

Unable to compel Gibbon's men to move any faster than they were—indeed, they were marching all night to reach him, after having traveled farther and faster from Petersburg than any other Union army unit—Sheridan fired off messages. To Brigadier General Joshua Chamberlain at V Corps, which had collapsed alongside the road to Appomattox Station early on April 9, Sheridan wrote, "If you can possibly push your infantry up here tonight, we will have great results in the morning." The note resulted in a flurry of bugle calls that put V Corps back on its feet.

Sheridan also shared his anxiety with Grant in a dispatch at 4:20 a.m. "If General Gibbon and the Fifth Corps can get up to-night we will perhaps finish the job in the morning. I do not think Lee means to surrender until compelled to do so." When Sheridan wrote the dispatch, the Cavalry Corps had been in ranks and under arms since 4 a.m., facing east toward Appomattox Court House.[46]

A pounding migraine had forced Grant to stop for the night at a farmhouse sixteen miles east of Appomattox Court House. While Grant bathed his feet in hot water and mustard and applied mustard plasters to the back of his neck and his wrists, his staff officers played a piano downstairs and sang. The music was just noise to the tone-deaf Grant, and it only aggravated his headache. He asked them to stop. When morning came, Grant's "sick headache" persisted despite his home treatments.[47]

Major General Edward O.S. Ord, the Army of the James's commander, reached Sheridan's headquarters just before sunup with excellent news: XXIV Corps and V Corps were just a couple of miles behind him. Sheridan's worries vanished.

As firing began in front of Sheridan's dismounted cavalrymen, the generals agreed that when the infantry arrived, it would take positions behind the cavalry. Until then, Sheridan's men would fight a delaying action, falling back when the pressure became too great.[48]

SHERIDAN WAS CORRECT IN believing that Lee would not surrender until there was absolutely no other option. While Sheridan was sleeplessly waiting for the Union infantry to reach his lines, Lee was discussing a last, desperate plan with his two remaining corps commanders, James Longstreet and John Gordon, and his nephew and cavalry chief, Fitzhugh Lee.

The once-powerful Army of Northern Virginia had been whittled down to a scarecrow force of no more than 15,000 infantry and cavalry—the equivalent of a single corps. Arrayed on three sides of the Rebels were more than 80,000 Union troops—the II, V, VI, and XXIV Corps, a brigade from XXV Corps, and the Cavalry Corps.

To Lee and his lieutenants, the road to Lynchburg offered a glimmer of hope. A hard-hitting infantry-cavalry assault might sweep aside Sheridan's cavalrymen if they were all that stood between Appomattox Court House and the Lynchburg road. The Army of Northern Virginia might yet reach the Blue Ridge and eventually join Joseph Johnston's army in North Carolina.

But if Yankee infantrymen reinforced Sheridan's troopers, the game was up. Even as Lee and his lieutenants were making their plan, Gordon thought it was little better than a forlorn hope. Come morning, however, Gordon's II Corps, with Fitzhugh Lee's cavalry and Longstreet's artillery, would spearhead the attack, while the rest of Longstreet's I Corps protected the rear.[49]

APRIL 9, 1865–APPOMATTOX COURT HOUSE—It was Palm Sunday, but no services were planned in the village; it was a day for fighting, not worship. Above the tree line the sun appeared as an orange disk, tinged by the fog hugging the hills and the dust from thousands of men already in motion.

From the crest of a small hill, Sheridan commanded a good view of the ground west of Appomattox Court House. Before daybreak, he had placed Custer's and Devin's divisions at the forefront, with Crook's and Ranald Mackenzie's divisions to their left.

A heavy line of Gordon's infantrymen and Fitzhugh Lee's cavalrymen emerged from Appomattox village and advanced steadily toward Custer's and Devin's dismounted troopers.

As the gunfire swelled to a sustained roar, Sheridan ordered Custer and Devin to conduct an orderly withdrawal to the right. That left the center open for the infantrymen from XXIV and XXV Corps, who at that moment were forming in the woods to the rear after having run the last two miles. V Corps was also just arriving. Sheridan ordered Mackenzie and Crook to hold their positions on the left as long as possible.

For the last time, the Rebels' high-pitched foxhunter's cry rang out over a contested battlefield. "The last charge of the war was made by the footsore and starving men of my command with a spirit worthy of the best days of Lee's army," wrote Gordon.

Refusing to sacrifice his men when thousands of reinforcements were so near at hand, Sheridan withdrew Mackenzie and Crook, ordering them to join Devin's and Custer's divisions on the right.[50] Gordon's men cheered loudly when they saw the Yankees pull back, briefly entertaining the hope that they might yet break out. They began marching up the Lynchburg road as the Cavalry Corps watched passively.

Then, the cheering stopped. Long lines of bluecoat infantry began emerging from the woods. In minutes, 10,000 troops from the XXIV and XXV Corps were standing shoulder to shoulder, facing the right side of Gordon's line. Ord's Army of the James had accomplished the extraordinary feat of marching 120 miles in just four days over muddy roads, in the rain and the heat, in the daytime and the nighttime.

One of Sheridan's staff officers found Joshua Chamberlain and his two brigades in the long V Corps column that was just arriving. Sheridan wanted Chamberlain to bring his men to the front immediately, the staff officer said. Chamberlain led his brigades into the woods behind Sheridan's cavalry and rode up to Sheridan to receive orders.

He was struck by Sheridan's warlike appearance astride Rienzi, "both, rider and steed, of an unearthly shade of darkness, terrible to look upon." With "a dark smile and impetuous gesture," Sheridan urged Chamberlain forward. "Now smash 'em, I tell you, smash 'em!" he cried.

The massed Union infantry divisions behind Sheridan now stretched for three miles and numbered 30,000, ranked three deep. As they faced the newly risen sun, their flags snapping in the breeze, the bluecoats began marching steadily toward Gordon's wraithlike troops. The Cavalry Corps, no longer a bystander, prepared to attack, with Custer in the lead.

The Rebels continued to advance down the road, but with all hope now gone of ever getting past the massed formations of enemy infantry. More V Corps units continued to pour from the woods.

And then, Fitzhugh Lee's cavalry and Gordon's II Corps suddenly recoiled from the nightmare visage of certain annihilation and withdrew to a nearby ridge.

The hilltop gave Sheridan a fine view not only of Gordon's and Fitzhugh Lee's troops but also of the village and Longstreet's corps in the valley beyond it, in ranks facing in the opposite direction, toward Meade's II Corps and VI Corps. Sheridan ordered Devin's and Custer's divisions to attack the Rebels, whose flanks they now overlapped.

But before the charge could properly begin, an aide galloped up to Sheridan with a message from Custer: the Rebels had shown a white flag. Lee had surrendered. It was over.

Chamberlain observed that everyone in the Union ranks seemed pleased with the situation—everyone except Sheridan. "He does not like the cessation of hostilities, and does not conceal his opinion," Chamberlain wrote.[51]

An equally pugnacious Custer, with his own truce flag and a phalanx of mounted troops, rode to where Longstreet was conferring with his officers. Custer brashly demanded that I Corps lay down its arms, or Custer and Sheridan would destroy it.

Longstreet angrily replied that he did not obey orders from Yankee subordinates. He then proceeded to lecture Custer about military courtesy, concluding, "Now, go and act as you and Sheridan choose, and I will teach you a lesson you won't forget!" Without another word, Custer rode back to his lines.[52]

ROBERT E. LEE HAD dressed carefully that morning in a new uniform, along with his ceremonial sword, gold spurs, and sash—all the while dreading the likelihood of his having to surrender the Army of Northern Virginia.

When Gordon's advance was well under way, Lee sent one of his staff officers, Colonel Charles Venable, to Gordon to find out how things were progressing. "Tell General Lee," said Gordon, "I have fought my corps to a frazzle, and I fear I can do nothing unless I am heavily supported by Longstreet's corps."[53]

At that instant, Lee knew that escape was impossible. According to Venable, Lee said, "There is nothing left me but to go and see General Grant, and I had rather die a thousand deaths."[54]

Lee summoned Longstreet to his field headquarters; Longstreet brought with him Major General William Mahone and Brigadier General E. Porter Alexander. Lee related what Gordon had reported and asked them what the army should do.

Longstreet replied with a question for Lee: would the destruction of the army aid the Confederacy in any way? Lee said that it would not. "Then your situation speaks for itself," Longstreet said. Lee turned to Mahone, who grudgingly agreed that the army must surrender.

When he was asked, Alexander proposed to Lee that the Rebels scatter to the hills like "rabbits or partridges in the bushes" and fight on—the guerrilla war strategy advocated by President Jefferson Davis. Lee patiently explained to Alexander why he would not do that. He refused to transform the Confederate army into "bands of marauders," he said, whose suppression would require the Union cavalry to "overrun many sections they may never have occasion to visit. We would bring on a state of affairs it would take this country years to recover from."[55]

Lee went looking for Grant to discuss surrender terms, while Longstreet and Gordon sought truces with their adversaries.

WEST OF APPOMATTOX COURT House, the shooting had largely stopped, but the situation remained muddled and nerve-racking. After the Confederates showed the white flag, Sheridan began riding toward Appomattox Court House to meet with the Rebel commander, Gordon.

He was suddenly fired upon from the woods to his right. Sheridan waved his hat, shouting that there was a truce, but his words were met with another fusillade. He ducked into a swale that shielded him from the woods and rode on.

As he neared the Confederate lines, some Rebels leveled their muskets at him. Gordon ordered the weapons lowered. When a soldier again raised his musket to fire at Sheridan, Gordon slapped it down and admonished the man for ignoring a flag of truce.

A Rebel tried to snatch Sheridan's flag, and Sheridan's color sergeant drew his saber to "cut the man down." Sheridan ordered the sergeant to take the flag back to his field headquarters. He sent a staff officer to Gordon to demand an explanation for the Confederates' conduct.

The emissary returned with an invitation from Gordon to join him and Major General Cadmus Wilcox. As Sheridan and his staff rode over, they encountered more firing by Gordon's men. Sheridan protested to Gordon that his troops had fired at him and were now shooting at Custer's and Devin's men.

"We might as well let them fight it out," said Sheridan. Gordon replied, "There must be some mistake."

After writing a note of protest to Lee, Sheridan suggested to Gordon that he send a staff officer to the brigade that was firing and order it to stop. Gordon had no staff officers available, so Sheridan volunteered Lieutenant Vanderbilt Allen to carry his order.

Sheridan recalled his and Gordon's previous encounters—at Winchester and Cedar Creek. "I had the pleasure of receiving some artillery from your Government, consigned to me through your commander General Early," he said, referring to the Rebel gun captured at Cedar Creek that bore those mocking words, written by a wag at Tredegar Works. Gordon retorted that while that was true, he had received two artillery pieces that morning "consigned to me through General Sheridan." His troops had taken the guns from Crook's division.

Reaching the brigade that refused to stop shooting, Lieutenant Allen informed its commander, Brigadier General Martin Gary, that a cease-fire was in effect and that Lee was surrendering. Gary said he would not acknowledge any order from a Yankee, adding, "I don't care for white flags; South Carolinians never surrender." Minutes later, a Confederate colonel rode up to repeat the order, and Gary reluctantly acquiesced.[56]

When Gordon brought up the subject of negotiations with Sheridan, the feisty Irishman testily reminded him that Lee had "attempted to break through [his] lines this morning" and that unconditional surrender was the only option. Later, Gordon peevishly wrote that Sheridan's bearing and conversation, "while never discourteous, were far less agreeable and pleasing than those of any other officer of the Union army whom it was my fortune to meet. . . . There was an absence of that delicacy and consideration which was exhibited by other Union officers."[57]

Sheridan was still fractious when Grant's staff officers rode up. They found him pacing unhappily. "Damn them, I wish they had held out an hour longer and I would have whipped hell out of them," he told Lieutenant Colonel Orville Babcock, Grant's aide-de-camp. A short time later, he asked Adam Badeau, one of Grant's military secretaries, "Is it a trick? Is he negotiating with Grant?" Holding up a clenched fist, Sheridan said, "I've got 'em—I've got 'em like that!"[58]

THE ENEMY GENERALS, WHO had devoted the past four years to one another's annihilation, now conferred. Ord and Longstreet joined Sheridan and Gordon. Longstreet, who had a copy of Lee's acceptance of Grant's surrender terms, told Sheridan that he feared Meade, ignorant of the situation, might attack his corps. Sheridan sent a staff officer to inform Meade of the current circumstances and another aide bearing Lee's acceptance letter to find Grant.[59]

Grant was on his way to Appomattox Court House when an officer rode up with Lee's message. "When the officer reached me I was still suffering from the sick headache," wrote Grant, "but the instant I saw the contents of the note I was cured."[60]

Lee arranged to meet Grant that afternoon at the brick home of Wilmer McLean, Rosser's host of the previous night. By the strangest coincidence, McLean had owned a farm near Manassas when the war's first major battle was fought there on July 21, 1861. After a shell hit the McLean home, the farmer moved his family to the quieter precincts of southern Virginia. But the war had again come to McLean's door.[61]

WHEN GRANT REACHED THE outskirts of Appomattox Court House, Sheridan, Ord, and some staff officers were waiting for him.

"How are you, Sheridan?" Grant asked.

"First rate, thank you. How are you?" replied Sheridan.

Grant nodded and, glancing at the village, asked whether Lee was there. Sheridan told him Lee was in a brick home up the road.

"Come, let us go over," Grant replied.

Grant aide Colonel Horace Porter wrote after this encounter, "No one could look at Sheridan at such a moment without a sentiment of undisguised admiration. In this campaign, as in others, he had shown himself possessed of military traits of the highest order."

Grant, Sheridan, Ord, and about a dozen staff officers rode to the McLean home, which Grant entered with Babcock, Sheridan, and Ord. When Sheridan and Ord were introduced to Lee and his aide, Colonel Charles Marshall, Sheridan was struck by the contrast between Lee and Grant. Lee, "tall, commanding," was dressed in a new uniform and bore a handsome sword, while Grant, much shorter, wore a soiled private's uniform, without sword or insignia, "except a pair of dingy shoulder straps."[62]

After the introductions were made, Sheridan and Ord joined McLean and the staff officers on the porch, while Grant and Babcock conferred with Lee and Marshall. Grant puffed on a pipe as he drafted the surrender terms. He confessed later to feeling "sad and depressed. I felt like anything rather than rejoicing at the downfall of a foe who had fought so long and valiantly." But the Southern cause, he added, was "one of the worst for which a people ever fought."

When the surrender document was copied and signed, Lee offered his sword to Grant; he declined it. Then, Babcock stepped onto the porch, "twirled his hat around his head once," and invited Sheridan, Ord, and the Union staff officers into the McLean parlor. They approached Lee almost reverentially, respectful of his reputation and elegant bearing—all except Sheridan.

He bluntly requested that Lee return the two dispatches that Sheridan had sent him that morning—those protesting being fired upon during the truce. Sheridan told Lee that he had not had time to make copies. Lee removed the notes from a breast pocket and handed them to Sheridan, saying, "I am sorry. It is probable that my cavalry at that point of the line did not fully understand the agreement."[63]

Lee turned to Grant and said that his men had no rations, but he was expecting several trainloads from Lynchburg. "When they arrive," he said, unaware that Sheridan's cavalry had seized them, "I should be glad to have the present wants of my men supplied from them." As all eyes turned toward Sheridan, Grant assured Lee that the Rebels would be fed as soon as possible. Sheridan told Grant that he would distribute the captured Rebel rations.[64]

Lee stepped outside, signaled to an orderly to bridle Traveller, and gazed across the valley toward his army as he put on his buckskin gauntlets. Every movement, every gesture, every glance by their dreaded nemesis became etched in the memories of the Union staff officers watching from the McLean porch.

Lee "smote his hands together several times in an absent sort of way," observed Newhall, as Traveller was brought around. Grant stepped onto the porch and touched his hat to Lee, who returned the salutation. He then departed on "his chunky gray horse," as Sheridan drolly observed. As Lee passed through his army's bivouac, cheers erupted from his men. Stone-faced, Grant mounted Cincinnati and rode away in silence.[65]

AFTER LEE AND GRANT had gone, the Yankee officers began furiously bidding for McLean's parlor furniture. Ord bought the table upon which Lee had signed the surrender agreement. Sheridan got the table where Grant had drafted the terms, handing McLean two $10 gold pieces—he had carried them throughout the war in case he was captured.

Sheridan presented the table to Custer as a gift for his wife, Libbie, with whom Sheridan had struck up a friendship in July during a dance on the presidential steamer *River Queen* while it was docked at City Point. Custer rode off with the table balanced on his shoulder. In a note to Mrs. Custer accompanying the gift, Sheridan wrote, "Permit me to say, Madam, that there is scarcely an individual in our service who has contributed more to bring this about than your very gallant husband."[66]

His buttery words to Mrs. Custer notwithstanding, Sheridan credited Grant with the Union victory. Before Grant took command, Lee had "never met an opponent he did not vanquish," and on the rare occasions when he did lose a battle, he always escaped. But in facing Grant, Lee was "for the first time, overmatched." Grant's "harmony of plan"—the coordination of campaigns on many fronts—forced the Confederacy to "yield to our blows."[67]

For his part, Lee wrote that the single factor most responsible for his defeat was his shortage of mounted troops. Lee had sent his principal cavalry force, under Wade Hampton, to the Carolinas to obtain fresh horses, leaving the Army of Northern Virginia with fewer than 5,000 cavalrymen to face Sheridan's 13,000 troopers. "Our small force of cavalry was unable to resist the united Federal cavalry under Sheridan," wrote Lee.[68]

THE CAVALRY CORPS WAS pointedly excluded from the April 12 surrender ceremony. Sheridan's lack of "delicacy" during his encounters with Gordon and Lee at Appomattox was surely one reason, but the Rebels' smoldering resentment of Sheridan's hard-riding troopers was probably the primary one. Lee had even requested that Sheridan's pickets not fraternize with the Rebels. While Sheridan undoubtedly felt the snub, there is no record of his thoughts about it.

Six generals from both armies met at the McLean house on April 10 to arrange the formal surrender by Lee's troops of their weapons, flags, and horses, and the Rebels' parole to their homes. While Generals Longstreet, Gordon, and Pendleton from the Confederate army and Union generals Gibbon, Merritt, and Charles Griffin haggled over these details, Sheridan and his Cavalry Corps, unwanted with the fighting now done, were setting out for Petersburg.

That morning, Sheridan had waited until the unusually late hour of 8 a.m., when both armies would be sure to witness it, to lead his Cavalry Corps, four abreast and in closed formation, through the middle of Appomattox Court House.[69] He and his men rode east from Appomattox at a shockingly leisurely pace compared with the swift, relentless pursuit that had ended in Wilmer McLean's parlor. At nighttime it seemed strange to the cavalrymen to make their camp without posting pickets. The reality that their war, at least, was over began to sink in.

THE CAVALRY CORPS WAS at Nottoway Court House when a telegraph operator happened to notice a bulletin being transmitted to General Meade. President Lincoln had been assassinated, it said. Sheridan dismissed the report as a "canard" and went to bed.

But it was true, and when Sheridan reached Petersburg, he was ordered to march to Sherman's aid in North Carolina with the Cavalry Corps and VI Corps. When the expedition was under way, a message from Army Chief of Staff Henry Halleck reached Sheridan's army on April 28 at South Boston, Virginia. Johnston had surrendered to Sherman, it said. The column retraced its steps to Petersburg.

Sheridan and his staff boarded a steamer to Washington, while the Cavalry Corps proceeded there on horseback. The troopers crossed the devastated, bone-littered northern Virginia countryside where, during the Overland Campaign, they had begun to crush the rebellion, and where they had lost so many comrades. They might have remembered beating Jeb Stuart's cavalry at Yellow Tavern, ensuring that it never again would ride circles around the Union army, or the three Shenandoah Valley triumphs that had broken the back of Jubal Early's army.

The Cavalry Corps had performed its most memorable service, however, during the past month—when it had smashed Lee's right flank, flushing him out of Petersburg, and had then stopped his army from escaping into the mountains. While his men might have time to savor their achievements, Sheridan would not. New orders awaited him in Washington.[70]

CHAPTER 13

Ruler of the Southwest

1865–1867

Their freedom had been given them, and it was the plain duty of those in authority to make it secure . . . and to see that they had a fair chance in the battle of life.
—PHIL SHERIDAN ON THE BLACK FREEDMEN DURING
RECONSTRUCTION[1]

His rule has, in fact, been one of absolute tyranny, without reference to the principles of our government or the nature of our free institutions . . . a resort to authority not granted by law.
—PRESIDENT ANDREW JOHNSON ON HIS REMOVAL OF
PHIL SHERIDAN FROM THE FIFTH MILITARY DISTRICT[2]

THE DAY AFTER HE REACHED WASHINGTON, DC, Phil Sheridan stared in dismay at the orders handed to him by one of Lieutenant General Ulysses Grant's staff officers. Dated May 17, the orders formally relieved him of his Middle Military District command—unsurprising, with the Shenandoah Valley secured for eight months. The surprise was that he was now commander of all US troops west of the

Mississippi River. "Your duty is to restore Texas, and that part of Louisiana held by the enemy, to the Union in the shortest practicable time."

If the Confederate commander in those states, Lieutenant General Edmund Kirby Smith, refused to surrender, Sheridan was to pursue Smith and his men as "outlaws." Sheridan would command more than 50,000 veteran bluecoats from Major General Edward Canby's Army of the Gulf; Major General J. J. Reynolds's Arkansas corps; IV Corps; XXV Corps; and two Cavalry Corps divisions. Grant's next words sent Sheridan out the door of his room at the Willard Hotel at a fast walk, on his way to see the general in chief: "You will proceed without delay to the West to arrange all preliminaries for your new field of duties."

If "without delay" meant what Sheridan feared, he would miss the Grand Review of the Armies scheduled for May 23 and 24. He had relished the opportunity to lead his beloved Cavalry Corps one last time, in a procession down Pennsylvania Avenue, under the proud gaze of the nation's leaders.[3]

SHERIDAN HAD RETURNED TO a capital whose atmosphere had markedly changed since the previous August, when he had met with Abraham Lincoln and Edwin Stanton to discuss his new assignment commanding the Army of the Shenandoah. At that time, Washington had just experienced the terror of Jubal Early's appearance outside the city, and uncertainty lingered over whether Early would return. Sheridan had dispelled that uncertainty by destroying Early's army in three decisive battles over one month.

The charged atmosphere that had previously defined Washington, with fear lurking so close to the surface, was now gone, replaced by a curious flatness—a postpartum letdown after the delivery of America from civil war and the shocking loss of Lincoln. The federal district still wore its widow's weeds—the White House flag hanging at half-staff, the black bunting draping the public buildings—but the Grand Review was expected to lift spirits and close out the mourning period.[4]

Vice President Andrew Johnson, a Tennessee Unionist, had humbly promised to carry out Lincoln's plan for reunification. Grateful that the bloodletting was finally over and still grieving over Lincoln's assassination, politicians had ceased their vicious partisanship. The rare truce would not last.

SHERIDAN ASKED GRANT TO delay his departure until after the Grand Review, because of his "strong desire to head [his] command on that great occasion." But Grant quietly refused. It was "absolutely necessary to go at once," he said. He pointed to a sentence in Sheridan's orders that read, "I think the Rio Grande should be strongly held, whether the forces in Texas surrender or not." There was a good reason for this—"a motive not explained by the instructions," said Grant.[5]

When Mexican president Benito Juarez's government defaulted on Mexican bonds held by Britain, Spain, and France, those nations had sent an expeditionary force in 1861 to coerce the payments. The British and Spanish troops soon left, but the French had remained at the urging of Mexico's clerics and conservatives, who saw the French as allies who might help them regain their former influence.

Claiming to represent Mexico's legitimate government, the priests, bishops, and wealthy landowners pronounced Mexico a constitutional monarchy and invited France's Napoleon III to appoint an emperor. He chose the Archduke Ferdinand Maximilian, the younger brother of the Austrian emperor. Maximilian established friendly relations with the Rebels in neighboring Texas, and during the war, goods flowed into Texas from Mexico, aiding the Confederacy.[6] In his opinion, Grant told Sheridan, Maximilian's reign in Mexico was no less than "a part of the rebellion itself, because of the encouragement that invasion had received from the Confederacy." The Civil War could not end until the French and Austrians were driven from Mexico, he said.

Even as Sheridan and Grant met, ex-Confederate troops were crossing the Rio Grande into Mexico under Maximilian's protection, carrying the weapons with which they had fought the Union. Grant wanted Sheridan to stop the exodus and to support Juarez and his allies in casting out the European usurpers.[7]

SHERIDAN REGRETFULLY LEFT WASHINGTON without realizing his wish to see in one place, one last time, his Cavalry Corps, the elite mounted troops with whom he had "gone through so many trials and unremittingly pursued and assailed the enemy." While Sheridan was traveling to St. Louis, Major General Wesley Merritt led the Cavalry Corps through Washington during the Army of the Potomac's parade on May 23; Major General William Sherman's Army of the West marched the next day. Massive crowds witnessed this final passing of the Union army—and loudly applauded when George Custer, his long blond hair blowing in the breeze, masterfully subdued his horse when it unexpectedly bolted toward the reviewing officers "like a tornado." At nighttime, the campfires of the armies of Grant and Sherman transformed Arlington Heights and the Potomac shoreline into blazing candelabra.[8]

In St. Louis, Sheridan boarded a steamboat for New Orleans. He had made this same journey a dozen years earlier as an adventure-seeking brevet second lieutenant en route to his first posting, with the 1st Cavalry at Fort Duncan, Texas.

That young man no longer existed. Sheridan had emerged from the ghastly abattoir divested of his youthful dreams and illusions about glory. At thirty-four, he was a tough, hard-eyed, clear-thinking warrior leader who had improbably scaled the summit of US military leadership.

NEAR THE MOUTH OF the Red River above Baton Rouge, a message from General Canby reached Sheridan: Kirby Smith had surrendered in New Orleans on May 26. The surrender absolved Sheridan of one objective and freed him to concentrate on the other: securing the Mexican-US border.[9]

Reaching the New Orleans headquarters of the Military Division of the Southwest—to be renamed weeks later the Military Division of the Gulf, responsible for Texas, Louisiana, Mississippi, and Florida—Sheridan read disturbing reports about organized groups of armed ex-Confederate soldiers marching through Texas on their way to Mexico. The reports only underscored the belief that he now shared with Grant: that the "vindication of republicanism," for which the Civil War had been fought, would not be complete until Maximilian was driven from Mexico.

Deciding to make an immediate show of force, Sheridan ordered four divisions of cavalry and infantry to Texas. Custer's 4,500 men, when they arrived in Alexandria, Louisiana, from the Grand Review, were sent to Houston; Merritt's 5,000 mounted troops were sent to San Antonio; and two infantry divisions from XXIII Corps, also placed under Sheridan's command, embarked for Galveston and Brazos Santiago, at the mouth of the Rio Grande. Units from his four other infantry corps would follow; Sheridan would have 52,000 combat veterans at his disposal.[10]

A US CAVALRY REGIMENT, one of several riding from the East to join Sheridan's command, was crossing the Mississippi River below Vicksburg when the troopers spotted a rowboat full of men towing two horses to the west bank. Their suspicions aroused, the cavalrymen went to investigate. But the men fled, abandoning the horses.

A week or two later, Sheridan received a letter from his old nemesis, Jubal Early—one of the men in the rowboat. Early wrote that he and other former Rebels were crossing the river to join Kirby Smith in Texas, unaware that Smith had already surrendered, when they were forced to abandon the two horses, which belonged to Early. Demanding compensation, Early added that further pursuit of him would be futile, because he would soon be "on the great blue sea." Sheridan bemusedly observed that if he had wanted to capture Early, he might have easily done so after Appomattox by merely riding to Early's home in Lynchburg. There is no record that Early's claim was ever paid.[11]

OUTWARDLY, NEW ORLEANS APPEARED unchanged by the war. Perhaps it was because the city had been under Union control since the arrival in spring 1862 of Admiral David Farragut's fleet and Major General Benjamin Butler's troops. Citizens hated "Beast Butler's" military regime, although he fed the hungry, employed the unemployed, and cleaned up the city, ridding it during the war of its annual yellow fever and cholera epidemics. After a new Louisiana state constitution was adopted in 1864, a Unionist administration began governing the state. The economy stirred back to life, although the old ruling class was largely excluded.

The city's social life went on much as it had before the war. Women still promenaded on Canal Street, and there were balls, parties, and dinners. Gaiety and sin continued to coexist easily with social and religious conservatism. The docks teemed with ships and laboring men; the streets were alive with jostling drays and wagons. The men pursued their traditional pastimes of gambling, horseracing, hunting, fishing, and drinking.

But behind the doors of many elegant homes, gentry in patched clothing dined on cornmeal and pork. And lurking unpleasantly in the background, like the pungent odor of raw sewage emanating from the gutters, was a virulent hatred of the Yankees, the Unionist politicians, and the black freedmen.[12]

SHORTLY AFTER ASSUMING HIS new command in New Orleans, Sheridan rode to the Mexican border "to impress the Imperialists . . . with the idea that we intended hostilities." He was convinced that "history will not excuse the attempted annihilation of a nation on the plea of nonpayment of a million or two of debts due."[13]

History might not excuse it, but Secretary of State William Seward appeared willing to do so, even if France's invasion was a flagrant violation of the Monroe Doctrine. Seward had remained at his post while recovering from the attempt made on his life on the night Lincoln was assassinated. He was unalterably opposed to US intervention in Mexico, determined instead to use diplomacy to reach a resolution.

In Brownsville, Texas, Sheridan began to rattle the saber loudly. He openly inquired about marching routes in Mexico and forage for horses and paraded his army up and down the east bank of the lower Rio Grande.

When Sheridan met with Grant in Washington in May, the commanding general had warned him that Seward opposed using troops "in any active way" on the border and counseled Sheridan to "act with great circumspection." Sheridan took this to mean that Grant was sanctioning him to conduct a "cold war" on the US-Mexican border.

Sheridan moved troops around, gathered intelligence, spread misinformation, and secretly supplied arms to the native Mexican insurgency. He demanded that Maximilian hand over the munitions that the ex-Rebels had given to the Imperialists in exchange for sanctuary. His calculated actions conveyed the impression that he was planning an invasion, which seemed entirely possible to many Mexicans; American troops from the last invasion had left just seventeen years earlier.

To Sheridan's disgust, Seward settled for the return of a few pieces of contraband Confederate artillery and the Imperial government's apologies, and then dropped the matter. "A golden opportunity was lost," Sheridan wrote, his frustration leaping off the page, "for we had ample excuse for crossing the boundary." The US government's passivity freed Maximilian to expand his control over most of Mexico.[14]

Undeterred, Sheridan launched a fresh "hostile demonstration," this time on the upper Rio Grande. At San Antonio, he ostentatiously inspected IV Corps and Merritt's cavalry division, as though readying them for a campaign. He then rode with a cavalry regiment to Fort Duncan, the place where he had begun his army career. There, opposite Piedras Negras, Sheridan again inquired about roads and forage. He sent a pontoon train to Brownsville and opened communications with Juarez. Rumors flew of an imminent US invasion of Mexico.

The actions hit their mark. The nervous Imperial government withdrew French troops from Matamoras, and thence from most of northern Mexico, all the way to Monterey. The French ambassador in Washington lodged a formal protest, prompting the skittish State Department to warn Sheridan to preserve strict neutrality on the border.

But Sheridan was already covertly supplying weapons and ammunition to anti-Imperialist insurgents being recruited in the areas that the French had abandoned. The arms, which Sheridan's records showed had been destroyed, were placed "at convenient places on our side of the river to fall into their hands."

Grant wrote to Sheridan that he was not sure this was legal, while at the same time fuming over the State Department's policy of using American troops as "a police force to protect a neutrality [Maximilian's] to build up a power that has done the United States so much harm and which contemplates so much more." Grant told Sheridan, "If I had my way I would use the United States forces to give to them [the Mexican republicans] the Rio Grande country as a base to start from."

The clandestine arms program continued; during the winter of 1865–1866, Sheridan sent Juarez's men 30,000 muskets from the Baton Rouge Arsenal. Still, Sheridan admitted that "it required the patience of Job to abide the slow and poky methods of our State Department," while at the same time restraining his combat veterans from crossing the Rio Grande into Mexico.[15]

SOME OF THE NEARLY 5,000 ex-Confederates living in Mexico had begun a colony at Cordoba, in the highlands above Vera Cruz. To attract new supporters to help prop up his sinking regime, Maximilian had promised large land grants to former Rebels and any colonists whom they could lure to Mexico from the South. Promotional material signed by former generals Sterling Price, John Magruder, and Dabney Maury circulated through the South; some states even named commissioners in anticipation of a surge of emigration to Mexico.

When the State Department did nothing about it, Sheridan, with Grant's authorization, published an order in April 1866 stating that anyone sailing to Mexico from Texas or Louisiana must first obtain a permit from his headquarters. The requirement doomed the colonization scheme.[16]

As the tide began to go out on Maximilian, a number of former Mexican republic generals began vying to succeed Juarez, whose presidential term had officially expired in December 1865. The contenders included the three C's: Juan Cortinas, Servando Canales, and Jose Maria Carbajal. Sheridan wanted a "uniter," and in his view, Cortinas and Canales were "freebooters" and unsuitable. Grant liked Carbajal, who had recently visited Washington to seek aid for the republicans. "Give him the benefit of advice and all the information you have," Grant told Sheridan. "I regret that we cannot give him direct aid."

But after interviewing Carbajal in New Orleans, Sheridan bluntly wrote, "He did not impress me very favorably. He was old and cranky, yet, as he seemed anxious to do his best, I sent him over to Brownsville." Carbajal didn't last; Canales deposed him in Matamoras. And so Sheridan decided to stick with Juarez and his general, Mariano Escobedo.[17]

Major Henry Young, Sheridan's former chief of scouts, had organized a bodyguard for Carbajal with Sheridan's reluctant consent and financial backing. But by the time Young reached the border with fifty men, Canales had already ousted Carbajal. And so, with Sheridan's blessing, Young decided to make contact with General Escobedo.

As Young and his men crossed the Rio Grande to meet Escobedo, a band of ex-Confederates and Mexican rancheros lying in ambush opened fire. Young and twenty-five of his men were either killed or drowned in the river. "I have never ceased to regret my consent," Sheridan confessed in his *Personal Memoirs*.[18]

Under Mexico's constitution, General Jesus Gonzales Ortega, who was president of the Mexican Supreme Court when Maximilian seized control of the country, was next in line to become president after Juarez. Living in exile in the United States, Ortega now attempted to claim the office. Sheridan irritably judged him to be "ridiculously late" and feared he might spoil the republican insurgency that was now gathering momentum under Juarez and Escobedo. After Ortega left New Orleans for the Rio Grande, Sheridan ordered Colonel John Sedgwick to arrest him when his ship docked. Sedgwick quietly took Ortega into custody at Brazos Santiago, ending his "further machinations," wrote Sheridan.[19]

By mid-summer 1866, Juarez's men, armed mainly with weapons Sheridan had secretly given them, controlled the territory along the Rio Grande and nearly all of northern Mexico down to San Luis Potosi. With each passing week, Maximilian's situation worsened. Sheridan's spies reported that the French were fortifying Vera Cruz and that the Empress Carlotta had sailed to France to beg Napoleon III for more aid.

But Napoleon wanted to cut his losses in Mexico and bring his army home to France. He would need every soldier soon. Prussia, having easily defeated Austria, was busily sweeping Germany's other states into its orbit, and Napoleon's regime was teetering. War with Prussia would curb its growing power and increase his, Napoleon believed.

In December, Sheridan learned that French soldiers were boarding ships at Vera Cruz. Confirmation came in early January 1867, in the form of an intercepted telegram addressed to French general Henri Pierre Castelnau in Mexico City. "Do not delay the departure of the troops; bring back all who will not remain there. Most of the fleet has left.—Napoleon."

With the French troops gone, in May 1867, Juarez's forces captured Mexico City and arrested Maximilian. On June 19, Maximilian was executed by a firing squad despite Secretary of State Seward's appeal for mercy.

Sheridan's "cold war" against Maximilian had succeeded brilliantly; it was no less than a tour de force in geopolitics—by a fighting general with no experience in international affairs. Sheridan's seat-of-the-pants brinkmanship on the border and his secret arms shipments to Juarez's insurgents had so destabilized Maximilian's regime that when Napoleon withdrew France's support, Maximilian could not survive.

Faith in Sheridan's ability to improvise had persuaded Grant to select him, over all his generals, for just this mission. And once more, Sheridan had proven to be Grant's most dependable troubleshooter, improbably ousting the French without using any force. "I doubt very much whether such results could have been achieved without the presence of an American army on the Rio Grande," Sheridan modestly wrote years later.[20]

SHERIDAN'S TRAINING AND EXPERIENCE had not prepared him for the complex problems and superheated political partisanship that he faced in Louisiana and Texas. A cold war strategy had worked in Mexico, but in the Southwest, diplomacy and a deft human touch were needed. Sheridan possessed neither.

In 1864, Louisiana Unionists wrote a new state constitution abolishing slavery and established a provisional government. But up-country Louisianans in the north and west remained loyal to the Confederacy, even after the war. Sheridan described them in a letter to President Andrew Johnson as "malcontents," adding that "this bitterness is all that is left. . . . There is no power of resistance left."[21]

Johnson implemented Lincoln's lenient Reconstruction plan in the hope of rapidly restoring the South to its place in the Union. He extended amnesty to former Rebels who took a loyalty oath and liberally granted pardons to those whose former high standing in the Confederacy made them ineligible for amnesty. By the end of 1865, every state except Texas had begun adopting a new state constitution and establishing a provisional government.

In the blink of the eye, former Rebels took control of state governments across the South. After the fall 1865 Louisiana state elections, ex-Rebels replaced nearly every Unionist elected official.

In his first State of the Union message in December 1865, Johnson pronounced the Union restored and declared his readiness to admit Southern senators and representatives to Congress. A staunch believer in states' rights and no friend of the black man, Johnson turned a blind eye when the reconstituted Southern states began enacting the so-called Black Codes, whose centerpieces were antivagrancy and labor-contract laws written to keep the new freedmen out of the cities, under the control of the whites, and working in the fields. The codes transformed the new freedmen into de facto slaves.

Sheridan wrote that the president's failure to demand civil rights for the new freedmen left the blacks "at the mercy of a people who, recently their masters, now seemed to look upon them as the authors of all the misfortunes that had come upon the land." Cruel Southern whites made the blacks at times wish they could repent their freedom. A Freedmen's Bureau official wrote that in Texas, blacks "are frequently beaten unmercifully, and shot down like wild beasts, without any provocation."[22]

The Black Codes and the former Confederates' swift return to power evoked cries in the North for harsher treatment of the South. In December 1865, congressional Republicans created a joint House-Senate Committee of 15 to reexamine the issues of Southern representation in Congress and black suffrage. The committee repudiated the provisional state governments approved by Johnson, asserting that only Congress could approve them.

AND SO BEGAN A titanic power struggle between Johnson and Congress over which branch of government would oversee postwar Reconstruction. Congress passed a bill giving the Freedmen's Bureau—hated bitterly in the South—new authority to protect former slaves and to try in military courts those who violated the rights of blacks. Johnson vetoed the bill, as well as the Civil Rights Act, which granted blacks the same rights as whites. The bills trampled on the states' prerogatives, the president declared.

Congress overrode both vetoes. It went on to approve and send to the states for ratification a proposed Fourteenth Amendment that extended citizenship rights to blacks, protected those rights against hostile state laws, and eliminated the old "three-fifths" clause from the Constitution. The latter provision had permitted the slave states to count, during every ten-year census, each slave as three-fifths of a white man to increase their representation in Congress. The clause's elimination, coupled with blacks' new citizenship rights, had the collateral effect of increasing the South's representation in Congress by twelve members.

The former Confederate states were required to ratify the Fourteenth Amendment before being fully restored to the Union with congressional representation. Tennessee, governed by Radical Republicans, ratified it, but the other ten states rejected it—Louisiana's legislature by a unanimous vote. Johnson tacitly supported the South's defiance and acted as if his vetoes had been upheld.[23]

Caught in the middle of the all-out war between the president and Congress were Sheridan and the other army commanders in the South who were responsible for implementing Washington's conflicting policies.

SHERIDAN SPENT JULY 1866 in Texas and with his troops along the Rio Grande. Juarez's and Escobedo's forces now controlled most of northern Mexico, but throughout Texas, Sheridan disgustedly observed, "a reign of lawlessness and disorder ensued." The courts and Texas's state government, dominated by ex-Confederates, condoned flagrant acts of violence and intimidation. Colonel Charles Griffin, the former commander of V Corps, wrote to Sheridan from Galveston, "There is scarcely an officer in this state, whose duty it is to arrest crime, that will turn or raise his hand against the scoundrels. I begin to believe that there is more disloyalty here now than in '61."

Indeed, in 1865 and 1866, five hundred white men were indicted for allegedly murdering blacks—without a single conviction. "Murder is considered one of their inalienable states' rights," a Northern visitor said of Texas. Small wonder, then, that when a reporter in Galveston asked Sheridan how he liked Texas, he replied, "If I owned hell and Texas, I would rent out Texas and live in hell."[24]

ON THE NIGHT OF July 30, 1866, an army officer met Sheridan's ship as it carried him back to New Orleans from Texas. Earlier that day, the officer reported, whites and New Orleans police had slaughtered dozens of blacks as they met at the Mechanics Institute to elect delegates for Louisiana's constitutional convention. As Sheridan grimly listened, the officer said that up to 40 men had been killed and 140 others had been injured. In the chaotic aftermath, Major Absalom Baird, the ranking officer in Sheridan's absence, had taken control of the city government.[25]

Sheridan was not especially surprised; he had feared an explosion of violence in New Orleans. Before leaving for Texas, he had warned Baird to be on guard. He was disappointed that his troops had been unable to defend the freedmen, who looked to the Union for protection.

Unlike many Union generals with Southern commands, Sheridan strongly supported and sympathized with the black freedmen. The government's obligation toward them, he believed, could not be more obvious. "Their freedom had been given them, and it was the plain duty of those in authority to make it secure, and screen them from the bitter political resentment that beset them, and to see that they had a fair chance in the battle of life," Sheridan wrote.[26]

BEFORE ADJOURNING IN 1864, the delegates to the Louisiana constitutional convention—all whites—had reserved the option of reconvening if needed. On June 23, 1866, they elected to do so in late July. Democrats and former Rebels were now running Louisiana, and Unionists knew that the survival of the Republican Party depended on giving the vote to the freedmen—and adopting new rules barring certain classes of ex-Confederates from state office. Before they could reconvene the convention, however, they had to elect new delegates to represent those parishes that during the 1864 convention were Confederate-occupied. At the meeting scheduled for July 30, delegates planned to discuss the new elections and proposed changes in the voting laws.

Every state official except Governor James Wells, the only statewide officeholder who was Republican, angrily condemned the convention and its goal of giving blacks the vote. Surprisingly, Wells supported black suffrage—surprising because he had become practically indistinguishable from his Democratic fellow officeholders in every other action that he took.

The threat of violence, as oppressive as the July heat and humidity, hung over the preparations for the meeting on Monday, July 30. Just three months earlier, Memphis police, firemen, and citizens had killed forty-six blacks during a three-day binge of violence that had destroyed hundreds of black homes, schools, and buildings.[27] Acting under the pretext of preemptive riot control, New Orleans policemen, most of whom were former Confederate soldiers, crowded into their precinct houses during the morning of July 30, armed with clubs, bowie knives, and new pistols on loan from the local gun shops. The sheriff swore in dozens of special deputies; they included members of the emerging white supremacy societies, local thugs, and citizens.

Lieutenant Governor Albert Voorhies had warned Major Baird that the convention would be dispersed because it violated municipal ordinances; Baird said the convention was legal, and if delegates were arrested, the military would release them.

So Voorhies telegraphed President Johnson, who assured him that if he obtained a court order blocking the convention, federal troops would back the police. Voorhies had no trouble persuading District Judge Edward Abell to forbid the meeting. Baird was not informed of Voorhies's backdoor correspondence with the president.[28]

Twenty-six nervous white delegates—a quorum required three times their number—gathered at the Mechanics Institute as about 170 black men, women, and children looked on. Then, in a show of support, about one hundred black men marched to the institute up Burgundy Street, which was lined with jeering white men.

During the march, someone fired a pistol. Both sides began heaving bricks, and the marchers hastened to the institute building and disappeared inside.

Police and citizens rushed up and poured a torrent of gunfire through the windows. When a white flag appeared, they stormed inside. A Confederate veteran who had lost both arms during the war exhorted the mob, "Kill every damned son of a bitch in the building, and [do] not let any escape."

The mob emptied its revolvers into the unarmed delegates and spectators. Police shot others cowering in the building yard. The wounded were stabbed and "pounded to jelly" where they lay. Dr. A. P. Dostie, a delegate and longtime Unionist, was specially singled out; he was shot through the spine, stabbed in the belly with a sword, and beaten. Others fled, only to be chased down. Blocks away, blacks with no involvement in these events were assaulted on the streets and beaten, stabbed, or shot dead.[29]

Cyrus Hamlin, son of former vice president Hannibal Hamlin and a Civil War veteran, wrote that "the wholesale slaughter and the little regard paid to human life" were worse than anything that he had seen during the war. Police threw wounded and dead blacks into jail cells indiscriminately and abandoned them there. A Sheridan aide who visited a precinct house reported that the jail was "more like a slaughter-pen for animals than a receptacle for human beings."[30]

MAJOR GENERAL WILLIAM SHERMAN of the Division of the Missouri shared his outrage over the mayhem with Sheridan. "It was no riot, it was an absolute massacre by the police which was not excelled in murderous cruelty by that at Fort Pillow."

Grant told Sheridan to continue martial law in New Orleans for as long as he believed it necessary to keep the peace, "and do not allow any of the civil authorities to act if you deem such action as dangerous to the public safety." Grant also forwarded to Sheridan several questions about the riot that the president wanted answered.[31]

In his responses to Johnson, Sheridan wrote that while the convention was the riot's immediate cause, its "remote cause" was the rising violence in New Orleans under the regime of Mayor John Monroe, who, "in the organization of the police force, selected many desperate men, and some of them known murderers." Sheridan told the president it was debatable whether Northerners could even reside in New Orleans, "whether they can be protected in life and property, and have justice in courts." Justice was unlikely: District Judge Abell, who presided over the city's only criminal court, had promised immunity to the rioters beforehand, and afterward, he convened a grand jury that indicted the victims, not the perpetrators.[32]

Sheridan protested when Johnson released an abridged version of his letter distorting his criticisms of the New Orleans officials. It was the beginning, Sheridan later wrote, of "Mr. Johnson's well-known political hostility toward me." Johnson notoriously made personal enemies of anyone who disagreed with him.[33]

The riot, coming on the heels of the one in Memphis, turned public opinion sharply against the Johnson administration. During a speech in St. Louis just before the midterm congressional elections, Johnson threw fuel on the fire by blaming the riot on Congress and a "radical conspiracy."

THROUGHOUT THE NORTH, FIERY wartime passions were rekindled. Northern newspapers overwhelmingly laid the responsibility on Johnson and his amnesties, pardons, and obvious sympathy for the defeated Confederates. "Blood is upon his hands, the blood of innocent, loyal citizens," wrote the *Chicago Tribune*, "who had committed no crime but that of seeking to protect themselves against rebel misrule, which he, Andrew Johnson, had foisted upon them."[34]

Always a fighter, Johnson tried to counteract the criticism by forming the National Union Party, a coalition of administration supporters, Democrats, and former Copperheads, and then going on a speaking tour.

Grant told Sheridan that Johnson no longer listened to Union loyalists. Fearing a resumption of the war, Grant quietly ordered all arms removed from Southern arsenals and sent to Northern storehouses.

Although there was no renewal of open hostilities, voters overwhelmingly rejected Johnson and his new party during the November 1866 election. Radical Republicans, vowing harsher measures for the "conquered provinces," won a veto-proof majority in Congress.[35] The House appointed a Select Committee on the New Orleans Riot—two Republicans and one Democrat—which, in its majority report, blamed city and state officials and criticized the president. The effect of Johnson's assurance to Lieutenant Governor Voorhies that federal troops would not interfere with police operations, the report said, "was to encourage the heart, to strengthen the hand, and to hold up the arms of those men who intended to prevent the convention from assembling."

Johnson's assigning blame to Congress for the riot was "an unwarranted and unjust expression of hostile feeling," the majority report said. In his minority report, the committee's lone Democrat contrarily asserted that blacks had "provoked" the deadly attack.[36]

THE RADICAL REPUBLICAN–DOMINATED CONGRESS began implementing its Reconstruction program on March 2, 1867. Over Johnson's veto, it enacted what became known as Reconstruction Act No. 1—creating five military districts to govern the ten Southern states that had rejected the Fourteenth Amendment. Sheridan became commander of the Fifth Military District, overseeing Texas and Louisiana.

No precedent for this existed in US history. Over the opposition of the president, one-third of the nation had been placed under martial law. The Reconstruction Act required the ten states to draft new constitutions establishing new governments that, hopefully, would ratify the Fourteenth Amendment and fully restore the states to the Union.

When the states did nothing, Congress passed a supplemental Reconstruction Act directing the military district commanders to register voters by September 1 to elect constitutional convention delegates. Barred from voting were ex-Confederate government officials and former US military officers who had gone on to serve in the Confederate army. But ex-Rebel soldiers, and even most officers, could vote if they pledged fealty to the United States. And for the first time, blacks could vote.

BEFORE MARCH ENDED, SHERIDAN issued General Orders, No. 1 to Louisiana and Texas. It made clear that the military now wielded veto power over all civilian government actions. Sheridan proceeded to remove the New Orleans judge and two elected officials whom he had long had in his sights for their roles in the riot eight months earlier. He had the authority for these actions under yet another supplemental Reconstruction Act, again passed over Johnson's veto, permitting district military commanders to remove any civil official who impeded Reconstruction.[37]

In a letter to Grant, Sheridan explained his reasons for removing New Orleans mayor John Monroe, Louisiana attorney general Andrew Herron, and District Judge Edward Abell. For at least nine months before the riot, Sheridan wrote, Abell had been "educating" the authors of the planned "outrage" and promising them immunity from prosecution. "He fulfilled his promise." Herron, he said, had prosecuted the victims instead of the rioters, "making the innocent guilty and the guilty innocent." And the mayor had encouraged the police to join the riot by assuring them they would not be punished if they did.[38]

Sheridan was aware that the removals, along with his aggressive drive to register Louisiana voters for the coming election of constitutional convention delegates, put him on thin ice with Johnson. The president's attorney general, Henry Stanbery, had issued an opinion restricting the commanders' authority over voter registration. Stanbery's opinion also limited those prohibited from voting to just former high-ranking Rebel officials. Grant, however, informed his military district commanders that the attorney general's opinion was "advisory" only and directed them to act on their own interpretations of the voter registration law. Sheridan, of course, chose to give "the most rigid interpretation to the law," excluding anyone from registering and voting if there was a question regarding his eligibility.[39]

Warned by W. H. C. King, editor of the pro-Democrat *New Orleans Times*, that more Louisiana blacks than whites were registering, Johnson ordered Sheridan to keep open the registration period past June 30, Sheridan's closing date. When he extended it until July 15, Johnson urged him to continue registration until August 1. Sheridan refused, knowing that the reason for the extensions was to register more ex-Rebels under Stanbery's more liberal rules.

OF THE FIVE DISTRICT commanders in the South, only Sheridan removed civilian officials. The other four seldom interfered in Southern civil affairs, and some of them openly opposed the Reconstruction policies.[40]

In New Orleans, Sheridan's actions and Congress's Reconstruction program were "bitterly and violently" denounced. He added to his unpopularity when the municipal government refused to investigate allegations of official malfeasance—and he reacted by firing the city comptroller, treasurer, surveyor, city attorney, and twenty-two aldermen. Sheridan then began removing officials in the outlying parishes—one of them a justice of the peace who prohibited black witnesses from testifying at a murder trial. Then, he purged the jury lists of everyone who was ineligible to vote.[41]

As Sheridan's removals piled up, Grant's support for the tough little general never wavered. "Every loyal man in this country admires your courage in civil affairs, as they did your military career," Grant wrote to Sheridan in May 1867.

Grant had quietly distanced himself from Johnson when the president's policies restored former Rebels to power. Even before Congress passed Reconstruction Act No. 1, Grant, with War Secretary Stanton's backing, had taken steps to protect loyalists from biased prosecution in the South, and he had authorized federal intervention when civilian authorities ignored local violence.

Grant and Stanton found themselves increasingly at odds with Johnson but in step with Congress. In appreciation of their support, Congress enacted the Command of the Army and Tenure of Office acts, which shielded Grant and Stanton from arbitrary dismissal by Johnson. Grant, Stanton, and Sheridan had become the Radical Republicans' most reliable agents of Reconstruction.[42]

SHERIDAN DEPLORED JOHNSON'S "DETERMINATION not to execute but to obstruct" Congress's Reconstruction program. His obstructionism, Sheridan wrote, "aroused among the disaffected element new hopes of power and place, hopes of being at once put in political control again . . . just as if there had been no war."

Pushing back against the president's refusal to carry out Congress's directives, Sheridan stretched his authority as far as he could. After the riot, he announced that former Union soldiers would comprise half of New Orleans's police force. He also integrated New Orleans's public transportation system—the first civil rights action of its kind in the South. Since before the war, blacks had been permitted to ride only in horse-drawn cars bearing a star. But in the spring of 1867, some blacks began riding in the unmarked cars reserved for whites. When the transit companies complained, Sheridan refused to intervene—many of his troops were black—and the separate conveyances were abandoned.[43]

Sheridan's cold war along the Mexican border had helped doom Maximilian's regime, but his aggressive tactics did not subdue the unreconstructed Rebels in Louisiana and Texas, Confederate states that had emerged from the war largely intact and unbowed. Instead of taming the rebellious elements, Sheridan's increasingly harsh measures only generated greater hostility, requiring yet more draconian actions.

THE LOUISIANA LEVEE BOARD disbursed millions of dollars in contracts, mainly to the commissioners' deserving supporters. In the spring of 1867, the levee commissioners' terms expired. The legislature, which had just appropriated $4 million for levee improvements, extended the board members' terms.

Governor James Wells, however, wished to utilize the $4 million to enhance his political influence, and so he pocket vetoed the extension and appointed his own board. Wells and the legislature approached Sheridan and asked him to choose between the dueling boards.[44] Sheridan pursued a course that managed to outrage both parties: he appointed his own board and dismissed the other two.

Wells angrily appealed to President Johnson, but Johnson would not overrule Sheridan. War Secretary Stanton, however, directed Sheridan to suspend his action until Stanton had read Sheridan's report on the affair.

Sheridan wrote the report on June 3, and on the day that he sent it to Stanton, he removed Governor Wells from office, having grown weary of Wells's "obstructions" of his attempts to reorder Louisiana's civil affairs. "If you will sustain me in this strong and just course I have taken," Sheridan wrote to Grant, "I think this State will come into the Union without any opposing party or part of the Secession element."

A loyal Unionist, Wells had been elected in 1865 with the Democrats' help, and he had supported Johnson's lenient postwar reconciliation. But when defiant former Confederates took control of the legislature, the governor repeatedly clashed with them over black suffrage, the state constitutional convention, and other issues. At the same time, Wells opposed many of the Reconstruction Act measures that Sheridan was implementing. The governor's independent positions angered both sides.

Sheridan removed Wells because he had failed to punish the perpetrators of the New Orleans riot and had replaced Unionists with ex-Rebels in state government. "His conduct has been as sinuous as the mark left in the dust by the movement of a snake," Sheridan told Stanton. Louisiana Democrats were not unhappy to see him go. The Democrat-leaning *New Orleans Times* punned, "All's well that ends Wells."

Wells did not make a graceful exit; he locked himself in the governor's office, emerging only when one of Sheridan's staff officers threatened to drag him out. Sheridan replaced Wells with Benjamin Flanders, who unequivocally supported Congress's Reconstruction program.

In his report to Grant, Sheridan explained that he was pursuing "a bold and firm course" in Louisiana because it was the only way that Reconstruction could succeed there. Grant assured Sheridan that he, Stanton, and Northern public opinion approved of Sheridan's conduct.[45]

JOHNSON HAD BEEN SEEKING a pretext for replacing Sheridan since he had swept out the mayor, aldermen, and other officials in March. On April 5, Grant had warned Sheridan that at the White House there was "a disposition to remove [him]," while adding, "Both the Secretary of War and myself will oppose any such move as will the mass of the people."

Sheridan knew that by firing Governor Wells, he had possibly provoked a final showdown with Johnson, who tended to act "with all the boldness and aggressiveness of his peculiar nature"—a description that also happened to fit Sheridan.

In July, the president sent Brigadier General Lovell Harrison Rousseau to New Orleans to monitor Sheridan's actions. Sheridan complained to Grant on August 3 that Rousseau, without authority, had interfered with Sheridan's command and even suggested his removal, allegations that Rousseau denied to Grant after Sheridan's letter appeared in New York newspapers.[46]

SHERIDAN COULD NO LONGER disguise his animosity toward the former Confederates who resisted his Reconstruction measures. To his former military aide, Frederick Newhall, Sheridan wrote, "If I am disliked, it is because I cannot and will not cater to rebel sentiment." It was of no consequence to him whether "the Southern States were readmitted tomorrow or kept out for twenty years. . . . The more I see of this people the less I see to admire."[47]

Sheridan's dislike of Texas had grown especially, and he did little to conceal it. He refused to allow a formal funeral procession in Galveston for Confederate general Albert Sydney Johnston when his remains were landed there, en route to Austin for burial. When Galveston citizens paid homage by marching in silence, Sheridan fired Galveston's mayor.[48]

He complained to Governor James Throckmorton that Texas authorities were refusing to prosecute people who attacked and robbed Unionists and blacks. To Grant, Sheridan wrote, "The condition of Freedmen and Union men in remote parts of the State is truly horrible. The Government is denounced; the Freedmen are shot and Union men are persecuted if they have the temerity to express their opinion. . . . My own opinion is that the trial of a white man for the murder of a Freedman in Texas would be a farce."

The situation was especially egregious in northeastern Texas. "It is currently reported in their counties that the object of the Governor in calling for troops for the frontier is to get the soldiers removed from the interior, so that there could be no interference in the perpetration of these fiendish activities," Grant wrote. Federal troops were no longer effective in Texas, Grant said; in Brownsville, citizens fired on a squad of soldiers. "The great number of murders of union men and freed men in Texas, not only as a rule unpunished but uninvestigated, constitutes what is practically a state of insurrection," Grant informed Stanton. "I would recommend the declaration of martial law in Texas."[49]

In April, when the murder rate soared, Sheridan had forwarded a communication from Colonel Griffin recommending Governor Throckmorton's removal. In his attached note, Sheridan told Grant, "I feel like Griffin on this subject, that he ought to be removed." But the violence had then receded, and Sheridan did not act. By July, however, the situation had become as impossible as ever, with the murders of large numbers of blacks and federal soldiers.

On July 24, Sheridan informed Grant that he wanted to shake up the civil government. "The laws are executed by those who hate the government and the military commander who is ordered to protect persons and property of its loyal citizens." He said he would initially make the changes "progressively, but if this does not make a change for the better, I will be forced to make many."

In a telegram on July 30, Grant assured Sheridan that he was free to "make such removals from civil offices, and appointments to fill vacancies, as you may deem necessary to secure a thorough practical execution of the laws of Congress in Texas."

That day, Sheridan removed Governor Throckmorton, and named Unionist E. M. Pease as his successor.[50]

President Johnson was busy trying to fire Stanton for carrying out Congress's Reconstruction policies. Grant protested to Johnson that Stanton had done nothing wrong and, moreover, was protected by the Tenure of Office Act.

But Johnson had long ago stopped listening to people who disagreed with him, and he demanded Stanton's resignation. When Stanton refused to submit it, Johnson suspended him and appointed Grant interim war secretary. It wasn't the last of Stanton, whose removal, return, and refusal to be turned out a second time would provide the impetus for impeachment proceedings against Johnson the following spring.[51]

With Stanton out of the way, Johnson turned to Sheridan, who, after removing Throckmorton, had proceeded to dismiss Shreveport, Louisiana's mayor and aldermen. On August 17, the president ordered Grant to reassign Sheridan to the Department of the Missouri. Grant objected, melodramatically urging,

> in the name of a patriotic people who have sacrificed Hundreds of thousands of loyal lives, and Thousands of Millions of treasure to preserve the integrity and Union of this Country, that this order be not insisted on. It is unmistakably the expressed wish of the Country that Gen. Sheridan should not be removed from his present Command. . . . I beg that their voice may be heard. Gen. Sheridan has performed his civil duties faithfully and intelligently. His removal will only be regarded as an effort to defeat the laws of Congress. It will be interpreted by the unreconstructed element in the South . . . as a triumph. It will embo[ld]en them to renew opposition to the will of the loyal Masses, believing that they have the Executive with them.

Johnson penned a long response in which he rejected each of Grant's arguments in turn, while reminding Grant that he was exercising his constitutional power as commander in chief. Sheridan's administration of the Fifth Military District, the president declared, "has, in fact, been one of absolute tyranny, without reference to the principles of our government or the nature of our free institutions . . . a resort to authority not granted by law."[52]

The news of Sheridan's dismissal got mixed reviews in the New Orleans press. The *Times* was glad to be rid of him and his "close adherence to the requirements of Congress." The *Bee*, resigned to the Radicals' reshaping the South either quickly or "little by little," favored the former approach. "General Sheridan sees the work that he has to do and does it promptly. That much is decidedly in his favor." The *Crescent* clearly regretted Sheridan's departure. "He has been daily more and more commending himself to general appreciation, as well as by the candor, directness and vigor with which he proceeds to his objects, as by the judicious character of some of his appointments."[53]

SHERIDAN REFLECTED THAT HE had "tried to guard the rights of everybody in accordance with the law" but acknowledged that his removal came as a relief. "I was not loath to go. The kind of duty I had been performing in Louisiana and Texas was very trying under the most favorable circumstances," but it was made worse by "the obstructions which the President placed in the way from persistent opposition to the acts of Congress as well as from antipathy to me."[54]

Despite everything, Sheridan had successfully overseen the registration of tens of thousands of black voters in Louisiana and Texas—indisputably his greatest achievement. He had punished the most odious instances of official corruption and misconduct. Even as his army was severely pared by postwar demobilizations from a peak of 52,000 men to just 7,000, he had attempted to protect loyal Unionists and blacks from the violence that permeated the Fifth Military District. He had made a maximum effort to carry out his mission, as he perceived it.

That said, Sheridan had displayed no aptitude for diplomacy. His forceful actions made him lasting enemies: even a decade later, he was accused in a $410,600 lawsuit of unlawfully seizing sugar and molasses from James Whalen's Killona Plantation; Whalen lost the litigation.[55]

JOHNSON INITIALLY CHOSE MAJOR General George Thomas of the Army of the Cumberland to succeed Sheridan in New Orleans. In a round-robin arrangement, Major General Winfield Scott Hancock of the Department of the Missouri was supposed to succeed Thomas, while Sheridan replaced Hancock. But because of Thomas's poor health, Sheridan and Hancock simply traded commands.

In instructing Sheridan to report to Fort Leavenworth, Kansas, Grant bluntly wrote, "You were right." All along, Grant had assured Sheridan that his dismissal, which both had known for months was inevitable, would not affect Sheridan's military career. Grant invited Sheridan to come to Washington for a vacation after reporting for duty at Leavenworth. "I know such a welcome awaits you as will convince you that Republicans are not always ungrateful and that there is still loyalty in the country."[56]

CHAPTER 14

Winter War on the Southern Plains

1868–1869

We don't want to exterminate or even to fight them. At best it is an
inglorious war, and for our soldiers . . . it is all danger and extreme
labor, without a single compensating advantage.

—GENERAL WILLIAM SHERMAN,
ON THE PLAINS INDIANS[1]

LATE IN THE AFTERNOON OF DECEMBER 1, 1868, as the metallic light began to fade, a long column of mounted figures appeared on the snow-covered rolling hills south of Camp Supply, the army's new depot in Indian Territory. It was Lieutenant Colonel George Custer and his 7th Cavalry, in triumphal array. Two days earlier, red-bearded California Joe, the famously bibulous scout who had once drunkenly attacked US cavalrymen by mistake, had brought the first news of the crushing blow struck by Custer and his men against the Indians who had terrorized western Kansas throughout the late summer and fall.

During raids on the growing settlements in the Saline and Solomon river valleys in August and September, renegades had slaughtered seventy-nine settlers and snatched away young women and children. Fifty miles to the south, at daybreak on November 27, the 7th Cavalry had struck back, smashing the sleeping Cheyenne winter encampment on the Washita River. The corpses of 103 warriors, women, and children were left strewn across the frozen ground.

Attacking the Indians in their winter camps was the novel strategy of Major General Phil Sheridan, who had conceded the futility of chasing warrior bands across the plains during the summertime. Now, Sheridan and his headquarters troops and contractors stood in ranks to welcome the victors.

The theatrical Custer turned it into a war pageant. The Osage scouts arrived first, their faces "fantastically painted," and prominently displaying their shields and quivers of arrows. Fresh scalps dangled from their spears, and their own plaited scalps were bedecked with long trains of feathers and silver ornaments. Conspicuous even amid this sybaritic display was the Osage warrior Trotter, bearing the meticulously decorated scalp of the renowned Cheyenne chief Black Kettle. The Osages whooped and fired their rifles into the air.

Behind them on a black stallion rode Custer, stone-faced and nearly unrecognizable in a full beard, buckskins, and fur hat, leading fifty-three captive squaws and children mounted on ponies and swathed to the eyes in red trade blankets. The eight hundred 7th Cavalry troopers brought up the rear as their band played the 7th Cavalry's anthem, "Garry Owen." Each officer lifted his saber as he passed Sheridan, who returned the salutes by raising his cap and smiling.

Of Custer, Sheridan had once said, "If there was any poetry or romance in war he could develop it." No better proof of Sheridan's observation existed than Custer's dramatic entrance at Camp Supply.

That night, at the 7th Cavalry's encampment a half mile from Camp Supply, the Osages performed what Sheridan described as a "hideous scalp dance." As the Osage drums pounded, the sister and niece of the late Black Kettle paid Sheridan a visit in his tent. Black Kettle's sister, Monahsetah, speaking for the captive women and children, politely asked Sheridan when he planned to murder them all. Nonplussed, Sheridan assured her that they would not be killed. The captives' spirits noticeably rose.[2]

SHERIDAN'S ELATION AT THE 7th Cavalry's triumph, however, was shot through with worry. Custer had informed him that Major Joel Elliot and sixteen men were missing. Custer hoped they would show up at Camp Supply or Fort Dodge.

Custer explained that he had been unable to conduct a thorough search for Elliot because he was being pressed by thousands of Indians who had come to Black Kettle's aid from nearby camps, and he had to protect his supply train. Sheridan thought Custer's explanation to be "a very unsatisfactory view of the matter." Still, he was proud of what his men had accomplished. "The blow that Custer had struck was a hard one, and fell on the guiltiest of all the bands—that of Black Kettle. It was this band that, without provocation, had massacred the settlers on the Saline and Solomon, and perpetrated cruelties too fiendish for recital."[3]

Sheridan was eager to see the battlefield for himself—and to try to find out what had happened to the Elliot party. A few days later, Sheridan, Custer, the 7th Cavalry, the Osage scouts, and a long supply train rolled out of Camp Supply and turned south toward Black Kettle's ruined camp.

BOTH SHERIDAN AND HIS predecessor commanding the Department of the Missouri, Major General Winfield Scott Hancock, had flailed impotently in their attempts to catch and punish the marauding Southern Plains Indian bands.

In 1867, Hancock had arranged a parley with the Cheyenne "Dog Soldiers"—warriors who eschewed the reservation for the free life of the plains—on the Pawnee Fork of the Arkansas River, but the Indians fled when they saw Hancock's troops. Hancock had sent Custer and the 7th Cavalry after them. The Indians scattered and continued robbing homes, killing and raping settlers, and kidnapping their children.

And then Hancock had suspended Custer for one year because he had force-marched his men from Fort Wallace to Fort Harker in July 1867—ostensibly to obtain supplies but actually so that he could visit his wife, Libbie.[4]

Having failed to subdue the Cheyenne and their allies, the government tried diplomacy; Congress organized an Indian Peace Commission. In October 1867, the commissioners negotiated a treaty with the Cheyennes, Arapahoes, Lipans, Comanches, and Kiowas at Medicine Lodge Creek in southern Kansas. Each tribe was assigned a reservation in the Indian Territory. The government pledged to pay an annuity and to provide food, clothing, teachers, schools, and doctors.

The Comanches and Kiowas were permitted to continue hunting buffalo in their traditional hunting grounds south of the Arkansas River. The Arapahoes and Cheyennes could hunt the buffalo between the Arkansas and Platte Rivers, so long as they did not interfere with the white settlers or the construction of the Union Pacific and Kansas Pacific Railroads. Most of the Indians who signed the treaty did not know what they were signing, and it was not explained to them.

Congress, immersed in impeachment proceedings against President Andrew Johnson, delayed ratifying the treaty for two years. Consequently, the promised goods and annuities were not sent to the reservations.[5]

By spring 1868, with the Indians facing starvation, the manifest failure of the treaty had become evident. Lieutenant General William Sherman, commander of the Division of the Missouri, wrote to his wife, "The poor Indians are starving. We kill them if they attempt to hunt and if they keep within the Reservations they starve." Many did not report to their reservations but went hunting instead. Others chose to go on the warpath.[6]

AFTER REPORTING TO FORT Leavenworth in August 1867 as the new commander of the Department of the Missouri, Sheridan had taken a long leave of absence. He visited his parents in Somerset, Ohio, then traveled to New York and thence to Washington.

There, Sheridan spent his days working with Generals Sherman and Christopher Augur on an army code of regulations and articles of war. At night, he socialized, enjoying it so much that he lingered in the capital through the early months of 1868. Sherman joked to his wife that he was urging Sheridan to return to work, but "he rather enjoys the parties." At the end of February, Sheridan finally left Washington for Fort Leavenworth.[7]

Early in the summer, Sheridan moved his headquarters to Fort Hays to be closer to the frontier. During an inspection tour of Fort Dodge, he met with a group of young Arapahoe and Cheyenne warriors, who told him their women and children were starving. Pitying them, Sheridan gave them a generous supply of rations.[8]

But in August, Comanches and Kiowas began raiding the Texas settlements, and about two hundred Cheyenne Dog Soldiers and Sioux and Arapahoe warrior bands rampaged through Kansas, Oklahoma, and Colorado. "A general outbreak was upon us," Sheridan wrote. The marauders rejected reservation life, resented the approaching Kansas Pacific Railroad, and scoffed at the counsel of their "peace chiefs."

From the Solomon and Saline river valleys to eastern Colorado, each attack wrought a heartrending tragedy. Daniel Wesaser's father was killed and his sister kidnapped, along with her child and Wesaser's six- and eight-year-old daughters. In a letter to Sheridan's headquarters, he wrote, "Their poor heart-broken mother is grieving herself to death for them. It is a hard trial; it looks like it is more than we can bear." The six-year-old was found frozen to death, and Wesaser's nephew was murdered; the others were never seen again.[9]

Acting Governor Frank Hall of the Colorado Territory reported that the Indians controlled the eastern territory up to twelve miles from Denver. "They are more bold, fierce, and desperate in their attacks than ever before," he wrote.[10]

In September, Sheridan sent Lieutenant Colonel Alfred Sully, the commander at Fort Dodge, with five hundred 7th Cavalry troopers and a company of the 3rd Infantry south into Indian Territory. A month earlier, Sully had enraged Sheridan by distributing arms to the Indians so that they could hunt buffalo. Now, Sully's ponderous column disappointed Sheridan, becoming a target for hit-and-run Indian attacks. It returned to Fort Dodge without accomplishing anything.

Another expedition by Colonel Eugene Carr's 5th Cavalry in northwestern Kansas was more energetic, but ultimately unsuccessful too. Despite waging a series of running fights, Carr's men were unable to force the Cheyenne Dog Soldiers to a decisive battle.[11]

The fleet warriors were as elusive as summer dust devils—there one minute, gone the next. They lived off the land, while the soldiers were tethered to supply trains—each infantry company requiring a six-mule wagon, and each cavalry troop, three wagons—to haul food, ammunition, and forage for the horses and mules. Unlike the Indian ponies, the army's livestock could not subsist solely on prairie grasses.

Moreover, scattered across Sheridan's Department of the Missouri were just 2,600 troops, 1,200 of them mounted, while the tribes in his jurisdiction could conceivably put 6,000 warriors in the field.

SHERIDAN RELUCTANTLY REINED IN his gut urge to strike back hard against the depredations. Instead, he concentrated his troops in the western Kansas forts, from which they might better protect—as much as it was possible—the settlers, the Santa Fe and Smoky Hill Trails, and the Kansas Pacific Railroad. Winter could not come soon enough this bloody year.[12]

There was a noteworthy exception to Sheridan's defensive program. Colonel George Forsyth, Sheridan's aide-de-camp, who had long lobbied Sheridan for a field command, was given a special "ranger" detachment. Its forty-seven men were all proven frontiersmen and sharpshooters. The unit was dubbed "Solomon's Avengers," in recognition of the settlers murdered along the Solomon River.

The Avengers went into action after warriors attacked a supply train near the Republican River. Forsyth's men followed the Indians to Arickaree Creek, a fork of the Republican River in northeastern Colorado Territory. Nearby were three large Indian villages of Sioux, Cheyenne, and Arapahoe, led by Sioux chief Pawnee Killer and Cheyenne warriors Tall Bull and Roman Nose.

At dawn on September 17, about seven hundred warriors attacked the Avengers and drove them to an island in Arickaree Creek. One of the first volleys of Indian gunfire killed Lieutenant Fred Beecher, a decorated Gettysburg veteran and a nephew of Henry Ward Beecher and Harriet Beecher Stowe. The company surgeon also died. Forsyth was wounded twice.

The warriors, however, ran into deadly accurate gunfire when they tried—three times—to overrun the sharpshooters, who were armed with Spencer repeaters capable of sustained fire of twenty rounds per minute. For eight days, the Indians ringed the besieged troopers, picking off their horses and denying them access to food and medicine.

Two scouts slipped through the cordon and alerted troopers at Fort Wallace, who ended the siege. The Avengers lost six killed and fifteen wounded on what became known as Beecher's Island, while killing about thirty-five Indians, including Roman Nose.[13]

At a meeting in Chicago in October 1868, the Indian peace commissioners, Republican presidential nominee General in Chief Ulysses Grant, and Lieutenant General Sherman, who oversaw the districts of Sheridan and other Western generals, reacted to the murderous Kansas raids by canceling the Indians' hunting and roaming privileges and resolving to force them, if necessary, onto their reservations. Commissioner Samuel Tappan objected that this was tantamount to a war of extermination. Sherman retorted that that was up to the Indians, and furthermore, a war against the Plains Indians was "not apt to add much to our fame or personal comfort." Sherman also urged the transfer of the Indian Bureau from the Department of the Interior to the Department of War; let the army manage the Indians, he said.

In a letter to Sherman, Sheridan wholeheartedly supported putting the army in charge. Under the present system, "there are too many fingers in the pie, too many ends to be subserved, and too much money to be made; and it is the interest of the nation, and of humanity, to put an end to this inhuman farce. . . . There should be one head [the army] in the government of Indians," he wrote.

Sheridan also told Sherman that the Medicine Lodge Treaty, in failing to punish the renegades who raided the settlements, had enabled them to grow "rich in horses, stock, and other property." "They should have been punished and made to give up the plunder captured," he wrote. But because they were not, the raiders must now be "soundly whipped, and the ringleaders in the present trouble hung, their ponies killed, and [subjected to] such destruction of their property as will make them very poor." He proposed to attack the Indians in their winter encampments, a strategy rarely used by the army and, therefore, likely to catch the Indians unawares.[14]

"Go ahead in your own way and I will back you with my whole authority," Sherman replied to Sheridan. "If it results in the utter annihilation of these Indians, it is but the result of what they have been warned [about] again and again."[15]

In choosing to mount a winter expedition, Sheridan knew that he faced daunting obstacles. Paralyzing blizzards and thirty-below-zero temperatures might envelope the Great Plains at any time from late fall until mid-spring, transforming the best-laid military plan into a desperate struggle for survival. Horses and mules, whose forage had to be brought when the snow covered the grasses, were especially vulnerable to the uncertainties of resupply—and snow, cold, mud, and vast distances made it virtually impossible for supply trains to keep up. Because winter campaigns required extensive planning and preparation without a guarantee of success, few had been attempted. But those who had been bold enough to attempt them had sometimes been richly rewarded.

The prototype was Colonel Kit Carson's expedition against the Navajos during the winter of 1863–1864. In five sweeps through the Navajos' New Mexico mountain kingdom, Carson and his New Mexico and California volunteers had destroyed the Navajos' crops and orchards, seized their livestock, and kept them constantly on the run. In March 1864, 6,000 Navajos—half the tribe—had surrendered, and by the end of the year, 8,000 had given up and gone into exile.[16]

Months later, on November 29, 1864, Colonel John Chivington and his Colorado militiamen wiped out a peaceful Cheyenne village that was under the protection of a government Indian agent and flying an American flag. In their unprovoked attack at Sand Creek in the eastern Colorado Territory, the soldiers slaughtered up to 150 men, women, and children, mutilating their bodies. A horrified government commission wrote that the soldiers' shocking actions "would put to shame the savage ingenuity of interior Africa."[17]

Before deciding to prosecute a winter campaign, Sheridan had not only consulted these historical antecedents but studied the meteorological records of western army posts to learn what kind of weather he should anticipate. He had also interviewed army officers, scouts, freighters, and settlers.

Most of them had advised against what Sheridan proposed. Famed mountain man and scout Jim Bridger, who was in his mid-sixties and living in St. Louis, had traveled to Fort Hays expressly to warn Sheridan not to proceed. "Blizzards don't respect man or beast," Bridger reportedly said.

But others familiar with the Plains winters told Sheridan that what he proposed was not impossible—if the troopers were properly clothed, fed, and sheltered. Sheridan listened to what they said.

His scouts, including a young man named William Cody, showed him on maps where the Indian winter camps were located—on the Washita River northwest of Fort Cobb in Indian Territory. Sheridan decided to take his chances with the elements in order "to strike the Indians a hard blow and force them onto the reservations."[18]

Sheridan laid out what would become his signature offensive strategy in the West: forces converging on an objective from different directions to deliver a knockout wallop. This one would be three-pronged, involving more than 3,000 men:

Colonel A. W. Evans marching east from Fort Bascom, New Mexico, with six troops of the 3rd Cavalry and two infantry companies; Brigadier General Eugene Carr leading seven troops of the 5th Cavalry southeast from Fort Lyon, Colorado Territory; and the principal strike force marching south from Fort Dodge, Kansas, with eleven troops of the 7th Cavalry, five infantry companies, and twelve companies of the Kansas 19th Volunteer Cavalry.[19]

Sheridan did not want Sully either to lead the operation or to command the 7th Cavalry. While Sully was one of the best-known Indian fighters in the West, his actions the previous summer had angered and disappointed Sheridan.

SHERIDAN HAD JUST ONE man in mind to lead the operation—the beau ideal of the light cavalry who had helped save the Union army during George Pickett's charge at Gettysburg, who had won a general's star at twenty-three, and who had burnished his glittering reputation in the Shenandoah Valley and at Five Forks, Sailor's Creek, and Appomattox Court House. Lieutenant Colonel George Custer was the kind of officer that Sheridan most liked: he was extraordinarily energetic, quick to act, aggressive, and willing to carry out any mission, even killing Indian civilians and destroying their homes.

But Custer was at home in Monroe, Michigan, serving out his one-year suspension for dereliction of duty. With Sherman's help, Sheridan got the last two months of Custer's sentence commuted. On September 24, Custer received a telegram from Sheridan. "Generals Sherman, Sully, and myself, and nearly all the officers of your regiment, have asked for you," Sheridan wrote. "Can you come?" Six days later—before Sheridan's request was officially approved—Custer reported to Sheridan at Fort Hays.[20]

Sheridan explained his plan, and Custer enthusiastically endorsed it. Custer would ride south toward the Washita River, "the supposed winter seat of the hostile tribes; to destroy their villages and ponies; to kill or hang all warriors, and bring back all women and children." It was not so different from the warfare in the Shenandoah Valley, where the Union cavalry's object was to destroy enemy forces, crops, and livestock.[21]

Custer liked the fact that the campaign would "dispel the old-fogy idea" that winter operations were impossible and, better still, force the Indians "to engage in a combat in which we should do for him what he had hither done for us; compel him to fight upon ground and under circumstances of our own selection."[22] He began preparing the 7th Cavalry for the expedition. While their horses were being reshod, the eight hundred troopers readied their clothing and gear and improved their marksmanship with twice-daily target practice.[23]

Custer's return was not welcomed by the 7th Cavalry, which disliked his strict discipline. Unlike the Wolverines, who had proudly served under him during the war, the 7th Cavalry troopers thought his command style unsuited to the frontier. They found his obsession with proper appearance especially irritating. But Custer had always been mindful of the impression he made, and he demanded as much of his regiment.

He infuriated his men when he seized their horses and reassigned them new mounts according to color—bays to four companies; sorrels to three companies; and chestnuts, browns, blacks, grays, and "brindles" to one company each. Captain Frederick Benteen, a company commander, described Custer's action as "not only ridiculous, but criminal, unjust, and arbitrary in the extreme."[24]

SHERIDAN SENT SULLY WITH a supply train to build a forward depot one hundred miles south of Fort Dodge for the winter campaign. Camp Supply soon stood at the confluence of Wolf and Beaver Creeks in the northwestern Indian Territory.

Sheridan rode there in November and experienced the ferocity of a Great Plains blizzard firsthand. Rain and snow drenched the troops, and powerful winds carried away their tents. Wet, cold, and shivering, Sheridan spent a miserable night huddled under a wagon, and "the gloomy predictions of old man Bridger and others rose up before me with greatly increased force." But he and his troops pushed on and arrived at Camp Supply on November 21 to find Custer and the 7th Cavalry waiting for them.[25]

But neither Evans nor Carr nor the 19th Kansas Cavalry had yet arrived. Scouts ranging the countryside could find no sign of them. While concerned about their absence, Sheridan decided to proceed anyway. He would prove to the Indians "that he would have no security, winter or summer, except in obeying the laws of peace and humanity." Custer, too, had no misgivings about marching into Indian Territory with just his eight hundred 7th Cavalry troopers, rather than the originally planned 3,000-man strike force.[26]

IT SNOWED ALL NIGHT November 21, and at reveille at 4 a.m. the next morning, snow was still falling, and two feet lay on the ground. Custer's bugler blew "Boots and Saddles," and the 7th Cavalry and its Osage and Kaw scouts mounted up. Visiting Sheridan's tent before leaving, Custer was asked by Sheridan what he thought of the snowstorm. "Nothing could be more to our purpose," Custer replied. "We could move and the Indian villages could not." As snow fell in "blinding clouds," the cavalry rode out of Camp Supply with Custer guiding by his compass and the 7th Cavalry band playing "The Girl I Left Behind Me."

On November 26, Major Joel Elliot struck a trail, less than a day old, of 100 to 150 warriors traveling southeast. Custer cut loose from his supply train, and the troopers followed the trail, carrying only what they needed.

All day and that night they pursued the warriors, who evidently were returning to their village from a raid on the Kansas settlements. About midnight, the soldiers reached the Washita River valley, where the raiders' trail ended at a cluster of lodges barely visible through riverside fog. Custer and his officers were certain they had located some of the Indians who had terrorized the Kansas settlements.

Through the rest of the night, the troopers quietly surrounded the village. To guard against discovery, officers forbade their men to build fires or even to stamp their feet to keep warm. Clutching their horses' reins, the troopers spent a "cold and comfortless night" in the subzero cold and snow, as the fog swirled about them.

November 27, 1868–Washita River, Indian Territory—As the sky became milky opaque in color, the cavalrymen could discern dozens of tall, white tepees in dense timber. It was the Cheyenne encampment of Black Kettle—the westernmost village of a chain of Indian encampments stretching for miles along the Washita River.

Custer had divided his regiment into four parts in order to encircle the village, without knowing how many warriors were in the camp or even which band they belonged to. Fortunately for him, Black Kettle's village contained just fifty Cheyenne lodges and three Sioux and Arapahoe tepees.

At daybreak, the troopers shed their overcoats and rations so as not to be encumbered when the shooting began. Then Custer gave the signal to his band to strike up "Garry Owen." The men cheered when they heard the familiar tune, off-key though it was when played on frozen instruments. The troopers stormed the village.

The Indians awakened to what must have been their worst nightmare—especially for Black Kettle and the other Sand Creek survivors. Black Kettle fired his rifle to alert his people; then he and his wife, Ar-no-ho-wok, leaped on a pony. A storm of bullets cut them both down before they could cross the river.

Those who were able to fought back desperately with rifles and bows and arrows. A few broke through the ring of troopers; others leaped into the Washita River, using the bank for cover. Squaws and children who stayed in the lodges were not harmed, but those caught in the melee were shot down. Some took their own lives; a Cheyenne woman disemboweled her baby before plunging her knife into her own breast. The troopers had control of the village within ten minutes, but the fighting continued.[27]

Alerted by the shooting, large numbers of mounted warriors from the other villages massed on a nearby ridge while the troopers ransacked the village and collected prisoners. Satanta's Kiowa warriors and Little Raven's Arapahoes had daubed on war paint and galloped to the Cheyennes' aid. With loud whoops, hundreds of them attacked Custer's cavalrymen.

The troopers withstood the attack, then counterattacked, driving away the warriors. The cavalrymen burned the village and, in an act of calculated destruction, slaughtered the Cheyennes' pony herd—eight hundred horses—after letting the surviving squaws choose mounts for their ride into captivity.

As the 7th Cavalry prepared to pull out of the charred village, littered with the bodies of 103 Cheyennes, including Chiefs Black Kettle and Little Rock, the troopers discovered that the Kiowas and Arapahoes had stolen their overcoats and rations—and killed Custer's dog, Blucher, with an arrow when it tried to chase them.

Major Elliot and sixteen men were unaccounted for. A scout told Custer that he had seen Elliot and his men chasing some Indians who had slipped away from the camp. Custer's men rode two miles in the direction that Elliot was last seen, but they did not find him or his men. With hundreds of Indian warriors nearby, the search was discontinued.

Custer led his regiment several miles down the valley toward the other encampments, hoping to draw the warriors away from Black Kettle's smoking village so that the supply train could safely approach. The troopers then reversed direction, drew rations and warm clothing from the supply train, and started back to Camp Supply. Custer's losses totaled four dead, fifteen wounded, and seventeen missing but presumed dead.[28]

THE 7TH CAVALRY, THIS time accompanied by Sheridan and the 19th Kansas Volunteer Cavalry, left Camp Supply on a clear, subzero morning in early December to view the Washita battleground and find out what had happened to Elliot and his men. The nearly 2,000 men and their supply wagons made steady progress despite the deep snows. When large buffalo herds stampeded the mules in the wagon train, Sheridan had to "throw out flankers" to shoot the leading bulls and turn away the herds. Packs of wolves devoured the fallen bison.

The 19th Kansas had already endured unexpected hardships just to reach Camp Supply, arriving too late to join Custer's expedition. Led by Colonel Samuel Crawford, who had resigned as Kansas governor to take the command, the 1,000 cavalrymen were itching to fight the Indians. They were amply supplied and armed with new Spencer carbines. After leaving Wichita on November 5, they had gotten lost and wandered the hills and valleys of southern Kansas for weeks, guided by their clueless scout, Apache Bill. Wet, cold, and half starved, the worn-out troops had straggled into Camp Supply on November 28.

As Sheridan's column marched on toward the Washita, a "blue norther'" swooped down upon them, lashing them with furious winds, freezing rain and snow, and achingly cold temperatures. Upon reaching the Canadian River, a detachment had to cut through the ice floes, their mounts emerging from the river bleeding and bruised. They built big drying fires on the opposite bank. The water refroze, trapping the wagons, and men had to wade in and chop them out with axes.[29]

That night, the winds blew down tents and extinguished the troopers' fires, reported De B. Randolph Keim of the *New York Herald*. Afraid to lie down for fear of freezing to death, the troopers tramped up and down in the camp all night as the equally miserable horses and mules "uttered melancholic moans."[30]

IN HIS REPORT TO General Sherman, Sheridan wrote, "There never was a more complete surprise" than Custer's daybreak attack on Black Kettle's camp, which "strongly reminded one of scenes during the war." Custer reported 103 Indians killed and the capture of fifty-three squaws and children, 875 ponies, 1,123 buffalo robes and skins, 535 pounds of gunpowder, 1,050 pounds of lead, 4,000 arrows, 700 pounds of tobacco, as well as rifles, pistols, bows, lariats, and large amounts of dried meat. Except for the captives, practically everything else was destroyed.[31]

In the Cheyenne lodges, Custer's men had found photos and daguerreotypes, clothing, and bedding taken from massacred settlers' homes; mail stolen from murdered couriers; and a large book, evidently a journal, in which nothing had been written. The Indians, however, had used the book to illustrate the recent fights of Black Kettle's band.[32]

ON DECEMBER 10, SHERIDAN, Custer, Keim, and several officers toured the battleground, escorted by a 7th Cavalry detachment. Yelping dogs stood watch over the frozen corpses of their Indian masters. As the group approached the charred village, they interrupted wolves and thousands of ravens and crows in their "carrion feast." The birds rose from the ground in a noisy, black mass and passed over the soldiers.

The dead warriors had been wound into blankets; some had been laid in trees, others under bushes. In a ravine, the soldiers found thirty-eight bodies.

Sheridan's party rode to a hilltop that commanded a view of the site. About one hundred yards away they came upon the naked body of a white man, riddled with arrows and bullet holes, his head smashed. It was one of Major Elliot's men.

Two hundred yards further, they found the others, nude, frozen, and hacked to pieces. "The poor fellows were all lying within a circle not more than 15 or 20 paces in diameter," wrote Sheridan, "and the little piles of empty cartridge shells near each body showed plainly that every man had made a brave fight."

All the bodies were mutilated, but none was scalped. Later, an account citing Indian sources reported that Elliot and his men were pursuing a group of women and children when a band of Arapahoes cut them off from the village. More warriors arrived, and Elliot's men dismounted and waged their last fight.[33]

In an abandoned Arapahoe village nearby, troopers made another dismaying discovery—the bodies of a white woman and a young boy. A Kansas trooper identified them: Clara Blinn and her two-year-old son, Willie, captives of Arapahoe raiders who had attacked their wagon train near the Arkansas River on October 7.

The army was well aware of Mrs. Blinn's plight; two of her letters had found their way to Colonel William Hazen, the commander at Fort Cobb. "If you could only buy us of [*sic*] the Indians with ponies or anything," she had written. Her son was weak, and she feared her captors were going to sell her into slavery in Mexico. Hazen had authorized an Indian trader to spend whatever was necessary to obtain her release.

Mrs. Blinn's ordeal had ended sometime after Custer's attack. She was shot at close range in the forehead and bludgeoned in the back of the head, after which "every particle of hair [was] removed." Her child was found nearby with a bruise on his cheek and his white curly hair dabbled with blood, suggesting that his head had been dashed against a tree. Black Kettle's sister, Monahsetah, blamed their deaths on the Kiowa chief Satanta.[34]

SHERIDAN CONCLUDED THAT CUSTER had struck "the most villainous of the hostile bands"—which had slaughtered settlers along the Saline and Solomon Rivers months earlier, "and whose hands were still red from their bloody work on the recent raid." He rejected others' portrayal of Black Kettle as a "peace chief." Too old to ride with his warriors, Black Kettle had instead incited them with "devilish incantations" to raid the settlements, then afterward he had shielded them. It was "a merited punishment, only too long delayed," Sheridan wrote.[35]

As commander of the southern Indian reservation district established after the Medicine Lodge Treaty, Hazen had labored throughout November to bring the tribes behind the shield of Fort Cobb, where they would be safe from attacks by the US cavalry. He was aware of what Sheridan was contemplating. "General Sheridan, still under the impression that these people are at war, may possibly attack them before I can collect them at this point," Hazen wrote.

But Hazen was selective about whom he chose to protect. He rejected the bands that had butchered settlers along the Solomon and Saline Rivers; he had judged Black Kettle's band to be one of them. A week before he was killed, the chief had implored Hazen to protect his people. "I have always done my best to keep my young men quiet," he told Hazen, but "some will not listen. . . . I have not been able to keep them all at home." Hazen told the Cheyennes and Arapahoes that he regretted being unable to give them sanctuary.[36]

Sheridan hoped to find other renegade Indians to attack along the Washita, but the camps near Black Kettle's were deserted; the Indians had fled, shooting dead hundreds of ponies to keep them out of the soldiers' hands. The wholesale slaughter pleased Sheridan. It was "a most cheerful indication that our campaign would be ultimately successful, and we all prayed for at least a couple of months more of cold weather and plenty of snow."[37]

When Hazen learned that Sheridan and Custer were marching toward the other Indian camps, he sent a note stating that all the bands east of Black Kettle's village were friendly and under his protection. They "have not been on the war-path this season," Hazen wrote.[38]

Of course, Hazen's message angered Sheridan, who had not forgotten about Hazen's expropriation of the eleven Rebel cannons claimed by Sheridan's division five years earlier on Missionary Ridge. This was another black mark against him in Sheridan's book. Hazen was no fonder of Sheridan.

His feelings toward Hazen notwithstanding, Sheridan could not very well flout Hazen's protection of the other Indian villages; Hazen reported directly to Sherman, except in military affairs, when he was answerable to Sheridan. Hazen clearly had the authority in this matter.

Custer wanted to attack Satanta's Kiowa camp anyway because of Monahsetah's accusation, but Sheridan forbade it. It was just as well that they did not, because Monahsetah had lied to protect the Arapahoes, who had killed the Blinns.

Sheridan fumed to Sherman that the binomial organizational structure was not working. As proof, he noted that government-issue flour, sugar, and coffee had been found in Black Kettle's camp—meaning his band had collected rations at the same time that it was raiding settlements. "Something should be done to stop this anomaly. I am ordered to fight these Indians, and General Hazen is permitted to feed them."[39]

THE EAST RANG WITH denunciations of Custer's "massacre" of Black Kettle's band, drowning out the Westerners' gratitude for the punishment finally meted out to the Kansas raiders. George Manypenny, the commissioner of Indian affairs, suggested that Custer might have attacked the wrong village. The superintendent of

Indian affairs, Thomas Murphy, heralded the late Black Kettle as "one of the truest friends the whites have ever had among the Indians," adding that "innocent parties have been made to suffer for the crimes of others."

The *New York Times* and *St. Louis Democrat* quoted from a private letter by an unnamed 7th Cavalry trooper who said that Custer had delighted in the slaughter of the ponies; Custer later learned that the author was Captain Frederick Benteen, embittered by the death of his friend Major Elliot. Thereafter, Custer and Benteen were sworn enemies.

The Reverend Henry Whipple, Episcopal bishop of Minnesota, deplored the "shameless disregard for justice" and the taking of "the most foolhardy course we could have pursued." Others claimed the army wished to exterminate the Plains Indians.[40]

The outcry must have puzzled Custer, Sheridan, and Sherman, who had planned and approved an operation that, excepting the deaths of women and children, resembled their punishing Civil War campaigns. Sherman heatedly denied that the army contemplated genocide. "We don't want to exterminate or even to fight them," he said. "At best it is an inglorious war, and for our soldiers . . . it is all danger and extreme labor, without a single compensating advantage."

Sheridan was convinced that the army's bête noir, the so-called Indian Ring—a nefarious, and largely imagined, cabal of politicians, federal bureaucrats, Indian agents, and businessmen—had manufactured the "hue and cry" to undermine the army's influence and shore up the Indian Bureau's authority. The Indian Ring had duped "some good and pious ecclesiastics," he wrote, and they had unwittingly become "the aiders and abettors of savages who murdered, without mercy, men, women, and children."

The Indians' serial rapes of female settlers always had especially outraged Sheridan, and the criticism of his campaign against Black Kettle's village inspired an unnecessarily explicit harangue on the subject in his annual report. The raiders, he said, raped the women "sometimes as often as forty and fifty times in succession, and while insensible from brutality and exhaustion forced sticks up their persons, and, in one instance, the fortieth or fiftieth savage drew his saber and used [it] on the person of the woman in the same manner."[41]

After everything had been alleged and denied, Edmund Guerriere, who claimed to have gone raiding with the Cheyennes, attested to Lieutenant Colonel J. Schuyler Crosby that many of the renegades in fact had been members of Black Kettle's and Little Rock's bands.[42]

FORBIDDEN BY HAZEN TO attack other Indian villages along the Washita, Sheridan set out for Fort Cobb. Along the way, Sheridan, Custer, and their large cavalry force passed what Custer described as "one continuous Indian village"—at least six hundred lodges extending twelve miles.

Sheridan wanted the Indians to turn over the raiders' ringleaders and stolen livestock. "I will compel them, if I can," he wrote to Sherman. Above all, Sheridan and Custer, believing Monahsetah's falsehood, wished to apprehend Satanta and Lone Wolf and force them to answer for the Blinns' murders.[43]

The Kiowas' camp was not far from Fort Cobb. Custer rode out to parley with Satanta and Lone Wolf, but they refused to come in. Sheridan got a different reception when he went there with his nearly 2,000-man cavalry force. "I am now your chief and you must obey me," Sheridan told them. "I am just as much your chief as you are the chiefs of your people."

Upon hearing Sheridan's unyielding words and seeing the impressive firepower arrayed against them, the two chiefs quickly became cooperative. They and a large contingent of warriors set out with Sheridan and Custer for Fort Cobb. Satanta and Lone Wolf assured Sheridan that their villages would follow in a few days after they had packed up all of their possessions.[44]

But as the party approached Fort Cobb, more warriors made excuses to leave, and soon just a handful of Kiowas remained. When Satanta tried to escape, Sheridan knew that his cooperation had been a sham. Cavalry officers overtook the sexagenarian chief before he got away. Sheridan placed Satanta and Lone Wolf under arrest.

After waiting in vain for two days for the rest of the Kiowas to appear at Fort Cobb, Sheridan learned that they were traveling in another direction, toward the Wichita Mountains southwest of the fort. "So I put on the screws at once by issuing an order to hang Satanta and Lone Wolf, if their people did not surrender at Fort Cobb within forty-eight hours," Sheridan wrote. Lone Wolf immediately sent a courier to summon the Kiowas to Fort Cobb.[45]

For Satanta and Lone Wolf, the wait was agonizing. Nightfall of the first day arrived with no sign of the tribe. Throughout the following morning, the two chiefs anxiously watched the distant hills and grew discouraged. Satanta sat beside his tent, wrapped in a blanket, "swaying back and forth, chant[ing] the most doleful and monotonous death-song," and scooped dirt into his mouth, wrote Colonel Horace Moore of the 19th Kansas.[46]

To Sheridan's disappointment, Satanta and Lone Wolf were spared the gibbet; their tribesmen began streaming into Fort Cobb during the afternoon of December 20. In his annual report, Sheridan wrote that he would always regret "not hang[ing] these Indians; they had deserved it many times; and I shall also regret that I did not punish the whole tribe when I first met them."[47]

MAJOR ANDREW EVANS'S MISSING 3rd Cavalry, a month overdue in joining Sheridan from Fort Bascom, New Mexico, pounced on a Comanche and Kiowa village sixty miles west of Fort Cobb on Christmas Day. After clearing the village with cannon fire, Evans's troopers skirmished most of the day with the warriors, killing twenty-five of them, while other soldiers burned the village's sixty lodges. A week later, Evans's men were on their way back to New Mexico.[48]

The other truant column, Colonel Eugene Carr's 5th Cavalry from Fort Lyon, reached the northern Texas Panhandle on December 30 only to turn around and return to Colorado.[49]

ON THE FIRST DAY of 1869, Sheridan was satisfied with what he had accomplished so far, but the job was not yet completed. "The Indians, for the first time, begin to realize that winter will not compel us to make a truce with then," he wrote to Sherman. He vowed to continue to campaign without letup until the Southern Plains warriors agreed to remain peacefully on their reservations.[50]

On New Year's Day, Sheridan met with twenty-one chiefs who came to Fort Cobb seeking peace. It mattered little to him, Sheridan told the chiefs, whether they went to their reservations or not; if they stayed out, "I will make war . . . winter and summer as long as I live," until they were wiped out. When Arapahoe chief Yellow Bear and Cheyenne chief Little Robe pledged their acquiescence, Sheridan replied, "If you come in here and do as I say, I will not be a bad chief to you."[51]

As promised, Yellow Bear's Arapahoes surrendered, but the Cheyennes—among them Little Robe's band—did not. Custer volunteered to take forty men to their camps to parley. Fellow officers told him it would be suicidal. As one officer bid Custer good-bye, he slipped him a pocket Derringer, so that "at the last moment I might become my own executioner" if the Indians massacred his party. Custer returned without having found the Cheyennes.[52]

On March 1, Sheridan sent Custer, with the 7th Cavalry and 18th Kansas, to bring in the holdout Cheyennes, "or give them a sound thrashing." This time, Custer located their village of 260 lodges.

The Indians, half starved and worn out from weeks on the run, held two captive white women, seventeen-year-old Sarah White and twenty-three-year-old Mrs. Anna Morgan. When the Cheyennes tried to slip away while the chiefs diverted Custer, he seized three chiefs as hostages. A tense standoff ensued. "I recall no more exciting experience with the Indians," Custer wrote in *My Life on the Plains*, never imagining his last day on earth in 1876.

Custer gave the Cheyennes an ultimatum: release the two women by sundown the next day and surrender at Camp Supply, or he would kill the chiefs, and the cavalry would attack the camp. Certain that Custer would do as he had threatened, the Cheyennes agreed to the terms.[53]

THE WINTER CAMPAIGN HAD smashed the power of the Southern Plains tribes. Sheridan had demonstrated that relentless campaigning alone, even without decisive battlefield victories, could break the Indians' fighting spirit. Sheridan had waged Grant's Overland Campaign in microcosm against a far weaker adversary, which he drove to the ends of its endurance by using winter as an ally.

Moreover, Sheridan had once more earned his men's deepest respect through the long days and nights of hard traveling, in blizzards and subzero cold. Private David Spotts of the 19th Kansas wrote in his diary that the men admired the major general for "camping in a tent when the weather was fair or foul, marching at our head in snow and rain, enduring all the hardships of wind and weather. He is not a young man, either, between 35 and 40 years old."[54]

The final act of the campaign occurred on July 11, when Colonel Carr, with eight companies of his 5th Cavalry troopers from Fort Lyon and three companies of Pawnee scouts, surprised Tall Bull's Cheyenne Dog Soldiers in their village at Summit Springs in northeastern Colorado Territory. The troopers killed fifty-two Indians, including Tall Bull (reportedly shot by scout William Cody), looted and burned eighty-two lodges, captured four hundred ponies, and ended the Dog Soldiers' reign of terror in the Republican River area between the Kansas Pacific and Union Pacific Railroads.[55]

ON FEBRUARY 15, 1869, Sheridan received a note from President-elect Grant inviting him to Washington for his inauguration on March 4. Grant's message also included this line: "I will, of course, give you the Military Division now commanded by Sherman." Sherman was succeeding Grant as general of the army.

Sheridan's promotion was a testament to Grant's confidence in his former Cavalry Corps commander's surpassing ability. Once more, Sheridan had proved that he was equal to practically any challenge—vanquishing the cream of the Confederate army, waging a cold war on the Mexican border, governing unreconstructed Rebels, or suppressing renegade Indians.

As commander of the Division of the Missouri, Sheridan would be responsible for the Departments of the Missouri, Dakota, and Platte—compassing hundreds of thousands of square miles between Canada and Texas and from Chicago to the Rocky Mountains. He was charged with protecting the settlements and railroads and keeping the peace, all with a pitifully small force of 10,000 troops.[56]

Delayed by the winter campaign in starting for Washington until early March, Sheridan and his party were riding north toward Fort Hays and the railroad that would take them to Washington when they intercepted a courier headed for Fort Dodge. As Sheridan suspected, the rider had a telegram for him.

Red-faced and with a catch in his voice, Sheridan read it aloud: he had been promoted to lieutenant general, making him the army's second-ranking officer. He produced a small bottle of whiskey; it was passed round to his staff officers, and a celebratory toast was offered: "To the health of the lieutenant general and the close of the campaign!"[57]

CHAPTER 15

Lieutenant General Sheridan

1870–1871

The people must be left nothing but their eyes to weep with after the war.

—SHERIDAN'S ADVICE TO PRUSSIAN LEADERS
DURING THE FRANCO-PRUSSIAN WAR[1]

THE SOUTHERN PLAINS WINTER CAMPAIGN of 1868 to 1869 was Lieutenant General Phil Sheridan's last field command. As the second-ranking army officer, he now no longer personally led men into battle; others would do the leading, while Sheridan, although still vigorous and just thirty-eight years old, would plan and direct.

One of Sheridan's first actions as William Sherman's successor was to move the Military Division of the Missouri headquarters from St. Louis to Chicago. Troops and supplies now moved on railroads rather than rivers, and Chicago was the West's rail center.

Cosmopolitan and bustling, with 300,000 residents, Chicago became Sheridan's first permanent residence since his boyhood days in Somerset, Ohio. Division headquarters was a building at Washington and La Salle Streets, opposite the courthouse.

He stayed at the Palmer House, a popular stopping place for army officers, before purchasing a home on South Michigan Avenue. He lived there with his younger brother Michael, who was his staff adjutant general and, of Sheridan's siblings, closest to him in spirit. Mary and Robert Lawrence kept house and cooked for the brothers. Mrs. Lawrence had served Sheridan since the Shenandoah Valley campaign.[2]

Sheridan quickly became a popular dinner guest in Chicago society because of his sociability, modesty, and fame and because he was an eligible bachelor. He enrolled at the Bournique School of Dance where, in classes arranged by Mrs. George Pullman, wife of the sleeping car inventor, he learned to waltz and polka and to perform a popular quadrille called "The Prairie Queen." His classmates included George Pullman, department store magnate Marshall Field, and Robert Todd Lincoln.[3]

Despite his renown, Sheridan remained unassuming. Once, when he was trout fishing in Wisconsin, an elderly farmer asked him to point out the famous General Sheridan. When Sheridan replied that he was in fact that general, the farmer refused to believe him. "How could a little man with such a low voice as yourn [sic] command a big army?"

The Earl of Dunraven described Sheridan as reserved on first acquaintance, though he quickly warmed to new company. He was "a delightful man," Dunraven wrote, "with the one peculiarity of using the most astounding swear words quite calmly and dispassionately in ordinary conversation."[4]

He spent freely. He purchased two farms and adjacent timberland in Polk County, Oregon, near the Grande Ronde Indian Reservation that he once superintended. Sheridan's papers detail a profusion of minor purchases that added up: an $11 goblet; a $24 ice pitcher; $14 worth of books from a New York bookseller; and, on the same day, $87 for books from a Chicago dealer.

"He could not save," his brother Michael wrote. "But possibly this was due as much to liberality as to lack of method, for if he had money on hand he gave it and spent it freely." Every former soldier with a hard-luck story found Sheridan to be a soft touch.[5]

SOON AFTER MOVING INTO the White House, President Ulysses Grant shocked his former army colleagues and alienated Western supporters by adopting a new Plains Indians program, the so-called Peace Policy. No longer would the tribes be treated as sovereign nations; no new treaties would be signed. Instead, the Indians would become wards of the government and, eventually, productive citizens—through civilizing and Christianizing.

The Society of Friends and former abolitionists had lobbied Grant to adopt the policy before his inauguration, amid the outrage over George Custer's attack on Black Kettle's Washita River camp. Grant asked the Quakers to recommend men of their faith as Indian agents and superintendents, and they soon occupied nine positions in Nebraska, Kansas, and the Indian Territory. The army assigned officers to the Indian Bureau to fill the rest.

Westerners denounced the Peace Policy. "If more men are to be scalped and their hearts boiled, we hope to God that it may be some of our Quaker Indian Agents, and not our frontiersmen who want and are trying to do something for the improvement of the country," asserted the *Leavenworth Bulletin*. The *Daily Colorado Herald* proposed transferring the Indian Bureau to the War Department. "Western people are the best judges in the matter," the *Herald* concluded.[6]

AT THE ACME OF this raging debate, Sheridan's troops attacked another Indian village in wintertime. Along Montana's Marias River in northern Montana, a band of Piegan Blackfeet Indians led by Mountain Chief had raided settlements and murdered settlers along the Canadian border. "Tell Baker to strike them hard," Sheridan wrote from Chicago. On January 23, 1870, Major Eugene Baker, brevetted for gallantry at Winchester in 1864, surrounded a Piegan village with detachments from the 2nd Cavalry and the Thirteenth Infantry.

Tragically, it was the wrong village. Mountain Chief's band did not live there. This village was riddled with smallpox, with six people a day dying on average. When a scout tried to warn Baker about the mistake, Baker had him arrested. The village chief, Heavy Runner, ran toward the soldiers waving a safe conduct pass from the Indian Bureau—and was shot dead.

The soldiers commenced firing freely into the village. When they stopped an hour later, 173 Piegans, including 53 women and children, lay dead in the crimson-spattered snow. Just one soldier was killed. The troopers burned the village and marched away with 140 prisoners and three hundred horses.

Mountain Chief, whose guilty band's camp lay ten miles away, quietly escaped to Canada. General Philippe Regis de Trobriand, the Montana district commander, pronounced the operation "a complete success."[7]

Because Trobriand's initial report did not state that the troopers had wiped out the wrong village, Sheridan's account compounded the horrific mistake: "After having been reportedly warned, they have at last received a carefully prepared and well-merited blow. . . . [I] cannot commend too highly" the troops who carried out the mission in bitter cold.[8]

From Washington, Sherman warned Sheridan to brace himself for a storm. It burst upon him in the weeks that followed. Vincent Colyer, secretary to the Board of Indian Commissioners, claimed that just 15 of the 173 dead were warriors, while the rest were noncombatants, including fifty children under age twelve, many killed "in their parents' arms."

Sheridan bitterly complained to Sherman that the Indian Ring, as represented by Colyer, was deliberately "deceiving the kind-hearted public . . . to get possession of Indian affairs so that the treasury can be more successfully plundered."[9]

The army closed ranks around Baker and Sheridan. "You may assure Col. Baker that no amount of Clamor has shaken our Confidence in him and his officers," Sherman wrote to Sheridan.[10]

Yet the barrage of criticism continued. The *New York Semi-Weekly Tribune* called the attack "a national disgrace." An editorial in the humanitarian journal *Bond of Peace* observed that "all the dispatches of Sheridan, Sherman and Baker on the late murderous and diabolical raid upon the Small Pox Camp of Pigeon [*sic*] Indians . . . in no measure excuse the disgraceful and wicked act." Wendell Phillips, the Boston abolitionist who advocated Indian citizenship, wrote, "I know only the names of three savages upon the plains—Colonel Baker, General Custer, and at the head of all, General Sheridan."[11]

The wholesale condemnations stung Sheridan more than had the outcry after Washita because Baker had clearly destroyed the wrong village; the humanitarians, the clergy, and the Eastern press were right. Worse, many of the people who had idolized him during the Civil War had now turned against him.

Never one to gracefully accept blame, however, Sheridan also believed that the Indians bore a collective responsibility when their fellow tribesmen raided and killed white settlers. Moreover, as he, Sherman, and Grant had understood during the Civil War, there would always be collateral damage.

Sheridan raised both of these charged moral issues in his and Baker's defense in a letter to Sherman. Women and children had died, he wrote, through the fault of the Indian raiders "whose crimes necessitated the attack." Furthermore, "during the war did any one hesitate to attack a village or town occupied by the enemy because women or children were within its limits? Did we cease to throw shells into Vicksburg or Atlanta because women and children were there?"

In the shared opinion of Sheridan, Sherman, and Grant, the deaths of Confederate noncombatants and the destruction of their crops and livestock were consequences of their support for the Rebel cause. War's Manichean imperatives legitimized barbarity.

While they were savaged in the East, Baker and Sheridan were lionized in the West for slaughtering the Piegan villagers. A petition signed by several hundred Wyoming Territory residents and sent to Sheridan expressed approval for his Indian policy and the "so-called 'massacre' of the Piegans by Colonel Baker." A resolution by Georgetown, Colorado, citizens asserted, "The war to the knife is the only way of avenging the many depredations that are daily being committed on the border."[12]

Caught between the diametrically opposed opinions of Easterners who advocated restraint and Westerners espousing unlimited aggression was the army, wrote Sheridan. "If we allow the defenseless people on the frontier to be scalped and ravished, we are burnt in effigy and execrated as soulless monsters, insensible to the sufferings of humanity. If the Indian is punished to give security to these people, we are the same soulless monsters from the other side."[13]

Fuel was added when an offhand remark made by Sheridan in January 1869 at Fort Cobb suddenly appeared in newspapers across the country. During a meeting with Southern Plains Indian chiefs, one of them introduced himself to Sheridan as "Me Toch-a-way. Me good Indian," to which Sheridan reportedly retorted, "The only good Indians I ever saw were dead." Transmogrified into "The only good Indian is a dead Indian," Sheridan's quip has resonated for more than a century.[14]

Besides tainting Sheridan and ruining Baker's reputation, the "Baker Massacre" doomed a proposal before Congress to transfer the Indian Bureau from the Interior Department to the War Department. The consensus was that the army could not be trusted to manage the tribes humanely.

IN MAY 1870, SHERIDAN was on his first inspection tour of the chain of Western forts for which he was now responsible when, upon reaching Helena, Montana, he learned that France and Prussia were at war. "I would like to go over as a spectator," he telegraphed Sherman. "Will you help me, and lay the matter before the President?" Permission was quickly granted.[15]

On his way to Europe, Sheridan visited Grant at his home in Long Branch, New Jersey. The president was pleased that Sheridan had elected to accompany the Prussians, not the French; he, like Sheridan, believed that the Germans would win, and Grant also regarded French emperor Napoleon III as a "usurper and a charlatan." Nor had he or Sheridan forgiven Napoleon for installing Maximilian in Mexico and creating a sanctuary for former Confederates.

In his letter of introduction for Sheridan, the president authorized his lieutenant general to visit Europe and to "return at his own pleasure." The letter described Sheridan as "one of the most skillful, brave and deserving soldiers developed by the great struggle through which the United States Government has just passed. Attention paid him will be duly appreciated by the country he has served so faithfully and efficiently."[16]

Sheridan and his inspector general and friend, Lieutenant Colonel James Forsyth, sailed from New York on July 27 on the steamship *Scotia*, reaching Liverpool on August 6. From there, they traveled to Berlin to meet the Prussian queen. Before their audience could be arranged, however, they received a telegram informing them

of an impending major battle. They hastily departed for the front, reaching the
Prussian army headquarters at Pont-a-Mousson, France, on August 17.[17]

France had declared war on Prussia in July, ostensibly over Prussia's secret
attempt to make Hohenzollern prince Leopold the king of Spain and King William
I's refusal to apologize to France for the action. Of course, there was much more to
it than that. Napoleon III was alarmed by the rise of Prussia's Northern German
Federation. Irrationally confident about the prowess of his French army, Napoleon
believed that he could defeat Prussia, shore up his tottering regime, and sharply
curb Prussia's expansionist dreams.[18]

William I had succeeded King Frederick William IV when he was declared mentally incompetent. Pragmatic and conservative, William began restoring the Prussian
army, where he had spent his career, to its onetime greatness. He named Albrecht
von Roon to be minister of war and Helmuth von Moltke as army chief of staff.
Together, they transformed the army into Europe's most efficient war machine.

Prime Minister Otto von Bismarck was the architect of the Northern German
Federation and a genius of statecraft. No more effective expedient existed to unify
the northern and the southern German kingdoms, Bismarck believed, than a war
with France, Germany's ancient enemy. Utilizing Germany's efficient railroad system, Von Moltke had swiftly mobilized 800,000 troops from across Germany to
march into France.[19]

On September 17, Sheridan and Forsyth rode in a hay wagon to German
headquarters, where Count Bismarck greeted them. His personal physician, Dr.
Moritz Busch, described Sheridan as "a small, corpulent gentleman of about forty-
five, with dark moustache and chin tuft, [who] spoke the purest Yankee dialect."

The next day, Sheridan and Forsyth accompanied Bismarck's party to the front.
When they were introduced to King William at the forward headquarters at Gravelotte, the king was wearing his Prussian Guards uniform.

They were just in time to witness the main German attack. Sheridan was ap-
palled when the German cavalry charged over an open field into "a dreadful fire
without the least chance of returning it. . . . The slaughter was terrible"—especially
so at a deep cut in the road, clogged with dead and wounded men and horses.[20]

After German infantry pushed back the French on the right, army headquarters
was moved to a spot on high, exposed ground. The German artillerists were confident that their Krupp guns had knocked out the French artillery and that the party
would be safe there.

Sheridan was not so certain. Surveying the battleground through a spyglass, he
saw French troops moving to the right. Turning to Bismarck, Sheridan warned him

that the French guns were going to fire on them at any minute. Bismarck urged the king to leave the hill; William refused.

Just then, two hundred French cannons roared to life and shells began falling around the king's party. The Germans hastily evacuated the high ground. Von Moltke then personally led a German infantry attack that drove the French from the field. Impressed by Sheridan's perception of danger from the French guns, Bismarck later wrote, "Sheridan had seen it from the beginning. I wish I had so quick an eye."[21]

That evening, the king's brother, Prince Frederick Charles—nicknamed the "Red Prince" because of his fondness for the hussar uniform of that color—shared a chunk of his stale black bread with Sheridan, who had not eaten all day. Sheridan then rode into a nearby town looking for water.

He was suddenly surrounded by a squad of hostile German troops who mistook his American army uniform for that of a Frenchman. "I thought my hour had come, for they could not understand English, and I could not speak German." Just when it seemed that Sheridan might be shot, an officer from the king's headquarters happened to ride by. Recognizing Sheridan, he ordered the soldiers to release him. After enjoying a laugh at the story, King William gave Sheridan a pass so that he could go wherever he pleased, in safety.[22]

Sheridan and Bismarck shared the upstairs of a home in Rezonville. The general and the chancellor went foraging for breakfast the next morning. Bismarck scrounged two eggs and two bottles of brandy, and Sheridan contributed four large sausages that he had purchased from a sutler's wagon. They ate and drank heartily before touring the Gravelotte battlefield.[23]

The place where the German cavalrymen were slaughtered was "sickening to an extreme," wrote Sheridan, and the ground was covered with thousands of German helmets that had been discarded during the fight. Sheridan was eager to inspect the abandoned French works for damage by the Germans' vaunted Krupp guns. "I was astonished . . . how little harm had been done the defenses by the German artillery," he wrote, despite the Germans' "serene faith" in its effectiveness.

During their battlefield tour, Sheridan and Bismarck found twenty wounded Germans whom the recovery parties had missed. They gave them water and brandy and stayed with them until army surgeons arrived.

While traveling together, Sheridan and Bismarck became friends. Sheridan admired the very qualities in Bismarck that Grant, Sherman, and others had praised in Sheridan: efficiency, practicality, energy, and the ability to work hard. They swapped hunting stories—Sheridan describing his expeditions in the Rocky Mountains, and Bismarck, his hunting trips in Finland.

Their friendship gave them the liberty of frankness. After the German cavalry debacle at Gravelotte, Sheridan bluntly told Bismarck, "Your infantry is the best in

the world, but it was wrong of your generals to advance their cavalry as they did."
In his *Personal Memoirs*, Sheridan expressed surprise that the general who ordered
the cavalry attack was not sacked.[24]

The Germans were besieging a French army in the fortress at Metz when a second French army attempted to march to its relief. It was also surrounded, at Sedan.
Near Sedan, Sheridan watched the Germans smash a French cavalry attack and
drive the French army back to its trenches. A courier emerged under a white flag,
bearing a note from the French emperor to King William: "Not having been able
to die in the midst of my troops, there is nothing left me but to place my sword in
your Majesty's hands."

The next day, September 2, Sheridan watched as Napoleon III rode out of Sedan
in a landau and met Bismarck at a cottage a mile from Donchery. After an hour's
discussion, the emperor agreed to surrender. The formal ceremony was held at
Chateau Bellevue, where Sheridan watched Prince Frederick Charles, who had
shared his stale bread, distribute a basketful of Iron Crosses to officers.[25]

Napoleon's capitulation rang down the curtain on France's Second Empire, but
the fighting did not end. The besieged army at Metz held out until the end of October. Tens of thousands of other French troops who had been fighting in the
provinces raced to defend Paris. King William's armies surrounded the capital with
240,000 troops. Four months of starvation and shelling lay ahead before the capital
surrendered on January 28, 1871.[26]

MEANWHILE, FRENCH GUERRILLAS—known as *francs-tireurs*, or free shooters—
ambushed German patrols and supply trains, sniped at them in villages, and murdered soldiers. This was a new phenomenon for the Prussians, and they were at a
loss over how to address it; in their experience, armies fought one another, while
civilians watched from the sidelines. The Prussians' frustration spilled over one
night at a dinner attended by Sheridan, Bismarck, and members of the Prussian
high command.

When Sheridan's opinion was sought, he surprised his hosts by asserting that
civilians should be roughly handled during wartime. During the American Civil
War, Prussian observers had deplored the mass casualties and the tactical operations
aimed at civilian property. But Sheridan was now forcefully advocating the targeting
of noncombatants' belongings. "The people must be left nothing but their eyes to
weep with after the war," Sheridan told them.

Dr. Busch wrote that Sheridan told his dinner audience, "The proper strategy
consists in the first place in inflicting as telling blows as possible upon the enemy's
army, and then in causing the inhabitants so much suffering that they must long
for peace, and for their government to demand it." Hang the insurgents and burn
their villages, he advised.

Sheridan's words took many of his listeners aback; Busch thought them "somewhat heartless . . . but perhaps worthy of consideration." They made sense, however, to Bismarck, who wanted a quick end to the war, fearing that if it continued for too long, France might rally and even find allies. He later told Dr. Busch, "The more Frenchmen suffered from the war the greater would be the number of those who would long for peace, whatever our conditions might be."

Bismarck adopted punitive measures against villages and suspected *francs-tireurs*. Henceforth, German troops, when fired upon, should "shoot down every male inhabitant" in that village. When reports reached Bismarck that German prisoners were being tortured and executed, he exhorted the army to hang or shoot all suspected *francs-tireurs* and to burn the villages that sheltered them—just as Sheridan had recommended. At Hericourt, a Prussian patrol burned the town after partisans fired on them. Near Orleans, three villages were reduced to ashes after guerrillas carried out ambushes and cut German telegraph wires. There should be "no laziness in killing," Bismarck exhorted.[27]

AFTER SPENDING SEVERAL WEEKS with Bismarck and the Prussian army command, Sheridan distilled his experiences in a letter to President Grant. He confessed to having "my imagination clipped" after observing the armies at Gravelotte and Sedan and the "many errors" he had seen committed by trained European troops.

"The men engaged on both sides were so scattered that it looked like thousands of men engaged in a deadly skirmish without any regard to lines, or formations," Sheridan told Grant. The French soldiers fought poorly. "I must confess to having seen some of the '*tallest*' running at Sedan I have ever witnessed," he wrote. "All my boyhood fancies of the soldiers of the great Napoleon have been dissipated, or else the soldiers of the 'little Corporal' have lost their élan in the pampered parade soldiers of the man of Destiny."

Sheridan admired the Germans' professionalism and fighting spirit—and was especially impressed by the infantrymen, who were "as fine as I ever saw, the men young and hardy in appearance, and marching always with an elastic stride." In his *Personal Memoirs*, Sheridan wrote that the German infantrymen left open intervals between files, "especially intended to give room for a peculiar swinging gait, with which the men seemed to urge themselves over the ground with ease and rapidity."

But he criticized the Germans' use of cavalry. Besides deploring the hopeless attack at Gravelotte, he sounded much as he had during his contretemps with General George Meade over the Cavalry Corps's role in the Overland Campaign: the Prussians had used their mounted forces to guard flanks and supply trains rather than as an independent force to destroy the French cavalry and communications lines.

American troops would have performed as well as the Germans under similar conditions, Sheridan said. "I can but leave to conjecture how the Germans would have gotten along . . . through the swamps and quicksands of northern Virginia." "There is nothing to be learned here professionally," Sheridan told Grant, "but it is a satisfaction that such is the case. There is much however which Europeans could learn from us."[28]

SHERIDAN AND FORSYTH EMBARKED on a grand tour of Europe. In Brussels, they paid respects to the Belgian king and queen. In Vienna, they dined with the prime ministers of Austria and Hungary. In Constantinople, they observed the women of the sultan's harem promenading in carriages on the esplanade. When the harem passed Sheridan and Forsyth, some women engaged in "a mild flirtation"—waving amber beads and "throwing us coquettish kisses." The sultan permitted Sheridan to inspect some of his troops during a review.[29]

Grant's letter of introduction gave Sheridan entrée to the king and queen of Greece and to Victor Emmanuel, the king of Italy, who happened to be an avid hunter. He invited Sheridan to hunt in the royal game preserve. After shooting buffalo on the Great Plains, Sheridan found Victor Emmanuel's preserve to be quite tame; from a stand, he killed four deer at fifteen paces. Urged to slaughter more, Sheridan, not wishing to disappoint his host, racked up seven more kills.

After visits to Milan, Geneva, Nice, Marseilles, and Bordeaux, Sheridan and Forsyth reached Paris in time to watch the Germans' triumphal entry into the capital, where the temporary government that succeeded Napoleon III had finally capitulated. The war, which claimed 320,000 lives on both sides, resulted in a peace treaty requiring France to forfeit Alsace-Lorraine, arousing intense resentment toward Germany. The Germans then withdrew—to crown King William I as emperor of a united Germany—and Paris's citizens revolted, sweeping away the conservative National Assembly and establishing the Paris Commune.

Sheridan and Forsyth left Paris in early March 1871 and visited England, Scotland, and Sheridan's ancestral home, Ireland. By then, other US Army generals had come to France to observe the war; they included Horatio Wright, Ambrose Burnside, and William Hazen.[30] Sheridan returned to the United States on May 24, 1871, ten months after beginning his leave of absence.[31]

UPON RETURNING TO CHICAGO, Sheridan learned that his brother Michael and his staff surgeon, Morris Asche, had organized a hunting expedition to the Great Plains in September and October for a glittering assembly of press moguls and business tycoons. They included James Gordon Bennett, publisher of the *New York Herald*; Charles Wilson, publisher of the *Chicago Evening Journal*; Anson Stager, president of Western Electric; Colonel Daniel H. Rucker, the army's assistant quartermaster general and Sheridan's future father-in-law; and New York financier Leonard Jerome, the future grandfather of Winston Churchill.[32]

Like the African safaris that would one day be all the rage for millionaires, celebrities, and aristocrats, buffalo hunts attracted the well-heeled adventurers of the 1870s. Sheridan's mission was to lead his guests to plentiful buffalo, deer, and antelope and to make sure that they killed a satisfactory number. But he knew it was just as important that his "tourists" also be entertained and sumptuously wined and dined.

For the makings of the celebratory feasts to be enjoyed along the way, sixteen wagons were filled with food, tents, supplies, and liquor, with one wagon used solely for hauling ice. The passengers, and their cooks, assistants, and baggage, rode in three army ambulances.[33] For entertainment, Sheridan sent for his favorite scout, twenty-five-year-old William Cody, inspiring what would one day become known as Buffalo Bill's Wild West Show.

Sheridan had made Cody's acquaintance in Kansas three years earlier, when Cody rode sixty-five miles through Indian-controlled territory, from Fort Larned to Fort Hays, to deliver an important dispatch to Sheridan. The message required an order to be delivered immediately to Fort Dodge, ninety-five miles away. When the scouts at Fort Hays declined the dangerous mission through Indian country, Cody volunteered. After resting four to five hours, he rode to Fort Dodge. There, after resting six hours, he returned to Fort Larned with more messages, then rode back to Fort Hays, covering 350 miles in less than sixty hours. Impressed by Cody's fearlessness and stamina, Sheridan hired him as a scout for the 5th Cavalry. In just one year, Cody fought in nine battles with Indians—more action than most soldiers saw during a career on the plains—and became chief scout.[34]

Eager to please his mentor, Cody was decked out in light buckskins and a sombrero and riding a snow-white horse when he greeted Sheridan and his guests at Fort McPherson, Nebraska. Before the entourage left the fort, the 5th Cavalry staged a review. Then, the caravan, with a one-hundred-man cavalry escort, set out for Fort Hays.[35]

All day long, the guests and their escorts slaughtered buffalo and whatever other game animals crossed their paths. Whenever a buffalo was killed, the party opened a bottle of champagne and toasted the successful hunter. At night, the hunters gathered around a blazing fire on the prairie, and Cody regaled the visitors with exciting stories about fighting the Indians. He advised them to take a shot of bourbon before breakfast, as he said Westerners did.

The tipsy, trigger-happy visitors littered the plains between Fort McPherson and Fort Hays with six hundred buffalo carcasses—taking the tongues and humps and leaving the rest to rot—along with the remains of hundreds of antelope, elk, and wild turkeys, and empty champagne bottles. Sheridan, an excellent shot and skilled hunter, bagged his share of game while drawing rough maps and sketching land features in his notebook. The guests returned home with warm feelings for Sheridan and the army—sentiments that would later translate into pro-army editorials and business contracts.[36]

THE SUCCESSFUL FALL 1871 hunt became the template for a more ambitious expedition. President Grant asked Sheridan to accompany Russia's Grand Duke Alexis, the twenty-one-year-old third son of Czar Alexander II, on another expedition. Alexis was on a goodwill tour of the United States, and Grant wished to show his gratitude for the czar's support of the Union during the Civil War. In January 1872, Sheridan and his staff met the grand duke and his retinue at Omaha's railroad station. From Omaha, the hunting party traveled west in high style on a special Union Pacific Railroad train to North Platte, Nebraska.

Sheridan had enlisted the commanders of the departments of the Platte and the Missouri to provide intelligence and supplies for the expedition. The meticulous planning resembled the preparations for a military campaign. Brigadier General John Pope, commander of the Department of the Missouri, monitored the southern buffalo herds' movements and telegraphed Sheridan with daily updates. Colonel Forsyth was in charge of mess arrangements, while Major General Edward O. C. Ord, commander of the Department of the Platte, converted Omaha Barracks into a supply depot for the hunt. Hundreds of army personnel were assigned to making sure the grand duke was well fed and entertained—and that he killed a buffalo.

Cody had been wildly popular with the guests of the previous hunting party, and so Sheridan arranged for him and one hundred Brule Sioux from Spotted Tail's band to be on hand. Another addition to the hunting party was Lieutenant Colonel George Custer, the army's flamboyant war hero and Indian fighter.[37]

Custer's buffalo hunting career began in Kansas during the 1867 Indian war, with a tragicomic incident that he recounted in *My Life on the Plains*. Custer wrote that he and his greyhounds had ridden miles ahead of his men in excited pursuit of a large buffalo. As Custer drew abreast of it and took aim with his pistol, his horse suddenly jerked. He grabbed at the reins with his gun hand—and accidentally shot and killed his horse. Luckily for him, his troopers found him afoot on the prairie before the Indians did. Custer had since become an accomplished buffalo killer and a skilled taxidermist.[38]

Escorted by the 2nd Cavalry, the splendidly appointed hunting party rode to a camp already prepared on Willow Creek, near present-day Culbertson, Nebraska, by Brigadier General Innis Palmer and troops from Fort McPherson. The 2nd Cavalry band heralded the grand duke's arrival by playing "Hail to the Chief."[39]

The next morning, Spotted Tail's band reported a large buffalo herd ten miles to the southwest. Sheridan, Alexis, Cody, Custer, and two Indians made the first attack. The grand duke got his first kill, and before that morning's hunt was finished, he had nine. A Sioux warrior delighted Alexis by killing a buffalo with one shot from a bow and arrow. That night, Spotted Tail's band staged a war dance before a giant bonfire with further illumination provided by Chinese lanterns hung from the trees.[40]

They rode the train to Denver, where city leaders organized a grand ball for the grand duke. They had just set out by train from Denver for St. Louis when Sheridan was informed that a large herd had been spotted near Kit Carson, Colorado. A second hunt was hastily organized.

This time, the eager hunters converged from several directions on the herd, and it scattered. In the melee, Sheridan's horse fell, and he ended up on foot. Just then, Alexis, Custer, and other hunters galloped over a hilltop while blazing away at some wounded buffalo—and they nearly bagged Sheridan, who flung himself to the ground to avoid the fusillade. Angrily leaping to his feet, Sheridan proceeded to heartily curse the wild shooters, sparing neither Custer nor Alexis. "It was a liberal education in profanity to hear him," a witness to the scene reported.[41]

Alexis returned to Russia with a slew of hunting trophies and stories. Later, Sheridan received a letter from Count Harry D'Offenberg of the Russian legation in New York conveying the czar's gratitude for the "cordial welcome and kind reception" accorded the czar's son.[42]

SHERIDAN REMINDED CODY THAT after the earlier expedition, publisher James Gordon Bennett had invited him to New York. He urged Cody to go, promising him a leave of absence with pay. Full of foreboding, Cody set out for New York, along the way stopping in Chicago and lodging with the Sheridan brothers.

To his surprise, Cody liked New York and loved the theater. And after more scouting in the West, Cody was invited back to New York in 1872 by Ned Buntline, who had written dime novels about "Buffalo Bill" Cody; Buntline wanted him to appear in his play *Scouts of the Prairie*. It was the beginning of Cody's show-business career, culminating in the Wild West Show and his tenure as the reigning celebrity of his era.[43]

BETWEEN THE TWO BUFFALO hunts, Sheridan was plunged into the middle of Chicago's worst disaster, the Great Fire. It began on October 8, 1871, near a barn owned by Patrick O'Leary (the story that the O'Leary cow kicked over a lantern proved apocryphal). With terrific intensity, the conflagration roared through the city's largely wooden structures, fanned by a thirty-mile-per-hour wind from the southwest. By the time rains tamped down the flames on October 9, the fire had incinerated 17,500 buildings in a three-and-a-half-square-mile area. More than two hundred people were dead, and a fourth of the city's 300,000 residents were homeless. As soon as the fire was brought under control, the looting began.

With his usual presence of mind in emergencies, Sheridan had organized residents to deliberately destroy buildings at key points in the fire's path, and the firebreaks had helped check its spread. Afterward, a delegation of city leaders sought Sheridan's help in feeding and sheltering the fire's victims. With Mayor R. B. Mason's consent and the backing of the War Department and President Grant, Sheridan sent for troops from Nebraska and Kansas and arranged for the delivery of 300,000 rations, tents, and blankets. By the next evening, some of the estimated 75,000 people left homeless by the fire were receiving government rations and shelter.

When looting and violence became widespread, the mayor asked Sheridan to restore order. Sheridan organized army units and 1,000 local volunteers to patrol the streets, and the law-and-order crisis subsided.

THE FIRE DESTROYED THE Division of the Missouri headquarters, all of its records, and all of Sheridan's letters, papers, maps, and journals. Army mules and horses perished—one of them Sheridan's beloved gray charger Breckenridge, captured on Missionary Ridge. The destruction of Sheridan's Civil War papers and journals deprived him of irreplaceable materials, making the composition of his *Personal Memoirs* exponentially more difficult. Future biographers, too, were deprived of insights that might have better explained the inner man.

The fire had one positive outcome, however. The Sheridan home, spared by the flames, became a temporary refuge for friends and army officers needing lodging. Put out of their home by fire damage, the Missouri division's quartermaster general, Colonel Daniel Rucker, his wife, and his teenage daughter, Irene, were invited by Sheridan to stay in his roomy home until they could find new quarters. Although busy and often absent, Sheridan managed to make the acquaintance of Irene—the young woman who would one day become his wife.[44]

CHAPTER 16

———

Final Conquest
of the Plains Indians

1874–1877

Send them powder and lead, if you will; but, for the sake of lasting
peace, let them kill, skin, and sell until the buffaloes are exterminated.
—SHERIDAN TO THE TEXAS LEGISLATURE,
SPEAKING AGAINST A BILL PROTECTING BUFFALO[1]

PHIL SHERIDAN'S WASHITA WINTER CAMPAIGN of 1868 to 1869 had forced the
Southern Plains Indians onto the reservations, where they had been promised food,
clothing, and education. The government, however, had largely reneged on these
promises. In 1874, the shortage of government rations had become critical. The
annual food allotment typically lasted just seven months—which was bad enough—
but in May 1874, no rations were delivered, and the Indians began to starve.

Worse, nature conspired to thwart their pitiful attempts to grow their own food.
Drought withered their crops. Then, as the Southern Plains baked in 110-degree
temperatures, locust swarms stripped the land of vegetation.[2]

In order to survive, the warriors rode south of the Cimarron River in search of
their onetime food staple—the buffalo. But everywhere they went, it seemed, teams
of white buffalo hunters were at work efficiently killing the shaggy beasts with their

powerful "Big Fifty" Sharps rifles. Having wiped out the buffalo herds in southern Kansas, the hunters, with the military's tacit approval, had moved into northern Texas, where vast herds still roamed the hunting grounds reserved for the tribes under the 1867 Medicine Lodge Treaty.

The buffalo hunters' wastefulness had long disgusted the Indians. After watching soldiers shoot up a small herd, cut out their tongues, and leave the carcasses to rot, the Kiowa chief, Satanta, had railed years earlier, "Has the white man become a child, that he should recklessly kill and not eat? When the red men slay game they do it so they may live, and not starve." The situation had worsened exponentially since then, until finally the combination of the omnipresent buffalo hunters, food shortages, and white rustlers' thefts on the reservations pushed the Indians to the breaking point.

That point came in 1874, when rustlers stole forty-three ponies from Little Robe, the popular Cheyenne "peace chief," and when buffalo hunters built a depot at Adobe Walls in the middle of the Indian buffalo hunting grounds in northern Texas. Adobe Walls, where Colonel Kit Carson and his Union troops had stood off the Kiowas in 1864, became the transit point from which the hunters shipped their hides to the railroad center at Dodge City, Kansas. From there, trains sped them to tanneries in the East.[3]

In May, a young Comanche shaman named Isa-Tai (in English the name roughly translated to "Wolf Shit") and half-breed leader Quanah Parker summoned the Comanches to a sun dance on the North Fork of the Red River. Isa-Tai, who claimed to be immune to white men's bullets and able to vomit ammunition, urged war against the whites. The Comanches sent runners to the Kiowa, Arapahoe, and Cheyenne camps and invited them to a grand council. At the meeting, war factions from all the tribes agreed to fight.[4]

BY JUNE 26, ABOUT seven hundred warriors had gathered near Adobe Walls. A few miles from the compound, they ambushed two hunters and tortured them to death.

Early the next morning, the outpost's twenty-nine buffalo hunters and storekeepers were jolted from their slumbers by war whoops and gunshots. Bizarrely, the Indians were guided by army bugle calls blown by a deserter from a black army regiment, and the buffalo hunters initially believed cavalry had come to their rescue.

The vast disparity in numbers might have suggested that the whites stood no chance. But the buffalo hunters, among them Bat Masterson, were all superb marksmen, and most were armed with "Big Fifties"—the .50-caliber cannons that fired three-inch bottleneck cartridges loaded with up to 110 grains of powder. One shot could kill a robust buffalo at six hundred yards.[5]

Unable to wipe out the stubborn hunters during the hours-long battle, the Indians settled for destroying all of their livestock, then left. The bodies of thirteen warriors lay outside the complex. Three hunters died.

A hunter who arrived later that day on horseback agreed to make the dangerous ride to Dodge City to summon help. At Dodge, the Kansas governor was contacted, and he notified the Missouri Department commander, Brigadier General John Pope.

Pope refused to send troops to Adobe Walls. The buffalo hunters had made thousands of dollars poaching on Indian hunting grounds, he said, and they had gotten what they deserved. Hunters in Dodge City were left to organize a relief force. By the time it reached Adobe Walls, the large war party had broken up and had gone raiding.[6]

IN A SPEECH, POPE once said that army officers serving on the frontier saw firsthand the conditions that forced Indians to go raiding, "beginning in injustice and wrong to the Indian, which he [the officer] has not the power to prevent; he sees the Indian gradually reach a condition of starvation impossible of long endurance and thus forced to take what he can get to save himself from dying of hunger, and cannot help sympathizing with him for doing so." But when the Indians went raiding, even out of desperation, the army had to act.[7]

Many frontier army officers, especially those who had fought in the Civil War, felt as Pope did. In his *Life on the Plains*, Colonel George Custer wrote, "If I were an Indian, I often think I would greatly prefer to cast my lot among those of my people adhered to the free open plain" rather than live on a reservation.[8]

Texas fell within Sheridan's jurisdiction, having been added to the Division of the Missouri in 1872. Sheridan, too, sympathized somewhat with the Indians' "fading out race," but he also believed that they should be held accountable for their crimes, just as whites were when they killed and robbed.

Sheridan supported the buffalo hunters, believing that the key to pacifying the Plains Indians was wiping out the buffalo, which provided them food, clothing, and shelter. Sheridan reproved Pope for not sending troops to Adobe Walls, and he complained about it to General of the Army William Sherman.[9]

With warrior bands now robbing and killing homesteaders and travelers, Sheridan began planning a Southern Plains campaign. But he first sought new authority to pursue the renegades onto their reservations. "Their reservations have furnished them with supplies with which to make the raids, and sheltered them from pursuit when they returned with their scalps and plunder," Sheridan grumbled.

Backed by his powerful patrons, Sherman and President Ulysses Grant, Sheridan received what he sought. On July 20, 1874, Interior Secretary Columbus Delano authorized the army, for the first time, "to punish the hostile Indians wherever found"—even in their reservation sanctuaries.[10]

SHERIDAN, SHERMAN, GRANT, AND pragmatic, hard-eyed army officers like them had understood for years that the solution to the Plains Indian "problem" was extermination of the buffalo. Sheridan's and Sherman's prosecution of "total war" during the Civil War had taught them that destroying an enemy's means of resupply and crushing his people's fighting spirit were as important as defeating him militarily.

As early as 1868, Sherman had warned Sheridan that the Indians would continue to terrorize the Republican River region so long as buffalo roamed there. "I think it would be wise to invite all the sportsmen of England and America there this fall for a Grand Buffalo hunt, and make one grand sweep of them all. Until the Buffalo and consequent[ly] Indians are out [from between] the [Kansas Pacific and Union Pacific] Roads we will have collisions and trouble." The following year, the *Army and Navy Journal* reported that Sheridan had proposed that ten army regiments be assigned to slaughter buffalo until too few remained to support the Indians.[11]

Yet, even in 1871, extermination seemed impossible; upwards of 10 million buffalo roamed the Great Plains. Since the early nineteenth century, when the Plains Indians' equestrian, bison-hunting culture had reached its apotheosis, the Indians had killed thousands every year, efficiently converting every kill into food, clothing, and shelter—at a rate of roughly six buffalo annually for every man, woman, and child. Conversely, soldiers, trophy hunters, and others killed thousands of buffalo out of casual blood lust—even from atop trains crossing the prairies, with passengers shooting buffalo along the right-of-way. All of these losses, even after attrition from disease, age, and predators were factored in, scarcely put a dent in the enormous herds.

BY THE TIME THE warriors attacked Adobe Walls in 1874, however, buffalo hunting had become highly lucrative—because German tanners had invented a novel process that turned buffalo hides into high-grade leather. Tanneries on the East Coast adopted the new process in 1871 and began buying hides for $3.50 apiece by the wagonload.

Teams of buffalo hunters and skinners armed with "Big Fifties" flooded the Great Plains. "It was like a gold rush," wrote Frank Mayer, who invested his $2,000 life savings in a hunting outfit and profited handsomely. From 1872 to 1874, millions of hides were shipped from Fort Dodge, Kansas—most of them killed north of the Arkansas River. "The vast plain, which only a short twelve months before teemed with animal life, was a dead, solitary, putrid desert," Major Richard Dodge, the commander at Fort Dodge, wrote in the fall of 1873. That year, hunters edged south into Indian Territory, where they were forbidden to hunt.

The army, although sworn to protect the reservation Indians from intruders, winked at the hunters' blatant poaching. An army officer once articulated the army's view to Mayer with startling clarity: "If we kill the buffalo we conquer the Indian. It seems a more humane thing to kill the buffalo than the Indian, so the buffalo must go."

Wright Moar wanted assurances that there would be no army interference before he moved his large-scale hunting operation into Indian Territory. He bluntly asked Major Dodge what he would do if Moar and others hunted inside the Indians' preserve. Dodge replied obliquely but unmistakably, "Boys, if I were hunting buffalo I would go where the buffalo are."[12]

SHERIDAN, SHERMAN, AND GRANT lobbied hard against every attempt to slow or stop the slaughter, although no government policy officially condoned it, and many army officers in fact objected to it. In 1874, at the urging of Sheridan and Sherman, Grant pocket vetoed a bill passed by Congress that would have made it illegal for a non-Indian to kill female buffalos or males in larger numbers than were needed for food.[13]

Sheridan discouraged the Texas legislature from passing a bill that would have saved the buffalo from extinction in Texas. In an address to a joint session in Austin, Sheridan said that instead of stopping the hunters from killing buffalo, Texas should give each of them a bronze medal, with a dead buffalo on one side and a "discouraged Indian" on the other. Buffalo hunters, Sheridan told Texas legislators,

> have done more in the last two years to settle the vexed Indian question than the entire regular army has done in the past thirty years. They are destroying the Indians' commissary; and it is a well-known fact that an army losing its base of supplies is placed at a great disadvantage. Send them powder and lead, if you will; but, for the sake of lasting peace, let them kill, skin, and sell until the buffaloes are exterminated. Then your prairies can be covered with speckled cattle, and the festive cowboy, who follows the hunter as a second forerunner of an advanced civilization.[14]

The army practiced what Sheridan preached to Texas leaders. At nearly every Southern Plains military post, buffalo hunters were provided with free ammunition—"all you could use, all you wanted, more than you needed," according to Frank Mayer—as well as a place from which to ship their hides.[15]

SHERIDAN WAS FREE TO prosecute the 1874 campaign against the Southern Plains Indians as he saw fit. "Act with vindictive earnestness, and to make every Kiowa & Comanche knuckle down," Sherman instructed him. Sheridan responded, "I propose, if let alone, to settle the Indian matter in the Southwest forever."[16]

His plan was for five columns—2,700 army infantry, cavalry, and artillery—to converge on the Texas Panhandle and relentlessly pursue the 1,200 Indians who had gone raiding. Colonel Nelson Miles would drive south from Fort Dodge, while Lieutenant Colonel John Davidson led troops westward from Fort Sill in Indian Territory, and Lieutenant Colonel George Buell moved west from Fort Griffin, Texas. Major William Price would push eastward from Fort Union in the New Mexico Territory, while Colonel Ranald Mackenzie marched north from Fort Concho, Texas.

Once the plan was made, Sheridan hastened to push the columns into the field without delay, even before they were battle ready. Speed was essential, he believed, to stop the troublemaking bands from coercing peaceful Indians to join them and "to prevent the accumulation of winter supplies from the buffalo herds."

Mackenzie's column was the plan's keystone. Sheridan had transferred Mackenzie and his crack 4th Cavalry from the Rio Grande area to participate in the operation. As Mackenzie marched north from Fort Concho, the other four columns would push the Indians into his path.[17]

Sheridan, Sherman, and Grant prized Mackenzie above all of their frontier field officers. He was a younger model of them: active, smart, coldly efficient, and utterly ruthless. He might have inherited the ruthlessness. His father, Alexander Slidell Mackenzie, while commanding the brig *Somers* in 1842, hanged three mutineers from the yardarm—one of them the son of War Secretary John Spencer. While a court of inquiry exonerated the elder Mackenzie, his naval career did not survive.

High-strung, intense, spartan in his habits, and, later in his life, increasingly unstable, Ranald Mackenzie graduated from West Point in 1862 and quickly earned a reputation as a fearless combat officer at Second Manassas, Chancellorsville, Gettysburg, and under Sheridan at Winchester and Cedar Creek. At Cedar Creek, although wounded twice while his regiment withstood Jubal Early's onslaught, Mackenzie refused to leave the field, even when Sheridan urged him to obtain medical treatment. This was Sheridan's kind of officer.

For his gallantry at Cedar Creek, Mackenzie was breveted a brigadier general at just twenty-four and given command of the Army of the James's cavalry. He fought beside Sheridan at Five Forks and Appomattox Court House. By then, Mackenzie had been wounded four times; outside Petersburg, a shell fragment tore off two fingers. Grant later wrote, "I regarded Mackenzie as the most promising officer in the army."[18]

On the frontier, Mackenzie was another Custer, with the same daring and dash, but without the theatrics or the surpassing ego. Significantly, he was one of the few Civil War leaders who successfully adapted his tactics to the exigencies of Indian fighting. His men called him "Three-Finger Jack," while the Indians knew him as

"Bad Hand." He achieved maximum results with minimum casualties, yet remained unloved by his men because he was severe and irascible.

Undoubtedly his irritability stemmed from the fact that he was in pain much of the time. He suffered from recurring fevers and from rheumatism in his right shoulder, left forearm, legs, and right knee—reminders of his Civil War wounds. Recently, Mackenzie had taken an Indian arrow in the thigh.

Superiors and subordinates alike recognized Mackenzie's gifts as a combat leader. He was one of the few officers, wrote one of his lieutenants, Robert Carter, "who was always ready and willing to assume the gravest responsibilities, and he would never hesitate to take the initiative while awaiting definite orders."[19] Because Mackenzie never hesitated, Sherman had sent him to track down and punish the Indians who slaughtered seven mule drivers in 1871. During another expedition in 1872, Mackenzie's troopers had attacked a Comanche village, killing twenty-five Indians.[20]

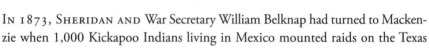

IN 1873, SHERIDAN AND War Secretary William Belknap had turned to Mackenzie when 1,000 Kickapoo Indians living in Mexico mounted raids on the Texas ranch country along the Nueces River. The raiders moved so swiftly that they were back across the Rio Grande in Mexico before US troops or local militia could respond. Sheridan transferred Mackenzie's 4th Cavalry to Fort Clark, replacing Colonel Wesley Merritt's 9th Cavalry, which had been largely ineffective.

Traveling to Fort Clark to meet with Mackenzie in April, Sheridan instructed him, strictly unofficially, to march into Mexico and destroy the Kickapoo village. Immediately after the meeting, Mackenzie told Lieutenant Robert Carter what Sheridan had said to him: "I want you to be bold, enterprising, and at all times *full of energy*, when you begin, let it be a campaign of *annihilation, obliteration* and *complete destruction*, as you have always in your dealings done to all the Indians you have dealt with. . . . I think you understand what I want done, and the way you should employ your force."

When Mackenzie asked Sheridan whose orders would give him the authority to violate Mexico's border, Sheridan exploded, pounding his fist on the table. "Damn the *orders*!" he shouted. "Damn the *authority*! You are to go ahead on your plan of action, and your authority and backing shall be General Grant and myself. With us behind you in whatever you do to clean up this situation, you can rest assured of the fullest support. You must assume the risk. We will assume the final responsibility should any result."[21]

Harassed by Texans during the Civil War, the Kickapoos had relocated to the Mexican province of Coahuila at the Mexican government's behest, to protect the citizens there from Comanche, Kiowa, and Apache marauders. The Kickapoos did their part, thereby gaining a sanctuary whenever they raided Texas—as well as buyers for the cattle, horses, and goods they stole during those raids.

In May 1873, Mackenzie's scouts located the Kickapoo village, and as darkness fell on May 17, Mackenzie, four hundred 4th Cavalry troopers, and two dozen black Seminole scouts crossed the Rio Grande into Mexico. Forty miles away lay the Kickapoo village outside Remolino.

The troopers rode all night. Dawn on May 18 found them outside Remolino. They attacked immediately and achieved complete surprise, killing at least nineteen women, children and old men—no warriors were present. They then rode off with forty prisoners, after burning the village and two others nearby. By late May 18, the weary cavalrymen were back in Texas—after having marched 160 miles without sleep in a day and a half.

Mackenzie's officers had assumed that he had written orders for the raid. When they learned that he did not, they were outraged. Had they known this, they told him, they would have refused to cross the river. Mackenzie, sounding like his father on the *Somers*, snapped back, "Any officer or man who had refused to follow me across the river I would have shot!"[22]

Sheridan jubilantly informed Sherman of the raid's success, but the commanding general, who had known nothing of it, frostily replied that he disapproved. The Texas legislature, however, extended its "grateful thanks" to Mackenzie and his men for "inflicting well merited punishment upon these scourges of our frontier." In his annual report, Sheridan defended the raid. "If the Mexican authorities cannot or will not protect our citizens from the attacks of Indians and freebooters from their side of the river, then it is the duty of the Lieutenant General to see that they are so protected."

Months later, the Kickapoos left Mexico, resettling in the Indian Territory; the Rio Grande was quiet for the next several years. Sheridan had broken the rules, and Mackenzie's bold gambit had succeeded brilliantly.[23]

THE CLIMACTIC BATTLE OF Sheridan's 1874 campaign occurred on September 28 in a magnificent setting of eight-hundred-foot-high rock walls and treacherous rockfalls. On the eastern edge of northern Texas's desolate Llano Estacado plateau, the capstone escarpment shears off into the second-largest canyon in the United States—the Palo Duro, with its maze of auxiliary canyons.

Sheridan's orders had gone out July 25, and the plan was working. In August, the marching columns of Miles, Davidson, and Buell had begun driving the Kiowas, Comanches, and Southern Cheyennes westward. The warriors and their families had withdrawn deep inside Palo Duro's labyrinth of interconnected canyons.[24]

Near the canyon mouth, Miles and his 744 troopers had fought a five-hour running battle with about two hundred warriors on August 30. In late September, Mackenzie's scouts penetrated the canyons and located several hundred Indian lodges in a warren of canyons, protected by the towering canyon walls. They had also found a steep, sketchy trail of switchbacks and breathtaking cliffs that led from the capstone into the canyon.

Mackenzie force-marched his men all night to reach the rim above Palo Duro Canyon. At first light on September 28, the 4th Cavalry began the descent. Amazingly, they reached the canyon floor without mishap or discovery by the Indians.

Mackenzie led the attack, which instantly emptied the Indian villages. Part of his command rode straight to the Indians' pony herd and seized 1,500 horses. The warriors counterattacked to retrieve their animals, but failed. Throughout the day, they harassed the cavalrymen with sniper fire from the canyon walls, giving their elders, women, and children time to escape.

The Indians melted away into the side canyons, but without their pony herd, lodges, or personal property. The troopers burned the lodges and, after selecting the 350 best ponies from the herd, shot the rest on the canyon rim. "It was a heavy blow," Lieutenant Carter wrote of the Indians' loss of their horses. "They were such valuable property that they were held in higher esteem than their squaws."

Sherman was pleased with the campaign's progress. "They go in with the relish that used to make our hearts *glad* in 1864–65," he told Sheridan.[25]

Sheridan had traveled to Fort Sill to better monitor the campaign. It was proceeding just as he had hoped: relentless cavalry attacks on the renegades' villages were forcing the bands to move repeatedly. Sheridan urged his commanders to keep up the pressure through the winter, until the Indians surrendered.

As they had during the Washita winter campaign of 1868–1869, Sheridan's troopers pursued the Indians to the ends of their endurance, fighting more than a dozen battles—each time destroying more Indian lodges, food, and supplies. The unyielding pressure, Sheridan wrote, gave the Indians "no opportunity or security to kill game or get food for their families, grazing for their stock, or safety for their lives, so their [*sic*] are now being captured or surrendering unconditionally and there is a fair prospect of a close of our labors before long."[26]

The Southern Plains tribes were experiencing the "total war" that Sheridan, Sherman, and Grant had practiced with such awful efficiency in Virginia, Georgia, and

South Carolina a decade earlier. Their two brightest protégés from the Civil War, Mackenzie and Custer, had become the brutal science's new avatars on the Great Plains.

IN LATE FEBRUARY 1875, bands of ragged, half-starved Kiowas, Southern Cheyennes, and Comanches began surrendering at the agencies. First, nearly three hundred Kiowas came in, followed in March by 820 Southern Cheyennes. The Comanches trickled in all that spring, with the last band of four hundred surrendering on June 2. The army had swept the country clean between Fort Sill and the Llano Estacado.[27]

Sheridan wanted to try the ringleaders for capital offenses before military tribunals and hang them. He also wished to send others to Eastern prisons if their cases were too weak to win convictions. The US attorney general approved Sheridan's exile plan but not the military commissions.

At Fort Sill in April 1875, as the Indian women wailed and wept, seventy-two warriors were shackled, placed in wagons, and sent on the first leg of their long trip to Fort Marion, in St. Augustine, Florida.[28] Sheridan's 1868–1869 and 1874–1875 campaigns had crushed the Southern Plains tribes and made the region safe for settlers.

WITH THE SOUTHERN PLAINS quiet, Sheridan could now concentrate on pacifying the turbulent Northern Plains. The Sioux and Northern Cheyennes, neglected and hungry on their reservations, were seething over encroachments on their tribal lands by settlers, gold prospectors in the Black Hills, and the Northern Pacific Railroad. Under the 1868 Fort Laramie treaties, the two tribes had received all of present-day South Dakota west of the Missouri River, including the Black Hills. The treaties also permitted the Indians to hunt buffalo north of the North Platte River so long as the herds lasted.

Red Cloud was the most prominent signatory, and he never reneged; two other Sioux chiefs, Sitting Bull and Crazy Horse, had not signed. Soon after the treaties were made, rumors began to circulate that the Black Hills abounded in mineral wealth—a portent of future trouble.

In early 1874, Sheridan began organizing an expedition into the Black Hills to find out if the rumors, now rampant, were true, as well as to assay the region's soil, timber, grass, and water resources and to locate a site for a military fort. On July 2, while Sheridan was completing his plans for the Red River campaign, Custer and the 7th Cavalry, which had been escorting Northern Pacific Railroad work crews in Montana, left Fort Abraham Lincoln in Bismarck, Dakota Territory, to explore the Black Hills.[29]

CUSTER'S EXPEDITION FOUND SURPRISINGLY plentiful timber, soil, grass, and water in the Black Hills, but most importantly, survey crews panned small amounts of gold in creeks near Harney Peak. The press reports caused prospectors to pour into the Black Hills. The gold rush was on.

With soldiers now needed to keep the miners out, Sheridan proposed the construction of two Black Hills forts, but Congress appropriated no money to build them. Consequently, supplies for the ceaseless army patrols, mainly conducted by Custer's 7th Cavalry, had to be hauled in from Fort Abraham Lincoln. Despite the army's efforts, by the summer of 1875 hundreds of white miners were panning the Black Hills's creeks and digging in the hillsides.

Even before Custer's expedition, there had been trouble at the Sioux agencies operated by the Indian Bureau. In February 1874, troops were summoned from Fort Laramie when Sioux from the Red Cloud Agency killed Lieutenant Levi Robinson as he led a wood-gathering detail. The prospectors' invasion of the Black Hills infuriated the Sioux war factions. Rumors of war began crowding out the rumors of gold.[30]

Powerless to keep out the prospectors, in September 1875 government commissioners offered to buy the Black Hills from Sioux leaders for $6 million or to lease the area for a $400,000 annuity. The Sioux rejected the offers. Chief Spotted Bear reportedly told the commissioners, "Our Great Father has a big safe. This hill is our safe."

After the parley's failure, War Secretary Belknap summoned Sheridan and George Crook to a White House meeting to discuss further action against the Sioux.[31]

AS THE SITUATION DARKENED on the Northern Plains, Sheridan was pulled away from his duties by two developments. Grant sent him to Louisiana in late 1874 to prevent Democrats from filling five disputed seats in the state house of representatives and taking control of the state assembly. The second interruption in his duties was more pleasant: Sheridan got married on June 3, 1875.

Unsurprisingly, the bride of the Civil War hero and second-ranking army officer was an army brat—Irene Rucker, the youngest daughter of Colonel Daniel Rucker, assistant army quartermaster general. Born at Fort Union, New Mexico, Miss Rucker, a devout Catholic educated in convents, was scarcely half the forty-four-year-old Sheridan's age. When she was a teenager, she and her family had stayed at Sheridan's home after the Great Chicago Fire damaged their house. But the courtship had not begun until a few years later, after a military wedding in which Miss Rucker was a bridesmaid.

They were married by the Right Reverend Thomas Foley, bishop of Chicago, in a private military ceremony at the Rucker home. The invited guests included President and Mrs. Grant, Sherman, War Secretary Belknap, and Generals John Pope, George

Crook, Christopher Augur, and Alfred Terry. The *New York Times* described the wedding as "quiet and unostentatious," with Sheridan wearing his full dress uniform and gold spurs. Among the numerous and expensive wedding gifts were a carriage and pair of horses, diamond earrings, and, from President and Mrs. Grant, a "seed pearl pin and earrings."[32]

IN LATE 1874, MISS Rucker, with several other ladies and Sheridan's staff, had accompanied the lieutenant general to New Orleans, ostensibly a stopover during a longer trip to Havana, Cuba. But suspicious New Orleans residents were certain that Sheridan had come to impose the will of the Republican Grant administration. They retained vivid memories of Sheridan's heavy-handed administration of the Fifth Military District.

Indeed, Sheridan bore secret orders from the president to reverse what Grant and other Republicans viewed as a Democratic power grab. So closely held were the details of this trip that neither Sherman nor the commander of the Division of the South knew anything about it. Sheridan was instructed to communicate by cipher with Belknap alone.

The 1874 elections had given the Democrats an apparent legislative majority, but the GOP-dominated election board ruled that each party had won fifty-three seats, with five in dispute, to be decided when the legislature convened in January. On January 4, Democrats in the state house of representatives, in a smoothly choreographed series of actions, seized control of the legislature and filled the five disputed seats with party members.

Grant had authorized Sheridan to use army troops to rectify the situation if necessary. And so, when Louisiana's Republican governor, William Kellogg, requested federal assistance, Sheridan acted. Army infantrymen marched into the legislative chamber with fixed bayonets and ejected the five Democrats. All the Democrats stormed out to convene a rump legislative session, while Republicans reorganized the House.[33]

To further secure his authority, Sheridan unilaterally incorporated the Department of the Gulf into his Division of the Missouri. He sought to replace the Gulf Department's commander, the former XIX Corps commander William Emory—an "old man, entirely unfitted for this place"—with protégé Mackenzie, but he ultimately withdrew Mackenzie's name because of "great dissatisfaction in Army circles."

Sheridan also sought Belknap's permission to round up the leaders of the anti-Republican White League—Confederate veterans who, just three months earlier, had battled city police in the streets. He wanted to try them in military courts. With Louisiana certain to be a pivotal state in the 1876 presidential election, Sheridan and Grant feared that the White League would prevent blacks from voting, thereby swinging the state to Democrats. But Sheridan did not get his military tribunal, despite warning Belknap of "the existence in this state of a spirit of defiance" that was a threat to loyal citizens.

The Civil War was a decade past, and Sheridan's resort to authoritarian Reconstruction-era tactics in Louisiana was extremely unpopular. Some Southern newspapers called for a revival of the war. State legislatures passed condemnatory resolutions, and Sheridan was denounced on the floor of Congress.

Grant and Belknap staunchly defended Sheridan—Grant in a message to Congress. After an ugly partisan fight, Congress appointed an investigatory panel.

In New Orleans, hostile crowds shadowed Sheridan wherever he went, and he received death threats. Congressman George F. Hoar of Massachusetts, in New Orleans with the investigatory committee, attested to the citizens' naked hostility toward Sheridan. Whenever Sheridan entered the dining room at the St. Charles Hotel for breakfast, Hoar wrote, "there were loud hisses and groans from nearly the whole assembled company." The guests would underline particularly venomous passages in the New Orleans papers and have a waiter carry them to Sheridan. "The General would glance at it with an unruffled face, and bow and smile toward the sender."

The congressional committee defended Sheridan's use of troops at the Louisiana legislature and brokered a compromise that calmed the volatile situation, at least until the 1876 elections: the Democrats got control of the House, while Republicans dominated the Senate.[34]

On November 3, 1875, a secret policy meeting was held at the White House that proved enormously consequential for the Northern Plains tribes. While no transcript exists, historian Robert Utley writes in *Frontier Regulars* that those attending included President Grant, Sheridan, Crook, War Secretary Belknap, Interior Secretary Zachariah Chandler, and Commissioner of Indian Affairs Edward Smith. Notably absent was General Sherman, who, fed up with Belknap constantly usurping his authority, had moved his headquarters to St. Louis in October 1874, virtually ceding control of army matters to Belknap.[35]

The meeting participants understood that there was no stopping the settlers, entrepreneurs, railroads, towns, and "civilization" from overrunning the once exclusive domain of the Plains Indians. There was no discussion of this; Manifest Destiny was so tightly interwoven into American orthodoxy as to be beyond moral or legal challenge.

And, indeed, the people were coming, like it or not: in 1870, an estimated 2.3 million whites lived in the West; by 1880, there would be 4.9 million. The only matter to decide was the technical problem of how to quickly and efficiently dispose of the Indians so that the whites could safely occupy vast areas that by treaty belonged to the Northern Plains tribes.

The secret meeting yielded two momentous decisions, neither occasioning public announcement. First, the army would withdraw troops guarding the Black Hills and not interfere with prospectors entering the Sioux's sacred grounds. Sheridan notified General Alfred Terry, his Department of the Platte commander, of this decision on November 9. President Grant, he said, had decided that his order forbidding miners to enter the Black Hills country "should not be rescinded, [yet] no rigid resistance by the military should be made to the miners going in. . . . Cause the troops in your command to assume such attitudes as will meet the terms of the President in this respect."

Secondly, Grant and his advisers decided to compel the northern tribes to quit their hunting grounds stretching west to the Big Horn Mountains and to force them to live permanently on their reservations. In December, runners carried instructions to the roaming bands to report to their reservations by January 31, 1876. After that date, the army would force those staying out to comply or kill them if they still refused. As expected, the hostile bands led by Sitting Bull, Crazy Horse, Gall, and others rejected the government ultimatum, setting the stage for the Great Sioux War of 1876.[36]

All of this was agreeable to Sheridan. The army was no longer burdened with the impossible assignment of keeping white prospectors out of the Black Hills. And the ultimatum promised to settle the problem of the fractious Northern Plains tribes. Since 1868, the Sioux had drawn rations at the agencies while raiding at will. The eastern Wyoming Territory had become virtually uninhabitable for white settlers and dangerous, too, for Crows, Shoshones, and Pawnees.

The president and his counselors also authorized Sheridan to mount a Northern Plains winter campaign immediately following the expiration of the January 31 deadline. While the leaders' faith in him must have gratified Sheridan, he also surely lamented Congress's refusal to grant his requests in 1874 and 1875 for two new forts. Sheridan had chosen the sites at the mouth of the Tongue River and on the Big Horn River after a personal reconnaissance. With those forts, the army might have swiftly seized control of the Powder River country. Without them, the soldiers had to march long distances before even beginning to campaign, eliminating the possibility of surprise.[37]

IN MAKING HIS NEW battle plan, Sheridan drew from the successful 1868–1869 and 1874–1875 campaigns. Army columns would converge from three directions on the Powder River country to destroy the wild bands' villages. While Sheridan's orders stated the operations "should be made without concert," he made it clear that he would not object if the commanders chose to work together.

Sheridan was concerned, however, that the campaign's late start—after the January 31, 1876, deadline for the Indians to report to their reservations—gave him too little time to locate and destroy the renegade bands before springtime restored their vaunted mobility. As the columns ventured out onto the cold plains, Sheridan renewed his request for the two new military posts in the Yellowstone Valley.[38]

Winters on the Northern Plains were harsher than those on the Southern Plains, Sheridan discovered. The weather was so bad in Bismarck that General Terry professed he could not send a column until springtime. Blizzards, temperatures reaching thirty below zero, and deep snow hampered the two remaining columns: George Crook, plodding north from Fort Fetterman, Wyoming, with twelve companies, and Colonel John Gibbon, marching east from Forts Ellis and Shaw with ten companies.

Gibbon found no Indians along the Yellowstone River, but when Crook's column reached the Powder River, his scouts spotted a Northern Cheyenne–Sioux village with 102 lodges. On March 1, Colonel Joseph Reynolds attacked with three hundred men and captured the village and the Indians' horses. The next morning, the Indians counterattacked and got back what they had lost. With his men suffering from frostbite because of the bitter cold, Crook limped back to Fort Fetterman.[39]

THE WINTER CAMPAIGN HAVING been a failure, Sheridan prepared for a summer campaign, working from the same blueprint. A total of 2,740 men in three columns, from the west, east, and south, would converge on the Powder River country.

Worrisome reports, however, were reaching Sheridan's Chicago headquarters of 1,000 lodges on the Little Missouri, representing Sioux, Northern Cheyennes, Northern Arapahoes, and others, and of additional warriors each day slipping away from the reservations. But Sheridan was convinced that while the bands might briefly unite in large numbers, they would quickly disperse. In this, he was tragically wrong.

He insisted that Custer, with General Terry in overall command of the 1,200-man column, lead the 7th Cavalry from Bismarck. But his favorite cavalry officer was under suspension, just as he had been prior to the Washita expedition. This time, Custer was being punished for more than dereliction of duty; he had offended the Grant administration.

Custer had testified at a congressional hearing convened to determine whether War Secretary Belknap had sold army trading post positions and presided over a corrupt sutler system that diverted supplies from the reservation Indians. Custer's testimony against Belknap and his sutlers was damaging enough, but the loquacious cavalry hero had then gone on to implicate Grant's brother, Orvil, and the president's brother-in-law.

In a letter to Grant, Sheridan tried to mitigate Custer's transgressions, but he had to admit, "Custer was in error, and I wish only to set it right." The unappeased Grant ordered Custer stripped of his command of the 7th Cavalry. As the time to begin the summer campaign drew near, Sheridan, Sherman, and General Terry all appealed to Grant to lift Custer's suspension. With great reluctance, the president permitted Custer's reinstatement.[40]

DURING THE 7TH CAVALRY'S leave-taking from Fort Abraham Lincoln, the troopers' doom-ridden wives wept copiously, and Libbie Custer witnessed an eerie vision. As she rode with the regiment onto the prairie, the troopers seemed to her to be marching simultaneously on the earth and in the sky. The result of an atmospheric phenomenon, Mrs. Custer's vision seemed ominously portentous.[41]

The supreme leader of the Sioux, Sitting Bull, also had a vision. After dancing for a day and a half during a "sun dance" ceremony, in which fifty pieces of flesh were cut from each of his arms, he reported seeing soldiers, horses, and some Indians falling from the sky, "like grasshoppers."[42]

At about the same time, Sheridan was writing to Sherman that he was "not at all sanguine" about the coming campaign but added, "We might just as well settle the Sioux matter now; it will be better for all concerned."[43]

CROOK WENT INTO ACTION first and fulfilled Sheridan's misgivings about the campaign. On June 17 at the Battle of the Rosebud—near where Reynolds was beaten on March 1—1,000 Cheyenne and Sioux warriors led by Sitting Bull and their war chief, Crazy Horse, attacked Crook's 1,100-man column from Fort Fetterman. While numerically equal to the Indians, Crook's men were overmatched in ability, and only their tenacious Crow and Shoshone auxiliaries prevented a disaster.

Still, it was a defeat, with Crook's losses totaling twenty-eight killed and fifty-six wounded. The Indians, who fought superbly for six hours before breaking off the attack, lost thirty-six dead and sixty-three wounded. Claiming victory, Crook withdrew to Little Goose Creek in northern Wyoming and did not stir from there for six weeks, except to hunt and fish.[44]

Sheridan was visiting the Sioux agencies and Camp Robinson while Crook was fighting for his life on the Rosebud. He departed for Chicago on June 18, not knowing about the Rosebud defeat or that Custer was about to enter a hornet's nest.[45]

PHILADELPHIA WAS IN A celebratory mood on July 4, 1876. Not only was it the centennial of the Declaration of Independence, but thousands of people—Generals

Sheridan and Sherman among them—were attending the first world's fair ever held in the United States, the Centennial International Exposition. A wildly popular exhibit was the gigantic hand and torch of Frederic Bartholdi's work in progress, "Liberty Enlightening the World"—the future Statue of Liberty.

Just after midnight, early on the Fourth of July, a band played the "Star-Spangled Banner," and the Liberty Bell was rung thirteen times before an audience of a quarter-million people gathered outside Independence Hall. Later that day, a Salt Lake City–datelined Associated Press report was handed to Sherman and Sheridan: Custer and five companies of the 7th Cavalry had been wiped out. The generals refused to believe the news; it was simply impossible.

The next day, however, a 15,000-word report from General Terry confirmed the AP story. Terry's report began, "Bismarck, D.T., July 5, 1876:—General Custer attacked the Indians June 25, and he, with every officer and man in five companies, were killed."

Custer had divided his regiment into three columns along the Little Big Horn River. Then, with 215 of his men, he had attacked an Indian village without realizing its enormous size until it was too late. As many as 2,000 warriors—Sioux, Northern Cheyennes, Blackfeet, Sans Arcs, Brules, and Northern Arapahoes—had wiped out Custer and all of his men before an hour had passed.[46]

No comparable military disaster had befallen the army in the United States' one hundred years of existence. And even though the Civil War's long casualty lists had numbed Americans to loss, the news of the violent death of the nation's best-known cavalryman and Indian fighter, along with two of his brothers (one of them, Tom Custer, the only Union soldier to win two Medals of Honor), a brother-in-law, a nephew, and more than two hundred others, sent a galvanic shock wave through the nation.[47] Eastern opinion, which had supported Grant's Peace Policy and condemned Custer's attack at the Washita River and the Piegan massacre, underwent a seismic shift. The *New York Times* declared that many Easterners now believed the Indians should be exterminated, "as though they were so many mad dogs." The *Nation* wrote, "Our philanthropy and our hostility tend to about the same end, and this is destruction of the Indian race."[48]

Sheridan sent Terry and Crook into Montana to hunt down the Indians that killed Custer and his men. But as he had predicted in early June, the great encampment had broken up, and the tribes had scattered. The army faced the old problem of chasing bands of warriors that would strike and run but not stand and fight. Never seeing the sense in prosecuting this kind of futile warfare, Sheridan began planning a Red River War–style winter campaign to destroy the Indians' means of sustenance and hound them until they surrendered or died.

The Custer massacre embittered Sheridan toward the Sioux, whom he now re-garded as his mortal enemy. Yet he refused to acknowledge his and the government's provocations—violating the Fort Laramie treaties by letting gold prospectors flood the Black Hills and forcing the Sioux onto their reservations. It was all the Indians' fault, Sheridan said. "They wanted to fight, and have been preparing for it for years back," he wrote. "It is their glory, their profession, and the only thing that stirs them up from absolute idleness."

Congress now belatedly approved construction of the two forts on the Yellow-stone River that Sheridan had thrice requested. It also authorized the enlistment of 2,500 new cavalry privates. Had the forts existed in 1876, Sheridan believed, there would have been no Great Sioux War, and Custer and his men would still be alive.

The forts could not be built until spring 1877 at the earliest. In the meantime, Sheridan sent infantry and cavalry units to the Sioux hunting grounds to harry the warriors. "There will be no letup on the hostile Indians on my part until they are finally subdued," Sheridan vowed.[49]

The Interior Department took the unprecedented step of voluntarily ceding control of the Sioux agencies to the army. Sheridan stationed troops at the agencies to dismount and disarm the renegade bands when hunger drove them there. He also sent Lieutenant Colonel Fred Grant, the president's oldest son, to the Sioux agencies to conduct a head count. Unsurprisingly, the Indian agents had submitted wildly inflated numbers, and only one-half of the Indians reported as present were actually on the reservations. The rest were with the wild bands, which explained why Crook and Custer had faced such surprisingly large numbers of hostile warriors.[50]

CUSTER AND FIVE COMPANIES of the 7th Cavalry had ridden off to attack the north side of the Sioux's sprawling village alongside the Little Big Horn River while Major Marcus Reno and three companies struck the south end. Four days before the battle, General Terry had told Custer that he planned to attack the village from the north while Custer, on the south side, blocked the Indians' escape. But Terry also said that if Custer reached the village before Terry, he should not wait if he be-lieved he could win. Custer had believed, and he had acted accordingly. Unfortu-nately for him, a bend in the river and the heavily wooded riverbanks concealed the village's terrible secret—its six great tribal circles stretching for miles, with 10,000 to 15,000 Indians.

The warriors' initial preoccupation with annihilating Custer's command gave Reno time to find a good defensive position and join forces with Captain Frederick Benteen, whose four companies had been held in reserve to prevent the Indians from escaping to the south. Together, they survived a two-day siege by the warriors who had wiped out Custer.

After studying battle reports and interviewing or corresponding with the officers involved, Sheridan concluded that the disaster was due both to Custer's tactical mistakes and the swiftness of his attack on the Sioux village. With no time to flee, the inhabitants could only stand and fight. Custer's failure to reconnoiter the village and his decision to divide his 650-man regiment into three columns had sealed his fate. The calamity resulted from "misapprehension and a superabundance of courage—the latter extraordinarily developed in Custer," Sheridan wrote to Sherman.[51]

Later, Sheridan confided to his childhood friend Henry Greiner, "Poor Custer, he was the embodiment of gallantry. . . . But I was always fearful that he would catch it if allowed a separate command. . . . He was too impetuous, without deliberation; he thought himself invincible and having a charmed life. When I think of the many brave fellows who went down with him that day, it is sickening."[52]

SHERIDAN PULLED IN TROOPS from all over the Division of the Missouri to pursue Sitting Bull, Crazy Horse, and the renegade bands. But the chase was laggardly under Terry and Crook. Crook, a good combat leader, had become unusually cautious after being bloodied on the Rosebud. The bookish Terry, a trained lawyer and excellent administrator, lacked confidence in his abilities as a field commander. They combined their columns into one force, 3,900 strong. But it required such a large supply train and moved so ponderously that it appeared Sitting Bull and Crazy Horse might run free forever.

This was disappointing, and a shake-up was needed. Eventually, Sheridan moved Terry and Crook to St. Paul and Omaha, respectively, to supervise the flow of supplies to the troops in the field. He appointed Colonels Nelson Miles and Ranald Mackenzie to run their field commands—Miles to command a new Department of the Yellowstone in Montana and Mackenzie to lead operations in the Black Hills, Wyoming, and Nebraska. To Sherman, Sheridan wrote that Miles and Mackenzie must "kill [the renegades] or compel them to take refuge at the several agencies."[53]

It was an inspired move. Crook and Terry excelled at getting supplies to the troops, and Miles and Mackenzie were aggressive, energetic, and utterly relentless. Miles would operate from a winter base at the mouth of the Tongue River in Montana, while Mackenzie's winter camp was located in Wyoming's Powder River country.

AT 4 A.M. ON October 23, 1876, Mackenzie and eighteen companies surrounded and pounced on the Sioux chief Red Cloud's camp. The attack was a complete surprise, and the soldiers seized the village and all of the band's ponies without loss of life. They disarmed and escorted the Indians to Fort Robinson.[54]

A month later, Mackenzie led 1,100 cavalrymen in a night march over the Big Horn Mountains in Wyoming. At dawn on November 25—five months to the day after the annihilation of Custer's command—the troopers charged through the 173-lodge Northern Cheyenne village of Lone Wolf and Dull Knife near the Red Fork of the Powder River. Although four hundred warriors resisted fiercely, they were driven from the village.

Before burning the lodges, the troopers confiscated loot from the Custer massacre: the regiment's silk guidon and memo books and Tom Custer's buckskin jacket. The Northern Cheyennes lost their lodges, six hundred horses, and thirty warriors killed. Five troopers died. The previously unassailable Northern Cheyennes never fully recovered from the blow struck by Mackenzie's men that day.

After chasing Sitting Bull around Montana for two months, Miles's scouts located Crazy Horse's camp on the upper Tongue River. On January 9, 1877, Miles's 5th Cavalry defeated five hundred Sioux and Northern Cheyenne warriors at Wolf Mountain.[55] Throughout the remainder of the winter, Miles and Mackenzie harried the Indians through blizzards and subzero temperatures. Their aggressive pursuit wore down their quarry.

THE TENSE 1876 PRESIDENTIAL election unexpectedly drained potential resources from Sheridan's campaign. The contest between Ohio's Republican governor, Rutherford Hayes, and Samuel Tilden, the Democratic governor of New York, was expected to be close, and Grant, Sherman, and Sheridan feared that a tie might reignite the Civil War. Sherman and Sheridan also believed that if Tilden won, he would replace them with former Confederates. President Grant ordered Sheridan to ready 4,000 troops from across the West to move east to preserve order if needed.

When the votes were counted, Tilden appeared to have narrowly won both the popular and electoral votes. But Republicans claimed that blacks had been illegally prevented from voting in Louisiana, South Carolina, and Florida, and they challenged Oregon's results too. If Republicans won all four states, Hayes would win by one electoral vote.

Congress named a fifteen-man electoral commission to determine who had won the four states. Grant asked Sheridan to go to Louisiana to protect the canvassing board. Sheridan was reluctant to leave Missouri division headquarters in the middle of the Great Sioux War, but he went anyway.

Sheridan's sudden appearance in New Orleans alarmed Democrats, certain that he had come to ensure that the canvassing board certified Hayes as the winner. He tried to reassure them that he was there only to safeguard the canvass. But then the all-Republican canvassing board threw out enough Democratic votes to give Hayes Louisiana's electoral vote. Disgusted with the process, Sheridan returned to Chicago.

A grand compromise by congressional Democrats and Republicans pronounced Hayes the winner and pledged to withdraw federal troops from the South, ending Reconstruction.[56]

IN JANUARY 1877, SITTING Bull, tired of running from Miles, announced to the Sioux that he was moving his Hunkpapas to the land of the "Great Mother"—Canada, so named by the Indians for the monarch who ruled England and her dominions, Queen Victoria.[57]

Between March and May 6, 1877—the day that Crazy Horse and 889 of his people came in to the Red Cloud Agency—thousands of gaunt, ragged, and frost-bitten hostiles surrendered at the agencies. Sheridan's troopers disarmed and dismounted them. Dull Knife, while surrendering his band of 524 Northern Cheyennes to Mackenzie, told the cavalry officer, "You were the one I was afraid of when you came here last summer."

The government compelled the reservation Sioux—threatened with denial of rations—to sign documents giving up the Black Hills and their hunting grounds. What the government had proposed to pay $6 million for in October 1875 it now obtained free of charge.

During the spring of 1877, Sheridan dispatched military crews to build the two forts in the Yellowstone Valley. Fort Custer was erected at the mouth of the Little Big Horn River. The second fort, at the mouth of the Tongue River, was named Fort Keogh, for Captain Myles Keogh, who died with Custer.

From Fort Keogh, Miles's command pursued the few straggling bands that had not yet come in to the Indian agencies. The last of them surrendered in September, ending the Great Sioux War and safeguarding the Yellowstone country for settlers, miners, developers, and railroaders.[58]

DURING THE SUMMER OF 1877, Sheridan and his staff made an inspection tour of Wyoming and Montana. As they traveled through the Big Horn Mountains, a zoologist with the party discovered a new butterfly species. He honored Sheridan by naming it *Theela sheridani.*

The peaceful Yellowstone Valley and the new forts, Custer and Keogh, inspired Sheridan with optimism; he foresaw an era of uninterrupted prosperity for the region. Already, he wrote, a growing population "[is] engaged in mining, grazing, and agricultural pursuits, pays taxes, builds farmhouses, and constructs fences, plows up the ground, erects school-houses, and founds villages . . . [adding] so much more to the trade, commerce and prosperity of the world."

In July, the party reached the Custer battlefield in southern Montana. Sheridan toured it with his aides, Sioux guides, and others—seventy men in all. The enlisted men killed in the battle were buried where they fell, while the remains of Custer and his officers had been sent to Fort Leavenworth to be shipped to their survivors. Custer was interred at West Point.

As Sheridan walked the grassy, shadeless hillside in the midday heat, trying to make sense of how his friend and his men had perished here, he conceived the idea of preserving the site as it was, as a national cemetery.[59]

CHAPTER 17

The
Conservationist
General

1882–1884

If authorized to do so, I will engage to keep out skin hunters and all other hunters, by use of troops. . . . I can keep sufficient troops in the [Yellowstone] park . . . and give a place of refuge and safety for our noble game.

—SHERIDAN IN AN 1882 REPORT[1]

BEGINNING IN 1871, Philip Sheridan had planned and sent four exploration expeditions into Yellowstone National Park. In 1882, he personally led a large expedition into the enchanted province of geysers and spectacular vistas.

Everything pleased him at first. The Union Pacific Railroad transported the expedition party to Green River Station in Wyoming. The party traveled by wagon to Lander and Fort Washakie, entering the park in mid-August. With Sheridan were his brother, Lieutenant Colonel Michael Sheridan, and a half-dozen Chicago friends, including Anson Stager, the head of Western Electric; fellow officers and a company of the 2nd Cavalry led by Captain J. N. Wheelan; and five Shoshone scouts. The party numbered 130 men and three hundred horses and mules.

Each day, the expedition followed Sheridan's unvarying routine of breaking camp by 6:15 a.m., marching fifteen to twenty-five miles, and stopping in the afternoon to enjoy the stunning scenery and to reel in brook trout from the clear streams and rivers. Good weather favored them each day. Following the course of the Snake River, they blazed the first trail connecting present-day Jackson Hole and the Thumb of Yellowstone Park.

In Yellowstone, they witnessed repeated eruptions of Old Faithful and many other geysers. Sheridan noted that the geysers had not changed since his visit in 1881, with the exception of the Sheridan Geyser, which had become "very violent" and whose crater now measured 125 feet, compared with 70 feet a year earlier.[2]

Sheridan enjoyed himself—until he left the park and encountered Northern Pacific Railroad construction crews that were extending the track to Livingston, Montana. Sheridan rode a work train into Billings, where enthusiastic railroad officials described their plan to transform Yellowstone National Park into a lucrative tourist destination.

DURING THE NORTHERN PACIFIC railroad's fitful march across the Northern Plains from Duluth toward its destination, Tacoma, there had been no more faithful protector of the railroad's interests than Sheridan's troopers from Fort Abraham Lincoln; they had guarded survey parties and track crews against Indian attacks. The army command and the executives of all the railroads shared wartime friendships, as well as an abiding faith in the nation's Manifest Destiny and the railroads' role as civilization's vanguard.

Not only had the army watched over the Northern Pacific as it marched west, but it had also guarded the construction crews of the Union Pacific and Kansas Pacific Railroads as they laid track across the Great Plains. And in 1877, when railroad workers went on strike in Chicago, St. Louis, Pittsburgh, and other cities in the East, President Rutherford Hayes had called on the army to restore order.[3]

AS THE RAILROAD OFFICIALS eagerly described their plans for Yellowstone, Sheridan's eyes narrowed, glinting with suppressed anger, and his pleasure with the wilderness trip ebbed. The Northern Pacific planned to lay an eighty-mile-long spur line into the park. Interior Secretary Henry Teller had tentatively granted the railroad's development company, Yellowstone Park Improvement Company, the exclusive rights to 4,400 acres on seven tracts.

The tracts were located at the park's most desirable locations, including Old Faithful, Mammoth Hot Springs, Lake Yellowstone, and the Grand Canyon of the Yellowstone. For an annual lease fee of just $2 per acre, the improvement company was permitted to cut all the timber that it needed for fuel and telegraph poles and to clear land for forage. Plans were already moving ahead for a large hotel near the geysers.

"I regretted exceedingly to learn that the National Park had been rented out to private parties," Sheridan wrote in his report, "for money making purposes, from which claims and conditions will arise that may be hard for the government and the courts to shake off."[4]

SHERIDAN HAD ENERGETICALLY PROMOTED Yellowstone since 1870, when he encouraged the first important exploration of the region. While inspecting military posts in Montana, Sheridan had met a mountain man who told him wild stories about "wonderland," as some Montanans called the strange region of geysers, volcanoes, and boiling springs to the south.

Sheridan was highly intrigued. When he reached Helena, a group of men approached him about mounting an expedition into the unmapped Yellowstone country. Sheridan agreed to provide a six-man cavalry escort led by Lieutenant Gustavus Doane; exploration, after all, was one of the army's manifold duties in the West. Led by Henry Washburn, the Montana Territory's surveyor general and a major general during the Civil War, the expedition confirmed everything that trappers and traders had been saying about the Yellowstone country since John Colter's famous exploration during the winter of 1807–1808.

In 1871, separate expeditions organized by Sheridan and Ferdinand Hayden of the US Geological Survey marched independently to the source of the Yellowstone River. The military expedition, led by Army Corps of Engineers captains John Barlow and David Heap, returned with satchels of scientific observations, surveying measurements, and detailed journals. All of Barlow's documents were destroyed in the Great Chicago Fire in October, but Heap had kept his own notes—and with them he drew the first accurate map of Yellowstone. An enduring legacy of this expedition was the christening of Mount Sheridan, a 10,308-foot peak overlooking Heart Lake.

Hayden's expedition was arguably more consequential than Sheridan's. It, too, was government sponsored, but the expedition's co-leader, Nathaniel Langford, worked for Jay Cooke, the financier behind the Northern Pacific Railroad. The railroad at that time was steadily advancing across the Dakota Territory toward the Montana Territory.

Two artists also traveled with Hayden: Thomas Moran, whose paintings Cooke had commissioned, and photographer William Henry Jackson. Their depictions of the stunning scenery attracted widespread attention.

The Hayden and Barlow-Heap expeditions produced a trove of incredible art-work and fresh, colorful accounts of mud pots, geysers, and waterfalls. When Jay Cooke had seen and heard it all, he vowed to turn the "Great Geyser Basin" into a public park.

Cooke and the Northern Pacific lobbied Congress hard to make Yellowstone the first national park. Hayden and Langford were the campaign's public faces. Jackson's iconic photos of the park were reproduced and bound in folios; each member of Congress got one.

By December, a bill transforming the wild country into a national park had been introduced. On March 1, 1872, President Ulysses Grant signed the law creating Yellowstone National Park, but without a cent appropriated for its management or maintenance. Fittingly, Langford became the park's first superintendent—without pay.[5]

The Northern Pacific's ambitious plans for the park were interrupted by the rail-road's collapse and Jay Cooke & Company's bankruptcy during the Panic of 1873. The railroad was stranded in Bismarck for six years before resuming its westward march.[6]

SHERIDAN ORGANIZED EXPLORATIONS TO Yellowstone in 1873, 1875, and 1876. Captain William Ludlow of the Corps of Engineers led the 1875 expedition, ac-companied by a young naturalist and Yale PhD, George Bird Grinnell, future editor of *Forest and Stream* magazine and a founder of the Audubon Society. The expedi-tion transformed Grinnell into one of the park's fiercest defenders.[7]

At the geysers, Ludlow and Grinnell were dismayed to discover that tourists had used hammers to steal ornamental rocks from the formations and had carved their initials into the remaining rocks. Nearly everywhere they went in the park, they saw the carcasses of butchered wildlife. Because no one was there to protect it, the park was under imminent threat; Superintendent Langford, forced to earn a living elsewhere, seldom visited.

In his report, Ludlow recommended that the War Department take over the park and send troops to police it until "a Civilian Superintendency, living in the Park, with a body of mounted police under his orders can suffice for its protection." Seventy citizens of Bozeman, Montana, signed a memorial to the interior secretary demanding the appointment of a salaried commissioner and assistants.[8]

SHERIDAN'S REPORT ON HIS 1882 expedition brimmed with passion. Clearly, he believed that Yellowstone was being degraded by neglect: 4,000 elk shot in one winter, 2,000 killed on the park's margins during the past winter, and large numbers of mountain sheep, antelope, deer, and other game destroyed as well. If nothing was done, all the game might be wiped out, Sheridan warned.

Make the park a big game preserve, he urged, and expand it 40 miles to the east and 10 miles to the south—adding 3,444 square miles. Such an expansion would displace no one from what was in fact "rough, mountain country, with an altitude too high for cultivation or winter grazing for cattle," he wrote.

Sheridan called for quick, decisive action and sought the support of sportsmen's clubs around the country for his plan to make the park a wild game refuge, protected by the army. "If authorized to do so, I will engage to keep out skin hunters and all other hunters, by use of troops from Fort Washakie on the south, Custer on the east, and Ellis on the north, and, if necessary, I can keep sufficient troops in the park to accomplish this object, and give a place of refuge and safety for our noble game."

Superficially, Sheridan's impassioned defense of the park wildlife appeared to be at odds with his earlier support for the annihilation of the Great Plains buffalo. But in Sheridan's view, there was no inconsistency: two wholly different issues were involved. The buffalo slaughter was necessary to suppress the Plains Indians; the wild game slaughter in Yellowstone served a narrow commercial interest and outraged his sensibilities as a lifelong hunter and former amateur ornithologist.[9]

In its enumeration of the serial game killings and its detailing of the Northern Pacific Railroad's plan to commercialize Yellowstone, Sheridan's report provoked public indignation. Just five hundred tourists a year on average visited the park, but with the Great Plains at peace and access to the park steadily improving, tourism was going to explode—and the legion of potential visitors wanted their park to remain pristine.

Sheridan reached out to potential allies to help him save Yellowstone National Park from developers, hide hunters, and vandals. Conservation-minded congressmen, chief among them Senator George Vest of Missouri, and naturalists such as Grinnell rallied under Sheridan's banner. Grinnell's *Forest and Stream* demanded that Congress take steps to protect Yellowstone from hide hunters and commercial exploitation.

But the Northern Pacific officials and their financial backers—the so-called railroad gang—were just as determined to not permit the public backlash to derail their plans. They dug in for a long fight.[10]

THE GREAT SIOUX WAR crushed the power of the Northern Plains Indians, and the Sioux—Sitting Bull and his defiant Hunkpapas in Canada excepted—settled on reservations in the Dakota Territory. But not all of the tribes were resigned to their fate as wards of the federal government.

The Northern Cheyenne and Nez Perce bridled at their resettlement on new reservations in Indian Territory and Idaho, respectively. Trouble continued to flare along the Rio Grande, with Lipans, Kickapoos, Comanches, and even Mexican revolutionaries mounting sporadic raids from Mexico into Texas. (Sheridan considered imposing martial law in the Texas border counties and occupying towns in northern Mexico, and Congress provisionally approved seizing Mexican territory if the raids continued, but the crisis passed.) And the White River Utes in Colorado and Geronimo's Chiricahua Apaches in Arizona rebelled at becoming farmers after having flourished for generations as hunter-gatherers.

But these uprisings between 1877 and 1886 were small affairs compared with the Great Sioux War, the Washita campaign, and the Red River War. And they were relentlessly quashed by Nelson Miles and Ranald Mackenzie, as well as others schooled in the hard-handed "total war" strategy pioneered by Sheridan, William Sherman, George Armstrong Custer, and George Crook.

Between 1868 and 1883, Sheridan directed the rise of a great chain of new forts across his sprawling Division of the Missouri to make it easier to suppress future Indian outbreaks quickly. It was frustrating work because budget constraints almost always required one fort to be abandoned when a new one was built. Worse, the Indian Bureau, which Sheridan believed deliberately moved its Indian agencies away from the forts to avoid the army's criticism of the agents' management, usually then belatedly discovered that it needed troops close at hand. And so the army was then required to build a new fort near the new agency. These unnecessary relocations cost "hundreds of thousands of dollars," Sheridan complained to Sherman.

The forts protected citizens and profited local businesses. Politicians, citizens, and businessmen ceaselessly petitioned Sheridan to station troops in their districts. To one such petition, Sheridan replied in exasperation, "If the wishes of the settlers on the frontier were to be gratified, we would have a military post in every county, and the Army two or three hundred thousand strong."[11]

But the rapid settlement of the West by whites was as effective a deterrent as the army forts. Each year, the Indians found themselves hemmed in further by forts, railroads, towns, and new roads to speed the proliferating settlers to their destinations.

SHERIDAN BEGAN TO OPENLY question whether treaties and military campaigns had been the best policies for dealing with the Plains Indians. "It would have been better if the Indians had been considered as part of the population of the United States, and dealt with generously," Sheridan wrote in one of his annual reports.

He also sharply criticized the Indian Bureau's management of the contractors that supplied the reservations, suggesting that lax oversight was the primary cause of the Indian wars of the 1870s. The contractors, Sheridan wrote in disgust, were interested solely in what would "best subserve their money-making interests. . . . I see enough to satisfy me that it is not the Government which is managing the Indians, it is the contractors, traders, and supply interests."

Sheridan told Sherman there was no question why the Indians had gone to war during the past several years. "The answer is hunger. This cannot be disguised." The Indians told him that they never received enough food or even the government's attention, except "after making war on its citizens and soldiers." "Many of the troubles that have occurred on the frontier have grown out of bad feeling superinduced by want of needed supplies," he wrote. The contractors delivered just part of what the government paid for and pocketed the rest as profit.

Sheridan's solution, which he expounded upon year after year, was to let the army manage the reservations; the army would cut costs by one-third and root out the corruption rampant among contractors and agents. But the army's bête noir, the so-called Indian Ring—the Indian Bureau, Interior Department, their contractors, and their congressional supporters—efficiently blocked every attempt to transfer control to the army.[12]

Failing to persuade Congress to give the War Department control of the reservations, Sheridan tried to thwart pork barrel military construction and scurrilous trading practices wherever he found them. He won some battles and lost others. He recommended revoking Belker & Company's permit to trade with the Indians after years of "irregular practices," notably dealing in smallpox-infected buffalo robes. Sheridan stopped a speculator's scheme to transfer Fort Kearney to North Platte, Nebraska, but failed to prevent Fort Abraham Lincoln from being built on a windy bluff near Bismarck. The Northern Pacific Railroad had claimed the more suitable nearby site on the plains for land development and track construction.

After the Great Sioux War, Sheridan urged the relocation of the Sioux reservations to the Missouri River to avert Indian–gold miner clashes in the Black Hills. Not only did the Black Hills treaty specify the relocation, but the Missouri River site had superior timber, soil, and game. But contractors and Indian traders, whose livelihoods would be damaged if trade goods were transported by boat rather than by railroad, persuaded President Grant not to move the agencies. Sheridan resignedly remarked to Sherman on Grant's concession to the businessmen, "He could not well help himself."

Sheridan objected to placing the Northern Arapahoes and Shoshones, which were ancient enemies, on the same Wyoming reservation. It was a "grave mistake," Sheridan said, adding that the Northern Arapahoes should have instead been paired with either the Sioux or the Southern Arapahoes. The decision stood.

Writing to Sherman in December 1878, Sheridan vented his frustration with the reservations' management: "We have occupied his [the Indian's] country, taken away from him his lovely domain, destroyed his herds of game, penned him up on reservations, and reduced him to poverty. For humanity's sake, then, let us give him enough to eat, and integrity in the agents over him."

Sherman wholeheartedly agreed. The army, he said, had become "the peripatetic police of civil Indian agents who are, in many cases, selected for no other reason than that of political expediency."[13]

THE ANNUAL REPORTS SUBMITTED by the army's military division commanders normally passed into the records unremarked upon, but Sheridan's 1878 report, unique in its bitterness and eloquence, attracted attention. In it, Sheridan blamed the government's "injudicious treatment" of the Indians and its failure to move the Sioux to the Missouri River for the 1876–1877 Great Sioux War. And he deplored the ridiculously heavy demands placed on the undermanned army to control the 192,000 Indians in ninety-nine tribes that resided in the 1 million square miles of Sheridan's Missouri Military Division. "No other nation in the world," he wrote, would have attempted to subdue the Plains Indians with fewer than 60,000 or 70,000 men, yet his forces on the plains never numbered more than 14,000, with one-third of them stationed along the Rio Grande. As a result, every encounter between troops and Indians became "a forlorn hope," with "the most barbarous cruelties staring [the soldiers] in the face in case of defeat."

The 1868–1869 Southern Plains war, he wrote, was the inevitable result of the region's rapid settlement and the government breaking every promise that it had made to the Indians. When the tribes reacted by robbing, raping, and murdering settlers across western Kansas, the government sent after them "an army too small to intimidate or even punish." Only "by the constant hammering of an inadequate force" was the military able to force the Comanches, Kiowas, Cheyennes, and Arapahoes onto the reservations, Sheridan wrote.

But there was nothing inevitable about the 1876–1877 Great Sioux War, he said. The Indians were not getting the food and supplies that they had been promised; some were half starving. "We took away their country, and their means of support, broke up their mode of living, their habits of life, introduced disease and decay among them, and it was for this and against this that they made war," Sheridan wrote with unusual asperity. "Could any one expect less? Then why wonder at Indian difficulties?"

The Indian Bureau had then inexcusably let thousands of Northern Plains Indians leave their reservations after they had received "their annuities and rations" and then return "well loaded down with plunder." "Kind treatment administered with steadiness and justice" might have forestalled the Plains Indian wars, Sheridan wrote, but there never was "much steadiness in the management of the Indians."

Sheridan's blunt cataloguing of the Indian Bureau's failures enraged Interior Secretary Carl Schurz, the onetime German revolutionary and Union army general. "There is, it seems to me, a certain fairness due from one branch of the public service to another" that his department did not receive from the War Department before Sheridan's report was made public, Schurz sputtered. He was highly offended, too, by Sheridan's "supercilious" tone. Schurz demanded that Sheridan supply proof of everything that he had said.

Sheridan responded by forwarding copies of reports dating to 1874 filed by his Division of Missouri field officers that pointedly described the desolation of the reservation Indians—reports that Schurz already possessed. Why was the Interior secretary challenging Sheridan's conclusions when he knew the facts very well? Sheridan wondered. "Surely the officers who guard his agencies and who are held responsible for lives and property on the frontier should have a right to report the causes of trouble without the danger of being lectured into silence by the Secty of the Interior," Sheridan wrote, suggesting that Schurz was trying to intimidate him and his subordinates into remaining quiet about the problems.

Schurz appointed his own committee to conduct its own investigation and make its own findings, without any of Sheridan's information. Then, to his credit, Schurz began implementing reforms, while insisting that the reservations must remain under civilian control—this being the reason for Schurz's actions.

At the inevitable congressional hearing that followed, Schurz accused the War Department of a long history of dishonest dealings with the Indians, dating to the Cherokee removal of 1838. Schurz's energetic response to Sheridan's report preempted the last serious attempt to move oversight of the reservations to the War Department—which had administered the Indian Bureau until its transfer in 1848 to the Interior Department.

Sheridan grumbled that the Interior Department could run its affairs to suit itself. "It's none of my business who they cheat as long as they don't cheat the Army."[14]

As the contretemps subsided in January 1879, the *St. Louis Times Journal* wrote, "If Mr. Schurz is in earnest in his professions of reform he should have thanked General Sheridan for calling the attention of the country to abuses that have been too long tolerated." Instead, Schurz had responded with an "absolute and contemptuous . . . style of treatment of General Sheridan," which deserved a "rebuke for its bad manners."[15]

MORE THAN ANY OTHER American, Sheridan had been responsible for safeguarding Western immigrants at the height of the Plains Indians' dominance—a blood-stained era of slaughter, rapine, and total war.* After dedicating more than a decade to smashing the power of the monarchs of the Great Plains—the Cheyennes, Sioux, Kiowas, Kickapoos, Apaches, Arapahoes, and Comanches—Sheridan now did something wholly unexpected. The most famous living Indian fighter in America decided to sponsor an ethnological study of the Plains Indians' culture before it vanished. He named two army officers from General Crook's staff, William Clark and John Bourke, to analyze the northern and southern tribes. The result was an essay by Bourke on the Arizona Moquis Indians' snake dance and Clark's landmark book *The Indian Sign Language.*[16]

Sheridan's sympathy for the conquered Plains Indians became evident when President Grover Cleveland sent him to arbitrate a dispute between cattlemen and the Southern Plains tribes in Indian Territory. The two sides were on the brink of open warfare.

Indian agent John Miles had persuaded the Southern Cheyenne and Arapahoe chiefs to lease 2.4 million acres to seven cattlemen for a ridiculously low two cents per acre. Tribal members were outraged when they learned what their chiefs had done. Cattlemen who had been left out of the deal egged on the protesters. John Miles's successor, Indian agent D. B. Dyer, sided with the chiefs and cattlemen and requested that federal troops be sent to protect them

In July 1883, Sheridan and Brigadier General Nelson Miles met with all of the involved parties. Two dissenting leaders, Little Robe and White Shield, complained that cattlemen were building fences everywhere. Others claimed that cowboys had shot and killed an Indian when he tried to stop cattle from being run across his property. Whites were stealing their horses and cattle, they said, and agency officials were shortchanging them on rations and supplies.

The chiefs who signed the deal confessed to Sheridan that they now regretted having done so. The cattlemen blamed the dispute on Indian troublemakers; the deal was fair, they said, and they had met all of the terms.

After Sheridan and Miles had listened to everyone, Sheridan recommended that President Cleveland order the cattlemen to leave the reservation. He proposed that agent Dyer be replaced with Captain Jesse Lee of the 9th Cavalry.

Cleveland removed Dyer and gave the cattlemen forty days to clear out their cattle, which soon joined the herds on the already crowded Texas and Kansas ranges. During the winter of 1885–1886, when storms killed hundreds of thousands of cattle on the southern plains, cattlemen bitterly blamed Sheridan.[17]

---

*Western historian Paul Hutton writes that between 1867 and 1884, under Sheridan's direct authority, army troops fought 619 battles against the Indians and lost 565 dead and 691 wounded—the unusually high killed-to-wounded ratio a result of the annihilation of Custer's command. See Paul A. Hutton, *Phil Sheridan and His Army* (Norman: University of Oklahoma Press, 1985), 345, 433n.

DURING SHERIDAN'S REINCARNATION AS a defender of the Plains Indians, he came to believe the reservations were so flawed that they should be abolished and the Indians gradually assimilated into society. He drew up a plan to wean the Indians and the US government from the reservation system. Each Indian family would receive an allotment of 320 acres of reservation land. The government would "buy" the unallocated Indian land from the tribes for $1.25 an acre, investing the money in government bonds. It then would sell that land to settlers, recouping the money it had paid the Indians.

The Interior Department would send the Indian families annual interest payments, at roughly 4 percent, on the bonds. The interest payments would build homes and schools and purchase farming equipment. The annual proceeds would have totaled as much as $1 million in the Dakota Territory and $223,000 in Montana. "The Indians are not poor, they are only incompetent at the present time to take care of their property," Sheridan wrote. They would receive the bonds' principal only when they were judged competent to manage their affairs.

The plan, generous and farsighted, was not adopted. Instead, in 1887 Congress approved the Dawes Severalty Act, which gave each family 160 acres and opened the surplus lands for settlement. The Indians were supposed to receive annual interest payments on the land sold to whites but only got occasional small payments.[18]

GENERAL OF THE ARMY William Sherman announced that he would go on the army retirement list on his sixty-fourth birthday, on February 8, 1884. It was now the turn of Sheridan, the last member of the great triumvirate that had led the Union army to victory in 1865, to become the army's commanding general. The promotion did not mean that Sheridan became a four-star general of the army like Sherman; he retained his three-star lieutenant general rank. The transition began on November 1, 1883, when Sherman stepped down from his command position while remaining on active duty for three months to instruct Sheridan in his new duties.[19]

At the age of fifty-two, Sheridan became the army's first general in chief whose entire adult life, thirty-four years, had been spent in uniform. Sheridan's immediate predecessors—George McClellan, Henry Halleck, Grant, and Sherman—had all graduated from West Point but resigned from the army as captains, then returned to serve during the war. None of the antebellum commanders of the US Army had attended West Point, and all had received their commissions as civilians.[20]

Reaching the pinnacle of his profession was not an unalloyed joy for Sheridan; he had to leave Chicago, where he had sunk deep roots over sixteen years. During the 1871 fire, Sheridan had won the city's abiding gratitude by swiftly restoring order and bringing food, clothing, and blankets to homeless residents. Chicago was where he and Irene had married in 1875, where their four young children had been born, and where some of his closest friends lived. But Washington, DC, would now become the Sheridans' home.

Thirty-one of Sheridan's Chicago businessman friends—including Marshall Field, George Pullman, Joseph Medill, and Philip Armour—made the transition easier by purchasing a roomy, three-story brick home in Washington for the Sheridans. Located at the corner of Rhode Island Avenue and Seventeenth Street, the four-year-old home, for which the benefactors paid $44,000, was a dozen blocks from the War Department. At one of the numerous receptions and dinners honoring Sheridan before his leave-taking, civic leaders presented him with the deed to his new home. In the accompanying letter, they wrote, "Citizens of Chicago . . . can never forget the great services rendered to their city by you at the time of its surest need."[21]

IN CANADA, SITTING BULL and 4,000 Sioux, joined in October 1877 by 150 bedraggled refugees from Chief Joseph's Nez Perce's band, remained the last major holdouts of the Great Sioux War. Sitting Bull "abruptly and disdainfully" spurned a delegation of US commissioners who wanted to discuss surrender terms. Miles agitated unsuccessfully for an across-the-border expedition on the order of Mackenzie's illegal Mexican raid against the Kickapoos.

One of Sheridan's great strengths was his ability to adapt a strategy to the situation, and he did so now. While publicly disavowing any plan to force the Sioux's surrender, "so long as they behave themselves and keep north off the Missouri," he quietly executed a plan to starve Sitting Bull into submission. He hinted at such a stealth program in a letter to Sherman in March 1878. "I think an international understanding to prevent the wild buffalo herd of that region from crossing the line to and fro, would be about as sensible as an understanding to control the Indians," he wrote.[22]

While there is no official US record of such an understanding, Canadian historian C. M. MacInnes wrote that beginning in 1878, US cavalry and Indian auxiliaries drove the buffalo southward whenever herds approached the border. Other early-twentieth-century Canadian historians, relying on eyewitnesses, related similar accounts.*

During this period buffalo hunters were also shipping tens of thousands of hides from Montana down the Missouri River each year. In a letter, Sheridan wrote, "If

---

* In *The Buffalo Hunters: The Story of the Hide Men*, American historian Mari Sandoz writes that a line of soldiers, Indians, and civilians turned the buffalos back whenever they began to cross the border, "and it was there, some said, shut in by this line of prairie fire and guns, that the greatest slaughter of the northern herd took place." See Mari Sandoz, *The Buffalo Hunters: The Story of the Hide Men* (Lincoln: University of Nebraska Press, 1978), 340.

I could learn that every Buffalo in the north herd were killed I would be glad. The destruction of this herd would do more to keep Indians quiet than anything else that could happen, except the death of all the Indians."[23]

Whether compelled by a clandestine US policy of deliberate starvation or not, hungry Sioux from Canada began straggling south into the reservations in small groups in 1879 and 1880. On July 19, 1881, Sitting Bull led 185 men, women, and children into Fort Burford and surrendered. Of the virtual annihilation of the northern buffalo herd, Sitting Bull bitterly commented, "A cold wind blew across the prairie when the last buffalo fell—a death wind for my people."[24]

THAT LEFT JUST ONE major Indian leader for Sheridan's generals to beat into submission—the wily Chiricahua Apache Geronimo. For two decades, Geronimo had alternately terrorized settlers on both sides of the border and lived quietly for years at a time. When in 1881 Geronimo's band left the San Carlos, Arizona, reservation and slaughtered dozens of settlers in southeastern Arizona and southwestern New Mexico, Sheridan appointed Major General George Crook to command the Department of Arizona.

In 1883, Crook tracked Geronimo down in Mexico's Sierra Madre mountain range and persuaded him to surrender. But two years later, Geronimo again broke out of the reservation and, with forty-two warriors and ninety-two women and children, fled to Mexico. Geronimo's band raided southern Arizona and New Mexico, leaving a trail of thirty-eight settlers' bodies. With 3,000 men, Crook gave chase, but the Chiricahuas disappeared into the mountains.

These latest killings brought Sheridan to Fort Bowie, Arizona, where he informed Crook that he would end the Apache scourge by sending the Chiricahuas and the Warm Springs Apaches to the East. But Crook persuaded him to wait until Geronimo was brought in; if their wives and children were removed, Crook's Apache scouts would stop aiding his troops. Sheridan reluctantly acquiesced, although he disapproved of using Apache scouts to track Apaches, believing they did not try hard enough.[25]

The disagreement marked the further erosion of the friendship between onetime West Point roommates Crook and Sheridan—a friendship that over the years had deteriorated into a strained working relationship. The process had begun twenty years earlier in the Shenandoah Valley with Sheridan's displeasure over the rout of Crook's VIII Corps at Cedar Creek and Crook's resentment over Sheridan's receiving all the credit for the victories at Winchester and Fisher's Hill, when the flank attacks that won both battles had been Crook's ideas.

Then, there had been Crook's inexplicable—to Sheridan—defeat at the Rosebud in 1876 and his six weeks of inactivity afterward, which Sheridan partly blamed for the Custer massacre. His laggardly pursuit of the Sioux over the next months

caused Sheridan to bring in Mackenzie and Miles. There had always been extenu-
ating circumstances, but Sheridan neither forgot nor altogether forgave failure, just
as Crook resented Sheridan's begrudging him credit during the Civil War. "I regret
that I learned too late that it was not what a person did, but it was what he got the
credit of doing that gave him a reputation," Crook wrote in his autobiography.[26]

Despite the souring relations between the two men, Crook, with his oddly parted
beard, had become the army's best-known, most innovative field commander. His
1872–1873 Tonto Basin campaign in north-central Arizona had forced 6,000
White Mountain Apaches and Yavapais to enroll at reservations. Crook was the
first to use Sioux scouts to track down renegade Sioux bands and Apaches to pursue
Apaches. He pioneered the use of the mule pack train, which could both travel
faster than wagon trains and go places wagon trains could not.[27]

Crook's second campaign against Geronimo ended in January 1886 in a two-
hour battle between one hundred of Crook's Apache scouts and Mexican militia.
The scouts and their leader, Captain Emmet Crawford, were riding to meet with
Geronimo when the militia confronted them, accused them of marauding, and
opened fire, fatally wounding Crawford. As Geronimo and his people watched, the
scouts, infuriated by the shooting of Crawford, picked off every militia officer.

While the battle had disrupted the meeting with Geronimo, the Apache leader
was weary of living as a fugitive. In March 1886, he and other Apache leaders met
with Crook and agreed to go into exile in the East for two years. But on the same
night, after drinking mescal, Geronimo was assailed by doubts and fled with twenty
men and thirteen women.[28]

Both President Grover Cleveland and Sheridan renounced the broken deal with
Geronimo anyway; they would accept only unconditional surrender. Sheridan in-
sinuated that the Apache scouts had allowed the chief to get away. "It seems strange
that Geronimo and his party should have escaped without the knowledge of the
scouts," he told Crook.

When Sheridan ordered Crook to stop pursuing Geronimo and to instead take
defensive precautions to thwart any raids, Crook asked to be relieved. Sheridan
promptly did so, sending Crook to the Department of the Platte. He appointed
his current favorite field commander, Nelson Miles, to replace him.

COLONEL RANALD MACKENZIE, SHERIDAN'S hard-driving campaigner, might
have appeared to be Crook's logical replacement. He had long been Sheridan's troubleshooter and had campaigned for years in the Southwest. But because of mental
illness, possibly early dementia, Mackenzie had been judged unfit for command
and forced into an early retirement.

"General Mackenzie was sent to Bloomingdale [Asylum, in New York] after a
full consultation with his friends," Sheridan informed Mackenzie's sister Harriet in

1883. Mackenzie was later discharged to live with relatives, but he steadily declined until his death in 1889, at the age of forty-eight.[29]

CROOK NEVER FORGAVE SHERIDAN, bitterly remarking in his autobiography, written after Sheridan's death, "The adulations heaped on him by a grateful nation for his supposed genius turned his head, which, added to his natural disposition, caused him to bloat his little carcass with debauchery and dissipation."

After he was promoted from field command, Sheridan certainly gained weight—his five-foot-five frame, which had carried 115 pounds after Missionary Ridge, now packed 200 pounds. His detractors suggested that his high color was due to heavy drinking, but Sheridan imbibed moderately. High blood pressure and the congenital heart problem that would end his life might better explain Sheridan's ruddiness.[30]

Miles was no more successful than Crook in tracking down Geronimo in Mexico, although not for lack of effort; his expedition logged 2,000 miles. But while the pursuit failed, Miles's summary exile of the Chiricahuas and Warm Springs Apaches to Florida—Sheridan's plan, which Crook had opposed—worked brilliantly. Geronimo's followers became so thoroughly demoralized that they gave up.

Geronimo surrendered unconditionally to Miles on September 4, 1886—becoming the last tribal leader to submit to the US government and concluding twenty years of Indian wars. Years later, while living at Fort Sill, Oklahoma, Geronimo earned money by selling his photograph and souvenir hunting bows inscribed with his name. He died at Fort Sill in 1909.[31]

AS THE ARMY'S COMMANDING general, Sheridan had charge of about 26,000 men—a smaller force than he had commanded in the Shenandoah Valley or at Five Forks. Moreover, he quickly discovered that the secretary of war was the de facto military commander—his departmental commanders reported directly to War Secretary Robert Todd Lincoln, the late president's oldest son. Often, Sheridan first learned of orders that had gone out with his supposed authorization when he read about them in the newspapers.

As had Sherman, Sheridan bridled at Lincoln's high-handedness, only to have the war secretary rebuke him, then rub it in by sending copies of the scolding to Sheridan's subordinate commanders. While his first months as commanding general were disconcertingly humbling, even humiliating, he found that his happy domestic life, comfortable salary, and high profile mitigated his dissatisfaction.[32]

REMOVED FROM DAY-TO-DAY DECISION making, Sheridan devoted himself to modernizing the army, a process begun by Sherman, who had been impressed by the reforms proposed by the brilliant warrior-scholar Lieutenant Colonel Emory Upton. Sheridan continued Sherman's effort to make the officer corps more professional:

upgrading the Artillery School at Fort Monroe, Virginia, and obtaining more funds for the School of Application for Cavalry and Infantry begun by Sherman at Fort Leavenworth—the basic training school for officers.

Sheridan crusaded to improve army marksmanship, and he succeeded Grant as president of the National Rifle Association. Upon his recommendation, the first army shooting team was formed; Sheridan oversaw the construction of army rifle ranges around the country. He arranged for marksmanship medals to be cast at the Philadelphia Mint.

Sheridan's keen interest in modern weapons inspired his promotion of breech cannons and the "magazine gun," which he called "the gun of the future." Yet, like nearly all Civil War–vintage officers, he was prejudiced against the Gatling gun. Spurned by most Union army officers even though the continuous-firing gun was available in 1862, the Gatling was not accepted by the American army until 1866.

Unwieldy as a cannon, the Gatling also wasted ammunition, Sheridan observed, and the gunner was highly vulnerable to sniper fire. When Brigadier General Alfred Terry requested more Gatlings, Sheridan replied that he didn't believe that the Gatling had killed a single Indian. "What we want on the frontier against Indians is more soldiers not new Gatling guns," Sheridan wrote.

Nor was he impressed by an innovation known as the "trowel bayonet," which he said was too cumbersome to carry on a rifle and would only encourage infantry-men to dig holes when they should be advancing.[33]

Sheridan represented the army at ceremonial events. He was grand marshal at the commemoration of the completed Washington Monument in 1885 and attended the unveiling of the Statue of Liberty. He was a pallbearer at the funerals of two former presidents, Ulysses Grant and Chester Arthur. And as the last of the Civil War's victorious triumvirate still in active service, Sheridan was an enormously popular keynote speaker at veterans' reunions. "You know we old cavalrymen are very clannish and look upon you as our leader," wrote the president of Pennsylvania's Grand Army of the Republic chapter, in asking Sheridan for a photo so that "a large crayon" could be made of it for the post. Letters such as this and autograph requests crossed Sheridan's desk almost daily.

Sheridan attended many reunions of Civil War veterans. Although he never put his private thoughts about the war to paper—at least not after his personal papers and journals were destroyed in the Great Chicago Fire—Sheridan, like thousands of veterans, evidently enjoyed the company of men who had shared the terror and exhilaration of combat. But he objected to the reunions' politicization by candidates for office, and he was uninterested in becoming a candidate himself. "I never had the presidential bee in my bonnet, and I don't intend to have it," Sheridan told an Associated Press reporter in 1887 after his name had surfaced for a potential candidacy. "There is nothing that would induce me to leave the profession [in] which nearly forty years of my life have been spent to enter upon a civil career."

BECAUSE HIS JOB WAS relatively undemanding, Sheridan was able to devote plenty of time to his family. The Sheridans had brought their four young children with them from Chicago to Washington, three girls and a boy born between 1876 and 1880: Mary, twin sisters Irene and Louise, and Philip Jr.

Sheridan was an attentive father, as well as an attentive son-in-law, performing a great service for his father-in-law, Colonel Daniel Rucker, the army's assistant quartermaster general. At Sheridan's quiet urging, President Chester Arthur compelled the retirement of sixty-six-year-old Quartermaster General Montgomery Meigs, whose son, the late Lieutenant John Meigs, was killed in 1864 in the Shenandoah Valley. Meigs's retirement cleared the way for Rucker, who was seventy years old, to at last reach the summit of the Quartermaster Corps after forty-five years of army service. Ten days as quartermaster general was enough for Rucker, who then followed Meigs into retirement with the rank of brigadier general.[34]

The Sheridans entertained frequently—their guests included the president, diplomats, cabinet members, judges, and congressmen. Irene Rucker Sheridan was one of Washington's most popular hostesses, sometimes receiving more than one hundred callers in a day in her high-ceiling sitting room with a bay window.

Sheridan preferred the library, with its red silk wallpaper covered with portraits of army friends, living and dead, and with shelves reaching to the ceiling, full of books. It was there, beginning in 1886, that he wrote his *Personal Memoirs* on a thick pad of white paper—necessarily lonely, tedious work that spanned a year and a half. Because his Civil War journals, reports, and diaries had been destroyed in the Great Chicago Fire, he had to piece it together from memory and the War Department's archives. Poor health forced him to conclude the memoirs with an account of his trip to Europe in 1870 and 1871.[35]

While the war secretary had arrogated to himself the army commander's authority in most important matters, Sheridan occasionally got his way in small concerns, such as the fight over the Confederate battle flags. In 1887, War Secretary William Endicott ordered the Rebel flags returned to the states from which they were captured. Endicott had not served in the Union army, and so he did not anticipate the howl of protest that his proposed action would evoke. Led by Sheridan, prominent members of the Grand Army of the Republic and Northern politicians violently objected. President Cleveland rescinded Endicott's order.[36]

SENATOR GEORGE VEST OF Missouri had been a Confederate congressman and a senator; unsurprisingly, he was a Democrat. Those credentials made him an improbable ally of Phil Sheridan. But Sheridan's years as a quasi public servant had made him a political pragmatist, and Vest happened to be chairman of the Senate Committee on Territories. He became Sheridan's most important partner in his crusade to protect Yellowstone National Park from developers, poachers, and vandals.[37]

"There is going to be a fight after all," George Bird Grinnell excitedly wrote in the January 11, 1883, issue of *Forest and Stream* magazine. "The Yellowstone Park is not to be put into the pockets of a few speculators without some resistance on the part of the representatives of the people. . . . The Park is for rich and poor alike, and every one should have an equal interest in it."[38]

Sheridan's report on the 1882 Yellowstone expedition had gotten results. Interior Secretary Henry Teller banned hunting inside the park, and, at Sheridan's urging, Vest took the first steps to protect the park by sponsoring a pair of resolutions in December 1882. Vest demanded that the Interior Department reveal all the concessions awarded inside the park. He also posed the question, How should the park be properly managed?

Vest got his answers, but he discovered that powerful interests were ready to thwart the changes that he sought. The Yellowstone Park Improvement Company and its parent company, the Northern Pacific Railroad, blocked Vest's attempt to curb the interior secretary's authority over the park. They also defeated his proposal to prohibit exclusive privileges and monopolies inside Yellowstone.

Vest persisted. In March 1883, he added an amendment to the Sundry Civil Appropriations Act that put the brakes on the park's development while also permitting the army to get a foot in the door. The amendment forbade the interior secretary to award monopolies or leases exceeding ten acres. No leases were permitted within a quarter mile of the geysers or Yellowstone Falls. Moreover, if trespassers, poachers, or vandals became major problems, the army could be deployed to protect the park.

This was an enormous setback for the Improvement Company, although it still controlled all ten acres where development was permitted. The company was determined to make the most of its ten-year lease. It quickly threw up temporary buildings: a boardinghouse, office, and stables.

The Improvement Company also accelerated construction of its 250-room National Hotel at Mammoth Hot Springs, which featured such rustic rarities as electricity, a six-by-twenty-two-foot kitchen range where fifteen cooks could work simultaneously, a barbershop, and a Steinway piano. The hotel's larder was stocked with elk killed inside the park—in defiance of Teller's January 1883 prohibition against hunting.[39]

The park superintendent now received a salary. His ten paid assistants patrolled the park to protect the game, timber, and scenic attractions from interlopers and vandals. There were not enough horses, so the policemen often had to patrol on foot, which severely reduced their effectiveness in the massive park. Consequently, poaching and vandalism continued.

Exacerbating these problems was the fact that no penalties were attached to the park regulations that the assistants ostensibly enforced; an offender might be expelled from the park and his equipment confiscated, but nothing more. In March 1884, the Wyoming Territorial Legislature attempted to fix the problem by extending its jurisdiction, laws, and penalties over the park. Two justices of the peace and two constables were hired. While uneven, enforcement improved; however, this state of affairs was not destined to last. Complaints about the haphazard justice meted out by the courts prompted the Interior Department to dispatch attorney W. Hallet Phillips to investigate. Startlingly, he found that Wyoming's authority over the park was invalid because Congress had never affirmed it.

At about the same time, Joseph Medill, chairman of the National Republican Party, and his traveling companions, who included a judge and a congressman, were hauled before a Wyoming justice of the peace for failing to extinguish a campfire properly. Medill's indignant account appeared in his *Chicago Tribune*, along with his opinion that a national park should be subject to national laws. But no federal laws applied to Yellowstone, and after Wyoming repealed its 1884 law, no state laws did either.[40]

CHESTER ARTHUR BECAME THE first president to visit the park. Sheridan had persuaded him to see it for himself—and to get in some excellent hunting and fishing while he was at it. Arthur had succeeded President James Garfield after Garfield's assassination in 1881. The former New York machine politician had surprised everybody by running a clean administration and signing into law the Pendleton Civil Service Act in January 1883.

The expedition Sheridan led in August 1883 was the most prestigious ever to visit Yellowstone. Besides Arthur, participants included Vest; War Secretary Lincoln; Montana governor J. Schuyler Crosby, who was a Sheridan staff officer during the war; Judge D. C. Rollins of New York; Western Electric president Anson Stager of Chicago; Sheridan's brother Michael and other members of Sheridan's staff; and a seventy-five-man 5th Cavalry escort commanded by Captain Edward M. Hayes. Sheridan barred newspapermen from the party. "If we have a newspaperman along, our pleasure will be destroyed," he said. Instead, Sheridan's brother and Hayes wrote dispatches that they sent by courier to the Associated Press.

At Fort Washakie, a delegation of Shoshones and Arapahoes presented Arthur with a pony for his daughter. Following the route that Sheridan had taken to Yellowstone from Green River, Wyoming, the previous year, the party left Fort Washakie at 5 a.m. on August 9. Later in the day, the president killed a trophy elk.

Arthur was an ardent fisherman, and in anticipation of the trip, he had bought $50 worth of gear. He and Vest put it to good use along the Snake River, together reeling in 105 pounds of trout in one afternoon.

When the expedition entered Yellowstone on August 23, Sheridan reminded his guests of the prohibition against hunting. The party spent a week touring the geysers and the waterfalls before leaving to board a train for home. After twenty-five days in one another's company, the men had become friends.

IF THERE WAS ANY question about Sheridan's motive for organizing the trip, his brother Michael answered it when he wrote in his later revision of Sheridan's *Personal Memoirs*, "General Sheridan was particularly gratified with what the journey had accomplished toward benefiting the Park, gaining for its future protection not only the good-will of his influential guests, but interesting the public in its preservation to such a degree that it became comparatively easy to induce Congress to safeguard it from speculators and plunderers."

The results were evident before the end of 1883. Writing in the December 20 issue of *Forest and Stream*, Grinnell observed, "The trip . . . is already, as we predicted last summer would be the case, resulting in action for the proper preservation of the Park." Indeed, with Sheridan's encouragement, Vest and Illinois senator John Logan had little trouble persuading Congress to deny the requests by Northern Pacific Railroad's straw man companies to build spur lines into the park in 1884 and 1885—one of them ostensibly to serve gold mines on the Clarks Fork River. Another attempt in 1886 also failed.[41]

Unable to get a toehold in the park, the railroad and its spin-offs, shell companies, and allies in Congress attempted to strip Yellowstone of its national park designation and restore it to the public domain. The shoddy administration of the park warranted it, declared the pro-development forces, although conditions had recently improved. In August 1886, a House-Senate conference committee zeroed out the park's budget; the supervisor and his assistants might remain but without pay.

Congress soon had reason to rue its decision. Interior Secretary Lucius Lamar of Mississippi, a professor, judge, and former Confederate official, had one viable option remaining—Vest's amendment to the 1883 Sundry Civil Appropriations Act—and he acted on it. Lamar requested that the War Department send troops to manage, supervise, and protect Yellowstone. Sheridan ordered Company M of the 1st Cavalry, stationed at Fort Custer, Montana, to enter the park and operate it until further notice.[42]

CAPTAIN MOSES HARRIS HAD won the Medal of Honor in West Virginia before serving under Sheridan in the Shenandoah Valley twenty-two years earlier. He commanded the fifty men of Company M who reached Mammoth Hot Springs during the evening of August 17, 1886.

The troopers discovered that most of the park's now unpaid administrators had left. Superintendent David Wear was grappling with an array of problems that he was powerless to address, chief among them being three large fires burning out of control and an outbreak of lawlessness.

Making his headquarters at Mammoth Hot Springs and christening it Camp Sheridan (it later became Fort Yellowstone), Harris began imposing order. He sent detachments to fight the fires—the first such federal fire control effort. Harris laid down rules for park visitors: no cutting green timber and no hunting or trapping. Campfires were restricted, and liquor sales were banned, except at the National Hotel. He forbade visitors to throw sticks, stones, or any obstruction into the geysers—including the tourists' favorite, laundry soap, which made them foam.[43]

The army's administration of the park was provisional—subject annually to renewal by Congress. But the military proved such an efficient manager that its tenure was routinely extended, and the government also sent soldiers to oversee three other parks. No one could have predicted that the temporary arrangement in Yellowstone would last the thirty-two years that it did, until the army ceded responsibility to the new National Park Service in 1918.

Epilogue

1885–1888

Not only was he a great general, but he showed his greatness with that touch of originality which we call genius.

—PRESIDENT THEODORE ROOSEVELT,
AT THE UNVEILING OF THE SHERIDAN EQUESTRIAN
STATUE IN WASHINGTON, DC, IN 1908[1]

PHILIP SHERIDAN, THE CONSUMMATE WARRIOR who never lost a battle, became an avuncular figure around Washington, DC. A *New York World* reporter described him in mufti as he attended to the army's business in the capital: "He wore upon the back of his round, bullet head an old-fashioned silk hat about two sizes too small; a short, light yellow-gray overcoat which had only two buttons and they were ready to fly off from the undue strain of Sheridan's round figure. The trousers were a gray plaid and fitted very snugly on the General's fat legs. His boots were thick-soled and un-blacked."

Sheridan had come far from the days when he habitually slept in a wrinkled, soiled uniform and often went without food. Although heavier, his hair now iron gray, he still bore himself with "the quick, elastic gait, erect figure, and soldierly presence acquired as a cadet," wrote his brother Michael.

Sheridan made many friends in the capital; people liked his amiable, low-key manner. "Politeness is a cheap commodity that every one may possess," he liked to say, sounding like an etiquette scold rather than the renowned combat leader that he was.[2]

Indeed, middle age mellowed Sheridan and made him more thoughtful. During a speech in 1887, he optimistically predicted "a period when war would eliminate itself," when diplomacy would replace killing. "Arbitration will rule the world."

Sheridan began to enjoy some of the fruits of his years of hard service. He bought a summer cottage at Nonquitt, Massachusetts, and began spending time on Buzzard's Bay. Next door to the Sheridans lived Louisa May Alcott, author of *Little Women*.[3]

BUT HIS ENJOYMENT WAS not destined to last. In November 1887, he complained to his physician, Army major Robert O'Reilly, that he had felt unwell for months. Indeed, he was flushed and short of breath. After examining the general, O'Reilly gave Sheridan the gloomy diagnosis: he had heart disease "of the mitral and aortic valves." Rest might prolong his life, but there was nothing then known to medicine that could cure him.

Although dismaying to anyone, the news was an especially hard blow for a man of seemingly iron constitution, who had spent a lifetime in robust health and endured years of fatigue and hardship without serious illness.[4] The disease progressed rapidly. On May 22, 1888, feeling ill and exhausted after returning to Washington from a Western inspection tour, Sheridan suffered a severe heart attack. Several more followed days later.

When Sheridan's medical condition became known, Congress hastily resurrected the rank of four-star general of the army, which had been permitted to lapse with William Sherman's retirement. The day that the bill was enacted, June 1, President Grover Cleveland signed it into law. Sheridan became the fourth general of the army in the nation's history, following in the steps of George Washington, Ulysses Grant, and Sherman.[5]

June brought more setbacks. After yet another heart attack, Sheridan said, "I nearly got away from you that time, doctor." Believing that the sea breezes at Nonquitt might be restorative, Sheridan's doctor and family arranged to move him there from Washington.

On June 30, Sheridan, gaunt and pale, and his family boarded the US man-of-war *Swatara*. After stopping at Baltimore to take aboard two Catholic nuns to serve as Sheridan's nurses, the ship continued to Massachusetts.

At Nonquitt in July, Sheridan briefly regained some of his strength and energy, and he read and revised proofs of his *Personal Memoirs*. But on August 5, he suffered a massive heart attack. With Irene by his side, Sheridan died at 10:30 p.m.[6]

THE NEWS TRAVELED FAST that another of the great triumvirate of Union generals from the war was dead—Ulysses Grant having died three years earlier. Now, only Sherman remained, and he would survive for just two and half years more.

On August 8, Sheridan's remains were placed aboard a special train with an honor guard escort from two veterans' groups: the Grand Army of the Republic and the Military Order of the Loyal Legion of the United States. As the funeral train rolled slowly toward Washington, people lined the tracks to pay tribute to Sheridan, and church bells tolled in towns along the way.

Sheridan's body lay in repose in Washington at his parish church, St. Matthew's Catholic Church, until his funeral on August 11. President Cleveland, his cabinet, the justices of the Supreme Court, congressmen and senators, diplomats, and military officers attended. Before the altar, blue and yellow flowers were arranged in the shape of a four-star general's shoulder strap. Prominently displayed was Sheridan's red-and-white swallowtail pennant, whose presence on battlefields in another era had assured victory.

Among Sheridan's pallbearers were a few surviving commanders from the war: Generals William Sherman, Wesley Merritt, and Christopher Augur. Dominican priests from a monastery near Sheridan's childhood home in Ohio chanted the ancient Office of the Dead. Cardinal James Gibbons delivered the homily, closing with the words, "Comrades and companions of the illustrious dead, take hence your great leader. . . . Though you may not hope to attain his exalted rank, you will strive at least to emulate him."[7]

After the service, the coffin was laid on a caisson as the Marine Band played "Nearer My God to Thee." To the beat of muffled drums, the procession passed slowly through Washington's streets and across the Potomac River to Arlington National Cemetery. Sheridan's gravesite, located on a hillside near Robert E. Lee's former home, looked east toward Washington.

After the seventeen-gun salute, the final services, and the lowering of the remains into the earth, the mourners dispersed—all but one. The last to leave Sheridan's gravesite was Sherman.[8]

SHERIDAN'S DEATH INSPIRED AN outpouring of eulogies from colleagues, former soldiers, Northern newspapers, and ordinary people. His improbable victory at Cedar Creek was usually invoked as proof of his greatness. His actions there were even retold in verse in "In Memoriam": "His plume alone, where 'er it shone,/Was worth ten thousand men;/'Twas he snatched victory from defeat,/Our hearty commander still;/When 'er we meet, his name we'll greet,/Our matchless Little Phil."[9]

In the former Confederacy, few mourned his passing. The *Clarke Courier* wrote, "It is not to be expected that any lamentations shall be heard in the Valley of Virginia over the death of this officer. . . . They can never forget as long as they live that he resorted to the use of the torch in order to bring them into subjection."[10]

IRENE SHERIDAN NEVER REMARRIED. She and her daughters later moved to another home on Massachusetts Avenue, just a block from Sheridan Circle. There she died in 1938—fifty years after her husband's death. Friends said that she often remarked, "I would rather be Phil Sheridan's widow than any living man's wife."

A May 19, 1930, *Time* magazine article reported that Senate Bill No. 319 proposed increasing Mrs. Sheridan's annual pension from $2,500 to $5,000, but the Senate Pensions Committee had reduced the amount to $3,600. Senator Lawrence Phipps of Colorado rose and protested the committee action, and the full Senate overrode the committee's recommendation, giving Mrs. Sheridan the $5,000 pension.

The Sheridans' three daughters, Mary and twin sisters Louise and Irene, proved as devoted to their father as was Mrs. Sheridan; they never married and continued to live in the Massachusetts Avenue house until their own deaths—Louise being the last to die, in 1969. It was said that each morning, the sisters would lean out the window of their home and call out "Good morning, Papa!" to the equestrian statue within hailing distance in "Papa's Circle."

Phil Sheridan Jr. graduated from West Point in 1902 and was an aide to President Theodore Roosevelt before going on to serve on the army's general staff. He died in 1918 at the age of thirty-eight, holding the rank of major. Young Sheridan, like his mother and sisters, is buried near his father in the family plot at Arlington National Cemetery.[11]

SEVEN CITIES AND FIVE counties are named for Sheridan. So, too, were an army tank and a fort outside Chicago. In 1890 and 1891, the government issued $10 treasury notes featuring Sheridan's image and, in 1896, a $5 silver certificate. In 1937, he appeared with Sherman and Grant on a commemorative stamp—one in a series honoring army and navy heroes.[12]

HENRY DAVIES, A FORMER Sheridan staff officer and Union general, wrote that at the start of the Civil War, Sheridan was just another "solitary and friendless second lieutenant" of infantry. His career really began when he was named commander of the 2nd Michigan Cavalry in Mississippi in 1862.[13]

His talents quickly attracted the notice of superiors. They saw that Sheridan planned carefully, but more importantly, he remained alert to opportunities that he might exploit. His rare ability to improvise quickly when conditions changed set him apart from other generals. Benjamin Crowninshield, a former Sheridan aide, wrote that Sheridan was continually "watching the troops in battle, seeing for himself what was done and taking advantage of the chances that offered."[14]

Sheridan's promptness at Stones River, Missionary Ridge, Yellow Tavern, Cedar Creek, Five Forks, and Appomattox Court House had redounded to the Union's great advantage. Sheridan also transformed the Cavalry Corps into a lethal offensive weapon that combined daunting firepower and mobility. Its development began at Yellow Tavern and continued in the Shenandoah Valley, before being showcased at Five Forks and during the pursuit of Lee's army to Appomattox.

Nearly alone among Civil War generals, Sheridan conducted operations in which cavalry, infantry, and artillery supported one another. British military historian Colonel G. F. R. Henderson wrote in *The Science of War,* "With one single exception . . . [American] generals seem to have been unequal to the task of handling the three arms together on the field of battle. The single exception was Sheridan, and his operations, both in the Shenandoah Valley and during the 'last agony' of the Confederacy, are well worth the very closest study."

Seventy years later, the pioneers of armored warfare did study the cavalry and the combined operations of Sheridan and other nineteenth-century practitioners. From their efforts emerged a new template for battle, the blitzkrieg, which also incorporated a new element that Sheridan and his contemporaries never could have imagined—the warplane.[15]

Another Sheridan legacy—strategic and tactical aggressiveness—remains a cornerstone of US military doctrine today. He articulated this view in evaluating the Army of the Potomac before Grant took command: "The army was all right; the trouble was that the commanders never went out to lick anybody, but always thought first of keeping from getting licked."

Sylvanus Cadwallader, the newspaper correspondent who traveled with Grant and observed Sheridan on the battlefield many times, wrote, "Probably no living soldier was ever more terrible in battle. . . . I think it no exaggeration to say that America never produced his equal, for inspiring an army with courage and leading them into battle." Despite his repeated exposure to danger, Sheridan led a charmed existence: he was never wounded. His ethos of offensive warfare inspired generations of imitators and innovators like him, including Theodore Roosevelt, Douglas McArthur, George Patton, and, arguably, the entire Marine Corps command.[16]

A LESS PRAISEWORTHY LEGACY is Sheridan's heritage of "total war," which he waged against the Confederacy and, later, the Plains Indians. Sheridan, Grant, Sherman, and President Abraham Lincoln came to believe that to win the war, they must destroy everything that sustained the Confederacy—and not shrink from extending the destruction to Southern civilians. Total war, as practiced by Sheridan in Virginia and Sherman in Georgia, proved diabolically successful.

By waging this pitiless kind of warfare, Sheridan and his small frontier army also crushed the Plains Indians. His army campaigned in the wintertime, burned the Indians' homes and possessions, and harried them until they gave up and returned to the reservations. The slaughter of buffalo to near extinction ensured that the Indians stayed there.

When Sheridan introduced the Prussian army to total war in 1870, he never imagined that his brutal prescription for suppressing French guerrillas would snowball into a murderous pathology during Germany's twentieth-century wars. "The people must be left nothing but their eyes to weep with after the war," Sheridan memorably told Prime Minister Otto von Bismarck and his staff when they asked him how to counteract the *francs-tireurs* during the Franco-Prussian War. His suggestion of reprisals against civilians initially shocked the Prussians, who believed that civilians should be exempted from war's killing and destruction.

But Bismarck saw the sense in this approach and adopted Sheridan's proposed countermeasures. Villages that harbored suspected guerrillas were reduced to ashes. "No laziness in killing" must be allowed, Bismarck told the Prussian army command.

The draconian measures inspired by Sheridan became German army doctrine in the early 1900s. "When you meet the foe, you will defeat him. No quarter will be given and no prisoners will be taken," Kaiser Wilhelm II told German troops about to embark from Bremerhaven for China and the Boxer Rebellion in July 1900. During the Boxer uprising, no European army matched Germany's 17,000 troops in the ruthlessness of their "cleansing operations." From December 1900 into 1901, German soldiers burned twenty-six villages and murdered, raped, and plundered the Chinese.[17]

In the new German General Staff manual issued two years later, *The Law of War on Land*, the harsher policy toward civilians was made explicit. "A war conducted with energy cannot be directed merely against the combatants of the enemy States and the positions they occupy, but it will, and must, in like manner seek to destroy the total intellectual and material resources of the latter," the manual stated. "Certain severities are indispensable to war, nay more, that the only true humanity very often lies in a ruthless application of them," because it shortens war's duration— exactly what Sheridan had told Bismarck. The manual liberated German soldiers from the Geneva Conventions with the words, "What is permissible includes every means of war without which the object of the war cannot be obtained."[18]

The German troops that invaded neutral Belgium in 1914 included detachments equipped with incendiary bombs—for burning villages and homes with people inside. A German officer concisely summed up the army's policy toward Belgian civilians, whom the invaders derisively called *schweinhundes* (pig dogs): "The innocent must pay with the guilty."[19]

A total of 5,521 Belgian civilians perished at German hands, according to historian Hew Strachan. German soldiers burned to the ground an estimated 25,000 homes and other buildings in 837 Belgian communities, including the cathedral city of Louvain.[20] L. H. Grondys, a Dutch neutral who observed the German invasion, wrote, "By their coldly calculated methods they have made war, that splendid and terrible phenomenon, a thing of sickening horror."[21]

During World War II, Germany waged total war on a vast scale, killing millions of civilians in Europe and Russia and annihilating 6 million Jews as part of Adolf Hitler's mad scheme of genocide. Assuredly, Sheridan cannot be blamed. But he planted the seed of an idea with Bismarck and his staff that later bore terrible fruit.

SEEMINGLY CONTRADICTORY TO EVERYTHING Sheridan represented was his fierce defense of Yellowstone National Park. He not only saved Yellowstone from commercialization but created the template for managing future national parks across the United States. Remarkably, Sheridan also understood that a park's ecosystem might surpass its boundaries and should be protected when possible. While he failed to convince Congress to expand Yellowstone's boundaries by 3,444 square miles, others recognized the wisdom of his vision; today, Yellowstone is bordered by national forests, wilderness areas, and Grand Teton National Park—which together largely comprise the ecosystem that Sheridan envisioned.

"The place is worthy of being a National Park, the geyser phenomena and the Yellowstone Canyon having no parallel in any nation," Sheridan wrote in his report on the 1882 expedition. Protect the park's game, he urged. "Let its life be made safe while in the National Park."[22]

IN 1908, PRESIDENT THEODORE Roosevelt dedicated a fourteen-foot-high equestrian statue of Sheridan and Rienzi in Sheridan Circle, six blocks from the home where Irene and the three Sheridan daughters then lived. The secretary of war, the army chief of staff, and members of the diplomatic corps were joined by thousands of people, who filled the grandstands erected for the occasion. Lieutenant Phil Sheridan Jr. pulled the cord to unveil his father's statue, as the Marine Band struck up "The Star Spangled Banner," and field guns fired a salute. Created by Gutzon Borglum years before he began his monumental work at Mount Rushmore, the statue shows Sheridan astride Rienzi, in the act of waving his hat to urge his men to follow him back to Cedar Creek.

"Not only was he a great general, but he showed his greatness with that touch of originality which we call genius," the president told the large crowd. "Indeed, this quality of brilliance has been in one sense a disadvantage to his reputation, for it has tended to overshadow his solid ability. We tend to think of him only as the dashing cavalry leader, whereas he was in reality not only that, but also a great commander." Among other things, Roosevelt credited Sheridan with developing "the system of campaigning in winter, which, at the cost of bitter hardship and peril, finally broke down the banded strength of those formidable warriors, the horse Indians."

Brigadier General Horace Porter, the former Grant aide who had observed Sheridan's leadership firsthand at Five Forks, told the crowd that Sheridan was "gifted with the ingenuity of a Hannibal, the dash of a Murat, the courage of a Ney. . . . The magnetism of his presence forged weaklings into giants, transformed routed squadrons into charging columns, and snatched victory from defeat."[23]

NOTES

PROLOGUE

1. George Forsyth, *Thrilling Days in Army Life* (New York and London: Harper & Brothers, 1900), 139.

2. Jeffry D. Wert, *From Winchester to Cedar Creek: The Shenandoah Campaign of 1864* (Carlisle, PA: South Mountain Press, 1987), 221–222; Philip H. Sheridan, *Personal Memoirs of P. H. Sheridan, General, United States Army* (New York: Charles L. Webster & Company, 1888), 2:74–76; William F. Drake, *Little Phil: The Story of General Philip Henry Sheridan* (Prospect, CT: Biographical Publishing Company, 2005), 314; Forsyth, *Thrilling Days*, 136.

3. Forsyth, *Thrilling Days*, 137; Sheridan, *Personal Memoirs*, 2:74–77.

4. Stephen Z. Starr, *The Union Cavalry in the Civil War*, vol. 2: *The War in the East from Gettysburg to Appomattox, 1863–1865* (Baton Rouge: Louisiana State University Press, 1981), 2:312. In his memoirs, Sheridan implausibly claims that he urged on his men with these words: "If I had been with you this morning this disaster would not have happened. We must face the other way; we will go back and recover our camp." Of course, this would not inspire a retreating soldier to turn around and fight. Sheridan undoubtedly was attempting to tamp down his reputation for colorful profanity. Sheridan, *Personal Memoirs*, 2:81.

5. Frank Flinn, *Campaigning with Banks in Louisiana, '63 and '64, and with Sheridan in the Shenandoah Valley in '64 and '65* (Lynn, MA: Press of Thomas P. Nichols, 1887), 225–226.

6. Forsyth, *Thrilling Days*, 140–142.

7. George Frisbie Hoar, *Autobiography of Seventy Years*, vol. 1 (New York: Charles Scribner's Sons, 1903), 1:208–209.

I. RISE FROM OBSCURITY

1. Papers of Philip Henry Sheridan, Reel 1, Manuscript Division, Library of Congress, Washington, DC (henceforth Sheridan Papers).

2. *New York Times*, February 18, 1888; Eric J. Wittenberg, *Little Phil: A Reassessment of the Civil War Leadership of Gen. Philip H. Sheridan* (Washington, DC: Brassey's, 2002), 142–144, 147; Sheridan, *Personal Memoirs*, 1:1–2; Joseph Hergesheimer, *Sheridan: A Military Narrative* (Boston and New York: Houghton Mifflin Company, 1934), 8–10;

Richard O'Connor, *Sheridan the Inevitable* (Indianapolis and New York: Bobbs-Merrill Company, 1953), 19.

3. *Historical Statistics of the United States* (Washington, DC: Bureau of the Census, 1975), 1:106.

4. Roy Morris Jr., *Sheridan: The Life and Wars of General Phil Sheridan* (New York: Crown Publishers, 1992), 11; Richard B. Morris, ed., *Encyclopedia of American History*. 6th ed. (New York: Harper & Row, 1982), 603; Sheridan Papers, Reel 101.

5. Sheridan, *Personal Memoirs*, 1:3.

6. Henry Greiner, *General Phil Sheridan as I Knew Him, Playmate-Comrade-Friend* (Chicago: J. S. Hyland and Company, 1908), 24–27.

7. Morris, *Sheridan,* 12–15; Greiner, *General Phil Sheridan*, 50–53; Hergesheimer, *Sheridan*, 18–22.

8. O'Connor, *Sheridan the Inevitable*, 29; Morris, *Sheridan,* 12–14; Sheridan, *Personal Memoirs*, 1:7; Hergesheimer, *Sheridan*, 18–22.

9. Greiner, *General Phil Sheridan*, 56; Morris, *Sheridan,* 15–17; Ezra J. Warner, *Generals in Blue: Lives of the Union Commanders* (Baton Rouge: Louisiana State University Press, 1964), 451–453; Hergesheimer, *Sheridan*, 26; James L. Morrison Jr., *"The Best School in the World": West Point, the Pre–Civil War Years, 1833–1866* (Kent, OH: Kent State University Press, 1986), 2, 15, 19, 23, 71.

10. Morrison, *"The Best School in the World,"* 77.

11. O'Connor, *Sheridan the Inevitable*, 31–32.

12. Sheridan, *Personal Memoirs*, 1:11–12; Morris, *Sheridan,* 21–22.

13. Sheridan, *Personal Memoirs*, 1:12–14; Morrison, *"The Best School in the World,"* 88–90, 94–97; Morris, *Sheridan,* 20, 22.

14. Morrison, *"The Best School in the World,"* 5–8, 16; Sheridan, *Personal Memoirs*, 1:14.

15. Sheridan, *Personal Memoirs*, 1:15–34.

16. J. P. Dunn, *Massacres of the Mountains: A History of the Indian Wars of the Far West* (New York: Harper & Brothers, 1886), 204; Thomas Stern, *Chiefs and Change in the Oregon Country* (Corvallis: Oregon State University Press, 1992), 2:318–319, 321–324, 335–345; Sheridan, *Personal Memoirs*, 1:69, 73–74; Morris, *Sheridan,* 28–29, 32–34.

17. Morris, *Sheridan,* 32–34.

18. Sheridan, *Personal Memoirs*, 1:35–52; Morris, *Sheridan,* 22.

19. Sheridan, *Personal Memoirs*, 1:59–60.

20. Dunn, *Massacres of the Mountains*, 211–212.

21. Sheridan, *Personal Memoirs*, 1:75–80.

22. Ibid., 80–83; Dunn, *Massacres of the Mountains*, 211–212; Morris, *Sheridan,* 34.

23. Sheridan, *Personal Memoirs*, 1:85–88.

24. Ibid., 90.

25. Dunn, *Massacres of the Mountains*, 217.

26. Sheridan, *Personal Memoirs*, 1:106–119.

27. Ibid., 100–101.

28. Morris, *Sheridan,* 37.

29. Bruce Catton, *The Civil War* (Boston: Houghton Mifflin Company, 1988), 24; Morris, *Sheridan,* 41; Sheridan, *Personal Memoirs*, 1:121–123; Sheridan Papers, Reel 1.

30. Sheridan, *Personal Memoirs*, 1:123; Morris, *Sheridan*, 43.

31. William E. Parrish, "Fremont in Missouri," *Civil War Times Illustrated* 17, no. 1 (April 1978): 8–10, 40–44; Sheridan, *Personal Memoirs*, 1:124, 126.

32. Morris, *Sheridan*, 44–46; Sheridan, *Personal Memoirs*, 1:126; Edward G. Longacre, "Justus McKinstry: A Rogue's Profile," *Civil War Times Illustrated* 17, no. 4 (July 1978): 15–19.

33. O'Connor, *Sheridan the Inevitable*, 57; Grenville Dodge, *The Battle of Atlanta and Other Campaigns* (Council Bluffs, IA: Monarch Printing Company, 1910), 139.

34. Sheridan Papers, Reel 1; O'Connor, *Sheridan the Inevitable*, 60; Sheridan, *Personal Memoirs*, 1:131–135.

35. Sheridan, *Personal Memoirs*, 1:136.

36. Shelby Foote, *The Civil War: A Narrative*. 3 vols. (New York: Vintage Books, 1958–1974), 1:372; David Coffey, *Sheridan's Lieutenants: Phil Sheridan, His Generals, and the Final Year of the Civil War* (Lanham, MD: Rowman & Littlefield Publishers, 2005), xv.

37. Foote, *The Civil War*, 1:373; Morris, *Sheridan*, 55; Sheridan, *Personal Memoirs*, 1:136–137.

38. Sheridan, *Personal Memoirs*, 1:138–139; Greiner, *General Phil Sheridan*, 235–236; Hergesheimer, *Sheridan*, 35–36; Foote, *The Civil War*, 1:374.

39. Sheridan, *Personal Memoirs*, 1:139; Morris, *Sheridan*, 58; Warner, *Generals in Blue*, 442–443.

40. Sheridan, *Personal Memoirs*, 1:139–143.

41. Warner, *Generals in Blue*, 195–197; Foote, *The Civil War*, 1:384; Sheridan, *Personal Memoirs*, 1:156–157.

42. O'Connor, *Sheridan the Inevitable*, 62; Morris, *Sheridan*, 65; Sheridan, *Personal Memoirs*, 1:145–152; Sheridan Papers, Reel 1.

43. Sheridan, *Personal Memoirs*, 1:153–154.

44. *War of the Rebellion: A Compilation of the Official Records of the Union and Confederate Armies* (henceforth O.R.), V. 17, Part II, 61.

45. Ibid., 155, 159–160; O.R., V. 17, Part I, 19–20; Part II, 62; Sheridan Papers, Reel 101.

46. Sheridan, *Personal Memoirs*, 1:160–161; Sheridan Papers, Reel 101.

47. Sheridan, *Personal Memoirs*, 1:162.

48. Ibid., 162–165; O.R., V. 17, Part I, 19–20; Part II, 62–63; David S. Heidler and Jeanne T. Heidler, *Encyclopedia of the Civil War* (Santa Barbara, CA: ABC-CLIO, 2000), 249–250.

49. O.R., V. 17, Part II, 66.

50. Sheridan Papers, Reel 1.

51. Morris, *Sheridan*, 72–73; Sheridan, *Personal Memoirs*, 1:166; Sheridan Papers, Reel 101.

52. Morris, *Sheridan*, 76–77; Sheridan, *Personal Memoirs*, 1:177–180; Greiner, *General Phil Sheridan*, 399.

53. Sheridan, *Personal Memoirs*, 1:181–182; Ulysses S. Grant, *Personal Memoirs of U.S. Grant*, ed. E. B. Long (Boston: Da Capo, 1982), 210.

2. STONES RIVER

1. O.R., V. 20, Part I, 350–351.

2. Earl J. Hess, *Banners to the Breeze: The Kentucky Campaign, Corinth, and Stones River* (Lincoln: University of Nebraska Press, 2000), 193; Foote, *The Civil War*, 2:86.

3. Sheridan, *Personal Memoirs*, 1:214–220.

4. Foote, *The Civil War*, 2:87.

5. Peter Cozzens, *No Better Place to Die: The Battle of Stones River* (Urbana: University of Illinois Press, 1990), 79–80; Morris, *Sheridan*, 99.

6. Sheridan, *Personal Memoirs*, 1:220–222.

7. Ibid., 222.

8. Foote, *The Civil War*, 2:87–88; James Lee McDonough, *Stones River: Bloody Winter in Tennessee* (Knoxville: University of Tennessee Press, 1980), 85–87; Colonel Francis T. Sherman, *Quest for a Star: The Civil War Letters and Diaries of Colonel Francis T. Sherman of the 88th Illinois,* ed. C. Knight Aldrich (Knoxville: University of Tennessee Press, 1999), 21–22; Morris, *Sheridan*, 105–109; Cozzens, *No Better Place*, 82–83.

9. O.R., V. 20, Part I, 348; Foote, *The Civil War*, 2:88; Sherman, *Quest*, 22–24; Sheridan, *Personal Memoirs*, 1:222–224; Cozzens, *No Better Place*, 109; O'Connor, *Sheridan the Inevitable*, 21–22, 84; Morris, *Sheridan*, 297; Frederick C. Newhall, *With General Sheridan in Lee's Last Campaign* (Philadelphia: J. B. Lippincott & Company, 1866), 17–19, 233; Greiner, *General Phil Sheridan*, 232, from J. W. Miller, Cincinnati *Commercial*; Wittenberg, *Little Phil*, 164.

10. Foote, *The Civil War*, 2:87; McDonough, *Stones River*, 86–87.

11. David R. Logsdon, ed., *Eyewitnesses at the Battle of Stones River* (Nashville, TN: Kettle Mills Press, 2002), 18–19.

12. O.R., V. 20, Part I, 348–349; Sheridan, *Personal Memoirs*, 1:243.

13. McDonough, *Stones River*, 111–112.

14. O.R., V. 20, Part I, 349; Sheridan, *Personal Memoirs*, 1:227–230; Morris, *Sheridan*, 109.

15. Foote, *The Civil War*, 2:90; Sheridan, *Personal Memoirs*, 1:227–230; McDonough, *Stones River*, 107–110.

16. Hess, *Banners to the Breeze*, 207–212.

17. Cozzens, *No Better Place*, 127.

18. Sheridan, *Personal Memoirs*, 1:226–232; McDonough, *Stones River*, 122.

19. William M. Lamers, *The Edge of Glory: A Biography of General William S. Rosecrans, U.S.A.* (New York: Harcourt, Brace & World, 1961), 227; Sheridan, *Personal Memoirs*, 1:244.

20. O.R., V. 20, Part I, 350–351; Sheridan, *Personal Memoirs*, 1:233–234.

21. Sheridan, *Personal Memoirs*, 1:234–235; Lamers, *The Edge of Glory*, 232–234.

22. Logsdon, *Eyewitnesses*, 57; Hess, *Banners to the Breeze*, 212; Foote, *The Civil War*, 2:91–93; McDonough, *Stones River*, 131–141; Sheridan, *Personal Memoirs*, 1:235.

23. Foote, *The Civil War*, 2:94–96, 726; Lamers, *The Edge of Glory*, 234–236; Hess, *Banners to the Breeze*, 216; Logsdon, *Eyewitnesses*, 63, 66–67, 77.

24. Foote, *The Civil War*, 2:96–102; Hess, *Banners to the Breeze*, 219–220; John Beatty, *The Citizen-Soldier: The Memoirs of a Civil War Volunteer* (Lincoln: University of Nebraska

Press, 1998), 206–207; Cozzens, *No Better Place*, 177–179, 192–194; Logsdon, *Eyewitnesses*, 90; Lamers, *The Edge of Glory*, 239; Hess, *Banners to the Breeze*, 219–224; Heidler and Heidler, *Encyclopedia of the Civil War*, 250.

25. John Russell Young, *Around the World with General Grant: A Narrative of the Visit of General U.S. Grant, Ex-President of the United States, to Various Countries in Europe, Asia, and Africa, in 1877, 1878, 1879*. 2 vols. (New York: American News Company, 1879), 2:304; Sheridan, *Personal Memoirs*, 1:247.

26. Morris, *Sheridan*, 84–85; Sheridan, *Personal Memoirs*, 1:186–188.

27. Sheridan, *Personal Memoirs*, 1:190–191; Morris, *Sheridan*, 84–85.

28. O'Connor, *Sheridan the Inevitable*, 76–77; Kenneth W. Noe, *Perryville: This Grand Havoc of Battle* (Lexington: University Press of Kentucky, 2001), 98, 141; Kenneth A. Hafendorfer, *Perryville: Battle for Kentucky* (Utica, NY: McDowell Publications, 1981), 122–123, 158; Cozzens, *No Better Place*, 12–13.

29. O.R., V. 16, Part I, 1081–1082; Warner, *Generals in Blue*, 294–295; Hafendorfer, *Perryville*, 316–326; Noe, *Perryville*, 147–159, 231; Sheridan, *Personal Memoirs*, 1:194–195.

30. Foote, *The Civil War*, 1:735; Hafendorfer, *Perryville*, 316–326; Sheridan, *Personal Memoirs*, 1:194–195, 200.

31. Hess, *Banners to the Breeze*, 87–99; Noe, *Perryville*, 215, 290; Hafendorfer, *Perryville*, 242, 301, 316–326.

32. Noe, *Perryville*, 257; Robert Underwood Johnson and Clarence Clough Buel, eds. *Battles and Leaders of the Civil War* (New York: Thomas Yoseloff, 1956), 3:57n. (Terrill was buried in the same grave as his brother, Confederate general Joseph Terrill, under a headstone that read, "God alone knows which was right." O'Connor, *Sheridan the Inevitable*, 366.)

33. Noe, *Perryville*, 380–385; Sheridan, *Personal Memoirs*, 1:197–199.

34. Noe, *Perryville*, 307–308.

35. Sheridan, *Personal Memoirs*, 1:198–200.

36. Ibid., 201.

37. Warner, *Generals in Blue*, 52, 174.

38. Sheridan, *Personal Memoirs*, 1:261; Hess, *Banners to the Breeze*, 226.

39. Sheridan, *Personal Memoirs*, 1:256–258.

40. Ibid., 341; Hergesheimer, *Sheridan*, 264.

41. Sheridan, *Personal Memoirs*, 1:240.

42. Captain Henry A. Castle, "Sheridan with the Army of the Cumberland," in *Military Order of the Loyal Legion of the United States, Commandery of the District* of *Columbia*, War Papers 34 (Wilmington, NC: Barefoot Publishing Company, 1993), 166–167.

43. Sheridan, *Personal Memoirs*, 1:206–207.

44. Ibid., 256–261.

45. Ibid., 261–267.

46. Ibid., 267–268.

47. Morris, *Sheridan*, 119–120.

48. Sheridan, *Personal Memoirs*, 1:271–274.

49. William F. G. Shanks, *Personal Recollections of Distinguished Generals* (New York: Harper & Brothers, Publishers, 1866), 161; Morris, *Sheridan*, 122–123; O'Connor, *Sheridan the Inevitable*, 104–105.

50. Peter Cozzens, *The Terrible Sound: The Battle of Chickamauga* (Urbana: University of Illinois Press, 1992), 78; Sheridan, *Personal Memoirs*, 1:215–216; O'Connor, *Sheridan the Inevitable*, 106–112.

51. Sheridan, *Personal Memoirs*, 1:249–250, 274–275.

52. Douglas Southall Freeman, *Lee's Lieutenants: A Study in Command,* ed. Stephen W. Sears, abr. ed. (New York: Simon & Schuster, 1998), 618–620; Foote, *The Civil War*, 2:709–712.

53. Lamers, *The Edge of Glory*, 321–322; Sheridan, *Personal Memoirs*, 1:275–276; Glenn Tucker, *Chickamauga: Bloody Battle in the West* (Dayton, OH: Morningside House, 1961), 276; Morris, *Sheridan*, 124–127.

3. DEFEAT AND VICTORY AT CHATTANOOGA

1. Young, *Around the World*, 2:626–627.

2. Foote, *The Civil War*, 2:728–729; Sheridan, *Personal Memoirs*, 1:278–279; Lamers, *The Edge of Glory*, 334–335.

3. Foote, *The Civil War*, 2:716–718; Tucker, *Chickamauga*, 175.

4. Foote, *The Civil War*, 2:718–722; Sheridan, *Personal Memoirs*, 1:278; Lamers, *The Edge of Glory*, 332.

5. Lamers, *The Edge of Glory*, 328–329; Beatty, *The Citizen-Soldier*, 341; Foote, *The Civil War*, 2:728–735; Tucker, *Chickamauga*, 298; Sheridan, *Personal Memoirs*, 1:280.

6. O.R., V. 30, Part I, 70.

7. Gates P. Thruston, "The Crisis at Chickamauga," in *Battles and Leaders of the Civil War,* ed. Robert Underwood Johnson and Clarence Clough Buel (New York: Thomas Yoseloff, 1956), 3:663–664; Charles A. Dana, *Recollections of the Civil War* (Lincoln: University of Nebraska Press, 1996), 115; Lamers, *The Edge of Glory*, 351, 251; Sheridan, *Personal Memoirs*, 1:283.

8. Sheridan, *Personal Memoirs*, 1:282.

9. Tucker, *Chickamauga*, 291–297.

10. Captain Edwin B. Parsons, "Sheridan," in *Military Order of the Loyal Legion of the United States, Wisconsin Commandery* (Milwaukee: Burdick, Armitage & Allen, 1891), 1:277.

11. Lamers, *The Edge of Glory*, 348–350.

12. Ibid., 351; William Rosecrans, "The Campaign for Chattanooga," *The Century* 34, no. 1 (May 1887): 134.

13. Sheridan, *Personal Memoirs*, 1:282–283; Dana, *Recollections*, 115; Foote, *The Civil War*, 2:739–740; Thruston, "The Crisis at Chickamauga," 663–664.

14. O.R., V. 52, Part I, 81; Rosecrans, "The Campaign for Chattanooga," 134; Sheridan, *Personal Memoirs*, 1:283.

15. Foote, *The Civil War*, 2:752.

16. Thruston, "The Crisis at Chickamauga," 664; O.R., V. 42, Part I, 81; Sheridan, *Personal Memoirs*, 1:283–287; personal communication with James Ogden III, historian,

Chickamauga National Military Park; Foote, *The Civil War*, 2:751, 758–760; Cozzens, *Terrible Sound*, 501; Castle, "Sheridan with the Army of the Cumberland," 178; John Bowers, *Chickamauga and Chattanooga: The Battle That Doomed the Confederacy* (New York: HarperCollins Publishers, 1994), vii.

17. Sheridan, *Personal Memoirs*, 1:302, 292.

18. Cozzens, *Terrible Sound*, 389; O.R., V. 30, Part I, 38.

19. Lamers, *The Edge of Glory*, 392; Foote, *The Civil War*, 2:784–785, 763; Morris, *Sheridan*, 138.

20. Foote, *The Civil War*, 2:784–785; Lamers, *The Edge of Glory*, 392; Morris, *Sheridan*, 139; Bruce Catton, *Grant Takes Command* (Boston and Toronto: Little, Brown and Company, 1969), 34.

21. Foote, *The Civil War*, 2:804; Harry Hansen, *The Civil War* (New York: New American Library, 1961), 470; for early Chattanooga, see the Hamilton County Tennessee Genealogy Society website at www.hctgs.org/History/early_chattanooga.htm.

22. Sheridan, *Personal Memoirs*, 1:294; Catton, *Grant Takes Command*, 42–44; Lamers, *The Edge of Glory*, 372–375; Johnson and Buel, *Battles and Leaders*, 3:719.

23. Sheridan, *Personal Memoirs*, 1:294–295, 297; O'Connor, *Sheridan the Inevitable*, 124–125.

24. Sheridan, *Personal Memoirs*, 1:295–296.

25. Ibid., 1:301–302.

26. Catton, *Grant Takes Command*, 56; Foote, *The Civil War*, 2:774, 880, 806–811.

27. Hansen, *The Civil War*, 468; Lamers, *The Edge of Glory*, 364–372.

28. William S. McFeely, *Grant: A Biography* (New York and London: W. W. Norton & Company, 1982), 149; Grant, *Personal Memoirs*, 344; Foote, *The Civil War*, 2:805–806, 834.

29. Brigadier General Joseph S. Fullerton, "The Army of the Cumberland at Chattanooga," in *Battles and Leaders of the Civil War*, ed. Robert Underwood Johnson and Clarence Clough Buel (New York: Thomas Yoseloff, 1956), 3:720–721; Foote, *The Civil War*, 2:841–842; O.R., V. 31, Part II, 188–189; Sheridan, *Personal Memoirs*, 1:303–304.

30. John Hoffman, *The Confederate Collapse at the Battle of Missionary Ridge* (Dayton, OH: Morningside, 1985), 16; Sheridan, *Personal Memoirs*, 1:308; Foote, *The Civil War*, 2:851–852; Morris, *Sheridan*, 144–145.

31. Foote, *The Civil War*, 2:853; Sylvanus Cadwallader, *Three Years with Grant* (Lincoln: University of Nebraska Press, 1996), 150–154.

32. O.R., V. 31, Part II, 190; James Lee McDonough, *Chattanooga: A Death Grip on the Confederacy* (Knoxville: University of Tennessee Press, 1984), 168–169.

33. O.R., V. 31, Part II, 190; Fullerton, "The Army of the Cumberland at Chattanooga," 725; Sheridan, *Personal Memoirs*, 1:310–311.

34. O.R., V. 31, Part II, 190–191; Sheridan, *Personal Memoirs*, 1:311.

35. Fullerton, "The Army of the Cumberland at Chattanooga," 725.

36. Ibid.; Hergesheimer, *Sheridan*, 141; Sheridan, *Personal Memoirs*, 1:312; Foote, *The Civil War*, 2:854–856.

37. Frank Burr and Richard J. Hinton, *The Life of General Philip H. Sheridan* (Providence, RI: J. A. & R. A. Reid, Publishers, 1888), 131; Hansen, *The Civil War*, 474; Foote,

The Civil War, 2:855–856; Sheridan, *Personal Memoirs*, 1:311–312; Sherman, *Quest*, 85; Fullerton, "The Army of the Cumberland at Chattanooga," 725–726.

38. MacArthur was his regiment's adjutant and its fourth color-bearer; the first had been shot, the second bayoneted, and the third decapitated. As MacArthur's famous son, Douglas MacArthur, told the (probably apocryphal) story decades later, Sheridan flung his arms around Arthur when he learned of his feat and told his comrades, "Take care of him. He has just won the Medal of Honor." It was not as simple as that; MacArthur would have to wait until 1890 to receive the medal. William Manchester, *American Caesar: Douglas MacArthur, 1880–1964* [Boston and Toronto: Little, Brown and Company, 1978], 14–15.

39. Foote, *The Civil War*, 2:855–856; O'Connor, *Sheridan the Inevitable*, 137; Dana, *Recollections*, 150.

40. Foote, *The Civil War*, 2:855–857; Fullerton, "The Army of the Cumberland at Chattanooga," 726; McDonough, *Chattanooga*, 199–200; Drake, *Little Phil*, 170; Hoffman, *The Confederate Collapse*, 12–15, 21, 25.

41. Sheridan, *Personal Memoirs*, 1:313–314; O.R., V. 31, Part II, 191.

42. O.R., V. 31, Part II, 191.

43. Sheridan, *Personal Memoirs*, 1:315–316; Hansen, *The Civil War*, 475.

44. Young, *Around the World*, 2:626–627; Catton, *Grant Takes Command*, 89–90; O.R., V. 31, Part III, 270.

45. O.R., V. 31, Part II, 192; William Babcock Hazen, *A Narrative of Military Service* (Boston: Tickner and Company, 1885), 279–235; Drake, *Little Phil*, 175; Sheridan, *Personal Memoirs*, 1:318–324.

46. O.R., V. 31, Part II, 192; Sheridan, *Personal Memoirs*, 1:321; Grant, *Personal Memoirs*, 340–341.

4. SHERIDAN'S CAVALRY CORPS

1. Horace Porter, *Campaigning with Grant* (Lincoln: University of Nebraska Press, 2000), 83–84.

2. McFeely, *Grant*, 151, 154.

3. Theodore Lyman, *Meade's Headquarters, 1863–1865: Letters of Colonel Theodore Lyman from the Wilderness to Appomattox*, ed. George R. Agassiz (Boston: Atlantic Monthly Press, 1922), 80; McFeely, *Grant*, 153.

4. Newhall, *With General Sheridan*, 41–45; General Henry E. Davies, *General Sheridan* (New York: D. Appleton and Company, 1897), 90–93; Starr, *The Union Cavalry*, 2:4–5.

5. Morris, *Sheridan*, 153; Sheridan, *Personal Memoirs*, 1:346.

6. Sheridan Papers, Reel 49.

7. Robert A. Doughty and Ira D. Gruber, eds., *The American Civil War: The Emergence of Total Warfare* (Lexington, MA, and Toronto: D. C. Heath and Company, 1996), 131–133; Catton, *Grant Takes Command*, 95–96, 143; Foote, *The Civil War*, 3:15–17; McFeely, *Grant*, 157.

8. Sheridan, *Personal Memoirs*, 1:327–330; Hergesheimer, *Sheridan*, 145–148.

9. Sheridan, *Personal Memoirs*, 1:336–339; Morris, *Sheridan,*, 150–152.

10. Ulysses S. Grant, *The Papers of Ulysses S. Grant, 1837–1885,* ed. John Y. Simon. 31 vols. (Carbondale: Southern Illinois University Press, 1967–2009), 10:124 (henceforth Grant Papers).

11. Sheridan, *Personal Memoirs,* 1:339.

12. Ibid., 340–341.

13. Ibid., 342–343.

14. Ibid., 343; Sheridan Papers, Reel 1.

15. Sheridan, *Personal Memoirs,* 1:346–347.

16. Ibid., 347. (The joke has been attributed to General Joe Hooker, who reportedly made the remark to cavalry officers. Drake, *Little Phil,* 196.)

17. Porter, *Campaigning with Grant,* 24.

18. Charles C. MacConnell, "Service with Sheridan," *Military Order of the Loyal Legion of the United States Papers, Wisconsin Commandery* (Milwaukee: Burdick, Armitage & Allen, 1891), 1:286.

19. Sheridan, *Personal Memoirs,* 1:353–354; Starr, *The Union Cavalry,* 2:40–41.

20. Starr, *The Union Cavalry,* 2:78–79; O.R., V. 33, 909.

21. O.R., V. 33, 909; Sheridan, *Personal Memoirs,* 1:354–357.

22. Gregory J. W. Urwin, *Custer Victorious: The Civil War Battles of General George Armstrong Custer* (Rutherford, NJ: Fairleigh Dickinson University Press, 1983), 125.

23. Starr, *The Union Cavalry,* 2:82; Sheridan, *Personal Memoirs,* 1:349–351; Davies, *General Sheridan,* 97.

24. Coffey, *Sheridan's Lieutenants,* 5.

25. Ibid., 5–9.

26. Starr, *The Union Cavalry,* 2:4–5, 69; Edward G. Longacre, *Custer and His Wolverines: The Michigan Cavalry Brigade, 1861–1865* (Conshohocken, PA: Combined Publishing, 1977), 27; Coffey, *Sheridan's Lieutenants,* 5; Porter, *Campaigning with Grant,* 160.

27. Starr, *The Union Cavalry,* 2:32–33.

28. Foote, *The Civil War,* 3:147.

29. Starr, *The Union Cavalry,* 2:86–87; Foote, *The Civil War,* 3:143, 146; Sheridan, *Personal Memoirs,* 1:357; Morris, *Sheridan,* 156.

30. Foote, *The Civil War,* 3:150.

31. Grant, *Personal Memoirs,* 402–404; Sheridan, *Personal Memoirs,* 1:360–361.

32. Grant, *Personal Memoirs,* 405–408; Starr, *The Union Cavalry,* 2:92–93; Sheridan, *Personal Memoirs,* 1:364–365.

33. Grant, *Personal Memoirs,* 411–412; Foote, *The Civil War,* 3:188–191.

34. Starr, *The Union Cavalry,* 2:93–94; Sheridan, *Personal Memoirs,* 1:365–366; Foote, *The Civil War,* 3:198–199.

35. Foote, *The Civil War,* 3:191–192, 198–200; Davies, *General Sheridan,* 98–101; Starr, *The Union Cavalry,* 2:93–95; Sheridan, *Personal Memoirs,* 1:367–369.

36. Foote, *The Civil War,* 3:196.

37. Starr, *The Union Cavalry,* 2:87–88.

38. Porter, *Campaigning with Grant,* 83–84; Sheridan, *Personal Memoirs,* 1:367–369.

39. Sheridan, *Personal Memoirs,* 1:369.

5. KILLING JEB STUART

1. Greiner, *General Phil Sheridan*, 232.

2. Sheridan Papers, Reel 85; Foote, *The Civil War*, 3:202, 224; James H. Kidd, *Riding with Custer: Recollections of a Cavalryman in the Civil War* (Lincoln: University of Nebraska Press, 1977), 287–295; Sheridan, *Personal Memoirs*, 1:370–373.

3. Kidd, *Riding with Custer*, 295.

4. Emory Thomas, *Bold Dragon: The Life of Jeb Stuart* (New York: Harper & Row, Publishers, 1986), 18, 56–58.

5. Ibid., 92, 128; Foote, *The Civil War*, 3:228.

6. Coffey, *Sheridan's Lieutenants*, 11–12; Warner, *Generals in Blue*, 108–109; Sheridan, *Personal Memoirs*, 1:372–375; O.R., V. 36, Part I, 817; Urwin, *Custer Victorious*, 136; Starr, *The Union Cavalry*, 2:100.

7. O.R., V. 36, Part I, 817; Sheridan, *Personal Memoirs*, 1:375–376; Starr, *The Union Cavalry*, 2:101.

8. John W. Thomason Jr., *Jeb Stuart* (New York: Charles Scribner's Sons, 1930), 496.

9. Foote, *The Civil War*, 3:227–229; Sheridan, *Personal Memoirs*, 1:376–377; Longacre, *Custer and His Wolverines*, 49; Hergesheimer, *Sheridan*, 182.

10. Thomason, *Jeb Stuart*, 492; Thomas, *Bold Dragon*, 289.

11. Starr, *The Union Cavalry*, 2:101.

12. Kidd, *Riding with Custer*, 298–300; Foote, *The Civil War*, 3:230–231; O.R., V. 36, Part I, 790; Thomason, *Jeb Stuart*, 497.

13. O.R., V. 36, Part I, 790–791, 818; Hergesheimer, *Sheridan*, 182; Sheridan, *Personal Memoirs*, 1:378–379; Starr, *The Union Cavalry*, 2:101–103.

14. Foote, *The Civil War*, 3:230–231; Thomas, *Bold Dragon*, 290–293; Starr, *The Union Cavalry*, 2:102–103; Thomason, *Jeb Stuart*, 499.

15. MacConnell, "Service with Sheridan," 289; Foote, *The Civil War*, 3:232–233; O.R., V. 36, Part I, 778.

16. Foote, *The Civil War*, 3:232–233.

17. Sheridan, *Personal Memoirs*, 1:381–382.

18. Ibid., 382–385; Urwin, *Custer Victorious*, 146–147; Drake, *Little Phil*, 218–219; Linus P. Brockett, *Our Great Captains: Grant, Sherman, Thomas, Sheridan, and Farragut* (New York: Charles B. Richardson, 1866), 225; Kidd, *Riding with Custer*, 310–312; Foote, *The Civil War*, 3:232–233; O.R., V. 36, Part I, 777–779, 791, 765, 819.

19. Foote, *The Civil War*, 3:224, 234; Sheridan, *Personal Memoirs*, 1:387; Starr, *The Union Cavalry*, 2:109.

20. Starr, *The Union Cavalry*, 2:107–109; Davies, *General Sheridan*, 102; Sheridan, *Personal Memoirs*, 1:391–392; MacConnell, "Service with Sheridan," 290; Grant Papers, 10:454; Grant, *Personal Memoirs*, 422–423; O.R., V. 36, Part I, 792; John S. Bowman, ed., *The Civil War Almanac* (New York: World Almanac Publications, 1983), 201; Foote, *The Civil War*, 3:221–222, 237–239, 241.

21. Foote, *The Civil War*, 3:279, 285.

22. Ibid., 277, 306; Kidd, *Riding with Custer*, 323–327; Starr, *The Union Cavalry*, 2:117–118; Sheridan, *Personal Memoirs*, 1:399–403.

23. Kidd, *Riding with Custer*, 331; Morris, *Sheridan*, 173–174.

24. Sheridan, *Personal Memoirs*, 1:406; Morris, *Sheridan,* 173–174; Foote, *The Civil War*, 3:281–282.

25. Foote, *The Civil War*, 3:282–283; Sheridan, *Personal Memoirs*, 1:406; Kidd, *Riding with Custer*, 332; O.R., V. 36, Part II, 411.

26. Sheridan, *Personal Memoirs*, 1:408–410; O.R., V. 36, Part II, 469–470; Foote, *The Civil War*, 3:284; Kidd, *Riding with Custer*, 335.

27. Sheridan Papers, Reel 85; Sheridan, *Personal Memoirs*, 1:414–416; Foote, *The Civil War*, 3:290–296, 304; Catton, *Grant Takes Command*, 277–278; O.R., V. 36, Part III, 628.

28. Sheridan, *Personal Memoirs*, 1:418–420; Foote, *The Civil War*, 3:307; Starr, *The Union Cavalry,* 2:117, 134.

29. Edward J. Stackpole, *Sheridan in the Shenandoah*, 2nd ed. (Harrisburg, PA: Stackpole Books, 1992), 121–122; Davies, *General Sheridan*, 310–317; Newhall, *With General Sheridan*, 19–20; Kidd, *Riding with Custer*, 263–264, 298.

30. Greiner, *General Phil Sheridan*, 232.

31. Eric J. Wittenberg, *Glory Enough for All: Sheridan's Second Raid and the Battle of Trevilian Station* (Washington, DC: Brassey's, 2001), 66–72, 82, 99; Starr, *The Union Cavalry,* 2:137–138.

32. Wittenberg, *Glory Enough for All*, 107–114; Urwin, *Custer Victorious*, 159–160; Foote, *The Civil War*, 3:307–309; Starr, *The Union Cavalry,* 2:137–139.

33. Wittenberg, *Little Phil*, 135–136; Wittenberg, *Glory Enough for All*, 87.

34. Sheridan, *Personal Memoirs*, 1:421–423; Wittenberg, *Glory Enough for All*, 135–139; Urwin, *Custer Victorious*, 160; Kidd, *Riding with Custer*, 348–360.

35. Sheridan, *Personal Memoirs*, 1:423–424.

36. Starr, *The Union Cavalry,* 2:143–145; Wittenberg, *Glory Enough for All*, 189; Catton, *Grant Takes Command*, 278; Sheridan, *Personal Memoirs*, 1:424–425; Davies, *General Sheridan*, 124; Foote, *The Civil War*, 3:309–310.

37. Foote, *The Civil War*, 3:316; Wittenberg, *Glory Enough for All*, 220–221.

38. Davies, *General Sheridan*, 125–126; Drake, *Little Phil*, 234; Sheridan, *Personal Memoirs*, 1:427–428.

39. Newhall, *With General Sheridan*, 24; Starr, *The Union Cavalry,* 2:145–147, 114.

40. Sheridan, *Personal Memoirs*, 1:428.

41. Wittenberg, *Glory Enough for All*, 223, 227–228, 233; Sheridan, *Personal Memoirs*, 1:427.

42. Newhall, *With General Sheridan*, 21–22.

43. Wittenberg, *Glory Enough for All*, 265–270; Sheridan, *Personal Memoirs*, 1:432–436.

44. Starr, *The Union Cavalry,* 2:179–207; Sheridan, *Personal Memoirs*, 1:439–442.

45. Sheridan, *Personal Memoirs*, 1:445, 454–455; Davies, *General Sheridan*, 130–132; Wittenberg, *Glory Enough for All*, 314; McFeely, *Grant*, 175; Foote, *The Civil War*, 3:310; Grant, *Personal Memoirs*, 411.

6. THE SHENANDOAH VALLEY

1. O.R., V. 37, Part II, 558.

2. Scott C. Patchan, *Shenandoah Summer: The 1864 Valley Campaign* (Lincoln: University of Nebraska Press, 2007), 1; Starr, *The Union Cavalry,* 2:151; Freeman, *Lee's Lieutenants*, 210–212; Sheridan Papers, Reel 1; Sheridan, *Personal Memoirs*, 1:464–465.

3. Wert, *From Winchester*, 7.

4. Morris, *Sheridan*, 184; Foote, *The Civil War*, 3:445–446; Lieutenant General Jubal A. Early, *A Memoir of the Last Year of the War for Independence in the Confederate States of America* (Lynchburg, VA: Charles W. Button, 1867), 38–40, 48; Starr, *The Union Cavalry,* 2:224–225.

5. Early, *Memoir*, 49–50; Foote, *The Civil War*, 3:446–447. Tourists and Virginia Military Institute cadets to this day adorn Jackson's gravesite with lemons in the belief that he habitually ate lemons for indigestion. However, Jackson biographer James I. Robertson Jr. wrote that this is largely myth; Stonewall enjoyed a wide variety of fruits and vegetables. James I. Robertson Jr., *Stonewall Jackson: The Man, the Soldier, the Legend* [New York: MacMillan Publishing USA, 1997], xi.

6. Grant Papers, 10:460; Early, *Memoir*, 56–58; Foote, *The Civil War*, 3:451–459.

7. Foote, *The Civil War*, 3:45.

8. O.R., V. 37, Part II, 223; Jeffry D. Wert, *Custer: The Controversial Life of George Armstrong Custer* (New York: Simon & Schuster, 1996), 168.

9. Bowman, *Civil War Almanac*, 216; Patchan, *Shenandoah Summer*, 157, 159, 251, 260–262.

10. Early, *Memoir*, 66–70; Patchan, *Shenandoah Summer*, 271–276; Foote, *The Civil War*, 3:460–461; Freeman, *Lee's Lieutenants*, 389; Sheridan, *Personal Memoirs*, 1:460–462.

11. O.R., V. 37, Part II, 433–434; Warner, *Generals in Blue*, 159–160; Sheridan Papers, Reel 1.

12. O.R., V. 37, Part II, 433–434.

13. George Gordon Meade, *The Life and Letters of George Gordon Meade*, 2 vols. (New York: Charles Scribner's Sons, 1913), 2:218–220.

14. Warner, *Generals in Blue*, 243–244; Patchan, *Shenandoah Summer*, 27; Sheridan, *Personal Memoirs*, 1:463–466; O.R., V. 38, Part V, 408; Morris, *Sheridan,* 182; McFeely, *Grant*, 185; O.R., V. 37, Part II, 558, 582.

15. Morris, *Sheridan,* 184–185; Sheridan, *Personal Memoirs*, 1:471–475, 484, 446–452.

16. Longacre, *Custer*, 242; O'Connor, *Sheridan the Inevitable*, 193–194.

17. Longacre, *Custer*, 242; George Thomas Stevens, *Three Years in the Sixth Corps* (Albany, NY: S. R. Gray, 1866), 388; Newhall, *With General Sheridan*, 13–14, 26–27.

18. John L. Heatwole, *The Burning: Sheridan's Devastation of the Shenandoah Valley* (Charlottesville, VA: Howell Press, 1998), 7, 13; Jay W. Simson, *Crisis of Command in the Army of the Potomac: Sheridan's Search for an Effective General* (Jefferson, NC, and London: McFarland & Company, 2008), 6; Coffey, *Sheridan's Lieutenants*, 48; Sheridan, *Personal Memoirs*, 1:467–468.

19. Wert, *Custer*, 170; Davies, *General Sheridan*, 142, 147; Hergesheimer, *Sheridan*, 151–152; O'Connor, *Sheridan the Inevitable*, 193–194.

20. Sheridan, *Personal Memoirs*, 1:469.

21. Ibid., 466–467; Wert, *Custer*, 175.

22. Longacre, *Custer*, 243–244; Sheridan, *Personal Memoirs*, 1:488–492.

23. Early, *Memoir*, 74; Kidd, *Riding with Custer*, 377; Wert, *Custer*, 175–177.

24. Major General Wesley Merritt, "Sheridan in the Shenandoah Valley," in *Battles and Leaders of the Civil War,* ed. Robert Underwood Johnson and Clarence Clough Buel (New York: Thomas Yoseloff, 1956), 4:503; Sheridan, *Personal Memoirs*, 1:492, 499–500.

25. Hergesheimer, *Sheridan*, 191; Sheridan, *Personal Memoirs*, 1:470–471.

26. Sheridan, *Personal Memoirs*, 2:8.

27. Early, *Memoir*, 79–81; Urwin, *Custer Victorious*, 177.

28. Sheridan, *Personal Memoirs*, 1:498–499.

29. Drake, *Little Phil*, 245.

30. Starr, *The Union Cavalry,* 2:249, 256.

7. TRIUMPH AT WINCHESTER

1. O.R., V. 43, Part II, 124.

2. Greiner, *General Phil Sheridan*, 325–326.

3. Ibid., 327–328.

4. Sheridan, *Personal Memoirs*, 2:5–6; Foote, *The Civil War*, 3:553.

5. Grant Papers, 12:64, 89–90, 96–97, 109, 118, 137, 139.

6. Grant, *Personal Memoirs*, 474; Abraham Lincoln, *Collected Works of Abraham Lincoln,* ed. Roy Basler, 8 vols. (New Brunswick, NJ: Rutgers University Press, 1953), 7:548.

7. John William De Forest, *A Volunteer's Adventures: A Union Captain's Record of the Civil War* (New Haven, CT: Yale University Press, 1946), 171–172.

8. Grant, *Personal Memoirs*, 474.

9. Foote, *The Civil War*, 3:553–554.

10. Sheridan, *Personal Memoirs*, 2:9–11.

11. John B. Gordon, *Reminiscences of the Civil War* (New York: Charles Scribner's Sons, 1903), 319–321; Sheridan, *Personal Memoirs*, 2:10.

12. Patchan, *Shenandoah Summer*, 15–18.

13. Sheridan Papers, Reel 85; Patchan, *Shenandoah Summer*, 30; Davies, *General Sheridan*, 157–158; Gordon, *Reminiscences*, 321; Sheridan, *Personal Memoirs*, 2:22–23.

14. Sheridan, *Personal Memoirs*, 2:24–25.

15. Flinn, *Campaigning*, 188; Morris, *Sheridan*, 200; Sheridan, *Personal Memoirs*, 2:25–26.

16. O.R., V. 43, Part I, 456; Wert, *Custer*, 182; Rutherford B. Hayes, *Diaries and Letters of Rutherford Birchard Hayes, Nineteenth President of the United States,* vol. 2, *1861–1865,* ed. Charles Richard Williams (Columbus, OH: F. J. Heer Printing Company, 1922), 498, 508; Gordon, *Reminiscences*, 323; Starr, *The Union Cavalry,* 2:274–277; Carlo D'Este, *Patton: A Genius for War* (New York: HarperCollins, 1995), 17; Kidd, *Riding with Custer*, 391–394; De Forest, *A Volunteer's Adventures*, 189; Morris, *Sheridan*, 200–201.

17. Sheridan was as good as his word. After the war, when Wright and her family lost their home in Winchester and she appealed to Senator Simon Cameron of Pennsylvania for compensation for her services, Cameron forwarded her request to Sheridan, jokingly advising him either to marry Wright or to find her a job. Sheridan sent her a watch and

chain as a token of his appreciation and got Wright a job at the Treasury Department, where she worked until retirement. Sheridan Papers, Reel 94; Drake, *Little Phil,* 460–461.

18. James H. Kidd, *One of Custer's Wolverines: The Civil War Letters of Brevet Brigadier James H. Kidd, 6th Michigan Cavalry,* ed. Eric J. Wittenberg (Kent, OH: Kent State University Press, 2000), 107; Grant Papers, 12:177–178n; Sheridan, *Personal Memoirs,* 2:28–29, 31; Porter, *Campaigning with Grant,* 298; O.R., V. 43, Part I, 61; O.R., V. 43, Part II, 124.

19. O.R., V. 43, Part I, 555.

20. Foote, *The Civil War,* 3:556–557; Starr, *The Union Cavalry,* 2:278–279; Sheridan, *Personal Memoirs,* 2:33–34.

21. George Crook, *General George Crook: His Autobiography* (Norman: University of Oklahoma Press, 1960), 129–131; Sheridan, *Personal Memoirs,* 2:36–37; O.R., V. 43, Part I, 27; Davies, *General Sheridan,* 315; Starr, *The Union Cavalry,* 2:279–280; Gordon, *Reminiscences,* 326; Hayes, *Diaries and Letters,* 2:511.

22. O.R., V. 43, Part I, 26; Grant Papers, 12: 192–193.

23. Hayes, *Diaries and Letters,* 2:514.

24. Starr, *The Union Cavalry,* 2:286–289.

25. Ibid., 281.

26. Grant Papers, 12:119; Sheridan, *Personal Memoirs,* 2:41–45; O.R., V. 43, Part I, 500–501.

27. Urwin, *Custer Victorious,* 191; Starr, *The Union Cavalry,* 2:293; Coffey, *Sheridan's Lieutenants,* xvi–xvii.

28. Grant Papers, 12:269.

29. Sheridan, *Personal Memoirs,* 2:53–55.

30. Early, *Memoir,* 91.

31. O.R., V. 43, Part I, 555–556, 558–559; Freeman, *Lee's Lieutenants,* 750–751.

8. BURNING THE VALLEY

1. Heatwole, *The Burning,* 99.

2. Sheridan, *Personal Memoirs,* 1:465.

3. Ibid., 486.

4. Ibid., 485–486.

5. Wert, *Custer,* 174; Michael G. Mahon, *The Shenandoah Valley, 1861–1865: The Destruction of the Granary of the Confederacy* (Mechanicsburg, PA: Stackpole Books, 1999), 115.

6. Drake, *Little Phil,* 250–251.

7. Mark E. Neely Jr., "Was the Civil War a Total War?" in *On the Road to Total War: The American Civil War and the German Wars of Unification, 1861–1871,* ed. Stig Förster and Jörg Nagler (Cambridge: Cambridge University Press, 1997), 33–34; Förster and Nagler, *On the Road to Total War,* 10–11; Joseph Wheelan, *Libby Prison Breakout: The Daring Escape from the Notorious Civil War Prison* (New York: Public Affairs, 2010), 19–20; see the website of the International Committee of the Red Cross at www.icrc.org.

8. Sheridan, *Personal Memoirs,* 1:487–488.

9. Lincoln, *Collected Works,* 8:151.

10. Jay W. Simson, *Custer and the Front Royal Executions of 1864* (Jefferson, NC, and London: McFarland & Company, 2009), 13–16; John F. Marszalek, *Sherman: A Soldier's Passion for Order* (New York: Free Press, 1993), 294.

11. O.R., V. 39, Part III, 162, 660; O.R., V. 44, 798.

12. James M. McPherson, "From Limited War to Total War in America," in *On the Road to Total War: The American Civil War and the German Wars of Unification, 1861–1871*, ed. Stig Förster and Jörg Nagler (Cambridge: Cambridge University Press, 1997), 306–307; O.R., V. 30, Part III, 403.

13. William Tecumseh Sherman, *Memoirs of General William T. Sherman*, 2 vols. (New York: D. Appleton and Company, 1875), 2:126–127.

14. Marszalek, *Sherman*, 285, 294–295, 382, 298–300; James A. Ramage, *Gray Ghost: The Life of Colonel John Singleton Mosby* (Lexington: University Press of Kentucky, 1999), 191; Grant Papers, 12:13, 15; O.R., V. 43, Part II, 552–553; V. 39, Part II, 378.

15. O.R., V. 43, Part II, 142–143.

16. McFeely, *Grant*, 186.

17. O.R., V. 43, Part I, 822, 841, 880; Ramage, *Gray Ghost*, 194–194.

18. Starr, *The Union Cavalry*, 2:48; C. W. Denison, *Illustrated Life, Campaigns and Public Services of Philip H. Sheridan* (Philadelphia: T. B. Peterson & Brothers, 1865), 122; James Joseph Williamson, *Mosby's Rangers: A Record of the Operations of the Forty-Third Virginia Cavalry* (New York: Ralph B. Kenyon, Publisher, 1896), 41–42; Freeman, *Lee's Lieutenants*, 151.

19. Ramage, *Gray Ghost*, 194–195; Wert, *Custer*, 174–175.

20. Williamson, *Mosby's Rangers*, 240–241; Wert, *Custer*, 185.

21. Williamson, *Mosby's Rangers*, 259, 261–263; Morris, *Sheridan*, 226–227; Heatwole, *The Burning*, 115; Starr, *The Union Cavalry*, 2:344–345.

22. Years later, an account found among the papers of Frank Shaver, another of the Rebels, corroborated this version. Shaver wrote that he shot Meigs in the head, and the third Rebel, Private F. M. Campbell, shot him a second time, in the chest. George F. Skoch, "In the Shadow of the Valley," *Civil War Times Illustrated* 23, no. 5 (September 1984): 37; Heatwole, *The Burning*, 90–92; Sheridan, *Personal Memoirs*, 2:50–52.

23. Skoch, "In the Shadow of the Valley," 37–38; Heatwole, *The Burning*, 97–98; Sheridan, *Personal Memoirs*, 2:52.

24. O.R., V. 43, Part I, 442; Heatwole, *The Burning*, 51–52.

25. Sheridan, *Personal Memoirs*, 2:55–56; O.R., V. 43, Part I, 916–917.

26. Merritt, "Sheridan in the Shenandoah Valley," 512–513; Heatwole, *The Burning*, 99, 62; Foote, *The Civil War*, 3:564.

27. Sheridan, *Personal Memoirs*, 2:55–56.

28. Greiner, *General Phil Sheridan*, 314.

29. Starr, *The Union Cavalry*, 2:302–303; Heatwole, *The Burning*, 151, 169.

30. Kidd, *Riding with Custer*, 397–399.

31. Heatwole, *The Burning*, 19.

32. Grant Papers, 12:269.

33. Drake, *Little Phil*, 347; *Daily Richmond Whig*, October 15, 1864.

34. O.R., V. 43, Part I, 560; Mahon, *The Shenandoah Valley*, 126.

35. Major General Thomas L. Rosser, *Riding with Rosser* (Shippenburg, PA: Bud Street Press, 1997), iv–v; Urwin, *Custer Victorious*, 170, 195.

36. Rosser, *Riding with Rosser*, 44–45.

37. Ibid., 45–47.

38. George B. Sanford, *Fighting Rebels and Redskins: Experiences in Army Life of Colonel George B. Sanford, 1861–1892,* ed. E. R. Hagemann (Norman: University of Oklahoma Press, 1969), 283.

39. Sheridan, *Personal Memoirs*, 2:56–57; O.R., V. 43, Part I, 431, 31.

40. Rosser, *Riding with Rosser*, 47; Greiner, *General Phil Sheridan*, 357; Sheridan, *Personal Memoirs*, 2:57–58; Longacre, *Custer*, 254.

41. Sheridan, *Personal Memoirs*, 2:58; Hergesheimer, *Sheridan*, 214; O.R., V. 43, Part I, 31, 447–448; Wert, *Custer*, 191.

42. Starr, *The Union Cavalry,* 2:301.

43. Rosser, *Riding with Rosser*, 49.

44. O.R., V. 43, Part I, 559.

45. Wert, *Custer*, 185; Longacre, *Custer*, 261–262; Simson, *Custer and the Front Royal Executions of 1864*, 87–88, 91.

46. O.R., V. 43, Part II, 920.

47. Sheridan Papers, Reel 1; Wert, *From Winchester*, 166–169; Gordon, *Reminiscences*, 328–329; Stephen Dodson Ramseur, *The Bravest of the Brave: The Correspondence of Stephen Dodson Ramseur*, ed. George G. Kundahl (Chapel Hill: University of North Carolina Press, 2010), 284.

48. Gordon, *Reminiscences*, 333–334; Wert, *From Winchester*, 174–175.

49. Lieutenant General Jubal A. Early, *Autobiographical Sketch and Narrative of the War Between the States* (Philadelphia and London: J. B. Lippincott, 1912), 438.

50. Gordon, *Reminiscences*, 334–335.

51. O.R., V. 43, Part I, 51.

52. Sheridan Papers, Reel 50, Box 55.

53. O.R., V. 43, Part I, 51.

9. MIRACLE AT CEDAR CREEK

1. Aldace F. Walker, *The Vermont Brigade in the Shenandoah Valley, 1864* (Burlington, VT: Free Press Association, 1869), 148.

2. Sheridan, *Personal Memoirs*, 2:62–63.

3. Ibid., 63–65.

4. Walker, *The Vermont Brigade*, 13; Wert, *From Winchester*, 170–171; Kidd, *Riding with Custer*, 406.

5. Urwin, *Custer Victorious*, 205.

6. Early, *Memoir*, 103–105; Foote, *The Civil War*, 3:567; Wert, *From Winchester*, 175–176; Gordon, *Reminiscences*, 336–337.

7. Flinn, *Campaigning*, 212; Gordon, *Reminiscences*, 337.

8. Gordon, *Reminiscences*, 338.

9. Walker, *The Vermont Brigade*, 133–134; Wert, *From Winchester*, 176.

10. Walker, *The Vermont Brigade*, 136–137; De Forest, *A Volunteer's Adventures*, 208–209.

11. Wert, *From Winchester*, 183–186.

12. Walker, *The Vermont Brigade*, 137.

13. Hayes, *Diaries and Letters*, 2:497, 511, 524, 528.

14. Wert, *From Winchester*, 186–191.

15. Early, *Memoir*, 106; Hergesheimer, *Sheridan*, 239.

16. Hergesheimer, *Sheridan*, 231; Captain S. E. Howard, "The Morning Surprise at Cedar Creek," in *Military Order of the Loyal Legion of the United States, Massachusetts Commandery* (Boston: The Commandery, 1900), 2:417; Wert, *From Winchester*, 190–191.

17. De Forest, *A Volunteer's Adventures*, 213, 220; Howard, "The Morning Surprise," 417.

18. Wert, *From Winchester*, 192–195; Richard Bache Irwin, *History of the Nineteenth Corps* (New York and London: G. P. Putnam's Sons, 1892), 420–423; De Forest, *A Volunteer's Adventures*, 213–217; Flinn, *Campaigning*, 218–223.

19. Walker, *The Vermont Brigade*, 139.

20. Kidd, *Riding with Custer*, 414–416; Walker, *The Vermont Brigade,* 133; Wert, *From Winchester*, 207–213.

21. Gordon, *Reminiscences*, 359.

22. Ibid., 341–34.

23. Rosser, *Riding with Rosser*, 56–57.

24. O.R., V. 43, Part I, 561–562.

25. D. Augustus Dickert, *History of Kershaw's Brigade* (Newberry, SC: Elbert H. Aull Company, 1899), 449; Wert, *From Winchester*, 218; John Worsham, *One of Jackson's Foot Cavalry* (New York: Neale Publishing Company, 1912), 276.

26. Sheridan, *Personal Memoirs*, 2:66.

27. Ibid., 66–67; Wert, *From Winchester*, 221; Drake, *Little Phil*, 306.

28. Sheridan, *Personal Memoirs*, 2:78–79; Forsyth, *Thrilling Days*, 142–143; Foote, *The Civil War*, 3:570.

29. Starr, *The Union Cavalry,* 2:312; Foote, *The Civil War,* 3:570; Wert, *From Winchester,* 223.

30. Flinn, *Campaigning*, 225–226.

31. Walker, *The Vermont Brigade*, 147.

32. Sheridan, *Personal Memoirs*, 2:82–83.

33. Walker, *The Vermont Brigade*, 148.

34. Sheridan, *Personal Memoirs*, 2:82–84.

35. Stevens, *Three Years*, 222.

36. Wert, *From Winchester*, 223; Walker, *The Vermont Brigade*, 148.

37. Thomas Lewis, *The Guns of Cedar Creek* (New York: Harper & Row, Publishers, 1988), 290–291; Sheridan, *Personal Memoirs*, 2:83–85.

38. Wert, *From Winchester*, 224; Irwin, *History of the Nineteenth Corps*, 431–432; Forsyth, *Thrilling Days*, 151; Hayes, *Diaries and Letters*, 2:527; Moses Granger, "The Battle of Cedar Creek," in *Sketches of War History, 1861–1865: Papers Prepared for the Ohio Commandery of the Military Order of the Loyal Legion of the United States*, ed. Robert Hunter (Cincinnati, OH: Robert Clark & Company, 1890), 3:125–126; Walker, *The Vermont Brigade*, 155; Urwin, *Custer Victorious*, 125; Sheridan, *Personal Memoirs*, 2:85.

39. Drake, *Little Phil*, 320; Granger, "The Battle of Cedar Creek," 126; Starr, *The Union Cavalry,* 2:314; Jonathan A. Noyalas, *The Battle of Cedar Creek: Victory from the Jaws of Defeat* (Charleston, SC: History Press, 2009), 61–62.

40. Forsyth, *Thrilling Days*, 152; Wert, *From Winchester*, 226–227; Noyalas, *The Battle of Cedar Creek*, 63; De Forest, *A Volunteer's Adventures*, 222.

41. Sheridan, *Personal Memoirs*, 2:86–87; Wert, *From Winchester*, 229–230.

42. Sheridan, *Personal Memoirs*, 2:88–89.

43. Forsyth, *Thrilling Days*, 160–161.

44. Starr, *The Union Cavalry*, 2:315; Gordon, *Reminiscences*, 347–348.

45. Noyalas, *The Battle of Cedar Creek*, 65; Urwin, *Custer Victorious*, 212; De Forest, *A Volunteer's Adventures*, 225, 223.

46. Greiner, *General Phil Sheridan*, 358; Sheridan, *Personal Memoirs*, 2:88–90; Walker, *The Vermont Brigade*, 152.

47. Gordon, *Reminiscences*, 348–350; Urwin, *Custer Victorious*, 214; Wert, *From Winchester*, 234.

48. Gordon, *Reminiscences*, 350.

49. Freeman, *Lee's Lieutenants*, 758–759; Wert, *From Winchester*, 236; Morris, *Sheridan*, 216–218.

50. Lewis, *The Guns of Cedar Creek*, 289–290; Wert, *From Winchester*, 238.

51. Lewis, *The Guns of Cedar Creek*, 253–254; Wert, *From Winchester*, 234.

52. Urwin, *Custer Victorious*, 215–216; Lewis, *The Guns of Cedar Creek*, 288; Forsyth, *Thrilling Days*, 160, 167; Sheridan Papers, Reel 1; Flinn, *Campaigning*, 230–231; Gordon, *Reminiscences*, 331; Walker, *The Vermont Brigade*, 153.

53. O.R., V. 43, Part I, 32–33; Sheridan Papers, Reels 11, 1.

54. Grant Papers, 12:327–328.

55. O.R., V. 43, Part I, 59–60.

56. Drake, *Little Phil*, 331.

57. Morris, *Sheridan*, 219; Lincoln, *Collected Works*, 8:58.

58. Noyalas, *The Battle of Cedar Creek*, 82; Morris, *Sheridan*, 220; Foote, *The Civil War*, 3:574. When Rienzi died in 1878, Sheridan had him stuffed. Rienzi today resides at the Smithsonian Institute. Noyalas, *The Battle of Cedar Creek*, 82.

59. David C. Whitney and Robin Vaughn Whitney, *The American Presidents* (New York: Prentice Hall Press, 1993), 140.

60. Sheridan, *Personal Memoirs*, 2:91–92; Starr, *The Union Cavalry*, 2:320; Urwin, *Custer Victorious*, 29; Dana, *Recollections*, 248–249.

61. Gordon, *Reminiscences*, 356–357, 364–365; Rosser, *Riding with Rosser*, 52; Stackpole, *Sheridan in the Shenandoah*, 364–365.

62. Freeman, *Lee's Lieutenants*, 758; Foote, *The Civil War*, 3:572; O.R., V. 43, Part I, 563.

63. O.R., V. 43, Part I, 560–564; Early, *Memoir*, 112–114.

64. Freeman, *Lee's Lieutenants*, 758, from Jedediah Hotchkiss, *Make Me a Map of the Valley: The Civil War Journal of Stonewall Jackson's Topographer*, ed. Archie P. McDonald (Dallas, TX: Southern Methodist University Press, 1973), 240–241.

65. William Tecumseh Sherman, *Home Letters of General Sherman*, ed. M. A. DeWolfe Howe (New York: Charles Scribner's Sons, 1909), 314.

66. O.R., V. 43, Part II, 552–553.

67. O.R., V. 43, Part I, 54.

10. THE END OF JUBAL EARLY'S ARMY

1. Early, *Memoir*, 125–126.
2. O.R., V. 43, Part II, 671–672.
3. Starr, *The Union Cavalry,* 2:342–343; Grant Papers, 12:397.
4. Sheridan, *Personal Memoirs*, 2:99.
5. O.R., V. 43, Part II, 687.
6. Ibid., 730; Starr, *The Union Cavalry,* 2:348–349; Morris, *Sheridan,* 229–230; Ramage, *Gray Ghost*, 232.
7. Sheridan, *Personal Memoirs*, 2:2–4; Newhall, *With General Sheridan*, 53–54.
8. Sheridan Papers, Reel 94; Sheridan, *Personal Memoirs*, 2:105; Hergesheimer, *Sheridan*, 287–288.
9. Sheridan, *Personal Memoirs*, 2:105–108; O'Connor, *Sheridan the Inevitable*, 237.
10. Gordon, *Reminiscences*, 374–375; Wert, *From Winchester*, 250.
11. O.R., V. 43, Part II, 882–884.
12. Ibid., 740–744; Sheridan Papers, Reel 50; Sheridan, *Personal Memoirs*, 2:103–104; Starr, *The Union Cavalry,* 2:337–341; Denison, *Illustrated Life*, 124–125.
13. O.R., V. 43, Part II, 830–831; Heatwole, *The Burning*, 224, 229–230.
14. Sheridan, *Personal Memoirs*, 2:112–113.
15. Sheridan Papers, Reel 94.
16. Sheridan, *Personal Memoirs*, 2:114–115.
17. Wert, *Custer*, 205–206; Simson, *Crisis of Command*, 99–100; Sheridan, *Personal Memoirs*, 2:112.
18. Sheridan, *Personal Memoirs*, 2:109–112; Sheridan Papers, Reel 94.
19. Urwin, *Custer Victorious*, 228; Sheridan, *Personal Memoirs*, 2:114.
20. Starr, *The Union Cavalry,* 2:371–374; Urwin, *Custer Victorious*, 228–230; Sheridan, *Personal Memoirs*, 2:116; Early, *Memoir*, 125–126.
21. Sheridan, *Personal Memoirs*, 2:118; Drake, *Little Phil*, 356.
22. Sheridan, *Personal Memoirs*, 2:118–120.
23. Starr, *The Union Cavalry,* 2:383; Early, *Memoir*, 129, appendix A; Wert, *From Winchester*, 248.
24. Sheridan, *Personal Memoirs*, 2:123; Drake, *Little Phil*, 358.
25. Starr, *The Union Cavalry,* 2:421; Morris, *Sheridan,* 240; Newhall, *With General Sheridan*, 33, 36; Sheridan, *Personal Memoirs*, 2:130.

11. WATERLOO FOR THE CONFEDERACY

1. Joshua Lawrence Chamberlain, *The Passing of the Armies: An Account of the Final Campaign of the Army of the Potomac* (Lincoln: University of Nebraska Press, 1998), 438–441.
2. Jay Winik, *April 1865: The Month That Saved America* (New York: HarperCollins Publishers, 2001), 29; Foote, *The Civil War*, 3:853; Sheridan, *Personal Memoirs*, 2:130; Starr, *The Union Cavalry,* 2:425–428; Cadwallader, *Three Years with Grant*, 306; Simson, *Crisis of Command*, 10; Wittenberg, *Little Phil*, 150.
3. Edward G. Longacre, *The Cavalry at Appomattox* (Mechanicsburg, PA: Stackpole Books, 2003), 39; Starr, *The Union Cavalry,* 2:425–426; Porter, *Campaigning with Grant*, 422.

4. Catton, *Grant Takes Command*, 437; Grant, *Personal Memoirs*, 531; Sheridan, *Personal Memoirs*, 2:128–129; Adam Badeau, *Military History of Ulysses S. Grant, From April, 1861, to April, 1865* (New York: D. Appleton and Company, 1882), 3:451.

5. Sheridan, *Personal Memoirs*, 2:132–133.

6. Gordon, *Reminiscences*, 386–392, 416.

7. Winik, *April 1865*, 33.

8. Foote, *The Civil War*, 3:840–842.

9. Sheridan, *Personal Memoirs*, 2:134–135; O.R., V. 46, Part III, 266; Chris Calkins, *History and Tour Guide of the Battle of Five Forks* (Columbus, OH: *Blue & Gray Magazine*, 2003), 54.

10. Starr, *The Union Cavalry*, 2:425–428; Sheridan, *Personal Memoirs*, 2:137–139.

11. Starr, *The Union Cavalry*, 2:432–433; Porter, *Campaigning with Grant*, 426–427; Wert, *Custer*, 214–215.

12. Starr, *The Union Cavalry*, 2:433; Sheridan, *Personal Memoirs*, 2:140; Newhall, *With General Sheridan*, 56, 61–62.

13. Sheridan Papers, Reel 50.

14. Porter, *Campaigning with Grant*, 428–429; Grant, *Personal Memoirs*, 531; Sheridan, *Personal Memoirs*, 2:143–145.

15. Sheridan, *Personal Memoirs*, 2:148; Starr, *The Union Cavalry*, 2:429–430; Longacre, *Cavalry*, 36; Ed Bearss and Chris Calkins, *Battle of Five Forks* (Lynchburg, VA: H. E. Howard, 1985), 10–13.

16. Porter, *Campaigning with Grant*, 431; Sheridan, *Personal Memoirs*, 2:148–152; Newhall, *With General Sheridan*, 64–70; Longacre, *Cavalry*, 68–74; Henry Edwin Tremain, *Last Hours of Sheridan's Cavalry* (New York: Bonnell, Silver & Bowers, 1904), 50.

17. Tremain, *Last Hours of Sheridan's Cavalry*, 54; Major General Wesley Merritt, "The Appomattox Campaign," *Military Order of the Loyal Legion of the United States, Missouri Commandery* (St. Louis: Smith & Owens Print Co., 1887), 1:112–113; Sheridan, *Personal Memoirs*, 2:153; Newhall, *With General Sheridan*, 70–72; Bearss and Calkins, *Battle of Five Forks*, 43, 45.

18. Porter, *Campaigning with Grant*, 432; Sheridan, *Personal Memoirs*, 2:154–156; Newhall, *With General Sheridan*, 88; O.R., V. 46, Part I, 1104.

19. Sheridan, *Personal Memoirs*, 2:156–157; Bearss and Calkins, *Battle of Five Forks*, 73–75; Calkins, *History and Tour Guide*, 68.

20. Hergesheimer, *Sheridan*, 299–301; Bearss and Calkins, *Battle of Five Forks*, 59–66; Sheridan Papers, Reel 94.

21. Catton, *Grant Takes Command*, 231; Grant, *Personal Memoirs*, 534–535.

22. Morrison, *"The Best School in the World,"* 6; William H. Goetzmann, *Exploration and Empire* (New York: W. W. Norton & Company, 1978), 316; Simson, *Crisis of Command*, 122–124; Warner, *Generals in Blue*, 541–542.

23. Porter, *Campaigning with Grant*, 434–435; Newhall, *With General Sheridan*, 93–95; Sheridan Papers, Reel 94.

24. Newhall, *With General Sheridan*, 95–99.

25. Porter, *Campaigning with Grant*, 435.

26. Sheridan, *Personal Memoirs*, 2:160–161; Newhall, *With General Sheridan*, 99.

27. Newhall, *With General Sheridan*, 99.

28. Foote, *The Civil War*, 3:870; Starr, *The Union Cavalry,* 2:447–448.

29. Calkins, *History and Tour Guide*, 180–181.

30. Freeman, *Lee's Lieutenants*, 779–781; Longacre, *Cavalry*, 88–89.

31. Bearss and Calkins, *Battle of Five Forks*, 77, 85, 89, 91; Drake, *Little Phil*, 388; Longacre, *Cavalry*, 86; Newhall, *With General Sheridan*, 105; Merritt, "The Appomattox Campaign," 116; Porter, *Campaigning with Grant*, 437.

32. Bearss and Calkins, *Battle of Five Forks*, 69–70; Chamberlain, *The Passing of the Armies*, 130.

33. Porter, *Campaigning with Grant*, 437–438.

34. O.R., V. 46, Part I, 835–836 (Warren's report); Ibid., 1105; Foote, *The Civil War*, 3:873; O'Connor, *Sheridan the Inevitable*, 254; Newhall, *With General Sheridan*, 122; Sheridan, *Personal Memoirs*, 2:163; Starr, *The Union Cavalry,* 2:449; Morris, *Sheridan,* 252; William Henry Powell, *The Fifth Army Corps (Army of the Potomac)* (New York: G. P. Putnam's, 1896), 809.

35. O.R., V. 46, Part I, 1105, 833; Grant, *Personal Memoirs*, 535.

36. Warner, *Generals in Blue*, 542; Sheridan Papers, Reel 94; Sheridan, *Personal Memoirs*, 2:167–168; Sheridan Papers, Reel 14.

37. Chamberlain, *The Passing of the Armies*, 153–154.

38. Porter, *Campaigning with Grant*, 438–441.

39. Newhall, *With General Sheridan*, 123; Foote, *The Civil War*, 3:873–875; Starr, *The Union Cavalry,* 2:453; O.R., V. 46, Part I, 54; Porter, *Campaigning with Grant*, 442.

12. THE RACE TO APPOMATTOX

1. Catton, *Grant Takes Command*, 462.

2. Starr, *The Union Cavalry,* 2:455; Winik, *April 1865*, 99; Newhall, *With General Sheridan*, 131.

3. Bearss and Calkins, *Battle of Five Forks*, 2; William Marvel, *Lee's Last Retreat: The Flight to Appomattox* (Chapel Hill and London: University of North Carolina Press, 2002), 202.

4. Foote, *The Civil War*, 3:279, 285; Marvel, *Lee's Last Retreat*, 5–6, 9, 202–203; Winik, *April 1865*, 99.

5. Emory Thomas, *Robert E. Lee: A Biography* (New York and London: W. W. Norton & Company, 1995), 352–353; Marvel, *Lee's Last Retreat*, 9, 11; Starr, *The Union Cavalry,* 2:454; Winik, *April 1865*, 104.

6. Winik, *April 1865*, 75; Freeman, *Lee's Lieutenants*, 786–788; Marvel, *Lee's Last Retreat*, 25–26.

7. O.R., V. 46, Part III, 529; Thomas, *Robert E. Lee*, 356; Starr, *The Union Cavalry,* 2:457; Winik, *April 1865*, 126–127; Freeman, *Lee's Lieutenants*, 789; Grant, *Personal Memoirs*, 561; Marvel, *Lee's Last Retreat*, 50; Calkins, *History and Tour Guide*, 126.

8. O.R., V. 46, Part III, 449, 528.

9. Sheridan, *Personal Memoirs*, 2:175; Marvel, *Lee's Last Retreat*, 45–46.

10. Longacre, *Cavalry*, 128–129.

11. Starr, *The Union Cavalry,* 2:463; Longacre, *Cavalry*, 130–132; Newhall, *With General Sheridan*, 144–146; Sheridan, *Personal Memoirs*, 2:177.

12. Sheridan, *Personal Memoirs*, 2:177; Foote, *The Civil War*, 3:914; Newhall, *With General Sheridan*, 149–150; O.R., V. 49, Part I, 582.

13. Cadwallader, *Three Years with Grant*, 312; Grant, *Personal Memoirs*, 546; Chamberlain, *The Passing of the Armies*, 205.

14. Freeman, *Lee's Lieutenants*, 791; Marvel, *Lee's Last Retreat*, 7, 63–65; Thomas, *Robert E. Lee*, 357.

15. Chamberlain, *The Passing of the Armies*, 210, 213–214.

16. Marvel, *Lee's Last Retreat*, 79; Sheridan, *Personal Memoirs*, 2:179; Starr, *The Union Cavalry*, 2:465.

17. Grant, *Personal Memoirs*, 548.

18. Marvel, *Lee's Last Retreat*, 71, 75, 77; Grant, *Personal Memoirs*, 549; Ezra J. Warner, *Generals in Gray: Lives of the Confederate Commanders* (Baton Rouge: Louisiana State University Press, 2000), 70.

19. Drake, *Little Phil*, 408–412.

20. O.R., V. 46, Part III, 609.

21. Sheridan, *Personal Memoirs*, 2:181–182.

22. Freeman, *Lee's Lieutenants*, 794.

23. Sheridan, *Personal Memoirs*, 2:180.

24. Ibid., 182–183.

25. Newhall, *With General Sheridan*, 174–175; Marvel, *Lee's Last Retreat*, 83–86.

26. Sheridan, *Personal Memoirs*, 2:180–181.

27. Foote, *The Civil War*, 3:918.

28. Sheridan, *Personal Memoirs*, 2:183; Winik, *April 1865*, 135–136.

29. Longacre, *Cavalry*, 156; Sheridan, *Personal Memoirs*, 2:185–186; Marvel, *Lee's Last Retreat*, 91; Starr, *The Union Cavalry*, 2:473; Newhall, *With General Sheridan*, 188.

30. O.R., V. 46, Part III, 610.

31. Sheridan, *Personal Memoirs*, 2:187.

32. Edward P. Tobie, *History of the First Maine Cavalry, 1861–1865* (Boston: Emery & Hughes, 1887), 418.

33. Freeman, *Lee's Lieutenants*, 801.

34. Newhall, *With General Sheridan*, 191–192; Sheridan, *Personal Memoirs*, 2:187–188.

35. Freeman, *Lee's Lieutenants*, 799–800; Starr, *The Union Cavalry*, 2:476; Sheridan, *Personal Memoirs*, 2:188).

36. Sheridan, *Personal Memoirs*, 2:188.

37. Grant, *Personal Memoirs*, 550–551; O.R., V. 46, Part III, 619; Thomas, *Robert E. Lee*, 359–360; Sheridan Papers, Reel 50.

38. Freeman, *Lee's Lieutenants*, 802–803; Marvel, *Lee's Last Retreat*, 143, 118–120; Thomas, *Robert E. Lee*, 359–360; October 5, 2011, interview with Sam Wilson Jr., chief ranger at Sailor's Creek Battlefield Historical State Park.

39. Newhall, *With General Sheridan*, 192–194.

40. Sheridan, *Personal Memoirs*, 2:188–189.

41. Ibid., 189–190.

42. Ibid., 190; Marvel, *Lee's Last Retreat*, 150–151; Starr, *The Union Cavalry*, 2:480.

43. O.R., V. 46, Part III, 654.

44. Grant, *Personal Memoirs*, 551.

45. Sheridan, *Personal Memoirs*, 2:191; Longacre, *Cavalry*, 180.

46. O.R., V. 46, Part III, 652–654; Chamberlain, *The Passing of the Armies*, 230–231; Starr, *The Union Cavalry*, 2:483.

47. Grant, *Personal Memoirs*, 552–553; Marvel, *Lee's Last Retreat*, 156–157.

48. Starr, *The Union Cavalry*, 2:483; Sheridan, *Personal Memoirs*, 2:191–192.

49. Thomas, *Robert E. Lee*, 361; Gordon, *Reminiscences*, 436–438.

50. Sheridan, *Personal Memoirs*, 2:192; Newhall, *With General Sheridan*, 208–210; Gordon, *Reminiscences*, 436–438.

51. Foote, *The Civil War*, 3:941–943; Newhall, *With General Sheridan*, 208–211; Chamberlain, *The Passing of the Armies*, 232–236, 244; Marvel, *Lee's Last Retreat*, 170–171; Longacre, *Cavalry*, 193; Sheridan, *Personal Memoirs*, 2:193–194.

52. Longacre, *Cavalry*, 194; O'Connor, *Sheridan the Inevitable*, 268.

53. Grant, *Personal Memoirs*, 556; Freeman, *Lee's Lieutenants*, 806–807; Winik, *April 1865*, 145–146.

54. Gordon, *Reminiscences*, 438.

55. Freeman, *Lee's Lieutenants*, 807; Winik, *April 1865*, 146, 150, 166.

56. Sheridan, *Personal Memoirs*, 2:194–197; Starr, *The Union Cavalry*, 2:485. Gary commanded the famous Hampton Legion. After the surrender, he rode to North Carolina and helped escort Jefferson Davis to the Deep South. Warner, *Generals in Gray*, 102.

57. Sheridan, *Personal Memoirs*, 2:197; Gordon, *Reminiscences*, 441–442.

58. Catton, *Grant Takes Command*, 462.

59. Sheridan Papers, Reel 85; Sheridan, *Personal Memoirs*, 2:198–200.

60. Grant, *Personal Memoirs*, 554.

61. Foote, *The Civil War*, 3:945–946.

62. Forsyth, *Thrilling Days*, 184–185; Porter, *Campaigning with Grant*, 468–469; Newhall, *With General Sheridan*, 217–218; Sheridan, *Personal Memoirs*, 2:200–201; Grant, *Personal Memoirs*, 556.

63. Grant, *Personal Memoirs*, 555–556; Newhall, *With General Sheridan*, 220; Winik, *April 1865*, 186; Sheridan, *Personal Memoirs*, 2:201–202.

64. Porter, *Campaigning with Grant*, 492; Marvel, *Lee's Last Retreat*, 180.

65. Newhall, *With General Sheridan*, 200.

66. Porter, *Campaigning with Grant*, 487; Wert, *Custer*, 167; Marguerite Merington, ed., *The Custer Story: The Life and Intimate Letters of General George A. Custer and His Wife Elizabeth* (Lincoln: University of Nebraska Press, 1987), 158–159. Today, the table resides at the Smithsonian Museum of American History.

67. Sheridan, *Personal Memoirs*, 2:202–203.

68. Starr, *The Union Cavalry*, 2:430.

69. Marvel, *Lee's Last Retreat*, 188; Starr, *The Union Cavalry*, 2:489–490.

70. Sheridan, *Personal Memoirs*, 2:205–208.

13. RULER OF THE SOUTHWEST

1. Sheridan, *Personal Memoirs*, 2:261–262.

2. Grant Papers, 17:280.

3. Sheridan, *Personal Memoirs*, 2:208–209.

4. Catton, *Grant Takes Command*, 490.

5. Sheridan, *Personal Memoirs*, 2:208–210.

6. Clarence C. Clendenen, *Blood on the Border: The United States Army and the Mexican Irregulars* (Toronto: MacMillan Company, 1969), 46.

7. Sheridan, *Personal Memoirs*, 2:210; Davies, *General Sheridan*, 255–256.

8. Porter, *Campaigning with Grant*, 507; Chamberlain, *The Passing of the Armies,* 327.

9. Sheridan Papers, Reel 85.

10. Sheridan Papers, Reels 83, 85; Sheridan, *Personal Memoirs*, 2:210–214.

11. Davies, *General Sheridan*, 257; Sheridan, *Personal Memoirs*, 2:211–212.

12. Joe Gray Taylor, *Louisiana Reconstructed: 1863–1877* (Baton Rouge: Louisiana State University Press, 1974), 5–8, 407–412.

13. Sheridan, *Personal Memoirs*, 2:214; Sheridan Papers, Reel 85.

14. Sheridan, *Personal Memoirs*, 2:210, 214–218.

15. Davies, *General Sheridan*, 258–259; Clendenen, *Blood on the Border*, 57–58; Grant letters in Sheridan Papers, Reel 17; Sheridan, *Personal Memoirs*, 2:216–218, 224–226.

16. Sheridan, *Personal Memoirs*, 2:218–219.

17. Grant letter in Sheridan Papers, Reel 17; Sheridan, *Personal Memoirs*, 2:219–222.

18. Sheridan, *Personal Memoirs*, 2:220–222.

19. Ibid., 223–224.

20. Felix Gilbert, ed., *The Norton History of Modern Europe* (New York: W. W. Norton & Company, 1970), 1117–1124, 1086; Clendenen, *Blood on the Border*, 58–59; Sheridan, *Personal Memoirs*, 2:226–228.

21. Davies, *General Sheridan*, 265–269; Taylor, *Louisiana Reconstructed*, 66–68; Sheridan Papers, Reel 17.

22. Sheridan, *Personal Memoirs*, 2:261; Eric Foner, *Reconstruction: America's Unfinished Revolution, 1863–1877* (New York: Harper & Row, Publishers, 1988), 200–201, 119; Taylor, *Louisiana Reconstructed*, 98–99.

23. Morris, *Sheridan*, 293–294.

24. Sheridan, *Personal Memoirs*, 2:232–233; James M. Smallwood, Barry A. Crouch, and Larry Peacock, *Murder and Mayhem: The War of Reconstruction in Texas* (College Station: Texas A&M University Press, 2003), 42–43; Sheridan Papers, Reels 3, 85; Foner, *Reconstruction*, 204; Drake, *Little Phil*, 452, from *Army and Navy Register* 4 (November 3, 1883): 8–9.

25. Sheridan, *Personal Memoirs*, 2:235.

26. Ibid., 2:261–262.

27. *United States House Select Committee Report on the New Orleans Riots* (Washington, DC: Government Printing Office, 1867), 4; Taylor, *Louisiana Reconstructed*, 104–105; Foner, *Reconstruction*, 261–262.

28. Ted Tunnell, *Crucible of Reconstruction: War, Radicalism and Race in Louisiana, 1862–1877* (Baton Rouge: Louisiana State University Press, 1984), 104; *United States House Select Committee Report*, 26; Taylor, *Louisiana Reconstructed*, 106–107.

29. Sheridan, *Personal Memoirs*, 2:238–239; George C. Rable, *But There Was No Peace: The Role of Violence in the Politics of Reconstruction* (Athens: University of Georgia Press, 2007), 53–54; Taylor, *Louisiana Reconstructed*, 109–110.

30. Foner, *Reconstruction*, 263; Rable, *But There Was No Peace*, 54; Taylor, *Louisiana Reconstructed*, 110–111.

31. *United States House Select Committee Report*, 548; Sheridan Papers, Reel 50; Taylor, *Louisiana Reconstructed*, 110–111.

32. Sheridan, *Personal Memoirs*, 2:238–239; Taylor, *Louisiana Reconstructed*, 139; Rable, *But There Was No Peace*, 55–56.

33. Sheridan, *Personal Memoirs*, 2:237; Taylor, *Louisiana Reconstructed*, 118.

34. Rable, *But There Was No Peace*, 57–58.

35. Sheridan Papers, Reel 17; Martin E. Mantell, *Johnson, Grant, and the Politics of Reconstruction* (New York: Columbia University Press, 1973), 19–20; Whitney and Whitney, *The American Presidents*, 146–147.

36. *United States House Select Committee Report*, 25, 27, 60; Sheridan, *Personal Memoirs*, 2:240–242.

37. Mantell, *Johnson, Grant*, 27; Taylor, *Louisiana Reconstructed*, 131–132; Joseph G. Dawson III, "General Phil Sheridan and Military Reconstruction in Louisiana," *Civil War History* 24 (June 1978): 134–135; Morris, *Sheridan*, 295; Sheridan Papers, Reel 85.

38. Sheridan, *Personal Memoirs*, 2:254–255.

39. Ibid., 259; Mantell, *Johnson, Grant*, 31–33.

40. Foner, *Reconstruction*, 307; Rable, *But There Was No Peace*, 109.

41. Sheridan, *Personal Memoirs*, 2:269–275.

42. Sheridan Papers, Reel 17; Mantell, *Johnson, Grant*, 24–25, 28–29, 3–4.

43. Sheridan, *Personal Memoirs*, 2:253, 261–263; Dawson, "General Phil Sheridan," 138; Taylor, *Louisiana Reconstructed*, 141.

44. Sheridan, *Personal Memoirs*, 2:265–266.

45. Ibid., 267–268; Taylor, *Louisiana Reconstructed*, 140–141; Tunnell, *Crucible of Reconstruction*, 100–103, 111; Dawson, "General Phil Sheridan," 138, 141–143; Sheridan Papers, Reels 17, 48.

46. Sheridan Papers, Reel 17; Sheridan, *Personal Memoirs*, 2:277–278; Grant Papers, 17:253–254.

47. Morris, *Sheridan*, 293–294.

48. Ibid., 268–270; Grant Papers, 17:39n.

49. Grant Papers, 17:38–39; Sheridan Papers, Reel 85.

50. Grant Papers, 17:255; Dawson, "General Phil Sheridan," 144.

51. Mantell, *Johnson, Grant*, 35–36, 81–84.

52. Dawson, "General Phil Sheridan," 144–145; Grant Papers, 17:279–281; Sheridan Papers, Reel 3.

53. Dawson, "General Phil Sheridan," 147.

54. Sheridan, *Personal Memoirs*, 2:277–278.

55. Sheridan Papers, Reels 101, 9.

56. Sheridan Papers, Reels 83, 17.

14. WINTER WAR ON THE SOUTHERN PLAINS

1. Carl Coke Rister, *Border Command: General Phil Sheridan in the West* (Norman: University of Oklahoma Press, 1944), 66–67.

2. Ibid., 78; US Congress, *Executive Documents from the Third Session of the 40th Congress, 1868–1869* (Washington, DC: Government Printing Office, 1869), Document No. 1, 20; Sheridan Papers, Reel 91; De B. Randolph Keim, *Sheridan's Troopers on the Borders:*

A Winter Campaign on the Plains (Lincoln: University of Nebraska Press, 1985), 121–123; Paul A. Hutton, *Phil Sheridan and His Army* (Norman: University of Oklahoma Press, 1985), 32; General George A. Custer, *My Life on the Plains*, ed. Milo Milton Quaife (Lincoln: University of Nebraska Press, 1968), 392–393; Sheridan, *Personal Memoirs*, 2:320.

3. Sheridan, *Personal Memoirs*, 2:320; House Executive Document No. 1, 41–2, 47.

4. Hutton, *Phil Sheridan and His Army*, 32–33.

5. Paul H. Carlson, *The Plains Indians* (College Station: Texas A&M University Press, 1998), 155–156; Stan Hoig, *The Battle of the Washita: The Sheridan-Custer Indian Campaign of 1867–1869* (Garden City, NY: Doubleday & Company, 1976), 24, 30; Davies, *General Sheridan*, 287–288.

6. Hutton, *Phil Sheridan and His Army*, 33–35.

7. Drake, *Little Phil*, 470.

8. Rister, *Border Command*, 62–64.

9. Sheridan, *Personal Memoirs*, 2:295–296; Sheridan Papers, Reel 76; Robert M. Utley, *Frontier Regulars: The United States Army and the Indian, 1866–1891* (New York: Macmillan Publishing Company, 1973), 143.

10. Sheridan Papers, Reel 76.

11. Hutton, *Phil Sheridan and His Army*, 48–51.

12. Davies, *General Sheridan*, 288–290; Utley, *Frontier Regulars*, 48.

13. House Executive Document No. 1, 40–3, 18; Sheridan, *Personal Memoirs*, 2:302–306.

14. Hoig, *The Battle of the Washita*, 185–186; Sheridan Papers, Reel 86; House Executive Document No. 1, 40–3, 20–21, 12.

15. Senate Executive Document No. 18, 40–3, 5.

16. Robert M. Utley, "Total War on the American Indian Frontier," in *Anticipating Total War: The German and American Experiences, 1871–1914*, ed. Manfred Boemeke, Roger Chickering, and Stig Förster (Cambridge: Cambridge University Press, 1999), 405–406.

17. James L. Haley, *The Buffalo War: The History of the Red River Indian Uprising of 1874* (Garden City, NY: Doubleday & Company, 1976), 8.

18. Rister, *Border Command*, 92, 96; House Executive Document No. 1, 41–2, 45–46.

19. Hoig, *The Battle of the Washita*, 74–75; Davies, *General Sheridan*, 289–290.

20. Nathaniel Philbrick, *The Last Stand: Custer, Sitting Bull, and the Battle of the Little Bighorn* (New York: Viking, 2010), 11–12; O'Connor, *Sheridan the Inevitable*, 301; Hutton, *Phil Sheridan and His Army*, 51; Dee Brown, *The Westerners* (New York, Chicago, and San Francisco: Holt, Rinehart and Winston, 1974), 235.

21. Keim, *Sheridan's Troopers*, 103; Utley, "Total War," 405.

22. Custer, *My Life on the Plains*, 263–264.

23. Drake, *Little Phil*, 483; Custer, *My Life on the Plains*, 264.

24. Philbrick, *The Last Stand*, 132; Rister, *Border Command*, 37–41.

25. Hoig, *The Battle of the Washita*, 77–78; Sheridan, *Personal Memoirs*, 2:310–312.

26. House Executive Document No. 1, 41–2, 45–46.

27. Sheridan Papers, Reel 9; Drake, *Little Phil*, 497–498; Custer, *My Life on the Plains*, 271, 288–337; Jerome A. Greene, *Washita: The U.S. Army and the Southern Cheyennes, 1867–1869* (Norman: University of Oklahoma Press, 2004), 129; Hoig, *The Battle of the Washita*, 93, 126–134.

28. Custer, *My Life on the Plains*, 347–380; Sheridan Papers, Reel 76; Hoig, *The Battle of the Washita*, 139, 140–143, 146; Utley, *Frontier Regulars*, 151.

29. Sheridan, *Personal Memoirs*, 2:324–326; Hoig, *The Battle of the Washita*, 102–111, plate facing 77; Drake, *Little Phil*, 501–503.

30. Keim, *Sheridan's Troopers*, 137.

31. Custer, *My Life on the Plains*, 388–389; Sheridan Papers, Reel 76.

32. House Executive Document No. 1, 41–2, 48.

33. Keim, *Sheridan's Troopers*, 142–150; Rister, *Border Command*, 107–108; Sheridan Papers, Reel 76; Sheridan, *Personal Memoirs*, 2:328; Hoig, *The Battle of the Washita*, 156–257.

34. Rister, *Border Command*, 117–118; Hoig, *The Battle of the Washita*, 96; Hutton, *Phil Sheridan and His Army*, 59, 84; Keim, *Sheridan's Troopers*, 150; Lonnie J. White, ed., "The Nineteenth Kansas Cavalry in the Indian Territory, 1868–1869: Eyewitness Accounts of Sheridan's Winter Campaign," in *Indian Wars of the Red River Valley*, ed. William Leckie (Sacramento, CA: Sierra Oaks Publishing Company, 1986), 30–32.

35. Sheridan, *Personal Memoirs*, 2:318–319.

36. Sheridan Papers, Reel 76; Hoig, *The Battle of the Washita*, 91–92.

37. Sheridan, *Personal Memoirs*, 2:330.

38. Hoig, *The Battle of the Washita*, 164.

39. Ibid.; Hutton, *Phil Sheridan and His Army*, 43, 83–85.

40. Hutton, *Phil Sheridan and His Army*, 95–97; Utley, "Total War," 411; Hoig, *The Battle of the Washita*, 161–162, 193–194.

41. Rister, *Border Command*, 66–67; Hutton, *Phil Sheridan and His Army*, 98; House Executive Document No. 1, 41–2, 48.

42. House Executive Document No. 1, 41–2, 47.

43. Custer, *My Life on the Plains*, 426; Sheridan Papers, Reel 76.

44. Sheridan Papers, Reel 76.

45. Sheridan, *Personal Memoirs*, 2:334–335; Custer, *My Life on the Plains*, 458.

46. Hoig, *The Battle of the Washita*, 167.

47. House Executive Document No. 1, 41–2, 49.

48. Utley, *Frontier Regulars*, 54; Sheridan Papers, Reel 76.

49. Hoig, *The Battle of the Washita*, 168.

50. Sheridan Papers, Reel 76.

51. Rister, *Border Command*, 136–138.

52. Custer, *My Life on the Plains*, 479; Sheridan, *Personal Memoirs*, 2:344.

53. Custer, *My Life on the Plains*, 566–569, 584, 589–608.

54. Davies, *General Sheridan*, 292–293; David L. Spotts, *Campaigning with Custer and the Nineteenth Kansas Volunteer Cavalry on the Washita Campaign, 1868–1869* (New York: Argonaut Press, 1965), 125.

55. Utley, *Frontier Regulars*, 157; Hutton, *Phil Sheridan and His Army*, 111–112.

56. Sheridan Papers, Reel 17.

57. Keim, *Sheridan's Troopers*, 307; Hutton, *Phil Sheridan and His Army*, 113–114; Sheridan, *Personal Memoirs*, 2:346–347; Rister, *Border Command*, 147.

15. LIEUTENANT GENERAL SHERIDAN

1. Moritz Busch, *Bismarck: Some Secret Pages from His History*, vol. 1 (London and New York: MacMillan, 1898), 171.

2. Hutton, *Phil Sheridan and His Army*, 153–154; Drake, *Little Phil*, 539; O'Connor, *Sheridan the Inevitable*, 320.

3. Drake, *Little Phil*, 546.

4. Philip H. Sheridan and Michael Sheridan, *Personal Memoirs of Philip Henry Sheridan, General, United States Army. New and Enlarged Edition, with an Account of His Life from 1871 to His Death, in 1888*, 2 vols. (New York: D. Appleton and Company, 1902), 2:578; Utley, *Frontier Regulars*, 142.

5. Sheridan Papers, Reels 7, 101; Drake, *Little Phil*, 547; O'Connor, *Sheridan the Inevitable*, 320.

6. Hoig, *The Battle of the Washita*, 194; Robert Winston Mardock, *The Reformers and the American Indian* (Columbia: University of Missouri Press, 1971), 87–88; Sheridan Papers, Reel 8.

7. Mardock, *The Reformers*, 67–68; Sheridan Papers, Reel 85; Hutton, *Phil Sheridan and His Army*, 190–191. The death total was probably higher; the Piegans reported more than two hundred killed.

8. Sheridan Papers, Reel 85.

9. Sheridan Papers, Reel 92; Hutton, *Phil Sheridan and His Army*, 192.

10. Sheridan Papers, Reel 91; Grant Papers, 20:119–120.

11. Mardock, *The Reformers*, 67–74; Drake, *Little Phil*, 55.

12. Sheridan Papers, Reel 92; Mardock, *The Reformers*, 67–74, 95.

13. Sheridan Papers, Reel 92.

14. *Oxford Dictionary of Quotations*, 3rd ed. (Oxford and New York: Oxford University Press, 1980), 505; Drake, *Little Phil*, 517; Hutton, *Phil Sheridan and His Army*, 180.

15. Sheridan, *Personal Memoirs*, 2:348–349; Sheridan Papers, Reel 48.

16. Sheridan, *Personal Memoirs*, 2:358–359.

17. Ibid., 360–363.

18. Gilbert, *The Norton History of Modern Europe*, 1117–1124, 1086; Otto von Bismarck, *Bismarck: The Memoirs* (New York: Howard Fertig, 1966), 2:100–101.

19. Gilbert, *The Norton History of Modern Europe*, 1110–1112; Bismarck, *Bismarck*, 2:99; Stig Förster and Jörg Nagler, eds., *On the Road to Total War: The American Civil War and the German Wars of Unification, 1861–1871* (Cambridge: Cambridge University Press, 1997), 2–3.

20. Busch, *Bismarck*, 90; Sheridan, *Personal Memoirs*, 2:363–374; Hutton, *Phil Sheridan and His Army*, 202.

21. Sheridan, *Personal Memoirs*, 2:374–376; Hutton, *Phil Sheridan and His Army*, 202–203.

22. Sheridan, *Personal Memoirs*, 2:378–380.

23. Ibid., 382–383.

24. Ibid., 384–386; Rister, *Border Command*, 164; Busch, *Bismarck*, 96, 98.

25. Sheridan, *Personal Memoirs*, 2:400–410.

26. Gilbert, *The Norton History of Modern Europe*, 1127; Sheridan, *Personal Memoirs*, 2:414.

27. Busch, *Bismarck*, 1717, 223–224; Geoffrey Wawro, *The Franco-Prussian War: The German Conquest of France in 1870–1871* (Cambridge: Cambridge University Press, 2003), 237–238, 264–265, 279.

28. Grant Papers, 20:216–217; Sheridan, *Personal Memoirs*, 2:398, 448–451.

29. Sheridan, *Personal Memoirs*, 2:431–436.

30. Ibid., 436–444, 452–453; Gilbert, *The Norton History of Modern Europe*, 1166–1167; Förster and Nagler, *On the Road to Total War*, 2–3; Jay Luvaas, "The Influence of the German Wars of Unification on the United States," in *On the Road to Total War: The American Civil War and the German Wars of Unification, 1861–1871*, ed. Stig Förster and Jörg Nagler (Cambridge: Cambridge University Press, 1997), 599.

31. Sheridan Papers, Reel 85.

32. Charles M. Robinson III, *The Buffalo Hunters* (Austin, TX: State House Press, 1995), 33–41; Hutton, *Phil Sheridan and His Army*, 207.

33. Hutton, *Phil Sheridan and His Army*, 207–208.

34. Sheridan, *Personal Memoirs*, 2:300–301; General Henry E. Davies, *Ten Days on the Plains* (Dallas, TX: Southern Methodist University Press, 1983), 28.

35. Robinson, *Buffalo Hunters*, 38–41; Hutton, *Phil Sheridan and His Army*, 208.

36. Davies, *General Sheridan*, 300; Sheridan Papers, Reel 101; Hutton, *Phil Sheridan and His Army*, 208; O'Connor, *Sheridan the Inevitable*, 321; Robinson, *Buffalo Hunters*, 39–41.

37. Sheridan and Sheridan, *Personal Memoirs*, 2:486; O'Connor, *Sheridan the Inevitable*, 322; Hutton, *Phil Sheridan and His Army*, 212–215.

38. Custer, *My Life on the Plains*, 79–85.

39. Sheridan and Sheridan, *Personal Memoirs*, 2:486–487.

40. Ibid., 488–490.

41. Hutton, *Phil Sheridan and His Army*, 215–216.

42. Sheridan and Sheridan, *Personal Memoirs*, 2:495.

43. Hutton, *Phil Sheridan and His Army*, 214–215; William F. Cody, *Buffalo Bill's Life Story: An Autobiography* (New York: Cosmopolitan Book Corporation, 1920), 250–258; Robinson, *Buffalo Hunters*, 43–45.

44. Sheridan and Sheridan, *Personal Memoirs*, 2:472–482; Karen Sawislak, *Smoldering City: Chicagoans and the Great Fire, 1871–1874* (Chicago: University of Chicago Press, 1995), 53; Hutton, *Phil Sheridan and His Army*, 209–212; O'Connor, *Sheridan the Inevitable*, 312–315; Drake, *Little Phil*, 539; Sheridan Papers, Reel 3; Davies, *General Sheridan*, 299.

16. FINAL CONQUEST OF THE PLAINS INDIANS

1. John R. Cook, *The Border and the Buffalo: An Untold Story of the Southwest Plains* (Chicago: Lakeside Press, 1938), 113.

2. Utley, *Frontier Regulars*, 214, 221; Haley, *The Buffalo War*, 401–402.

3. Carlson, *The Plains Indians*, 159–160; Robinson, *Buffalo Hunters*, 18; Haley, *The Buffalo War*, 401–404.

4. Robinson, *Buffalo Hunters*, 76; Haley, *The Buffalo War*, 52–53, 56–57.

5. Robinson, *Buffalo Hunters*, 85; Haley, *The Buffalo War*, 69–70, 29.

6. Robinson, *Buffalo Hunters*, 86–87; Haley, *The Buffalo War*, 76–77; Carlson, *The Plains Indians*, 159–160.

7. Charles M. Robinson III, *Bad Hand: A Biography of General Ronald S. Mackenzie* (Austin, TX: State House Press, 1993), 57.

8. Custer, *My Life on the Plains*, 22; Hutton, *Phil Sheridan and His Army*, 145.

9. Sheridan and Sheridan, *Personal Memoirs*, 2:496; Hutton, *Phil Sheridan and His Army*, 246–247.

10. Sheridan Papers, Reel 13, Box 7; House Executive Document No. 1, 43–2, 27–29.

11. Sheridan Papers, Reel 17; David D. Smits, "The Frontier Army and the Destruction of the Buffalo," *The Western Historical Quarterly* 25, no. 3 (Autumn 1994): 317.

12. Carlson, *The Plains Indians*, ix–x; Philbrick, *The Last Stand*, 110; Smits, "The Frontier Army," 327; Utley, *Frontier Regulars*, 213; Haley, *The Buffalo War*, 21–27; Robinson, *Buffalo Hunters*, 103, 56–58, 66–67.

13. Smits, "The Frontier Army," 330.

14. Cook, *The Border and the Buffalo*, 113.

15. Smits, "The Frontier Army," 332.

16. Hutton, *Phil Sheridan and His Army*, 248.

17. William Leckie, ed., *Indian Wars of the Red River Valley* (Sacramento, CA: Sierra Oaks Publishing Company, 1986), 1–2; Haley, *The Buffalo War*, 188.

18. Robinson, *Bad Hand*, 13–38; Grant, *Personal Memoirs*, 583.

19. Robinson, *Bad Hand*, xvi–xvii, 106, 156–157; Robert G. Carter, *On the Border with Mackenzie* (Austin: Texas State Historical Association, 2007), 549.

20. Haley, *The Buffalo War*, 170. The Kiowa chief Satanta, known as the "Orator of the Plains" for his long speeches derogating the whites, actually boasted to Sherman at Fort Sill, where the Kiowas were seeking rations and sanctuary, about having killed the muleteers. Sherman angrily ordered his arrest after a tense confrontation in which someone fired an arrow at the general. Sherman ordered Satanta and fellow Kiowas Big Tree and Satank sent to Texas to stand trial for murder. Satank was killed just outside the fort while trying to escape. A Texas jury convicted Satanta and Big Tree and sentenced them to death, but Governor Edmund Davis commuted their sentences to life in prison. In 1873, over the objections of Sheridan and Sherman, the two Kiowa leaders were released as part of Grant's Peace Policy. After the Red River War, Satanta was returned to prison in Huntsville, Texas, where in 1878 he would throw himself off the prison's top story and die. Utley, *Frontier Regulars*, 209–212; Hutton, *Phil Sheridan and His Army*, 233–235; Rister, *Border Command*, 189–190.

21. Carter, *On the Border*, 422–423.

22. Ibid., 465, 458; Hutton, *Phil Sheridan and His Army*, 217–218, 222–224; Clendenen, *Blood on the Border*, 67–70; Robinson, *Bad Hand*, 143.

23. Hutton, *Phil Sheridan and His Army*, 224–226; Robinson, *Bad Hand*, 153–154; Clendenen, *Blood on the Border*, 71; Sheridan Papers, Reel 86.

24. Keim, *Sheridan's Troopers*, 181; Haley, *The Buffalo War*, 105.

25. Carter, *On the Border*, 488–495; Robinson, *Bad Hand*, 171–172; Haley, *The Buffalo War*, 173–182; Sheridan Papers, Reel 39.

26. Robinson, *Bad Hand*, 180; Haley, *The Buffalo War*, 188.

27. Utley, *Frontier Regulars,* 226–232; Hutton, *Phil Sheridan and His Army*, 257–260.

28. Rister, *Border Command*, 196; Utley, *Frontier Regulars*, 232–233; Hutton, *Phil Sheridan and His Army*, 258; Custer, *My Life on the Plains*, 533–534n.

29. Ralph K. Andrist, *The Long Death: The Last Days of the Plains Indians* (New York: Collier Books, Macmillan Publishing Company, 1993), 133–134; Carlson, *The Plains Indians*, 155–156; Utley, *Frontier Regulars*, 242–243; Custer, *My Life on the Plains*, 609n; Drake, *Little Phil*, 558–559.

30. House Executive Document No. 1, 43–2, 24–25; Sheridan Papers, Reels 6, 7; Utley, *Frontier Regulars*, 240, 244; Hutton, *Phil Sheridan and His Army*, 291–294.

31. Utley, *Frontier Regulars*, 245; Drake, *Little Phil*, 559.

32. Sheridan Papers, Reel 7; Hutton, *Phil Sheridan and His Army*, 273–274; Drake, *Little Phil*, 556–557; Rister, *Border Command*, 199; *New York Times*, June 1875.

33. Foner, *Reconstruction*, 554–555; Hutton, *Phil Sheridan and His Army*, 265–267; O'Connor, *Sheridan the Inevitable*, 328–331. Sheridan's cipher key can be viewed on Reel 6 of his papers.

34. Sheridan Papers, Reel 6; Hoar, *Autobiography*, 1:208–209; Hutton, *Phil Sheridan and His Army*, 267–272; O'Connor, *Sheridan the Inevitable*, 330–331; Foner, *Reconstruction*, 555.

35. Utley, *Frontier Regulars*, 246; Marszalek, *Sherman*, 387.

36. Sheridan Papers, Reel 7; Utley, *Frontier Regulars*, 247–248; Hutton, *Phil Sheridan and His Army*, 299–300; Carlson, *The Plains Indians*, 142, 160–161.

37. Hutton, *Phil Sheridan and His Army*, 282–283; Rister, *Border Command*, 202.

38. Sheridan Papers, Reel 7; Hutton, *Phil Sheridan and His Army*, 300–301.

39. Hutton, *Phil Sheridan and His Army*, 303; Rister, *Border Command*, 204.

40. Philbrick, *The Last Stand*, 44; McFeely, *Grant*, 428–435; *New York Times*, March 29, 1876; Sheridan Papers, Reel 7.

41. Philbrick, *The Last Stand*, 18–20.

42. Utley, *Frontier Regulars*, 236, 239; Philbrick, *The Last Stand*, 69.

43. Sheridan Papers, Reel 7.

44. Philbrick, *The Last Stand*, 55, 93–94; Utley, *Frontier Regulars*, 256.

45. Hutton, *Phil Sheridan and His Army*, 312–313.

46. Philbrick, *The Last Stand*, 286; Utley, *Frontier Regulars*, 267–268.

47. Philbrick, *The Last Stand*, 141, 314.

48. Mardock, *The Reformers*, 144.

49. Sheridan Papers, Reel 7; Hutton, *Phil Sheridan and His Army*, 322.

50. Sheridan Papers, Reel 7; Utley, *Frontier Regulars*, 267–268; Rister, *Border Command*, 210.

51. Philbrick, *The Last Stand*, 99; Sheridan Papers, Reels 7, 104.

52. Greiner, *General Phil Sheridan*, 357.

53. Utley, *Frontier Regulars*, 268–269, 278; Sheridan Papers, Reel 91.

54. Robinson, *Bad Hand*, 204.

55. Sheridan Papers, Reel 86; Robinson, *Bad Hand*, 215–221; Utley, *Frontier Regulars*, 277; Hutton, *Phil Sheridan and His Army*, 325.

56. Whitney and Whitney, *The American Presidents*, 160–161; Hutton, *Phil Sheridan and His Army*, 276–279.

57. Utley, *Frontier Regulars*, 278–279.

58. Philip H. Sheridan, *Annual Report to the Secretary of War, 1877* (Washington, DC: Government Printing Office, 1877), 1:55–56; Sheridan Papers, Reel 8; Robinson, *Bad Hand*, 232–233; Hutton, *Phil Sheridan and His Army*, 325; Utley, *Frontier Regulars*, 272, 280–281.

59. Sheridan Papers, Reels 8, 9; *Annual Report of the War Secretary, 1878*, in House Executive Document No. 1, Part 2, 45–3.

17. THE CONSERVATIONIST GENERAL

1. Philip H. Sheridan, *Report of an Exploration of Parts of Wyoming, Idaho, and Montana in August and September 1882* (Washington, DC: Government Printing Office, 1882), 18.

2. Ibid., 6–17; Aubrey L. Haines, *The Yellowstone Story: A History of Our First National Park*, 2 vols. (Yellowstone National Park, WY: Yellowstone Library and Museum Association, 1977), 1:263.

3. Sheridan was inspecting forts in the West when Chicago's 11,000 rail workers struck in October 1877 and returned after the crisis ended. Hutton, *Phil Sheridan and His Army*, 175.

4. Sheridan Papers, Reel 86; Sheridan, *Report of an Exploration*, 17; Haines, *The Yellowstone Story*, 1:259–263; Hutton, *Phil Sheridan and His Army*, 39, 264, 354–355. An example of the army command's long-standing friendships with railroad executives was Grenville Dodge, chief engineer of the Union Pacific Railroad (UPRR) and the commander of General William Sherman's XVI Corps during the Atlanta campaign. When UPRR vice president Thomas Durant tried to change Dodge's route across Wyoming in 1868, Generals Grant, Sherman, and Sheridan came to Dodge's rescue. At a meeting with Dodge and Durant at Fort Sanders, Wyoming, Grant, then a candidate for president, informed Durant that his proposed changes to Dodge's plan were unacceptable. Durant backed down. Afterward, Dodge escorted his three friends to his home in Council Bluffs, Iowa.

5. Paul A. Hutton, "Phil Sheridan's Crusade for Yellowstone," *American History Illustrated* 19, no. 10 (February 1985); Hutton, *Phil Sheridan and His Army*, 161–165; Haines, *The Yellowstone Story*, 1:138, 155, 164–173; H. Duane Hampton, *How the U.S. Cavalry Saved Our National Parks* (Bloomington: Indiana University Press, 1971), 25–28.

6. Haines, *The Yellowstone Story*, 1:179.

7. *Concise Dictionary of American Biography*, 2nd ed. (New York: Charles Scribner's Sons, 1977), 380; Haines, *The Yellowstone Story*, 1:204.

8. Haines, *The Yellowstone Story*, 1:203–205; Hampton, *How the U.S. Cavalry Saved Our National Parks*, 39–40.

9. Sheridan, *Report of an Exploration*, 18; Sheridan, *Personal Memoirs*, 1:31–32. While stationed near Eagle Pass, Texas, in 1854 and 1855, Sheridan made "stick traps" to catch and study wintering birds along the Rio Grande. He reported snaring meadowlarks, quail, plover, bluebirds, and mockingbirds.

10. Haines, *The Yellowstone Story*, 2:40.

11. Sheridan Papers, Reels 9, 10; Hutton, *Phil Sheridan and His Army*, 156.

12. Utley, *Frontier Regulars*, 290–291; Hutton, *Phil Sheridan and His Army*, 334, 182; Sheridan, *Annual Report to the Secretary of War*, 59; Keim, *Sheridan's Troopers*, viii; Sheridan Papers, Reels 9, 10.

13. Hutton, *Phil Sheridan and His Army*, 158–159; Sheridan Papers, Reels 86, 8, 91.

14. Sheridan Papers, Reels 86, 91; Hutton, *Phil Sheridan and His Army*, 337–340; O'Connor, *Sheridan the Inevitable*, 344–345.

15. Sheridan Papers, Reel 91.

16. Hutton, *Phil Sheridan and His Army*, 341–342.

17. Ibid., 360–362; Rister, *Border Command*, 218–221.

18. Sheridan Papers, Reel 91; Howard R. Lamar, ed., *The Reader's Encyclopedia of the American West* (New York: Thomas Y. Crowell Company, 1977), 290–291.

19. Warner, *Generals in Blue*, 443; Sheridan Papers, Reel 14.

20. Davies, *General Sheridan*, 1.

21. Rister, *Border Command*, 221–222; Drake, *Little Phil*, 602–603.

22. Sheridan Papers, Reels 104, 9, 10.

23. Smits, "The Frontier Army," 335, 337; C. M. MacInnes, *In the Shadow of the Rockies* (London: Rivingtons, 1930), 145–146; Sheridan Papers, Reel 12.

24. Utley, *Frontier Regulars*, 287; Smits, "The Frontier Army," 338. Sitting Bull later joined *Buffalo Bill's Wild West Show* for two national tours, charging for his autograph. In 1890, amid the Ghost Dance religious revival sweeping the Sioux nation, rumors reached Indian agent James McLaughlin at the Standing Rock Agency that Sitting Bull planned to participate. As reservation police attempted to arrest him at his cabin on December 15, 1890, a fight broke out. When the shooting stopped, Sitting Bull, a teenage son, six bodyguards, and six policemen lay dead. Lamar, *The Reader's Encyclopedia*, 1120.

25. Lamar, *The Reader's Encyclopedia*, 436–437; Utley, *Frontier Regulars*, 382–383.

26. Crook, *General George Crook*, 141.

27. Utley, *Frontier Regulars*, 194.

28. Hutton, *Phil Sheridan and His Army*, 366–367; Utley, *Frontier Regulars*, 384–386; Sheridan Papers, Reel 14.

29. Sheridan Papers, Reel 14; Robinson, *Bad Hand*, 326–328.

30. Crook, *General George Crook*, 264–265, 134; Greiner, *General Phil Sheridan*, 413.

31. Sheridan and Sheridan, *Personal Memoirs*, 2:564–565; Lamar, *The Reader's Encyclopedia*, 436–437.

32. Hutton, *Phil Sheridan and His Army*, 349–350; Drake, *Little Phil*, 605–606.

33. Sheridan and Sheridan, *Personal Memoirs*, 565; Paul A. C. Koistinen, "The Political Economy of Warfare in America, 1865–1914," in *Anticipating Total War: The German and American Experiences, 1871–1914*, ed. Manfred Boemeke, Roger Chickering, and Stig Förster (Cambridge: Cambridge University Press, 1999), 72–73; Hutton, *Phil Sheridan and His Army*, 160–162; Sheridan Papers, Reels 9, 14, 7. A week before the Battle of the Little Big Horn, Custer chose not to bring a Gatling gun, believing it would slow him down. Utley, *Frontier Regulars*, 258.

34. Hutton, *Phil Sheridan and His Army*, 140–141, 148; Sheridan Papers, Reel 14; Drake, *Little Phil*, 594, 617.

35. Rister, *Border Command*, 221–222; Drake, *Little Phil*, 619. After Phil Sheridan died in 1888, Brigadier General Michael Sheridan, aide to his older brother for a quarter century, added 124 pages to the memoirs to complete the story. The "new and enlarged" Volume II was published in 1902.

36. Hutton, *Phil Sheridan and His Army*, 349–350.

37. *Biographical Dictionary of the United States Congress, 1774–1989* (Washington, DC: Government Printing Office, 1989), 1983.

38. *Forest and Stream*, January 11, 1883, 1.

39. Haines, *The Yellowstone Story*, 1:267–269, 272; 2:59, 209–211; Hampton, *How the U.S. Cavalry Saved Our National Parks*, 58–61.

40. Haines, *The Yellowstone Story*, 1:292–304, 312, 323; Hampton, *How the U.S. Cavalry Saved Our National Parks*, 68–74. In 1894, Congress passed the Lacey Act, placing Yellowstone under the jurisdiction of Wyoming's federal courts. Hampton, *How the U.S. Cavalry Saved Our National Parks*, 123.

41. Thomas C. Reeves, "President Arthur in Yellowstone National Park," in *Montana: The Magazine of Western History* (July 1962): 19–20, 24, 27; Sheridan and Sheridan, *Personal Memoirs*, 2:539–550; Hutton, "Phil Sheridan's Crusade"; Hutton, *Phil Sheridan and His Army*, 359; Haines, *The Yellowstone Story*, 2:36–37; *Forest and Stream*, December 20, 1883.

42. Haines, *The Yellowstone Story*, 1:324–326; Hampton, *How the U.S. Cavalry Saved Our National Parks*, 79–80.

43. Hampton, *How the U.S. Cavalry Saved Our National Parks*, 82–85; Haines, *The Yellowstone Story*, 2:3.

EPILOGUE

1. *New York Times*, November 25, 1908.

2. Sheridan and Sheridan, *Personal Memoirs*, 2:573, 577; O'Connor, *Sheridan the Inevitable*, 349, 84.

3. Hutton, *Phil Sheridan and His Army*, 147; Drake, *Little Phil*, 608.

4. Sheridan and Sheridan, *Personal Memoirs*, 2:565; Drake, *Little Phil*, 621.

5. Sheridan and Sheridan, *Personal Memoirs*, 2:565–566; Sheridan Papers, Reel 14.

6. Sheridan and Sheridan, *Personal Memoirs*, 2:566–568; Drake, *Little Phil*, 622–624.

7. Sheridan and Sheridan, *Personal Memoirs*, 2:568–570.

8. Drake, *Little Phil*, 624–625; O'Connor, *Sheridan the Inevitable*, 357; Sheridan and Sheridan, *Personal Memoirs*, 2:570. Sheridan's name was carved into the entablature above

one of Arlington's eastern entrances. Known as "Sheridan's Gate," it stood until 1971. See "The History of the Sheridan Gate at Arlington National Cemetery," Arlington National Cemetery, www.arlingtoncemetery.net/sheridan-gate.htm.

9. Sheridan Papers, Reel 101.

10. Heatwole, *The Burning*, 232.

11. Morris, *Sheridan*, 390–393; O'Connor, *Sheridan the Inevitable*, 357; *Time* 15, no. 20 (May 19, 1930).

12. For images of the stamp and the $5 treasury note, see www.answers.com/topic/philip-sheridan.

13. Davies, *General Sheridan*, 306–307.

14. Benjamin W. Crowninshield, *A History of the First Regiment of Massachusetts Cavalry Volunteers* (Boston and New York: Houghton, Mifflin and Company, 1891), 38; Hergesheimer, *Sheridan*, 266–267.

15. Peter McCarthy and Mike Syron, *Panzerkrieg: The Rise and Fall of Hitler's Tank Divisions* (New York: Carroll & Graf Publishers, 2002), 19–25; Colonel G. F. R. Henderson, *The Science of War* (London and New York: Longman's, Green, and Company, 1908), 279.

16. Newhall, *With General Sheridan*, 231; Henderson, *The Science of War*, 256; Starr, *The Union Cavalry*, 2:493; Cadwallader, *Three Years with Grant*, 305; Hergesheimer, *Sheridan*, 266–267, 16.

17. Sabrina Dabringhaus, "An Army on Vacation? The German War in China, 1900–1901," in *Anticipating Total War: The German and American Experiences, 1871–1914*, ed. Manfred Boemeke, Roger Chickering, and Stig Förster (Cambridge: Cambridge University Press, 1999), 463–471.

18. E. Grimwood Mears, *The Destruction of Belgium: Germany's Confession and Avoidance* (London: William Heinemann, 1916), 7–8.

19. Jeff Lipkes, *Rehearsals: The German Army in Belgium, August 1914* (Levven, Belgium: Levven University Press, 2007), 558.

20. Hew Strachan, *The First World War* (New York and London: Viking, 2003), 49; Lipkes, *Rehearsals*, 13; Wawro, *Franco-Prussian War*, 309–310.

21. L. H. Grondys, *The Germans in Belgium: Experiences of a Neutral* (New York: D. Appleton and Company, 1916), v–vi.

22. Sheridan, *Report of an Exploration*, 17–18.

23. Greiner, *General Phil Sheridan*, 423–425; *New York Times*, November 25, 1908.

BIBLIOGRAPHY

PERIODICALS CONSULTED

The Century, 1881–1930.

Civil War History: A Journal of the Middle Period (Kent, Ohio) 24 (June 1978).

Civil War Times Illustrated, Harrisburg, Pennsylvania, 1959–.

Daily Richmond Whig, 1861–1869.

Forest and Stream Magazine, 1873–1930. Available at University of North Carolina's Davis Library, microfilm serial 1–31, reels 208–235.

Montana: The Magazine of Western History, Helena, Montana, 1955–.

New York Times, 1851–.

Time 15, no. 20 (May 19, 1930).

Western Historical Quarterly, Western Historical Association at Utah State University, Logan, 1970–

BOOKS AND ARTICLES

Andrist, Ralph K. *The Long Death: The Last Days of the Plains Indians*. New York: Collier Books, Macmillan Publishing Company, 1993. First published in 1964.

Badeau, Adam. *Military History of Ulysses S. Grant, From April, 1861, to April, 1865*. Vol. 3. New York: D. Appleton and Company, 1882.

Bearss, Ed, and Chris Calkins. *Battle of Five Forks*. Lynchburg, VA: H. E. Howard, 1985.

Beatty, John. *The Citizen-Soldier: The Memoirs of a Civil War Volunteer*. Lincoln: University of Nebraska Press, 1998.

Bierce, Ambrose. "Chickamauga." *The Norton Anthology of American Literature*. Vol. 2, 312–319. New York: W. W. Norton & Company, 1979.

———. *Phantoms of a Blood-Stained Period: The Complete Civil War Writings of Ambrose Bierce*, edited by Russell Duncan and David J. Klooster. Amherst: University of Massachusetts Press, 2002.

Biographical Dictionary of the United States Congress, 1774–1989. Washington, DC: Government Printing Office, 1989.

Bismarck, Otto von. *Bismarck: The Memoirs*. New York: Howard Fertig, 1966.

Black, Jeremy. *The Age of Total War, 1860–1945*. Westport, CT: Praeger Security International, 2006.

Boemeke, Manfred, Roger Chickering, and Stig Förster, eds. *Anticipating Total War: The German and American Experiences, 1871–1914.* Cambridge: Cambridge University Press, 1999.

Bowers, John. *Chickamauga and Chattanooga: The Battle That Doomed the Confederacy.* New York: HarperCollins Publishers, 1994.

Bowman, John S., ed. *The Civil War Almanac.* New York: World Almanac Publications, 1983.

Broadwater, Robert P. *The Battle of Perryville, 1862.* Jefferson, NC: McFarland & Company, 2005.

Brockett, Linus P. *Our Great Captains: Grant, Sherman, Thomas, Sheridan, and Farragut.* New York: Charles B. Richardson, 1866.

Brown, Dee. *The Westerners.* New York, Chicago, and San Francisco: Holt, Rinehart and Winston, 1974.

Burr, Frank, and Richard J. Hinton. *The Life of General Philip H. Sheridan.* Providence, RI: J. A. & R. A. Reid, Publishers, 1888.

Busch, Moritz. *Bismarck: Some Secret Pages from His History.* Vol. 1. London and New York: MacMillan, 1898.

Cadwallader, Sylvanus. *Three Years with Grant.* Lincoln: University of Nebraska Press, 1996.

Calkins, Chris. *History and Tour Guide of the Battle of Five Forks.* Columbus, OH: *Blue & Gray Magazine,* 2003.

Carlson, Paul H. *The Plains Indians.* College Station: Texas A&M University Press, 1998.

Carter, Robert G. *On the Border with Mackenzie.* Austin: Texas State Historical Association, 2007.

Castle, Captain Henry A. "Sheridan with the Army of the Cumberland." In *Military Order of the Loyal Legion of the United States, Commandery of the District* of *Columbia,* 2: 159–183. War Papers 34. Wilmington, NC: Barefoot Publishing Company, 1993.

Catton, Bruce. *The Civil War.* Boston: Houghton Mifflin Company, 1988. First published in 1960.

———. *Grant Takes Command.* Boston and Toronto: Little, Brown and Company, 1969.

Chamberlain, Joshua Lawrence. *The Passing of the Armies: An Account of the Final Campaign of the Army of the Potomac.* Lincoln: University of Nebraska Press, 1998.

Chickering, Roger. "Total War: The Use and Abuse of a Concept." In *Anticipating Total War: The German and American Experiences, 1871–1914,* edited by Manfred Boemeke, Roger Chickering, and Stig Förster, 13–28. Cambridge: Cambridge University Press, 1999.

Childs, George W. *Recollections of General Grant: With an Account of the Presentation of the Portraits of Generals Grant, Sherman, and Sheridan at the U.S. Military Academy, West Point.* Philadelphia: Collins Printing House, 1890.

Civil War Papers Read Before the Commandery of the State of Massachusetts, Military Order of the Loyal Legion of the United States. Vol. 1. Boston: F. W. Gilson Company, 1900.

Civil War Society. *Civil War Society's Encyclopedia of the Civil War.* Princeton, NJ: Philip Lief Group, 1997.

Clendenen, Clarence C. *Blood on the Border: The United States Army and the Mexican Irregulars*. Toronto: MacMillan Company, 1969.

Cody, William F. *Buffalo Bill's Life Story: An Autobiography*. New York: Cosmopolitan Book Corporation, 1920.

Coffey, David. *Sheridan's Lieutenants: Phil Sheridan, His Generals, and the Final Year of the Civil War*. Lanham, MD: Rowman & Littlefield Publishers, 2005.

Concise Dictionary of American Biography. 2nd ed. New York: Charles Scribner's Sons, 1977.

Cook, John R. *The Border and the Buffalo: An Untold Story of the Southwest Plains*. Chicago: Lakeside Press, 1938.

Cozzens, Peter. *No Better Place to Die: The Battle of Stones River*. Urbana: University of Illinois Press, 1990.

———. *The Terrible Sound: The Battle of Chickamauga*. Urbana: University of Illinois Press, 1992.

Crook, George. *General George Crook: His Autobiography*. Norman: University of Oklahoma Press, 1960.

Crowninshield, Benjamin W. *A History of the First Regiment of Massachusetts Cavalry Volunteers*. Boston and New York: Houghton, Mifflin and Company, 1891.

Custer, General George A. *My Life on the Plains*, edited by Milo Milton Quaife. Lincoln: University of Nebraska Press, 1968.

D'Este, Carlo. *Patton: A Genius for War*. New York: HarperCollins, 1995.

Dabringhaus, Sabrina. "An Army on Vacation? The German War in China, 1900–1901." In *Anticipating Total War: The German and American Experiences, 1871–1914*, edited by Manfred Boemeke, Roger Chickering, and Stig Förster, 459–476. Cambridge: Cambridge University Press, 1999.

Dana, Charles A. *Recollections of the Civil War*. Lincoln: University of Nebraska Press, 1996.

Davies, General Henry E. *General Sheridan*. New York: D. Appleton and Company, 1897.

———. *Ten Days on the Plains*. Dallas, TX: Southern Methodist University Press, 1983.

Dawson, Joseph G., III. "General Phil Sheridan and Military Reconstruction in Louisiana." *Civil War History* 24 (June 1978): 133–151.

De Forest, John William. *A Volunteer's Adventures: A Union Captain's Record of the Civil War*. New Haven, CT: Yale University Press, 1946.

Denison, C. W. *Illustrated Life, Campaigns and Public Services of Philip H. Sheridan*. Philadelphia: T. B. Peterson & Brothers, 1865.

Dickert, D. Augustus. *History of Kershaw's Brigade*. Newberry, SC: Elbert H. Aull Company, 1899.

Dodge, Grenville. *The Battle of Atlanta and Other Campaigns*. Council Bluffs, IA: Monarch Printing Company, 1910.

Doughty, Robert A., and Ira D. Gruber, eds. *The American Civil War: The Emergence of Total Warfare*. Lexington, MA, and Toronto: D. C. Heath and Company, 1996.

Drake, William F. *Little Phil: The Story of General Philip Henry Sheridan*. Prospect, CT: Biographical Publishing Company, 2005.

Dunn, J. P. *Massacres of the Mountains: A History of the Indian Wars of the Far West*. New York: Harper & Brothers, 1886.

Early, Lieutenant General Jubal A. *Autobiographical Sketch and Narrative of the War Between the States*. Philadelphia and London: J. B. Lippincott, 1912.

———. *A Memoir of the Last Year of the War for Independence in the Confederate States of America*. Lynchburg, VA: Charles W. Button, 1867.

Flinn, Frank. *Campaigning with Banks in Louisiana, '63 and '64, and with Sheridan in the Shenandoah Valley in '64 and '65*. Lynn, MA: Press of Thomas P. Nichols, 1887.

Foner, Eric. *Reconstruction: America's Unfinished Revolution, 1863–1877*. New York: Harper & Row, Publishers, 1988.

Foner, Philip S. *The Great Labor Uprising of 1877*. New York: Monad Press, 1977.

Foote, Shelby. *The Civil War: A Narrative*. 3 vols. New York: Vintage Books, 1958–1974.

Förster, Stig, and Jörg Nagler, eds. *On the Road to Total War: The American Civil War and the German Wars of Unification, 1861–1871*. Cambridge: Cambridge University Press, 1997.

Forsyth, George. *Thrilling Days in Army Life*. New York and London: Harper & Brothers, 1900.

Freeman, Douglas Southall. *Lee's Lieutenants: A Study in Command,* edited by Stephen W. Sears. Abr. ed. New York: Simon & Schuster, 1998. First published in three volumes from 1942 to 1944.

Fullerton, Brigadier General Joseph S. "The Army of the Cumberland at Chattanooga." In *Battles and Leaders of the Civil War,* edited by Robert Underwood Johnson and Clarence Clough Buel, 3:719–726. New York: Thomas Yoseloff, 1956.

Gilbert, Felix, ed. *The Norton History of Modern Europe*. New York: W. W. Norton & Company, 1970.

Goetzmann, William H. *Exploration and Empire*. New York: W. W. Norton & Company, 1978.

Gordon, John B. *Reminiscences of the Civil War*. New York: Charles Scribner's Sons, 1903.

Granger, Moses. "The Battle of Cedar Creek." In *Sketches of War History, 1861–1865: Papers Prepared for the Ohio Commandery of the Military Order of the Loyal Legion of the United States,* edited by Robert Hunter, 3:100–143. Cincinnati, OH: Robert Clark & Company, 1890.

Grant, Ulysses S. *The Papers of Ulysses S. Grant, 1837–1885,* edited by John Y. Simon. 31 vols. Carbondale: Southern Illinois University Press, 1967–2009. Available online on the Mississippi State University Libraries website at library.msstate.edu/usgrant/the _papers.asp.

———. *Personal Memoirs of U.S. Grant,* edited by E. B. Long. Boston: Da Capo, 1982.

Greene, Jerome A. *Washita: The U.S. Army and the Southern Cheyennes, 1867–1869*. Norman: University of Oklahoma Press, 2004.

Greiner, Henry. *General Phil Sheridan as I Knew Him, Playmate-Comrade-Friend*. Chicago: J. S. Hyland and Company, 1908.

Grondys, L. H. *The Germans in Belgium: Experiences of a Neutral*. New York: D. Appleton and Company, 1916.

Hafendorfer, Kenneth A. *Perryville: Battle for Kentucky*. Utica, NY: McDowell Publications, 1981.

Haines, Aubrey L. *The Yellowstone Story: A History of Our First National Park.* 2 vols. Yellowstone National Park, WY: Yellowstone Library and Museum Association, 1977.

Haley, James L. *The Buffalo War: The History of the Red River Indian Uprising of 1874.* Garden City, NY: Doubleday & Company, 1976.

Hampton, H. Duane. *How the U.S. Cavalry Saved Our National Parks.* Bloomington: Indiana University Press, 1971.

Hansen, Harry. *The Civil War.* New York: New American Library, 1961.

Hayes, Rutherford B. *Diaries and Letters of Rutherford Birchard Hayes, Nineteenth President of the United States.* Vol. 2, *1861–1865,* edited by Charles Richard Williams. Columbus, OH: F. J. Heer Printing Company, 1922.

Hazen, William Babcock. *A Narrative of Military Service.* Boston: Tickner and Company, 1885.

Heatwole, John L. *The Burning: Sheridan's Devastation of the Shenandoah Valley.* Charlottesville, VA: Howell Press, 1998.

Heidler, David S., and Jeanne T. Heidler. *Encyclopedia of the Civil War.* Santa Barbara, CA: ABC-CLIO, 2000.

Henderson, Colonel G. F. R. *The Science of War.* London and New York: Longman's, Green, and Company, 1908.

Hergesheimer, Joseph. *Sheridan: A Military Narrative.* Boston and New York: Houghton Mifflin Company, 1934.

Hess, Earl J. *Banners to the Breeze: The Kentucky Campaign, Corinth, and Stones River.* Lincoln: University of Nebraska Press, 2000.

Historical Statistics of the United States: Colonial Times to 1970. 2 vols. Washington, DC: Bureau of the Census, 1975.

Hoar, George Frisbie. *Autobiography of Seventy Years.* Vol. 1. New York: Charles Scribner's Sons, 1903.

Hoffman, John. *The Confederate Collapse at the Battle of Missionary Ridge.* Dayton, OH: Morningside, 1985.

Hoig, Stan. *The Battle of the Washita: The Sheridan-Custer Indian Campaign of 1867–1869.* Garden City, NY: Doubleday & Company, 1976.

Hotchkiss, Jedediah. *Make Me a Map of the Valley: The Civil War Journal of Stonewall Jackson's Topographer,* edited by Archie P. McDonald. Dallas, TX: Southern Methodist University Press, 1973.

Howard, Captain S. E. "The Morning Surprise at Cedar Creek." In *Military Order of the Loyal Legion of the United States, Massachusetts Commandery.* Vol. 2, 415–425. Boston: The Commandery, 1900.

Hutton, Paul A. *Phil Sheridan and His Army.* Norman: University of Oklahoma Press, 1985.

———. "Phil Sheridan's Crusade for Yellowstone." *American History Illustrated* 19, no. 10 (February 1985): 10–15, 7.

Irwin, Richard Bache. *History of the Nineteenth Corps.* New York and London: G. P. Putnam's Sons, 1892.

Johnson, Robert Underwood, and Clarence Clough Buel, eds. *Battles and Leaders of the Civil War.* Vols. 3–4. New York: Thomas Yoseloff, 1956.

Keim, De B. Randolph. *Sheridan's Troopers on the Borders: A Winter Campaign on the Plains.* Lincoln: University of Nebraska Press, 1985.

Kidd, James H. *One of Custer's Wolverines: The Civil War Letters of Brevet Brigadier James H. Kidd, 6th Michigan Cavalry*, edited by Eric J. Wittenberg. Kent, OH: Kent State University Press, 2000.

———. *Riding with Custer: Recollections of a Cavalryman in the Civil War.* Lincoln: University of Nebraska Press, 1977.

Koistinen, Paul A. C. "The Political Economy of Warfare in America, 1865–1914." In *Anticipating Total War: The German and American Experiences, 1871–1914*, edited by Manfred Boemeke, Roger Chickering, and Stig Förster, 57–76. Cambridge: Cambridge University Press, 1999.

Kundall, George G., ed. *The Bravest of the Brave: The Correspondence of Stephen Dodson Ramseur.* Chapel Hill: University of North Carolina Press, 2010.

Lamar, Howard R., ed. *The Reader's Encyclopedia of the American West.* New York: Thomas Y. Crowell Company, 1977.

Lamers, William M. *The Edge of Glory: A Biography of General William S. Rosecrans, U.S.A.* New York: Harcourt, Brace & World, 1961.

Leckie, William, ed. *Indian Wars of the Red River Valley.* Sacramento, CA: Sierra Oaks Publishing Company, 1986.

Lewis, Thomas. *The Guns of Cedar Creek.* New York: Harper & Row, Publishers, 1988.

Lincoln, Abraham. *Collected Works of Abraham Lincoln,* edited by Roy Basler. 8 vols. New Brunswick, NJ: Rutgers University Press, 1953. Available online through the Abraham Lincoln Association website at quod.lib.umich.edu/cgi/t/text/text-idx?page=browse&c=Lincoln.

Lipkes, Jeff. *Rehearsals: The German Army in Belgium, August 1914.* Levven, Belgium: Levven University Press, 2007.

Lippitt, Francis J. *A Treatise on the Tactical Use of the Three Arms: Infantry, Artillery, and Cavalry.* Harrah, OK: Brandy Station Bookshelf, 1994.

Logsdon, David R., ed. *Eyewitnesses at the Battle of Stones River.* Nashville, TN: Kettle Mills Press, 2002.

Longacre, Edward G. *The Cavalry at Appomattox.* Mechanicsburg, PA: Stackpole Books, 2003.

———. *Custer and His Wolverines: The Michigan Cavalry Brigade, 1861–1865.* Conshohocken, PA: Combined Publishing, 1977.

———. "Justus McKinstry: A Rogue's Profile." *Civil War Times Illustrated* 17, no. 4 (July 1978): 15–21.

Luvaas, Jay. "The Influence of the German Wars of Unification on the United States." In *On the Road to Total War: The American Civil War and the German Wars of Unification, 1861–1871*, edited by Stig Förster and Jörg Nagler, 597–619. Cambridge: Cambridge University Press, 1997.

Lyman, Theodore. *Meade's Headquarters, 1863–1865: Letters of Colonel Theodore Lyman from the Wilderness to Appomattox,* edited by George R. Agassiz. Boston: Atlantic Monthly Press, 1922.

MacConnell, Charles C. "Service with Sheridan." In *Military Order of the Loyal Legion of the United States, Wisconsin Commandery.* Vol. 1, 285–293. Milwaukee: Burdick, Armitage & Allen, 1891.

MacInnes, C. M. *In the Shadow of the Rockies*. London: Rivingtons, 1930.

Mahon, Michael G. *The Shenandoah Valley, 1861–1865: The Destruction of the Granary of the Confederacy*. Mechanicsburg, PA: Stackpole Books, 1999.

Manchester, William. *American Caesar: Douglas MacArthur, 1880–1964*. Boston and Toronto: Little, Brown and Company, 1978.

Mantell, Martin E. *Johnson, Grant, and the Politics of Reconstruction*. New York: Columbia University Press, 1973.

Mardock, Robert Winston. *The Reformers and the American Indian*. Columbia: University of Missouri Press, 1971.

Marszalek, John F. *Sherman: A Soldier's Passion for Order*. New York: Free Press, 1993.

Marvel, William. *Lee's Last Retreat: The Flight to Appomattox*. Chapel Hill and London: University of North Carolina Press, 2002.

McCarthy, Peter, and Mike Syron. *Panzerkrieg: The Rise and Fall of Hitler's Tank Divisions*. New York: Carroll & Graf Publishers, 2002.

McDonough, James Lee. *Chattanooga: A Death Grip on the Confederacy*. Knoxville: University of Tennessee Press, 1984.

———. *Stones River: Bloody Winter in Tennessee*. Knoxville: University of Tennessee Press, 1980.

McFeely, William S. *Grant: A Biography*. New York and London: W. W. Norton & Company, 1982.

McPherson, James M. *Abraham Lincoln and the Second American Revolution*. New York and Oxford: Oxford University Press, 1991.

———. "From Limited War to Total War in America." In *On the Road to Total War: The American Civil War and the German Wars of Unification, 1861–1871*, edited by Stig Förster and Jörg Nagler, 295–309. Cambridge: Cambridge University Press, 1997.

Meade, George Gordon. *The Life and Letters of George Gordon Meade*. 2 vols. New York: Charles Scribner's Sons, 1913.

Mears, E. Grimwood. *The Destruction of Belgium: Germany's Confession and Avoidance*. London: William Heinemann, 1916.

Melville, Herman. *Collected Poems of Herman Melville*, edited by Howard P. Vincent. Chicago: Packard and Company, 1947.

Merington, Marguerite, ed. *The Custer Story: The Life and Intimate Letters of General George A. Custer and His Wife Elizabeth*. Lincoln: University of Nebraska Press, 1987. First published in 1950.

Merritt, Major General Wesley. "The Appomattox Campaign." *Military Order of the Loyal Legion of the United States, Missouri Commandery*. Vol. 1, 108–131. St. Louis: Smith & Owens Print Co., 1887.

———. "Sheridan in the Shenandoah Valley." In *Battles and Leaders of the Civil War*, edited by Robert Underwood Johnson and Clarence Clough Buel, 4:500–521. New York: Thomas Yoseloff, 1956.

Military Order of the Loyal Legion of the United States War Papers. Wilmington, NC: Broadfoot Publishing Company, 1993. Multiple volumes. First published in 1891.

Morris, Richard B., ed. *Encyclopedia of American History*. 6th ed. New York: Harper & Row, 1982.

Morris, Roy, Jr. *Sheridan: The Life and Wars of General Phil Sheridan.* New York: Crown Publishers, 1992.

Morrison, James L., Jr. *"The Best School in the World": West Point, the Pre–Civil War Years, 1833–1866.* Kent, OH: Kent State University Press, 1986.

Neely, Mark E., Jr. *The Civil War and the Limits of Destruction.* Cambridge, MA: Harvard University Press, 2007.

———. "Was the Civil War a Total War?" In *On the Road to Total War: The American Civil War and the German Wars of Unification, 1861–1871*, edited by Stig Förster and Jörg Nagler, 29–51. Cambridge: Cambridge University Press, 1997.

Newhall, Frederick C. *With General Sheridan in Lee's Last Campaign.* Philadelphia: J. B. Lippincott & Company, 1866.

Noe, Kenneth W. *Perryville: This Grand Havoc of Battle.* Lexington: University Press of Kentucky, 2001.

Noyalas, Jonathan A. *The Battle of Cedar Creek: Victory from the Jaws of Defeat.* Charleston, SC: History Press, 2009.

O'Connor, Richard. *Sheridan the Inevitable.* Indianapolis and New York: Bobbs-Merrill Company, 1953.

Oxford Dictionary of Quotations. 3rd ed. Oxford and New York: Oxford University Press, 1980.

Parrish, William E. "Fremont in Missouri." *Civil War Times Illustrated* 17, no. 1 (April 1978): 4–10, 40–45.

Parsons, Captain Edwin B. "Sheridan." In *Military Order of the Loyal Legion of the United States, Wisconsin Commandery.* Vol. 1, 275–284. Milwaukee: Burdick, Armitage & Allen, 1891.

Patchan, Scott C. *Shenandoah Summer: The 1864 Valley Campaign.* Lincoln: University of Nebraska Press, 2007.

Philbrick, Nathaniel. *The Last Stand: Custer, Sitting Bull, and the Battle of the Little Bighorn.* New York: Viking, 2010.

Porter, Horace. *Campaigning with Grant.* Lincoln: University of Nebraska Press, 2000.

Powell, William Henry. *The Fifth Army Corps (Army of the Potomac).* New York: G. P. Putnam's, 1896.

Pyne, Henry R. *Ride to War: The History of the First New Jersey Cavalry.* Piscataway, NJ: Rutgers University Press, 1961.

Rable, George C. *But There Was No Peace: The Role of Violence in the Politics of Reconstruction.* Athens: University of Georgia Press, 2007.

Ramage, James A. *Gray Ghost: The Life of Colonel John Singleton Mosby.* Lexington: University Press of Kentucky, 1999.

Ramseur, Stephen Dodson. *The Bravest of the Brave: The Correspondence of Stephen Dodson Ramseur*, edited by George G. Kundahl. Chapel Hill: University of North Carolina Press, 2010.

Reeves, Thomas C. "President Arthur in Yellowstone National Park." In *Montana: The Magazine of Western History* (July 1962): 18–29.

Reid, Whitelaw. *Ohio in the War: Her Statesmen, Her Generals, and Soldiers.* 2 vols. Cincinnati, OH: Moore, Wilstach & Baldwin, 1868.

Rister, Carl Coke. *Border Command: General Phil Sheridan in the West*. Norman: University of Oklahoma Press, 1944.

Robertson, James I., Jr. *Stonewall Jackson: The Man, the Soldier, the Legend*. New York: MacMillan Publishing USA, 1997.

Robins, Captain Richard, ed. *Toasts and Responses at Banquets Given Lieut.-Gen. P. H. Sheridan . . . by the Military Order of the Loyal Legion of the United States, Commander of the State of Illinois, March 6, 1882–1883*. Chicago: Knight & Leonard, Printers, 1883.

Robinson, Charles M., III. *Bad Hand: A Biography of General Ronald S. Mackenzie*. Austin, TX: State House Press, 1993.

———. *The Buffalo Hunters*. Austin, TX: State House Press, 1995.

Rosecrans, William. "The Campaign for Chattanooga." *The Century* 34, no. 1 (May 1887): 131–135.

Rosser, Major General Thomas L. *Riding with Rosser*. Shippenburg, PA: Bud Street Press, 1997.

Royster, Charles. *The Destructive War: William Tecumseh Sherman, Stonewall Jackson, and the Americans*. New York: Alfred A. Knopf, 1991.

Sandoz, Mari. *The Buffalo Hunters: The Story of the Hide Men*. Lincoln: University of Nebraska Press, 1978.

Sanford, George B. *Fighting Rebels and Redskins: Experiences in Army Life of Colonel George B. Sanford, 1861–1892*, edited by E. R. Hagemann. Norman: University of Oklahoma Press, 1969.

Sawislak, Karen. *Smoldering City: Chicagoans and the Great Fire, 1871–1874*. Chicago: University of Chicago Press, 1995.

Scheibert, Justus. *A Prussian Observes the American Civil War*. Columbia: University of Missouri Press, 2001.

Shanks, William F. G. *Personal Recollections of Distinguished Generals*. New York: Harper & Brothers, Publishers, 1866.

Sheridan, Philip H. *Annual Report to the Secretary of War, 1877*. Washington, DC: Government Printing Office, 1877.

———. "From Gravelotte to Sedan." *Scribner's Magazine* 4, no. 5 (November 1888): 515–535.

———. Papers of Philip Henry Sheridan. Library of Congress. 104 microfilm reels. 1985.

———. *Personal Memoirs of P. H. Sheridan, General, United States Army*. New York: Charles L. Webster & Company, 1888.

———. *Report of an Exploration of Parts of Wyoming, Idaho, and Montana in August and September 1882*. Washington, DC: Government Printing Office, 1882.

Sheridan, Philip H., and Michael Sheridan. *Personal Memoirs of Philip Henry Sheridan, General, United States Army. New and Enlarged Edition, with an Account of His Life from 1871 to His Death, in 1888*. 2 vols. New York: D. Appleton and Company, 1902.

Sherman, Colonel Francis T. *Quest for a Star: The Civil War Letters and Diaries of Colonel Francis T. Sherman of the 88th Illinois*, edited by C. Knight Aldrich. Knoxville: University of Tennessee Press, 1999.

Sherman, William Tecumseh. *Home Letters of General Sherman*, edited by M. A. DeWolfe Howe. New York: Charles Scribner's Sons, 1909.

———. *Memoirs of General William T. Sherman.* 2 vols. New York: D. Appleton and Company, 1875.

Simon, John Y., ed. *The Papers of Ulysses S. Grant.* 31 vols. Carbondale: Southern Illinois University Press, 1967–2009.

Simson, Jay W. *Crisis of Command in the Army of the Potomac: Sheridan's Search for an Effective General.* Jefferson, NC, and London: McFarland & Company, 2008.

———. *Custer and the Front Royal Executions of 1864.* Jefferson, NC, and London: McFarland & Company, 2009.

Skoch, George F. "In the Shadow of the Valley." *Civil War Times Illustrated* 23, no. 5 (September 1984): 35–39.

Smallwood, James M., Barry A. Crouch, and Larry Peacock. *Murder and Mayhem: The War of Reconstruction in Texas.* College Station: Texas A&M University Press, 2003.

Smits, David D. "The Frontier Army and the Destruction of the Buffalo." *The Western Historical Quarterly* 25, no. 3 (Autumn 1994): 312–338.

Spotts, David L. *Campaigning with Custer and the Nineteenth Kansas Volunteer Cavalry on the Washita Campaign, 1868–1869.* New York: Argonaut Press, 1965.

Stackpole, Edward J. *Sheridan in the Shenandoah.* 2nd ed. Harrisburg, PA: Stackpole Books, 1992.

Starr, Stephen Z. *The Union Cavalry in the Civil War.* Vol. 2: *The War in the East from Gettysburg to Appomattox, 1863–1865.* Baton Rouge: Louisiana State University Press, 1981.

Stern, Thomas. *Chiefs and Change in the Oregon Country.* Vol. 2. Corvallis: Oregon State University Press, 1992.

Stevens, George Thomas. *Three Years in the Sixth Corps.* Albany, NY: S. R. Gray, 1866.

Strachan, Hew. *The First World War.* New York and London: Viking, 2003.

Taylor, Joe Gray. *Louisiana Reconstructed: 1863–1877.* Baton Rouge: Louisiana State University Press, 1974.

Thomas, Emory. *Bold Dragon: The Life of Jeb Stuart.* New York: Harper & Row, Publishers, 1986.

———. *Robert E. Lee: A Biography.* New York and London: W. W. Norton & Company, 1995.

Thomason, John W., Jr. *Jeb Stuart.* New York: Charles Scribner's Sons, 1930.

Thruston, Gates P. "The Crisis at Chickamauga." In *Battles and Leaders of the Civil War,* edited by Robert Underwood Johnson and Clarence Clough Buel, 3:663–664. New York: Thomas Yoseloff, 1956.

Tobie, Edward P. *History of the First Maine Cavalry, 1861–1865.* Boston: Emery & Hughes, 1887.

Tremain, Henry Edwin. *Last Hours of Sheridan's Cavalry.* New York: Bonnell, Silver & Bowers, 1904.

Tucker, Glenn. *Chickamauga: Bloody Battle in the West.* Dayton, OH: Morningside House, 1961.

Tunnell, Ted. *Crucible of Reconstruction: War, Radicalism and Race in Louisiana, 1862–1877.* Baton Rouge: Louisiana State University Press, 1984.

United States Congress. *Executive Documents from the Third Session of the 40th Congress, 1868–1869.* Washington, DC: Government Printing Office, 1869.

————. *Executive Documents from the 41st Congress, 1869–1871* (3 Sessions). Washington, DC: Government Printing Office, 1871.

————. *Executive Documents from the 43rd Congress, 1873–1875* (2 Sessions). Washington, DC: Government Printing Office, 1875.

United States House Select Committee Report on the New Orleans Riots. Washington, DC: Government Printing Office, 1867.

United States War Department. *Annual Reports of the Secretary of War.* Washington, DC: Government Printing Office, 1868–1886.

————. *War of the Rebellion: A Compilation of the Official Records of the Union and Confederate Armies.* 69 vols. Washington, DC: Government Printing Office, 1909. Available online through the Cornell Library website at digital.library.cornell.edu:80/m/moawar/waro.html.

Urwin, Gregory J. W. *Custer Victorious: The Civil War Battles of General George Armstrong Custer.* Rutherford, NJ: Fairleigh Dickinson University Press, 1983.

Utley, Robert M. *Frontier Regulars: The United States Army and the Indian, 1866–1891.* New York: Macmillan Publishing Company, 1973.

————. "Total War on the American Indian Frontier." In *Anticipating Total War: The German and American Experiences, 1871–1914*, edited by Manfred Boemeke, Roger Chickering, and Stig Förster, 399–414. Cambridge: Cambridge University Press, 1999.

Walker, Aldace F. *The Vermont Brigade in the Shenandoah Valley, 1864.* Burlington, VT: Free Press Association, 1869.

Warner, Ezra J. *Generals in Blue: Lives of the Union Commanders.* Baton Rouge: Louisiana State University Press, 1964.

————. *Generals in Gray: Lives of the Confederate Commanders.* Baton Rouge: Louisiana State University Press, 2000.

Wawro, Geoffrey. *The Franco-Prussian War: The German Conquest of France in 1870–1871.* Cambridge: Cambridge University Press, 2003.

Wert, Jeffry D. *Custer: The Controversial Life of George Armstrong Custer.* New York: Simon & Schuster, 1996.

————. *From Winchester to Cedar Creek: The Shenandoah Campaign of 1864.* Carlisle, PA: South Mountain Press, 1987.

Wheelan, Joseph. *Libby Prison Breakout: The Daring Escape from the Notorious Civil War Prison.* New York: Public Affairs, 2010.

White, Lonnie J., ed. "The Nineteenth Kansas Cavalry in the Indian Territory, 1868–1869: Eyewitness Accounts of Sheridan's Winter Campaign." In *Indian Wars of the Red River Valley*, edited by William Leckie, 22–43. Sacramento, CA: Sierra Oaks Publishing Company, 1986.

Whitney, David C., and Robin Vaughn Whitney. *The American Presidents.* New York: Prentice Hall Press, 1993.

Williamson, James Joseph. *Mosby's Rangers: A Record of the Operations of the Forty-Third Virginia Cavalry.* New York: Ralph B. Kenyon, Publisher, 1896.

Winik, Jay. *April 1865: The Month That Saved America.* New York: HarperCollins Publishers, 2001.

Wittenberg, Eric J. *Glory Enough for All: Sheridan's Second Raid and the Battle of Trevilian Station.* Washington, DC: Brassey's, 2001.

————. *Little Phil: A Reassessment of the Civil War Leadership of Gen. Philip H. Sheridan.* Washington, DC: Brassey's, 2002.

Worsham, John. *One of Jackson's Foot Cavalry.* New York: Neale Publishing Company, 1912.

Young, John Russell. *Around the World with General Grant: A Narrative of the Visit of General U.S. Grant, Ex-President of the United States, to Various Countries in Europe, Asia, and Africa, in 1877, 1878, 1879.* 2 vols. New York: American News Company, 1879.

INDEX

Abell, Edward, 220, 221, 222
Abraham Lincoln, Fort, 272, 273, 286, 291
Adobe Walls, Northern Texas, 264–265
African American soldiers, 189, 199
African Americans
    integrate New Orleans public transportation, 224
    murdered, 218–219, 219, 220, 226
    slaves, 89, 209
    suffrage for, 219, 222, 223, 228, 275, 282
    in Texas, 217, 218, 226
Alcott, Louisa May, 308
Alexander, E. Porter, 202, 203
Alexis, Grand Duke of Russia, 260, 261
Alger, Russell, 15, 18
Allegheny Mountains, 101, 116
Allen, Vanderbilt, 203, 204
Amelia Court House, 189–190
Anderson, Richard, 69–70, 102, 104
    divisions at Sailor's Creek, 194, 195
    leaves Shenandoah Valley, 108–109
    relieved of command, 197
Antietam, 59
Apache Indians, 289
    Geronimo (Apache chief), 297, 298
    surrender, 299
Appomattox Court House, 200–208
    Confederate brigade refuses to surrender, 203–204
    truce at, 187

Appomattox River, bridges burned, 193, 196
Appomattox Station, 198
Arapahoe Indians, 231, 232, 239, 245, 291
Arkansas Corps, 210
Army, United States, modernization, 299–300
Army and Navy Journal, 266
Army Corps of Engineers, 5, 287, 288
Army of Northern Virginia, 41, 60, 66, 68, 75, 207
    at Appomattox, 198–199
    on eve of surrender, 200
    march to Appomattox, 197
    officers urge surrender, 197
    in retreat, 188–190, 192
    shortage of horses, 206–207
    surrenders, 202–207
    targeted by Grant, 99
Army of the Cumberland, 26, 32–33
    at Chattanooga, Tennessee, 47–48
    hiatus, 33, 34
    regroups, 37
    Rosecrans relieved of command, 46
    at Stones River, Tennessee, 21–29
Army of the Gulf, 210
Army of the James, 91, 193, 201
Army of the Ohio, leadership problems, 29–32
Army of the Potomac, 49, 60, 67–68
    Cavalry Corps, Union. *see* Cavalry Corps, Union

Petersburg, march to, 171–175
  condition of roads, 173–174
  Custer at, 177
  inappropriate music played, 176
  rain, and condition of roads, 173,
    174, 175
Petersburg, Union troops enter, 189
Petersburg, Virginia
  casualties, 92, 172
  Confederate Army retreats, 188–189
  mine exploded, 100
  rain, and condition of roads,
    173–174
  under siege, 172
  surprise attack, 100–101
Phil Sheridan and His Army (Hutton),
    294
Philadelphia Academy of Fine Arts, 156
Philadelphia Inquirer (newspaper), 132
Philadelphia Mint, casts marksmanship
    medals, 300
Pickett, George
  defense of Petersburg, 181, 183
  at Dinwiddie Court House, 177, 178
  at Five Forks, 185
  at Petersburg, 176
  Pickett's Charge, 75, 176, 236
  relieved of command, 197
Piedras Negras, Mexico, 6, 214
Piegan Blackfeet, 251
Pig Foots (boy gang), 2
Pillow, Fort, 220
Pio Pio Mox Mox (Indian chief), 7
Plains Indians, 229, 231, 234
  dispute, with cattlemen, 294, 295
  ethnological study, 294
  form war party, 264–265
  moved to reservations, 263–264
  starving, 263–264, 265
  wars, as preventable, 290–293
Pleasonton, Alfred, 58, 59, 76
Polk, Leonidas, 23, 27, 40, 43
Ponies, shot, 242, 243, 271

Pope, John, 16, 260, 265, 274
Porter, Horace, 65, 71, 115, 173–174,
    174–175, 176, 178, 179, 180,
    182, 185, 314
Potato famine, Ireland, 2
Potomac River, 102
Poverty, of Confederates, 164–165, 172,
    190, 192, 196
  emergency rations sent, 165
Powder River, 276, 277
Powell, William, 127, 134
  division at Battle of Cedar Creek, 142
  division sent to destroy Virginia
    Central Railroad, 164
Presidential election, 1876, contested,
    282
Presidential election, Mexico, 215
Prisoners of war
  executed, 127, 128, 133–134
  intelligence from, 152
  officers, 155, 163, 195
  released, in reward for cooperation,
    165
  taken at Five Forks, 183
  taken at Sailor's Creek, 195
Prisoners of war, Confederate, 79, 86,
    87–88, 115
  guerrilla fighters, 163
Prisoners of war, Union, 58, 76, 108
Prussia, 216
  Franco-Prussian War, 249, 253
Pullman, George, 250, 296
Pullman, Mrs. George, 250
Pulque, 6

Quakers, 108–109, 250–251

Railroad workers, strike, 286
Ramseur, Stephen Dodson, 97, 111, 112,
    135, 141
  fatally wounded and captured, 155
Rape, of settlers by Indians, 243
Rapidan River, 65, 66